CW01336796

A TABLE OF CONTEN

DISCLAIMER:

Although, as with any work of fiction, the author admits to some presiding influence upon his writing from his general knowledge and from the experiences of his life, any close resemblance to reality of the events or characters described in this book is purely coincidental.

The author reserves the right to alter this work for future print runs or editions.

THE PERFECT LAUNCHPAD:

A Satire on the Dark Energy inside a Software House

A SUMMARY OF *"THE PERFECT LAUNCHPAD"*

I have written a comedy which is set against the background of the computer industry. My chief character is the belligerent and domineering director of a software house (adapted from its original function: that of a warehouse), who believes that his systems are the ideal foundation for every business. But besides being a bully, he is a coward; and to protect himself from his own insecurity, he has hired a couple of "bouncers" from a nightclub who assist in the dismissal of staff – by ensuring they leave quietly and without creating a scene. He thinks of himself as enterprising, although his business has been built off the back of his wife's dowry.

All of the characters have their tics and eccentricities. His wife is tremendously large and unhealthy, and is subject to "pica" – an irrational desire to eat foreign objects that are not food, such as the bathroom sponge. She is not attractive to her husband, who would prefer to do away with her; although even he must admit that her money is essential to his enterprise. The director himself is no oil painting. Nor is the Chief Programmer, who suffers from head lice, and an obsession with technology that goes well beyond his daily duties. His previous incumbent was high on the autistic spectrum; whilst the cleaner is a tiny woman who has spouted five offspring, and manifests a slight resentment of her place in society, coupled with an unwillingness to "put herself about" much.

I have used the narrative as a springboard for satirizing many different aspects of employment and society: obesity, office politics and the abuse of power within this setting - combined with the psychology of *learned helplessness* amongst office workers, who fear for the safety of their jobs; the obscurity of programming languages, and the bizarre confusions that may result; the fastidiousness of health and safety, coupled with an ignorance of the most basic of its protocols; the fear and hatred that rich people have for tax inspectors; the frustration of being trapped in an unproductive marriage; the verbosity of legalese ... and much else besides.

The Chief Programmer has been virtually defrauded of his money by his avaricious boss, and the undercurrents of anger are explored in a surreal setting, in which the tables are turned and the "ruled" become the "rulers": with the fearsome strength of the bouncers being turned against the director himself - with humiliating effect.

The narrative blurs the hinterland between the sea of imagination, and the land of software reality: with elements plucked from the art of programming to feed an increasingly fantastical setting.

A COMPANION PIECE TO "*THE PERFECT LAUNCHPAD*"

To Begin With

This prologue is to put my readers "in the frame", so to speak, for the forthcoming adventure - which I have laid on for them with the only magic tool that I possess: a head full of ideas, blessed in a baptismal font of words. And if a nymph presides over this fountain, as over similar objects in nature, then let her help me sculpt this foreword into a safety barrier against a barrage of criticism, that the gist of my tale has been drawn up by someone who has lost his mind!

The Setting

For the benefit of those readers who have never worked in a software house, it is a company entirely devoted to the development of computer systems. It is often centred inside the cheapest and most spacious real estate that money can buy, which also lies not too far from public amenities. A popular choice is a warehouse; and this, as it so happens, is the location I have selected for my story.

My decision to set a comedy in an apparently humourless industry has been met with incredulity by my friends. Surely I was attempting to get blood out of a stone? Well, there is no appreciable blood inside - or upon - a stone ... unless a sharp edge of it has been used to take a life; but, squeeze tightly upon this *particular* rock of collective memories, and an abundance of humour will eke out.

But Why, Oh Why, a Software House?

I have worked with computers, in one capacity or another, for most of my adulthood; and the industry which envelops them is familiar to me. Sometimes my labour was contracted out by agencies to software houses, and I must confess: they can be highly eccentric in the way they go about getting things done. But their directors would never be tempted into self-mockery, for they conduct every aspect of their daily grind with an attitude of the utmost seriousness (nay, pomposity even). Software houses are obsessed with jargon for its own sake; and with producing reams and reams of useless documentation. And by these extreme measures, do they sincerely aim to blind the innocent client with science. Should he ever complain that, for his substantial (and ever-increasing) outlay, he is not receiving satisfaction, the volumes of paperwork in colour-coded folders are always close at hand - as evidence that the wheels of production have been revolving furiously for the fulfilment of his needs! It is usually *he*. (Ladies, be not alarmed by my exclusion of you. Would you *prefer* to be considered dupes?)

Sometimes fulfilment appears simple to achieve, and yet - truthfully – it is laced with more Gordian Knots than could be embroidered by all the seamstresses of Mount Olympus. Therefore, the client's heartfelt desires may be refused upon the grounds that the budget will be hopelessly exceeded. And, sometimes, fulfilment may actually be attained by a relatively simple process, but one which must be made to appear complicated, in order to ensure the proper payment of funds ... although you may *call* this "extortion", and I shall not argue with you.

Sample Software Houses

There was a software house at which I worked (the company shall remain anonymous) where I was testing a system, and discovered an error. The response by the manager was to insist that there was no error. My counter-claim was breezed over, like a deceased sheep upon barren moorland. The prevailing culture was to let the client play guinea-pig; and if he should later choke upon something indigestible, to levy a handsome fee for fixing it. The project had already overrun its allotted schedule, and the House of Software began to arm its firing squad. I later discovered, long after I had left, that the organization I worked for had been sued in court by the utility company that was its client. And the judge passed sentence thus, 'You shall be taken to the place from whence you came, and from there to a place of execution. You shall be hung by the neck until the body of the Software House be dead. And may God have mercy on its soul.' I jest. He didn't really say this, but there *was* an indictment requiring it to be removed to its homeland of America, and never to do business in the United Kingdom again.

Whilst I will admit that my story is sustained by outrageous fantasy, I find I am surprised - as I reflect upon it – by how much of what I wrote is the literal truth! One software house where I had a contract was called Sound Techniques Ltd. It used to be a recording studio, and they never bothered to change the name! And, for a while, I was part of an office team in Catholic Ireland - situated, it saddens me to say, in a reconstituted house of God.

My very first appointment in software development was in a strange location indeed. The arrangement was open plan, something which I was new to in those days, and the system "under construction" was for a bank. I was intrigued by the so-called "menus", and by the concurrent sight of a huge chemical processing plant in the near vicinity, which I couldn't miss whenever I peered out of a certain window. Somehow, the juxtaposition of the two things – the list on the screen, and the processing plant - must have made an deep impression upon my young mind, for I fantasized to a senior colleague how the menu items might be a cover-up for a phenomenon more sinister ... such as "Soylent Green", or something equally inappropriate. But when he swallowed my idea, I am not sure it went down too well.

Real-Life Characters

My managers and colleagues have, by turns, been either staid or colourful; and challenging or personable. One rather lovable old programmer was a doppelgänger for Einstein, and would talk incessantly to himself as he went about his business. When you were in the gents, you knew if he was occupying one of the cubicles, since he could be heard mumbling some arcane bit of computer code.

At another place, there was an old coder who must have been looking to retire soon after I met him. His name was Adam. Every afternoon, Adam would retrieve an apple (just one, never two!) from the top of the metal cabinet beside his desk, where it had perched all morning, waiting to be mashed up between his teeth. And every day, this alone comprised his lunch. He would crunch into the flesh of the fruit with evident delight, whilst standing quite still, and thinking profoundly about whatever was the leading technical issue of his day, - which I don't suppose involved either Eve or a pet serpent. But, then again, who knows?

Programming Oddities

And – Ah! The acquired taste of certain programming languages ... infuriating to the novice, but a gift to satire. One recalls to mind when several variables are concatenated, and the result is *nothing*, whenever at least one of these variables is "null"!

I think there are occasions when turning the syntax of online code into an object of fun is almost mandatory. Take PHP, for example. If you use one equals sign for setting a value, it will never work. If you employ two equals signs to "pop a question", the question is never answered. Why, pray? Well, *one* equals sign will set the field to the "comparison value", irrespective of what it was before you asked the question!

If variable_a is currently "2", and you posit a condition, if variable_a = "3" ... with the intention of performing certain actions if it is ... then variable_a is inadvertently set to "3" and the actions nested within the "if" statement will *always* be performed.

How so? It works like this ... one equals sign for asking a question, two for an assignment where the value is not null; and three for an assignment, where the value is null.

'Oh, that's simple enough,' I hear you say.

'Well, yes,' is my reply. 'It *is* simple enough; but I must protest that such a conception is not natural! If the functionality of the hard shoulder, by the side of the road upon which cars drive, were suddenly to be controlled by some arbitrary rule, involving the ambient light in the sky, - the new ruling might be understood *well enough*; but who among us would not *occasionally* forget it? (Oh, but wait! A foolhardy idea like this has already occurred to someone with power and authority: and said potentate decrees ... "Let the side of a motorway be designated as a *hard shoulder* (to cry upon, perhaps, – after the inevitable accident?) during a certain time of day; and as an *extra runway* for the "boy racers" of the tarmac, at another period of the day. What was this legislator thinking? Decent rules are predicated upon the sound principle that they are easy to remember; and not upon the opposite of this - that they are easy to forget!

And don't get me started on the multi-layered processes of online programming. One language to paint the screen (HTML), one to read from the screen (PHP), and one to feed what is read from the screen into the database (MYSQL) ... a database which, unlike in days of yore, will not be inside the computer on your desk – oh, no! Why that would be *far* too simple. Rather, it will be stored snugly inside a server, perhaps two hundred miles away from where you are sitting! Yes, three languages, all interacting, and - in many cases - all three appearing on the same line! And all jet-setting hundreds of miles back and forth with every press of the return key!

Now, I am pondering a dialogue with a far-off database, via a screen that lies a foot or two from our focussed eyes. Shall I liken it to a conversation with a zombie inside our lounge? Every time you say something, you must wait while the terminally dumb person (a.k.a. "dumb terminal") consults his brain, which is in a secure compound in the north of England. Pity the poor courier, who carries the message such a distance, and posts it through his letter-box; waiting patiently to be handed the reply, - that must be relayed, forthwith, across country, back to your comfortable lounge. Yet ... never fear, for this particular courier cycles at 200 miles per second. (Sound waves, you are but junior partners!) And then there's a road block.

Is it like a modern clinic, with a polyglot of health professionals, all misunderstanding each other – with Chinese whispers – because each speaks in a different native tongue, *which is never English*? No? Oh well, - perhaps not, then.
And contrast with earlier methods of instructing your computer to do something, whereby one language was enough.

"One ring to rule them all,
And in the darkness join them"

Thank you, Gollum.

And yet ... Rejoice! All is open source. So we must not complain. You get what you pay for – and, in this case, you have paid nothing. There are, of course, alternatives, but they would probably bankrupt a systems developer of modest, private means.

And what of the annoying and frequent habit of the PHP interpreter to throw up an entirely meaningless "HTTP 500" error: an issue which, by now, may have been resolved ... somewhat. And how could I re-construe any of this to be funny in a human setting? Please read my narrative to find out. But before you do, dare I mention how complex a computer system can be? It may comprise a hundred thousand lines – each with either a logical condition, or an instruction. And if the syntax on even one line proves faulty, the entire house of cards could fall! We must hope that an infinitesimally small syntax error does not one day ignite a process leading to nuclear war.

A friend once warned me about getting bogged down in too much detail. He said something like,

'First, you are examining the stem of a plant giving rise to a leaf; and then, you see the leaf itself; before finally gazing at the serrations on the leaf ...'

At this point, I sympathised with his critique, and by mistake mentioned "microvilli", which exist at an acute level of magnification – although not in plants. But afterwards, just like any obsessive-compulsive, I returned to my detail. For how could I do otherwise?

And now, I feel another comparison coming on. It is building up inside me like a cobra's venom, and I must spit it out. If computer programmers proceeded at the same rate of acceleration through their tasks ... as the parliamentarians, during their withdrawal of our nation from the European Union, – it might take them (collectively) a hundred years just to display "Hello, World" on a computer screen, before the system went down, and the whole human race with it! It seems that the leaders of our nation can only handle one subject at a time. And three and a half years of Brexit brings home how pedantic the whole political process is: indeed, one might be forgiven for thinking that the negotiators' time would be no less profitably spent, counting the hairs on the legs of a flea! They arm themselves with vacuous phrases, and even talk of "prorogation": a 1000-year-old Norman term which - previously - no ordinary, living mortal has ever heard of.

Have you, at any point in your life, found yourself stationed at premises where there is a Timer on the toilet door, installed to assess how much valuable company time is being "wasted" in the lavatory? This was a reality in one American software house – and a friend of mine reported the same feature in a software house he had once worked in! Yes, they actually did this. In fact, in the case of my own experience, I do believe there was a video-camera installed as well. Of course, the equipment was attached to the main entrance of the lavatory, and not to the insides of cubicle doors! But, by now, the intrusion may have been taken a step further, so that a programmer's private taste in newspaper copy might be discreetly observed; and, out of this, his political persuasions ascertained, - as he (or she) sits on the not-so-royal throne, and reads and rustles each massive printed sheet.

Such equipment for spying was the brain-child of the scruffiest director imaginable. He had unkempt hair and holes in his jeans, long before the days when this became fashionable; and this, in spite of the fact that the prevailing culture of the company required that all about him should behave in a business-like fashion, and be dressed smartly in suits. He further pleaded ignorance of the length of my contract, on the very first day of my assignment (after I had travelled thousands of miles to take up my post). Yet he had arranged the contract! And he subsequently revealed his comparative ignorance of the software he would have us use: being easily swayed by one of the programmers who was demonstrating it to him, even though it seemed to offer nothing but default functionality.

On another occasion, I was outsourced to a software house in England. One day, the sociable and jolly boss decided to throw a party at his residence for the benefit of his staff; and, during the course of the evening, as everyone began to let their hair down ... there suddenly appeared the plump backside and ample bosoms of a woman, entirely naked and running along the landing, and up or down the stairs, whilst the big boss chased her away from prying eyes and into a safe haven! But it was only his girlfriend. So that's alright, then.

Elements of Ruthlessness

At one software house, the prevailing habit in the boardroom was to reassure the technical personnel that their jobs were completely safe, and that they should surely stay (at least) until Christmas, in order to receive some huge bonuses that were earmarked for them. In reality, you could have received the sack. But I was fortunate. I got two £20 Marks and Spencer vouchers. And promises may be even more hollow than that. If you are virtually guaranteed an extension by your agent, in advance of the client having seen you, then you can be confident of not getting one. If there is no such promise, then you might be lucky. But every job is only safe - until it isn't.

A polite and personable young documenter once introduced himself to me, the very day he had joined the team. He was keen to shake the hands of his new colleagues and to say, 'Hello'. Three days later, he came over to shake my hand again. This time, it was to say, 'Good bye'. A Beatles song comes to mind.

And what about the following set up (to facilitate a dismissal): taking an unwitting staff member out to the pub for his birthday, attempting to get him drunk, and then - upon his return to the office, - the manager telling him he has drunk too much, and is therefore unfit for work ... so would he please leave ... forthwith; to be followed, only days later, by the termination of his contract? Somewhat Machiavellian, I think.

When I was working in Ireland, a Dublin agent attempted to put my mind at rest on the subject of job security. She told me confidently that sackings were rare; and then she admitted, in the next breath, that within the last day or two, approximately 100 freelancers had been laid off - simultaneously! You could get angry, but you have to see the funny side of it as well.

An old friend of mine, a fellow contractor, once booked time off from a busy contract. During his vacation, his mother died. He rang his line manager.

'Could I have some compassionate leave?' he wondered.

'Why, of course.'

He took his compassionate leave, and, upon his return, was ushered into the boardroom ... and you can guess what came next. His deadlines were not being met, and so he was fired.

'Contractors are as disposable as Kleenex tissues,' I paraphrase the words of a former manager of mine. But at least he was truthful.

The large tale which follows is for the benefit of certain clueless IT managers (and this is not a catch-all phrase, for some of them are knowledgeable, and appreciative of their team's hard graft) - so that they may better understand the near-madness manifested by employees in their honest attempt to deliver their units of work on time. A former manager once told me a story about a technical person who would drive to his place of work on his motorbike each day. He was systematically becoming more and more stressed by his office duties. One day, these duties finally "got to him". He drove to the front entrance, through the door, and – still on the saddle and revving his engine, - up the stairs, along the corridor, and into his team leader's office. Once there, he made himself comfortable in his boss's chair, removed his boots and socks; and thence proceeded to take the weight off his bare feet, by placing them on the table! After this, he simply sat back, and waited for his team leader to arrive. Oh! To be a fly on the wall that day! The encounter would have been something to marvel at.

Comedy or Satire?

Certain aspects of a contractor's life just have to be made fun of. But is it comedy or satire? I hope to achieve laughter – but also to make people think. Too often, in consideration of television sitcoms or stand-up comedians, the word "satire" is used to describe an art form which is pure "comedy"; and there is nothing wrong with that. The exponents must be bold and imaginative, but their performances are conducted without any expectation of altering the world.

I would frequently wake up in the middle of the night, with my mind still in the throes of invention, like the propellers of an aircraft after the engine has been switched off. Thus was I transported to a light-switch, and thence to a pencil and paper ... to scribble something down. And afterwards, thankful for having emptied my mind of its mild burden, I would click the light off and settle down once more into my pit. But, alas! Another thought was winging its way into my head, and pressing me for its inclusion. And so the cycle (just documented) would be acted out all over again.

With the constant oscillation betwixt light and dark beyond the witching hour, it must have seemed to my neighbours as if I was sending messages to aliens in Morse code; not that there are any aliens in our inner courtyards - unless you count foxes, with their anguished screeches after nightfall.

I have lampooned the computer industry (especially software houses), and the office routine as a whole, but this is only a springboard, from whence I may dive into a bewildering array of questionable things. Capitalism does not escape my critical eyes; nor modern abstract art, with special attention devoted to "concept art"; nor the common misuse of English, nor the rambling of legal practitioners, whose phraseology resembles a foreign language. You have seen how the obscure syntax familiar to technical maestros is not allowed to escape either. Nor is religious practice unblemished by my scrutiny ... but, my dear church-goers, please rest easy – for it not "affairs of the spirit" which concern me. In fact, I *allow* my characters (nay, positively *encourage* them) to refer freely to Holy Scripture, in order to demonstrate how far removed they are from salvation, themselves, or from *any* notion of inner purity! My intention is never to denigrate spiritual faith – but to hold a light up to the bizarre and hypocritical misuse of religion in peculiar circumstances ... which, I am sure you will agree, can often be hilarious.

So, take this either as a threat or a promise. You may lock up your daughters and your legal papers, your bibles and your most cherished political beliefs – yet, still, shall the runny mead of my rich satire seep through the cracks in the safe, and imbue them all!

Not so Humorous

And what can you make of a faintly cold office environment, where warm relations somehow exist between two people who have only just met: two persons whose bond is suddenly so strong as to make others feel excluded? Finding this to be decidedly odd, I approached a friend and colleague for enlightenment; and received, for my answer, not words, but a behaviour ... he stepped gingerly across the room and gave me one of those "special handshakes". Then I knew. He could see the misuse of secrecy and power, but could not verbalise his knowledge openly - and so he revealed it with discretion.

On one occasion, at another site where I worked, I was witness to a lengthy interaction between a superior and an underling, consisting entirely of sign language. I perched myself comfortably upon an empty desk in front of them, in order to "enjoy the show". And I was surprised to notice that neither party was inhibited either by my presence, or by my curiosity. It was as if I was watching two actors in a silent film: I, transparent as a ghost, and they, with no knowledge of my existence. Could either one, or both, of the interlocutors be deaf? Or was the theme the same as for the previous paragraph?

Many years ago, my introduction to the arcane art of computer programming was a TOPS course arranged at a site in Farringdon, London. On day one, the trainees were told that the organisation hosting this induction, both traces and records information on "virtual criminals". What does that even *mean*, I wondered? It sounded like a dark activity. Our dazed expressions, or our furrowed brows, must have called for some further explanation, and we were told,

'Will anyone who is not comfortable with this situation please leave now.' And this, in the worst unemployment crisis since the Great Depression. Everyone there desperately needed this training for the growth of their careers. If any of those present had a moral dilemma, it was Hobson's choice: damned if you leave, damned if you stay. I wanted the exposure to programming, but also wished to reassure myself on one point. I asked: would the code I create be used for the purpose of holding or processing this sensitive information? To my relief, I was told by the tutor that each student's output was "coursework" only – and would not be "misappropriated" (my word, not hers).

Of Questionable Hardware, and Defamation

In the course of the narrative, I draw attention to the inflammatory nature of certain Dell laptops. (Years ago, the culprit, a Sony battery, was identified, and the 400 or so faulty devices were requisitioned.) I have an old Dell model myself, and I can confirm that it has been a great little work horse, which has never caught fire or blown up; although I did have the battery replaced at one point.

One of my creations, a sentient beetle, makes mention of military hardware. I am not a weapons specialist, and so it is all "hearsay" to me. And it is, in any case, only true as far as my fictional characters know. It may be that their sources are wrong; but they are all the more human for that (yes - even the beetle).

To Finish Up

Many dramas have some overriding characteristic: it might be funny, tragical or didactic. And some even have substantial claims made for them - as possessing all of these features. But these stories struggle to maintain their standards. My *own* focus, however, does not waver from the first line to the last. Let me express the hope that my novel shall meet with readers whose minds are as broad and bright as an avenue lined with gorgeous trees – and who can swallow my Chaucerian sense of ribaldry, without so much as a hiccup. Indeed, anyone in search of political correctness will not find it here.

Generally speaking, I have many serious ideas on my agenda, and much to write, while I have lead in my mechanical pencil and life in my mind. So I must pour all of my present hilarity into this humble offering (which is punctuated with so many serious notes as well); lest I taint my other, more solemn and poetic offerings with my jests, and (like a composer) scramble the notes of my harmony. Whether, in so doing, I have finally purged myself of my comedic nature ... only time will tell.

PART ZERO: THE PREAMBLE

Close to a forgotten tract of English coastline which (owing to an oversight on the part of the deity who presides over this landscape) may not exist outside of unreality, there is a conspicuous row of buildings offering public services to the community at large. These include a software house, a sandwich shop, a firm of financial advisors, a chapel with accompanying cemetery, and a funeral parlour. What brought them here is a matter of arcane speculation: for there is only a small customer base in the locality. Perhaps here, like nowhere else, the freehold land is cheap? (In a world of illusion, how may it be otherwise?) And, somehow, the businesses are blossoming. The proprietors are "beside themselves with *un*holy joy" – to marinate a sweet old phrase – as the soil of coincidence feeds the flower of invention.

And rumour, like a fungus, has spores to sow. (For there is "dark matter" everywhere, though it may not be perceptible to the naked eye.) Rumour brazenly announces that the director of the software house was slave-driving his most potent member, until that member drooped (a pun issued with apologies to Masters and Johnson); and that the producer of *handmade sandwiches* added the *coup de grâce* with her toadstools. Did the director liaise with her, in order to receive backhanders from the clergyman and the funeral director for lucrative services rendered: such as liturgies, musicianship on the church organ, and the dedication of a burial plot? Nicely rounding it all off, a financier has been summoned to offer guidance to the bereaved on the thorny issues of tax evasion, and the laws of inheritance. Oh, joy!

As the sole creator of all the characters in this work, the author has his own opinions. (I say "sole creator"; although, now and again, the narrator has, for the playful entertainment of his readers, split his own psyche into a First Person and a "Descriptor".) He is confident that the "sarnie lady" is chaste in her intentions, and that she always uses mushrooms and never toadstools. However, as any mycologist knows, it is possible to be poisoned by mushrooms; and, furthermore, she is not above using stale ingredients in her sandwiches.

A financial advisor and a clergyman may have been unable to conceive of such a wicked plot. But yours truly cannot vouch with any certainty for the director of the software enterprise, who has become a white, middle-class racist, and a law unto himself since being released into the virtual world. Indeed, the author (just like his own creator, when *He* is quizzed by infidels with respect to the foul play of Western governments) refuses to be held to account for the actions of those who began life as mere figments of his imagination.

In fact, it is for the sake of realism that I relate my story in the present tense. After all, it would be implausible to forge a chain of events - born as a possibility out of the past, and actually occurring in the future (that is experienced as "the present" when you and I arrive there) ... because in real time, we have only the *here and now* to play with. A carpenter must fashion his Pinocchio out of whatever grain of wood becomes available to him. (Do I hear your approval? I am so glad.) Anyhow, the past tense is for the conventional narrator, which I am not. And as for the future ... who knows?

And the funeral director? He is a dark horse – whose efficacy in the internment of bodies is unknown. The womb of fancy is still sore from the moment of his birth ...

'I could not squeeze out another one like him,' she says. 'His big head stretched my sensitive vulva, as he forced himself into the rarefied air of the printed page. Ouch! I would have taken Mifepristone and aborted him, but for the advice of my gynaecologist' Ah! Dearest Fancy, preferred over the faculties of intellect and wit; and, so often, the exit strategy of both.

God-Fearing Funeral Services & Son is last in the terrace of practical enterprises. It is conspicuous for the absence of a patrilineal name, and for its failure to supply the plural form of the final noun. Its controller is an ambitious gentleman, who lost all of his family before he had acquired the power of speech; and who was lucky enough to be adopted at the age of three by a rich, elderly couple who suckled him on a lethal mixture of fine food and exaggerated praise. He grew fat on the one, and smug on the other. And yet, still, a sense of his own misfortune in starting life as an orphan shines forth like the rising sun, and nourishes a rabid desire to succeed. In some ways, he is not unlike the director of our software enterprise, whom you are just about to meet.

******

The forthcoming narrative explores various idioms. It may, by turns, be prosaic, poetic, or dramatic. It may even be religious. I have bequeathed something for everyone. All of the events take place within a short time frame, and a few of the *Dramatis personae* are *in absentia* for a while. Most of them may well be "beyond the pail". Notwithstanding, as I am ever the humble democrat, - I shall leave the *ultimate* reckoning of the good or bad character of each of my creations for others to decide.

PART THE FIRST: INSIDE THE LAUNCHPAD

Picture a warehouse. It has no distinguishing features. You might surmise that it is a place of storage and nothing more. Yet, in this consideration, you would be wrong. Inside it are many Portakabins, each illuminated by a series of dull, eco-friendly light bulbs – which are, in truth, friendly only to the wallet, and hostile to the eyes ... the eyes of office workers at their desks, who longingly imagine that what is seeping through the window, and illuminating the exterior space, is natural sunlight. Hanging from the ceiling are cheap chandeliers, bought from a charity shop nearby; and some brightly coloured bulbs of the botanical kind, with their roots cruelly confined by tiny flower-pots.

Enter .... the director of the enterprise. The in-house cat is following him, hopeful of a tasty snack, and purring with wet lips in anticipation of this booty. Unfortunately, her lips are not the only parts of her which are wet. Her real name is *Pia*, but she has been nicknamed "Puddles" for a reason you can guess. The director is proceeding apace, across the floor of a huge open plan area, less aware of the feline than of his own deportment. He glides through his domain, much as a blue-blooded royal patrols his florid palace - or his duchy of Cornwall. And yet there is nothing grand about his surroundings: for although they are lit by the human spirit – it is a spirit of inflated pride, and of fantastic aspiration. The director holds his chin high in the air, and his nose points towards a materialistic heaven – from whence he catches a whiff of higher things. Amongst them, are the petrol fumes of a Rolls Royce that he is determined shall be his one day; as well as the homely smell of a Vispring mattress, cradling him in his foetal position and stuffed, not with cotton wool, but with warm notes hot off the presses of the Bank of England .... each, with the Queen's head still fuming slightly. Meanwhile, the headboard of his dreams is constructed out of gold florins and silver coins, glinting with sun kisses like a rivulet of Mammon; and, all the while, his imaginary love-nest is flavoured with the scent of a perfect woman ... but let's not get carried away.

He opens a door, and then another door, and finds himself in one of the mini-Portakabins: which is, strange to tell, inside another Portakabin All around is a huge open plan area. In another incarnation, it could have made a splendid auditorium. For now, it remains the innards of an unremarkable building.

'But won't your employees suffer from an absence of sunlight?' He has been asked. The director explains, without irony:

'We believe that the more thoroughly immersed the staff are in their software environment, the fewer distractions they will have, and the more devoted they will be to their labours. My instruction is for the clocks to go forward by one hour when they arrive, and back by one hour before they leave. This has been named, after this House of Software, as "The Perfect Launchpad Time". I hasten to add that I swiftly restore Greenwich Mean Time when the staff are absent: for I, being unique among human beings, realise that the orbit of the earth cannot be altered via the setting of mechanical timepieces.'

'But why place a smaller cabin within a larger one? I fear your staff will suffer from claustrophobia.'

'We ...' he responds (meaning himself, of course; but applying greater cogency to his argument, by implicating the approval of other, non-existent, people, with the easy affectation of a royal who need brook no contradiction; and obviously not invoking the "We" of the Holy Trinity, for *that* would be sacrilege) ... '*We* contend that if a thing is worth doing, it is worth doing well – which is to say, it should be done without fluency, without simplicity, and always without compromise'.

The windows of the Portakabins are constructed from laminated plastic, and, near where he is standing, hangs an imposing portrait of Winston Churchill, with the following caption underneath: "A riddle, wrapped in a mystery, inside an enigma": except that this time, the subject is not the Soviet Union, but the intricacies of computer programming. Many a frustrated programmer has pondered these words; and one or two have picked obsessively at the outermost layer of a plastic window or two, until it separates from its fellows – curling, like a translucent wave upon the sea. Just as the wave is about to become a tsunami, the one who is illegally fiddling will part company with it, and attack the adjacent window in his tiny act of sabotage. In this way, the layers are never unravelled completely. Nor does the offender allow the skin below his cuticles to be cut, and deposit a spot of blood. At all costs, he must escape detection. For if caught red-handed, what would be his defence? Perhaps it would be that such behaviour is only skin-deep, and disguises a deep state of problem-solving reflection?

Outside the Portakabins, in the open plan area, there are two bronze statues. The first is a near-replica of the late nineteenth century sculpture by Hugo Reinhold. You know the one. It is informed by Darwin's theory of evolution – and is, itself, a mock-up of Rodin's The Thinker, depicting a thoughtful ape sitting on top of a pile of books, one of which is 'The Origin of Species'. The slight modification, in the present context, is that the ape is now seated in front of a computer. It is a parody of a parody. Beside it, is a second sculpture, also in bronze, showing an oversized thumb and forefinger peeling the rings from a huge onion ... each sheet of gossamer representing yet another layer of confounded logic – susceptible to the powers of human understanding, only after the previous ring has been rolled away. In the original incarnation, the ape is pondering his place in the natural order of things. Here, the creature's eyes are fixed on the allium vegetable beside him, rather than on the computer, - acknowledging how much of a programmer's thinking occurs 'outside the box'.

In a broader context, the art work stands for the doomed attempts of every new technician to unpick the futile attempts of the last, or to "stand and deliver" in an impractical timescale. The present incumbent (just in the author's line of vision), is a mere stripling of less than twenty years. And, just for good measure, he is struggling with a further unpalatable truth. This is, that the area designated to him has been smelling of a pungent vegetable since he arrived that morning. For the life of him, he cannot discover the source of the odour. Every so often, his tongue sallies forth with distress signals, such as 'Oh!' and 'Oh, no!' The culprit has been sellotaped to the underside of his desk, and is – in fact - a partially decayed onion! It is a gift in kind, from the misanthropic employee who last sat in his chair, to whichever upstart would replace him.

But hearken! The youth's nearly-suppressed effusions are acquiring some more words, 'Oh, dear! It can't be. Not him. No, pleeeaaaase ...!'

At this very second, the director of the whole enterprise has appeared, and he is admiring the sculptures. The notification sent to him from his olfactory bulb has been put into a holding pen, marked, "To be attended to shortly". Meanwhile, he is conceiving a little pun, intended for the three unsuspecting underlings who have formed a queue by his side. It will be something to do with a need to *go wireless*, as the current connections are *not long enough in the blue tooth*. When the pun has been released, the effect turns out to be no more welcome than the gas which presently invades the air. The attendees are silent, excepting one who has been employed long enough to have acquired a smidgen of Dutch courage. The courageous one expresses his superiority over the other two by groaning quietly at his boss's feeble touch of whimsy (which is only the latest of many touches). And the aforementioned school-leaver (who feels like Livingstone, hunting for the source of the Nile) imitates this audible groan. Foolish Boy!

The director sniffs, like a hound alerted to the scent of a rotten fox.

'You're supposed to eat breakfast at home,' he remarks.

'It is not my *breakfast*,' the voice of innocence replies. He means to emphasise the lack of ownership with the word, *my*, but his courage fails him at the final moment: leaving the emphasis to rest, instead, upon the word, "breakfast".

'Well, I hope it is not your *last supper*.'

Soon afterwards, the boy chances upon the guilty bulb. But alas! The director has moved on.

A Change of Tone

And now, on a friendlier note, we must celebrate the handshakes between the various pieces of electronic equipment. Oh! We can only guess at what felicitous greetings must occur – or at how busy these pieces must be, seizing each other's peripherals so warmly, in a virtual kind of way. (It is a wonder they ever get any work done!) And, thank God, it *is* in a virtual way, for we would not wish the effluent from private quarters to attenuate the circuits.

Often, this festival of neighbourliness may be presided over by "Blue Tooth", which, acting less like a dentist than a sermonizing priest, requires that the two devices who are in communion should be "joined, through interdependency, so as to form a couple". Ah! How romantic! How much more amicable is a union such as this, than what commonly holds sway between the director of this forlorn enterprise - and his wife, whom I shall now introduce.

******

In fact, there she is now - in the wake of the big chief himself. Heads are turning, and she is acknowledged as a supernova in her own right. For a while, she has been puzzling over the belligerent behaviour of her mobile telephone. Upon being switched on, it says, "Optimizing app 1 of 125" – and thereupon initiates a process which takes twenty minutes before the device is finally "open for business". When it is switched off, it simply comes on again. It does not respond to obedience training - and, deciding not to use it after all, she removes the battery. She complains,

'I do hope I shall never have to lift the battery from the engine of my car when I park by the supermarket. I haven't got room for it in my handbag!'

Amidst the flow of extraordinary communications, the natural effusions of the First Lady's perfume creates an olfactory handshake with every unsuspecting nostril in the vicinity. She has actually adorned herself with a cosmetic which is musk-based - applied from a phial she reuses and never rinses out, and which she keeps in her handbag at all times, since 'you never know when you might need to create a big impression'. The potion is remarkably pungent, and, when she catches up with her misogynist Prince Charming, he is wondering why a liquid infused with a male hormone is worn by females as an aphrodisiac for the male sex.

He and his spouse begin to speak of how rosy their future appears to be.

'Our new business is putting down roots and behaving like a hardy annual,' she says. Alas! She says too much.

'Ha! Ha!' he coughs, and pretends it is an allergic reaction to her perfume. His interjection is actually brought on by an indigestible morsel of dialogue that he has lately heard, which impels him to instant reflux. She tuts.

'It is *my* business, not *ours*,' he thinks. His cough is a warning that he will not be standing for any sub-standard behaviour during the course of the forthcoming meeting, scheduled for that morning.

'After all,' he reasons silently, 'If I must put up with nonsense from my wife, I will certainly not take it from anyone else'.

She tuts again. An affair of the heart hath reached a sad impasse when the rhythms of a husband's thoughts are prompted by his wife's tutting.

Freddie, the Cleaner

Now, it is widely known that Mr Propotamous has given summary dismissals to many of his staff; and sometimes the act of firing goes to their heads. In the list of casualties is a former cleaner named Freddie; who, with a passionate and generous heart, would attend to the potted plants of the big boss, keeping them in the springtime of their beauty. Yet too often this heart of his is impregnated with a sharp spite, or envy, – twinned with an absolute dearth of rationality.

Freddie's response to his disappointment was to open a shoe-polishing business right outside the front door of the software house, calling out to all-comers, whilst on his hands and knees, 'Let your footsteps rise and shine!' until Mr Propotamous requested that he should 'leave upon the instant'.

But still, he hovers. One day, he is seen taking his two infant grandsons for a walk. This consists of packing them into a supermarket trolley, and thence pulling it up the precipitous hill which leads to the offices ... thereupon to occupy the same forbidden place upon the street as before.

Freddie used to take his hyperactive grandchildren - whose intelligence he does not rate highly - for bouts of intense activity in the park. It is a process known to him as "draining the vegetables". But he has stopped this in recent years, as he finds it too strenuous.

Subsequently, he has embellished his behaviour with another strange habit. He detains employees *en route* to work

- in order to spy upon them, or to relate some pointless story about elderly residents in his neighbourhood, whom nobody knows. Rumour has it that he is lonely and craves human company, but Rumour can surmise nothing of his silent intentions; and, for all I know, via these well-engineered delays he may be enacting a rare form of revenge upon the House of Software. What follows is a conversation of his, conducted when he was in full flight earlier on today, - and recorded in the diary of a person on Pilate's payroll who was running late.

"'Excuse me, but I used to be employed in the same offices as you. Remember me?' And without waiting for a reply, Freddie rambles on ... 'Well, I chanced upon a certain Ms Gray on the way to where I am now; and *do you know* she has only one lung, and suffers from a complexion far paler and more sickly than her surname - with pimples, and a blackhead known as Popeye. She staggers forth daily upon that steep hill she calls home, with *two* walking sticks ... one in each hand; and these, she manages like an Alpine skier who has gone off-piste (as well as off-colour); but Mrs Aquiline, whose skin is still as fresh and florid as the day that it was made, - has only *one* stick. It is created from the finest maple, and at the top of it there is a knob, that has been carved to resemble the face of her dearly departed husband. Picture her thus! *Just one stick, mind*. And this contrast – in spite of the fact that M/s Gray is 92 years young, and Mrs Aquiline is all of 95. 'Tis certain that the gifts of relative health are a travesty of justice – as are the gifts of relative mirth!' (He laughs as he sees me flinch.) 'Now hold your horses right there ... I forbid you to leave ... It would be most rude, for I have more to say. *Watch out!* I still have a grudge against the last person who didn't let me finish.' And thus does he go on and on, waving his arms about like a madman, so as to indicate comparison and extent, - until I am left with no alternative but to turn around and run for it."

An Aberrant History is a Dangerous Thing

The director is relentlessly misanthropic. But why? In the search for clues, one may prefer to recount how he is provoked by tiny lapses of good judgement - or forgetfulness - in others, and overlook how his character was originally formed. In this respect, one stands in the laboratory of life, treating some alteration to the hue of a liquid here, or the occurrence of a thunderclap and flash of artificial lightening there, - as a *Son et Lumière* and nothing more.

But aided by the magnifying glass of family history, one examines at his peculiar name (which I have withheld from the public gaze until now). Even the priest at the child's christening elevated his eyebrows to an altitude somewhere above Lord Hereford's Nob (speaking figuratively, of course), as he said the words: 'I name this child ... Pilate ... Hodgkin ... Propotamous.' The child was later advised to change his name, which (in adulthood) he duly did, to Pilate *Henry* Propotamous – leaving the most offending articles unaltered because he found their pomposity somewhat edifying. In his current line of employment, he has been nicknamed "PHP", after the online programming language. He does not seem to mind. And, in fact, this pseudonym is faintly appropriate, for he does have a tendency to dabble in the technicalities of his profession, and compound a problem or two, – before handing everything over to someone else to clean up. The well-attuned reader will be reminded of Pontius Pilate, who, one Spring day two thousand years ago, caused an Almighty problem (note the capital "A") by failing to get his hands dirty - and washing them instead. At present, he (the twenty-first century Pilate, that is) is fully engaged in the *dabbling* stage of the spin cycle. Later, and just at the point when the problem becomes insoluble, he shall wash all traces of his iniquity with imaginary soap suds.

His father wanted to give him the name of a biblical character, and felt Pilate to be 'a relatively blameless guy'. His excuse was: 'Well, I couldn't exactly call my only son "Jesus", for that would be disrespectful.' Clearly, Pilate's father was not from South America. Oh! To be rich in respect, but poor in action. Daddy was devoted to bible studies, yet unfortunately suffered from occasional bouts of mental illness; whilst mummy was a victim of dipsomania. The result was a strange Christian name, arrived at through a lethal mixture of the bible, drunkenness and madness; with the bible providing the alternatives, and the drunkenness and madness conspiring to make the selection. Once daddy and mummy were finally restored to their respective states of sanity and sobriety, - the vicar had already been informed of the infant's name, and recorded it in the pages of his catalogue.

Pilate was picked on in primary school on account of his preposterous name; then he was picked on in senior school on the same account; and thirdly (but not lastly) he was picked on in his first office role – although there were other reasons for this; for, by that time, the deposit of spitefulness which he had already endured, was exceeding the threshold permitted for that emotional account: and violent outbursts would stem the flow of mockery. Yet it never occurred to Pilate, during these early days, to follow through and alter what he should be known by. His parents, who were Jehovah's Witnesses, had instilled in him the tenet that it is no more correct to alter your patrilineal name, than to have a blood transfusion: on the basis that your name is as much a part of you as your blood platelets, or your DNA.

Sadly, his torments did not end with others taking his name in vain. There was also the small issue of his father interminably reciting, of an evening, the least inspiring parts of the bible, melded with an impression of the lounge vibrating in sympathy with the heave and sigh of his mother snoring (after a reckless dose of whisky). Such things would drive him into the arms of Beelzebub. Yet, even today, he is strangely unaware of whose embrace it is, since he is wont to invoke the holy book himself, - and with great relish (albeit when it happens to suit *him*, and usually for some slightly crooked end). He accompanies his wife at church services of various denominations. You might call the two of them "spiritual vagrants". Upon occasion, he has even been known to depict himself as less a company director, than a prophet with devoted followers.

But now, dear reader, I must unlock a small episode from the vault of Pilate's past. He would wish it to remain hidden, but – like him – I am a disciple of my own temptation. It began one morning, long ago, when he was in the foothills of his adolescence. He remembers the day well. The sun was beating down on him through his bedroom window. His rabbit lay beside him, soft and warm and helpless. A fire in his loins had been kindled by a demon in a saucy dream. And when he awoke, he decided to rape his bunny rabbit multiple times, before running the sperm-drenched object through the spin drier. But never fear! It was a crime without consequence, for the inseminated party was but a furry toy which – without so much as a pip-squeak - would take the rap of animate things.

Pilate recalls the focus of his first date, a rebellious adolescent girl with posh parents; and with a penchant for cooking. That would-be date is still as vivid as anything in the present tense. His diary entry for that day reads:

"She undertakes to feed me. The agreed time is 2pm. I am held up and ten minutes late. Her door is locked shut. She will not open. Outside, my cooked meal has been deposited on the ground in a plastic dish, normally reserved for the family dog. Two pigeons have begun pecking at the gravy and mashed potato. Beside the food is a piece of extra-strong Kleenex tissue marked with a felt-tip pen: "Stuff the meal. I'm not in the mood.""

******

When he was a little older, he kept a boxer puppy whom he named "Smut", on account of its tendency to leave a record of where its nose and mouth had been, in a trail of slime like that which exudes from the orifice of a giant snail. Unfortunately, on one occasion a damp patch was sustained in the area of his trousers which covered his genitals. He was teased mercilessly in school, as to the true nature of the offending effluent. Then, one day without warning, the creature went missing and was never seen again. At around this time Pilate was baby-sitting his friend's giant millipede. He was enticed by its smooth locomotion, but somewhat put off by the multiple pairs of legs; and he decided, whilst "under the influence" (you make take that how you will) to go one better and purchase the ever-popular Royal Python, *Python regius*. This charming reptile is (nowadays) famous for its innumerable colour sequences, achieved through selective breeding; and (always) for its endearing habit of curling up into a tight ball whenever it is feeling shy. Whether a forensic examination would have revealed what the puppy-shaped bulge in its stomach was, who can tell? No matter, Pilate was very devoted to his new pet (which was a mature female specimen, touted to be of record length), and its mealtimes were always a shared pleasure.

Once, when the serpent had become rather stout, and sloughed its skin, he remarked upon how the discarded tissue resembled one half of his mother's tights – and, in the end, he saved two skins, which he intended to use for cross-dressing, until he found they didn't fit. Later on, he insisted that one of them be employed as a Christmas stocking, which, to his great chagrin, Santa Claus left empty. But why would he expect otherwise? Well, his family were non-conforming in a church of non-conformists, and had chosen to reinstate the convention of Yuletide.

Pilate was an only child, and doted on by his relatives, to the extent of becoming (in their eyes) someone who could do no wrong. And he always thought of himself as highly entrepreneurial. While still a young child, an aunt - who was rich in money but poor in health, - gave him a lavish present for his birthday. It matters not what this present was: only that she was nearing her end, and wanted to 'go out with a flourish of kindness'. Recognising the huge price tag attached to the object, he hovered around her, like a little vulture, anticipating more free gifts to come.

The cogs of his canny brain turned around and around. He cajoled from her various boons of moderate worth, and thought discreetly to himself,

'While I am on a roll I might as well milk the situation for all it's worth.' Then, one fine day, the opportunity arose for him to speak with disarming frankness. 'After all, auntie,' he reasoned, 'What use is your money to you now? Where you are going you won't need it.' He perceived a touch of brutality in his words, and so he softened his tone,

'Heaven awaits, auntie! Heaven awaits!'

His aunt instructed him to keep the expensive gift a secret from his parents, in case they were embarrassed by the extreme limits to which her Christianity had lead her, and by the concomitant fact that they could neither afford to recompense her; nor to be generous to the boy in equal measure. Then, just before Christmas of that year, she passed away. He began plea-bargaining with his parents – saying that he would do the Christmas shopping for them that they had ear-marked for him, on the double condition that they give him the money to buy his own present, and that it be more money than they would normally spend themselves – as he was saving them time. After all, 'time is money,' he reasoned.

Their "present" to him was a substantial wad of notes to "purchase" the gift he had already received from his aunt. This left him free to pose with the unspent allowance, like Rockefeller: and make his friends go green with jealousy. During this time, he bought many decorative things, including a gilt-edged hammer.

'No one knows what I have done,' he thought. 'And if ever I should come under suspicion for misappropriating money, I shall make a pretence of not remembering how I came by such an unusual device.'

Leadership Style and Peculiar Staff

Pilate insists, 'I have no time to talk to my staff. Don't they realise how busy I am? They must email me, and make no bones about our respective desks being within a stone's throw of each other. In fact, I shall, forthwith, send out (by email) to each and every one of them, a missive with no fewer than twenty-seven attachments: on the subject of office etiquette.'

Pilate fritters away his time: on Facebook, to improve his social life – so far, without effect; on Twitter – to "noisily" express his opinions, and so emulate another president known to all (who heads a union - not of people, but of states); in sending emails, or text messages, – to those who are within earshot of him; and via LinkedIn – when searching for fresh technical wizards, whom he can poach from other companies. He is also intending to employ Instagram and WhatsApp, but is not sure what for. And the more methods of indirect contact that he employs, the less he truly communicates.

Pilate may be likened to the famous English Chemist, Henry Cavendish, who was so reticent that he felt driven to undertake all of his business transactions through the depositing and receiving of faceless messages; except that Pilate is not actually shy. He is just retiring – or, to pluck a more suitable phrase from the lexicon, "lazy".

His chief programmer, Dmitri, is prepared to parley with others of inferior capability; but he would prefer to touch base with his laptop; and so, in conversation, he looks the other way, for he *is* (perhaps) a little shy. In a soliloquy, he was once overheard to say,

'In the past, many have felt that they could give me short shrift, on the understanding that I, who am ever reasonable, shall not respond in kind. It is a back-handed compliment, I suppose, but it is one I could well do without.'

******

Mr Propotamous is in his private office. He oscillates back and forth in his executive armchair, and almost senses his mother's hand upon his shoulder, - day-dreaming that he is a toddler once more, and being gently rocked to sleep. Each time he leans forward, he peers through a minute portal in the breeze block wall, onto the open plan area below. He delights in his snug hideaway, and refers to that little window as his "spyhole". It admits a view of a mezzanine floor with some potential for grandeur; and, below this floor, his staff may be seen as they arrive each morning. From his vantage point he derives a feeling of empowerment. He murmurs with pleasure:

'They are here because they *have* to be here, whereas I am here by choice. I command every movement of their bodies and their minds. And – Oh! - what a circus act it is! The code operates like magic. It casts a spell upon the medium, who cannot be released - except by solving the conundrum which confounds him. A mild dose of autism prevails, causing the technical wizards to move through the public gallery outside their Portakabins, looking quite lost. How therapeutic it is for me to watch other men at work ... men who have forgotten the most basic principles of social interaction. Or perhaps, they never learned them (in lieu of their future careers). They are, shall we say, experientially challenged, and have difficulty in wearing the facial expression which is appropriate for each social situation that arises.'

Mr Propotamous keeps a journal, in which he makes occasional entries as he peers through his spyhole. One day, he may donate this journal to the annals of ethology; but, for the time being, he is reluctant to part with something that gives him so much pleasure. He verbalises the notes he has made, his voice fluctuating like the tone of an actor practising for a part in a play:

'It is as if the jobbing programmer, on a tranquil day, retains the embers of a fire – with the ebb and flow of dialogue not quite strong enough to wash them away. Can his face, like memory foam, ever reclaim its puffy innocence? We shall see.'

Mr Propotamous enlarges upon his thesis (if we may bestow such a flattering term upon it),

'The developer will put on some emotional garb at the outset of a conversation, which is usually one of strained concentration; and then, like to one in a tuxedo and a tight bow-tie, he simply forgets to change into something more comfortable.'

And there is more ...

'My minions enter the Servants' Quarters at 9am, with cables hanging out of their ears, like tightly-woven dreadlocks formed from a superabundance of earhole hair. They are deep in conversation with a second personality – much as a schizophrenic might be. Thankfully, the mysterious "medium" only *appears* to be inside their skulls – and has, in fact, a legitimate source. So they are *compos mentis*. Thank God! Yet it is an irony of their profession that, once disconnected from their mobile phones, and after a day in which their software wishes have not been consummated, they will *appear* to have grown more sane, whereas in fact they have moved nearer to the point of madness.'

'Ah! Multi-tasking ... always and forever ... surfing the net, checking their emails, conversing upon Skype ... Dear me! In a valiant attempt to perform *every act at once*, they end up doing *nothing very well*.'

The director contrasts their condition with his great sanity. He feels a resemblance to God, and reflects,

'I preside over a well-organised chaos: like an entomologist with his termite mound. And I inhabit an Officer's *Mess* – in the primary sense. But I know exactly where everything is.'

And, in order to retain his mental faculties at the peak of their performance, the director occasionally takes down a book of detective stories from the highest shelf of his wall unit, and reads a page or two; before returning to the infamous spyhole.

On one occasion, as his shift draws slowly to a close, a coder is attending to his terminal. Our hero-boss is transfixed by him, and cooing with satisfaction. Suddenly, the coder's attention switches to the rear end of his desktop machine, as he disentangles some wires from various solid objects, such as ice-cream and chocolate bar wrappers, and attaches a new peripheral. In order to do the job properly, he realises that he must descend to the ground and look behind the visual display unit, so that he can better see how the male parts might connect with the female. He moans quietly, for he is a little portly, and has not often bent his knobbly knees like this since he crawled out of his mother's vagina. Surely, the last time was when his old gymnastics master insisted upon it? He offers up a little prayer to his maker that he might get 'the wretched piece of merchandise up and running in a jiffy'; and, in the process of whispering his divine request, he quite forgets himself. Amazingly, in the white heat of the moment, - he rises, genuflects, and makes the sign of the cross. And then he falls to his knees once more, with his hands clasped together. Surely, he is not about to mortify himself before the altar of an electronic god? He leaves his prayer, and continues with his labours for several minutes as if nothing has happened ... until he realises that something *has* happened. He pauses and begins to sweat. He stares into space, moving his lips silently. And then, he splutters out the following words with a look of horror on his face:

'Oh, my God! What did I just do? Did I really do what I think I just did? Did I, in fact, genuflect and cross myself with my forefinger?'

And so a stream of reflection is set in motion, but this time with no accompanying act of supplication (for he is in a panic). His short-term memory crystallises in that stream, as clearly as the face of Narcissus might, were the supernatural being of that name to gaze into it; but, unlike Narcissus, this coder is rapidly falling *out of love* with himself. Then he completes his soliloquy with a verdict that few would disagree with: 'I must have lost my marbles. Did anyone see them as they rolled away?'

******

While all of this is going on, Pilate is gazing through his tiny (aforementioned) hole and photographing events with his digital camera. What he sees may serve as evidence in a court of law – though of what, he is not yet certain. Suddenly, he receives the message, "Please wait ... Stitching pictures". Pilate examines the result, and scribbles in his notebook,

'A perfect triptych: programmer descends to his knees; programmer rises, and them parleys with his maker; programmer's face is fixed with grave concern. And I thought the overarching mood of the day was temperate and normal!

Like the elements in chemistry – it seems my staff will freeze at different temperatures.'

******

As Pilate delights in his tiny portal, and revels in his most private of quarters, he celebrates his financial ascendency with a bottle of champagne.

'Lucky the man who likes what he can have,' he remarks blandly, whilst swallowing a mouthful of gas. He then hiccups repeatedly, – before satisfaction is achieved by way of a very loud belch ...

'This is an explosive product for the middle classes,' he muses – sounding rather like Guy Fawkes. 'And it is couched in mystery, with the only formally accepted example hailing from the Champagne region of France. Therein, lies a miraculous formula that attempts to break with the laws of physics ... and bring to birth a fluid child that is, in point of fact, less liquid than gas, and – hmm - to my taste buds, somewhat sour: a concoction so special that it must be patented. But why, oh why – a formula for the produce of only *thisssss region*?' he asks audibly, slurring his words in a slovenly, drunken fashion. 'Could this be the one true place where a special gas uniquely miscible with wine, may be mined or refined? Ah, but no! The gas is not added as an after-thought, but is the naturally occurring "trapped wind", bottled in the *tirage* part of the fermentation process. Well, then. When I have had a glass (or three) of the same, and it is starting to repeat on me ... a great conversion becomes possible. I must simply hold my breath, and stick my head into a barrel of "still vino" from the self-same area.' (He yawns dramatically, and holds his head, which is beginning to sag, - as if he is a neonate with a weak neck.) 'Oh, my mind ... how vexed am I? And shall the peripatetic greenhouse gas within me - be prejudicial to the elevated exit at the front (as in a cow), or to the *alternative* (baser) exit from the posterior? If the posterior is to be preferred, then the aforementioned miraculous conversion slips beyond my reach.' He ponders this conundrum for a while ... and resolves it thus: 'but I could squat, butt-naked and fully immersed, inside the tub – and then the aeration phase may be completed.'

And now, he falls asleep - whilst his stomach rumbles with the unsettling rhythms of a volcano.

What follows is an unsettling dream.

Pilate pictures himself in a café where his least-favourite music is playing.

'Do you only stock "Rap", "House", or "Garage"?' he asks the proprietor politely, hoping the present track can be replaced.

'Why certainly not, sir... Would you prefer some futuristic form of these specialities (yet to be conceived of), such as "Hotel", "B&B" or "Heathrow runway" ...? Or the rough strains of "Garden Shed", perhaps? And what piping hot beverage would *Sir* like to order ...? What little tincture would match the mood of the music, in the manner of all good synaesthesia?'

'I'll have a thimble of deadly nightshade, please.'

******

Now reflect, for a moment, on the combined intelligence operating in an Information Technology Unit. Think, also, of how *normal human behaviour* is sacrificed for the arcane arts of systems development to have their day. And ponder, for a while, upon the creative tension leaking out of staff, through physical tics and crazy sentences; and then reflect upon what they might become. Audience, I give you ... One elderly programmer, fortified by a rich spirit, as *l'exemple parfait* of "the mature fruitcake". As a matter of fact, the director has only recently said 'goodbye' to him (before issuing him out with God's speed through the back door).

He bears a striking resemblance to the physicist, Albert Einstein, and he is also thought to have had full-blown Asperger's Syndrome. The said technophile and "celebrity" - for this is what he became during his brief tenure, - did have valuable knowledge, and (when a small morsel of this had been articulated) he would occasionally be cornered by someone with a query. His reaction to this could go one of two ways. If he admired the intellect of the questioner, he might be helpful. And if he did not – nay, if he even disagreed with the phrasing of the question, or with any premise subtly embedded within it, - he might choose to test the questioner's patience. This was achieved by locking his own eyes with those of the unfortunate, - a task not easy to perform, for "Einstein" suffered from a condition known as "Strabismus". Herein, the two eyes point in different directions, – an outcome which prompted that nasty man, Mr Propotamous, to give out incessant taunts – with reference to a general lack of focus. But our strange genius had a special way of bringing his whole visual system into play. He would tilt and rotate his head slightly, like a seagull: so capturing, with both eyes, the fullness of the person before him. In the process, he would also open his lips and hum a melody from Ira Gershwin, and bare his teeth in order to perform a tap dance upon them with his soiled and jagged nails. It was as if his fingers were the legs of Fred Astaire, and his dentition were a piano, decked out with various keys: some white, and some a shade of off-white or caramel (tinctured, perhaps, by the imbibing of too much coffee). Such a display would continue until the question was fully formed. At that point, the guru would gingerly put his fingers – with their tap-dancing fingernail "shoes" - back into his pockets, shut his mouth, and walk quietly away; leaving his opposite number in a state of open-mouthed astonishment.

Fortunately, there was a soft side to Einstein as well. On occasion, he would serenade a bowl of fruit with "My Darling Clementines". And at lunchtime, he would buy floral displays to take home to his non-existent wife. Inside the office, bouquet in hand, he moved like a ballet dancer with splayed feet. Needless to say, he was imagining a level of grace beyond his capabilities. As flower heads showered the carpet, like confetti at a wedding, he imagined himself to be stepping through his code - and examining its procedural logic. Occasionally, when he listened to Johann Strauss on his iPod, his indelicate movements would form themselves into a waltz. He called it his "structured walk through".

And he was also named "der mumbler", on account of his low-voiced, running commentary upon things. He mumbled over lunch. He mumbled during every visit to the lavatory. You knew he was in there, because you could hear the mantra from the cubicle:

'If this is a literal ... and that is a boolean which alternates between *Yes* and *No* ... then more conditions are required in one pass through the procedure ... a case statement, perhaps ...? Now, let me see ... switch ($a) { case add ... mmmmm'. At this juncture, he might pause, and then (arriving at a temporary conclusion) shuffle his feet with excitement.

When he was moving through the open plan area, he would occasionally retrace his logic, - shuffling backwards, to compensate for a miscalculation. This ensured that he did not arrive too soon at his destination, which could either be his desk, or *le grand* coffee pot in the kitchen. Of course, no one else could concentrate while he was doing all of this - and so he was fired: but not, unfortunately, before he had lost the company a valuable contract with the Ministry of Defence, who decided (after speaking to him during a visit to the software house) that they should "look elsewhere".

It was a sad turn of events, for, in the early days, our superstar of the virtual world was an especially productive member of the team. This was due to the great powers of concentration he displayed; and to his unfailing ability to come up with a solution, no matter how challenging the problem. He never took a day's sick leave – except once, when he was concerned about his stooping gait, and was prevailed upon by his doctor to visit an osteopath to discuss the possibility of having a bit of 'scaffolding work' done on his spine. Not surprisingly, Einstein became less productive as the months went by. He used to scour manuals for the syntax applicable for certain "verbs", and would readily apply the most terse and ingenious methods in software development: most especially in "Sequel" (the pet name of programmers for SQL, or Structured Query Language). And he was latterly observed to be working on his autobiography, The Sequel Life of Benjamin Disrami (his true name); and to be reading Tolstoy during his lunchtime and coffee breaks. Relating to the latter, his mumblings became his undoing:

'If Pierre_Bezuhov_will_meet_Napoleon

Then if Napoleon_must_die ...' etcetera, etcetera ...

Yes, dear reader, he had cast his lot with the mentally insane ... and was attempting to render the whole of War and Peace into pseudo-code.

His last legacy to the intellectual life of the department was no less strange. He had become exceedingly disillusioned with the bank which held his current account and received his generous salary; and so he expressed his intention to transfer his savings into the COBOL compartment known as "Working Storage". To this day, no one quite knows what he meant.

The Boss's Curriculum Vitae

The director had once worked as a computer programmer himself. He was a practitioner in the art of "C". But he was not a very good one. His mood was often aggravated by the requirement for every condition to have its inferences contained within a couple of "short and curlies" (or "curly brackets" to you and me). The modern family of low-level languages (such as C, Java and PHP) came to be regarded by him as the "short and curly brigade"; but not Python or Ruby-on-Rails. 'Ah, my precious Ruby! So like Pascal, she could be his half-sister!' quoth he. After a while, he became fed up with the pressure of being under someone else's thumb, – and decided that, from here on, he would call the shots. But he is less "the sheriff" than he would have us believe. He is subject to the eagle eyes of tax inspectors, of whom he says: 'They are swine - pure and simple! Idle porcine beasts, I say! But they are not *edible* swine, else they would serve a culinary function, and feed my starving foot soldiers!' (These are his underrated and overworked underlings). 'Instead of this, the vultures nourish only that fathomless layabout whose name is *The Treasury*, – and, towards this end, they bereave me of my hard-earned savings! (By this he means, all of the money which has been hard-earned for him by others.) 'And – while we are on the subject - how, may I ask, are *tax evasion* and *tax avoidance* two different things? Methinks word conjurors are evading the proper use of our mother tongue! Or *avoiding, evading or eluding* it. Let some linguistic devil conjure an entrapment for them! Or, Vietnamese-style, may they stumble into a covered hole - and be impaled upon a spike tainted with filth! And then we'll see how well they can split hairs; or be split, like hairs - or hares, in the teeth of hounds.'

He has inaugurated a small business once before. To raise capital, he gathered together a number of investors via some high-profile marketing; and through the promise of generous returns on shares. Having reigned in a satisfactory sum of money, he reconstituted the shares with a fresh "product split", through which the shareholders lost two-thirds of their investment; and he then placated the anger they felt, by stating the half-truth that he had the largest shareholding, and would stand to lose the most money. In summary, he *did have*, but he *would not*. One of the shareholders, Dmitri, was more forthright than the others; and so, in a tempestuous meeting, this brave soul indicated his wish to form a resolution against the director. Now, usually in such a scenario the individual would be voted down – being viewed as some kind of an apostate, a rogue intent upon rocking the boat until he is the only one left sitting in it. But, in this case, the motion was carried, giving the minor shareholders, collectively, a majority share of the company: and, therefore, control over its future fortunes. The director saw that he was cornered. He was terrified that nearly everyone would sell their shares, and reduce the value of his own holding. So he decided, with complete legality, to bring his venture into the first chapter of liquidation.

'Their collective voice must not become more powerful than my own,' he thought deviously, 'and so I shall simply take that voice away; and, unlike when a voice is hoarse in wintertime, no lozenge in existence shall restore its clarity and its purpose.'

And so he declared himself bankrupt, and the shares became worthless. Then he stashed his capital into an offshore account, not liable for taxation. (This is thanks to a succession of Her Majesty's Governments, whose representatives have countenanced such measures. And why shouldn't they? For they have funds of their own which require a safe haven.)

'I feel Christmas has come early this year! It is time to be merry,' he sings to himself, whilst performing a jig and wringing his hands. 'Ah, "insolvency"! That dreadful state which is suffered by the poor, but enjoyed by the rich as they pass on their debt to the poor ... or (at least) to the *public purse*! I shall keep my money overseas until the resulting furore has subsided. Then, I shall re-deploy it to inaugurate one more "initial public offering" - and so invite a fresh bunch of suckers to hand me their money. I have no qualms about this. My God believes in freedom – and so do I."'

Our colourful sinner is aided and abetted by his well-connected wife, who originally supplied an essential cash injection. In short, he is a modern paragon of enterprise.

The rebellious shareholder (previously mentioned) had worked as a sole trader for a while, developing novel software for the marketplace. But he was getting nowhere fast. So Pilate purchased his "plc" for a nominal fee, altered one or two things in the look and feel of the flagship system, and then re-packaged it as his own, - levying an inflated charge from the same client who had previously paid his rival a pittance. In spite of this daylight robbery, *said client* was blinded by the science of a prettier screen layout. The sole trader was one Dmitri Bosphorus-Deux, a computer nerd of French extraction. His nickname is "DB2", which is also the name of IBM's famous database development tool - although Dmitri pretends to be oblivious to this. And because he had fallen upon hard times, Pilate even offered him a job - on the understanding that there would be no legal proceedings initiated, out of vengeful thoughts. In fact, to add salt to a festering wound, the new employee is contractually obliged to defend the director's good name! What else can he do? He is driven by a need "to put bread on the table".

It would seem that Pilate has thought of everything. Surely, he would be content to relax and feather his nest? Not he!

'I am an astute man possessed of high energy and purpose,' he says, revelling in a positive self-concept.

Thus does he ascend the ladder of success, occasionally brushing aside those links to others who would hold him back; or pausing to brush up his technical know-how to a level which, he feels, 'is commensurate with my exalted position'.

The Technical Skills of Pilate

Pilate likes to think of himself as versatile, and as someone who leads from the front. He is a self-professed man of principle - who would never ask his troops to fight a battle, without waving his own sabre in the fray. Presently, he is sitting in his office; and his machine has been misbehaving all day. He has learned that, when disconnected from the system, he must log in again in order to log out. And there are other distractions. He reaches for the Headex pills he keeps in a draw beneath his desk.

'Damn it!' he expostulates. 'So many moving parts. God-forsaken commercial videos! Advertising banners! Allies of Satan! Pop up. Drop down. Pop up. Drop down. Like a Jack-in-a-Box, in love with perpetual motion!' He paints the air blue with a hotchpotch of rage and profanity.

'Lord sssssssssssod it!' he says with feeling. 'Fie upon you, and upon all who sent you!' But "Lord Sod It" suffers the insult in silence. And while Pilate is fast and loose with his typing, the venerable Lord warns him about "sticky keys".

'And sod the stickiness as well!'

Next on the agenda is a disobedient mouse.

'It seems that a mouse is even less amenable when trapped inside a machine (and visible there in the form of a cursor), than when independent of it,' observes Pilate. As he speaks, his forefinger moves to the far right; mouse goes half way; forefinger moves to the left; mouse prefers centre ground; forefinger moves furiously in a dazzling array of directions; mouse is belligerent, and refuses to cooperate at all! Finger slumps through over-exertion; mouse has become perfectly still. Then, quite suddenly, mouse revives itself - and rushes about like a maniac on amphetamines!

Today, he has for some time been struggling to access a sensitive email account, which his computer (the unfortunate victim of his stupidity) is telling him has been dormant for a long period. In fact, he has, this very moment, begun to compose the substance of an email highlighting a small technicality, which he would like the service provider to read, just as soon as he can ascertain where to send it:

To Whom it may concern:
Dear Sir or Madam,

I hate to disabuse you of any false notions that are extant amongst your associates, - but I must point out, in the interests of our glorious Mother Tongue, that when you claim to be "authenticating", you are, in point of fact, "authorizing". A website is not a restaurant. We are verifying our privileges in order that we may peruse our private data. We are *not* assessing the spices of an Indian curry. This is my polite rejoinder. With gratefulness, please amend where appropriate.

Forever Yours,
Pilate Henry Propotamous

He believes it to be a worthy note, but unfortunately the Spellchecker disagrees. His fingers slip as he is typing, so that "please" becomes "pleeeaaaase" - which is re-interpreted as "steeplechase"; whilst "rejoinder" is turned into "reindeer". Being short-sighted, he has accepted the superior wisdom on offer, and saves the message in his Drafts Folder – to be sent later.

After this, a vision of his adolescent love-interest floats into his conscious mind. His memory of her vital limbs and her strong will is still vivid: and it casts its long shadow over him, like a presiding spirit. After a disagreement many moons ago, she left a dog's dinner for him on the hessian mat outside her front door ... but she is now an old maid with whom he occasionally communicates with relish: for all animosity attached to that event has long since been forgotten. With the present-giving season just around the corner, his email reads, 'Wishing you a lovely Christmas with scrummy mince pies' - which the overworked and underpaid spellchecker changes to: 'Wishing you a *lonely* Christmas with *scummy* mince pies'. He posts his message in perfect innocence, for how can he doubt the puissance of modern software, when he is determined to be made rich by it?

Quite suddenly, a fresh cloud of grumpiness surrounds him. He is facing an electronic brick wall – prompting him to type a series of letters and digits into a field supplied, in order to prove that he is the person he says he is, and that the screen used for accessing his account is the one in front of him. He has already had to prove that he is not a robot, but there is worse to come.

The prompts appear in an oblong window, and they look as if they were written by someone who is suffering from *Delirium tremens*. Furthermore, each time he reproduces a mixture of letters and digits, he is presented with another mixture. Soon, the requirement to type spurious strings of characters and digits metamorphoses into a request to name the animal that he sees. The requirement is easy enough - a cat, a dog, a monkey, a giant panda. All of these he instantly recognises. And then there are the giant lizards of olden days. His eyes sparkle with delight.

'Ah! I'm good at these!' he exclaims. 'Now that one's a stegosaurus' (he dutifully types the word) '... and that's a diplodocus' (still dutiful and still typing; and then he stops) '... or is it the less streamlined brontosaurus ... hang on ... wasn't there some issue about the *brontosaurus* being a miss-reading of the fossil record ...? Dmitri ...? *Dmitri* ...?' He calls for the one whose shareholding he has shrunk to zero, and whose software he stole (and whom he also "rescued" with a second-rate bout of employment). But Dmitri is not available; and, anyhow, Dmitri's primary area of expertise is not the Jurassic period of the dinosaurs, but the much-vaunted "Age of the Personal Computer". Pilate moves through the options on the display unit in his usual shambolic way, until he cries out, as if in pain:

'Good God! Do I espy a sailing boat with legs ... or is it a Mudskipper? And what do we have here ...? An axolotl - the "Peter Pan of salamanders", as I like to call it. I always get those two little monsters mixed up!' And so, being somewhat mixed up himself, he gives up the ghost for the time being; and his weary spirit is disembodied and sails off, for a siesta, to the fabled Land of Nod.

******

When he awakes, Pilate is being summoned by a junior programmer to advise upon the execution of a set of procedures.

'If I check with the big boss before I run each procedure, then what can possibly go wrong?' the foolish lad reasons. 'I will have covered myself – if not in glory, then at least in a safety blanket.'

The ensuing conversation is punctuated with module names, and goes something like this:

'So, shall I fire off ACC_APP_ONE now?'

'Umm,' is the indeterminate reply. The boss is still rubbing the sleep out of his eyes, as the appropriate button is pressed.

'And shall I run *this procedure* as well: APP_TWO?'

'Hmm - Yea,' says Pilate in response. He really wishes the pest would go away, but he is instantly faced with another question, and then another.

'What about *the subroutine*?' the questioner pursues his goal. And with all the confidence of youth, he is pressing the "Accept" button in lieu of an affirmative response.

'Yes ... Yea ...' replies Pilate with alacrity, to every query that is floated. But he is not really concentrating. Moments of golden silence pass, and the boy raises yet another scenario, looming like a Welsh hillock in a grey downpour.

'Yea – yes, of course!' exclaims Pilate, this time with growing impatience, as the employee continues to Accept and Enter, Accept and Enter, parrot-fashion. Then, quite suddenly, Pilate breathes in deeply and poses, like a peacock with bloated lungs, before holding forth with authority,

'Hold on. No ... that's not right!' But, alas, it is too late. The scene is set, the final button has been pressed, and the instructions contained within the most destructive module of all, are obediently executed by the mild-mannered machine.

'I could just terminate these processes ... or reverse-engineer them ... couldn't I?' asks the voice of youth, who places his trust in the benevolence of fortune.

'My dear boy! The withdrawal method was long ago proven to fail. Even *you* should know this!' The young man is respectfully quiet, and the big boss resigns himself to the loss of a few critical files. A scapegoat must be found. It's a hard world, and there's no rest for the wicked. Perhaps the failure to include the question, 'Are you sure?' could be employed to bring the perpetrator to justice? Pilate dismisses his underling with an abbreviated wave of the lower arm. Alone again, he attempts to access one of his personal accounts; and, again, he encounters difficulty. So he switches his "dumb terminal" off. Ah! How aptly named these units are? He has been thinking that he might open his forthcoming meeting with a passionate metaphor, wherein he is the central processing unit, and his staff are the *dumb terminals* ... or maybe not. He powers the device up again; and he rejoices in the ensuing success:

'Off and on! It usually works.' But not for long, does it work.

When Pilate is at war on the keyboard, a dual effect sometimes occurs ... Pilate calls the players in this kaleidoscope his "blackout curtains". The curtain to the left carries the words: "Start typing to search for apps, files and settings". And the curtain to the right tells him, "ACTION CENTRE: No new notifications" - or complains about not being able to perform the latest batch of (entirely superfluous) updates.

Sometimes the curtains work independently of each other; but when they operate in unison, an "insufficiency of light and website" remains. Pilate notices there are no folds manifest in the textiles; and so, he reasons, 'the fabrics must have been stretched to their utmost limit, in a malicious attempt to blot out my online world.'

He brings his fist down on the keyboard (a method which proves less successful than pressing the on-off switch), and he grunts with all of the contempt that a biological mechanism, born of millions of years of evolution, ought to have for a collection of mere circuit boards. The computer is not responding. The director rises, and will stroll through his premises again, – checking, *en route*, that his employees are at their desks. After all, some of them, like the ill-fated files, may have gone missing. But before he departs, Pilate thumps the terminal upon its ill-fated head; and then delivers one final blow to the keyboard. He truly believes in this procedure. He has seen it work. It is (he would have us know) only a *light* fist. He is proceeding cautiously for, if there is not only "Intel inside", but an expert system with a modicum of artificial intelligence, - 'why then,' he fantasises, 'it is *just possible* that I might be hauled before a tribunal conducted by the Royal Society for the Protection of Animals. Can an expert system be regarded as an animal, or a sentient being? Perhaps a robot could be? Well, I'm not taking any chances.' He reasons thus:

'Great worlds! Where else may consciousness reside,
But in the sum of our complexities?'

******

As Mr Propotamous patrols his premises, he assigns tasks for the day to anyone who is idle. On his walkabout, he remembers, with satisfaction, how his removal of Benjamin Disrami, alias "Einstein", was, in its detail, a replica of a certain employer's dismissal of him – during the nine to five era of his life, before he cast out on his own. Generally, power is seized by those who lust after it the most, - and who have neither the aptitude (nor the requisite virtue) to use it constructively. So it was with this manager. But the energy of a superior being (like Mr Propotamous) cannot be wasted on settling a feud; especially when the "target" of his venom is rarely to be found at the point of contact, being either too high to aim at – or in the process of moving on. No. If vengeance is sought, then it is easier to have satisfaction at the cost of whomsoever is within range. And even if *whomsoever* should be an adorable donkey, or innocent as a lamb, *he* or *she* must bear the entire load from the gun barrel. How else can it be?

Now – back to the employee whom Mr Propotamous failed to see eye to eye with. The famous Mr Disrami was well-liked, if eccentric. Therefore, a trap had to be set for him. Opportunity knocked when his birthday came to pass. He was cajoled away from his desk, and into the local bar for a pub meal, whereupon he was plied with alcoholic beverages by several devious colleagues (who were in league with the boss). Whilst under the spell of their bogus generosity, a jocund conversation held sway.

'Such charity is unprecedented,' uttered the dupe, who was full of joy.

'Here - have another one.'

'You are too kind. Let me buy *you* one.'

'No. You are our guest of honour.'

'Oh! I shouldn't.' After administering another two pints, the revellers exclaimed,

'Here! Throw *that* down your neck!' Mr Disrami looked at them sheepishly, as something stronger slides across the table towards him. 'Please ... we insist.'

When Mr Disrami got back to his desk after lunch, he was uncharacteristically late. Trouble was brewing, and Mr Propotamous cornered him. Straight away, the victim deflected the attention with an apology,

'Sorry I'm late back, sir. The guys insisted on taking me out for a little birthday celebration.' He looked so happy as he said this.

'I think you can go home now.' The sourness of the reply was received like a special brand of sharp humour.

'What? A special dispensation on my birthday?' the victim replies. He was positively beaming now; and it was one of those rare occasions when he was not mumbling.

'You can go home.' Mr Propotamous nodded as he spoke. He was not joking.

'Why? What's up?' the employee's smile was beginning to fade.

'You've had too much to drink.'

'No. I'm fine – really.'

'I think you've drunk too much – really.'

'Is everything alright?'

'You need to go home. Right now. Just take the afternoon off.'

'Yes ...?'

'Yes. And the rest of the week, as well.'

We round off this tale with a short extract from Pilate's diary:

'... and so, as the unwanted human, a.k.a. "waste product", was in the process of being excreted, he was given to understand that – were he to protest - a trumped up charge of intemperance would be levelled against him, and stand as a black mark on his employment record for evermore. With this threat in the air, and even though the despised man claimed never to have been an habitual drinker, he agreed to go quietly, and save himself a bloody discharge.'

So much for the evil machinations of the office.

Following this injustice, a modest sprinkling of self-criticism rained down upon Mr Propotamous (for anything more than a light drizzle would be strictly off limits). But eventually the director consoled himself by misquoting that sonorous and touching work of literature, A Tale of Two Cities: 'It is a far, far better thing that I do now, in controlling the fate of others, than I have ever done by being controlled myself.' He also wishes his country were not controlled from Brussels, but that is another matter.

After indulging himself in these reflections, the chieftain retreats to a private room, to have another go at checking one of his email accounts. One message is about PPI, and another (from eBay) proclaims insincerely,

'We're giving you £10 just because we miss you.'

He once created a Facebook account and has not used it since. But, like a faithful dog, it never forgot him. After a few seconds, his email account is finally open, and he is reading out loud, "Do you know Priscilla Slurpensworth or Eustace Crotch-Hurts?" He gazes wistfully at the screen as another message arrives in his inbox: "Henrietta Fluck and Luce

Jackhole have unfriended one another. Peter Pubic is deeply disturbed by this. Do you want to know why?' And then, the last of the present crop of useless messages suddenly appears: "Do you know Brett Badshit or Gemima Chuzzlewack? They recently joined Freda Guano and Neil By-Mouth in Sicily, and have uploaded photographs of their holiday." He does *not* know these people, and ponders,

'Why are they contacting me? Is it something they ate? Perhaps the Mafia will take them out?'

Pilate opens another virtual window, and for a few minutes watches a video on the sexual revolution of 1960s. Then he yawns so widely, that he almost gives himself lockjaw. At last, he settles down to watch his favourite Reality TV programme on BBC iPlayer, "Brand New: Ugly as Gargoyles and Fat as Pigs". Unfortunately, within seconds of the opening credits, his online problems return. Spurious messages are spooled to the screen: "Sorry! We are unable to provide you with this video. We did not find it on the content delivery network." He is impressed by the electronic show of manners, but he soon tires of the forthcoming blockade ...

"This content doesn't seem to be working" ... "Insufficient bandwidth to stream the program" ... "The connection to the server was reset when the page was loading". The director, ever the one to blame others (even when they are inanimate), exclaims,

'Well! How very surreptitious! That server of ours is a slippery customer.'

And now, just to delay the venerable director further, the telephone rings. He responds with impatience:

'Yes?'

'Hail, you! May I spick wit Meeeester Propota-mouse, pleassss?' It is a cold caller.

'Yes.'

'Wheel, sour, we would lick to spick wit yow tide-ay abit your retail abbots: especially wit respect to your liquid intake and output.'

'Not now.'

'Sire, we are not ceiling anything. It eeeeeeze just a quack survey for the Department of Urology at a famous uni.'

'I thought I'd made this number X-Directory.'

'Sire? You need an X-Ray?'

Pilate puts the receiver down, for he is rapidly approaching that time of life when an enlarged prostate snuggles up to the bladder and the colon, as if it is a lonely heart. And, being a normal red-blooded male, he doesn't want to talk about it.

As the internet connection returns, the first virtual window to appear hosts the arrival of yet another email from Facebook, "Good news! You have two messages from Priscilla Slurpensworth."

Long-Suffering Dmitri

The director wishes to petition his star performer, Dmitri, for a little assistance. He would have addressed his enquiry to the young man with whom he recently collaborated in destroying valuable data, – but where would be the point?

'I'll have to give that Foolish Boy his marching orders soon,' he decides.

The personage with whom he would prefer to communicate is in the gents, and is presently processing two oversized portions of gristly steak (which he consumed for lunch).

Dmitri is morbidly obese, and has taken no serious exercise since he was at school, and then only reluctantly. His frame of reference is that the brain is a muscle, which uses energy at one sixth of the rate of other muscles. And so he gets his workout while sitting down. Further to this, he is the self-proclaimed *Fuehrer of ideas*, and so, by an act of transference, he reckons his own body fat may even be burned through the busyness of those around him.

Dmitri has hirsute nostrils, flourishing beyond the watchful eyes of the Forestry Commission; and he is far too preoccupied to train the undergrowth with a pair of tweezers. He is married to his work, and takes computer manuals home with him every weekend to read. Like "Einstein", he is a demon for detail. He is also under duress, and constantly needs to add flying buttresses to his wall of politeness. Unlike "Einstein", he is unencumbered by any psychiatric condition (so far as we know), and is a smooth talker - whose words are alternately brushed with undercoats of fatigue or slime. As yet, no occasion for treachery has arisen; but he is ever vigilant. From time to time, he is given the task of team leading, although – according to the corresponding entry in Pilate's journal – 'he is ill-suited to lead, having developed the lip-smacking, cap-raising servitude of other "items" on the payroll, such as Claire Format and Dexter Rotatory'. He appears solitary, except for a skin condition he carries around with him on his head (which kindly affords shelter to micro-organisms.)

Dmitri, whilst pondering his broken business dreams, will tend to sound like a seafarer, 'I was once intrepid, but now a change in the direction of the wind fills my sails with disquiet – and my body and soul too! And the effect carries over. If I should enter the sea, the water feels colder than the air; and yet, alighting upon dry land once more, the temperature of the air seems magically to have changed places with that of the sea, and become the chillier of the two! Thus does my *flesh* follow my *soul*, and every alteration in my circumstances makes me fearful.'

Myfanwy, reflecting upon literal meanings, will reply, 'Oh, you loveable and silly man! The English coastline is the same for everyone.'

'I am speaking metaphorically,' is always his defence.

Dmitri is a sensitive and private man. He discovered early in life that he could fill his time satisfactorily, by performing actions purely for their intrinsic pleasure. Among such pastimes were variations of Solitaire such as the Rubik's Cube, and, of course, the odd game of chess against himself: wherein he would study the juxtaposition of the pieces in scrupulous detail before making his move – as if persuading a fly on the wall that it really mattered - before switching the board around and, with equal intensity, "batting for the other side". But what to do for a career? Upon discovering the art of computer programming, he had found his place in the cosmos.

The First Lady, Myfanwy Esquelle

The director's wife has miscellaneous qualities. She is part Welsh, and part Italian. She likes to emphasise the Italian, as she has spent much of her life in Milan, - which is touted as the centre of fashion, although she knows nothing of *chique* attire. To be honest, she does look somewhat Mediterranean. She also speaks with an accent which is, by turns, Welsh or Italian, depending upon which of these locations was most recently included in her travel itinerary. Either way, her voice lilts romantically, and would lull a suitor's attentions - until he laid his eyes upon her. Her name is *Myfanwy Esquelle*. She has the same mindset as her husband, and feels that anything which sounds high-flown cannot be a bad thing. When she appears, as if out of nowhere, her husband is apt to remark (insincerely),

'Your presence here delights me, but I did not expect you back so soon.' To which his wife may respond,

'Perhaps your *wishing* me back was a telepathic allure more powerful than your *expectation*.'

Indeed, both of them are literate to a high degree – and given to examining language under a microscope, so that, in a perfect flight of fantasy, the spoken word becomes like a coarse mineral, subject to a discrete chemical assay.

From time to time, Myfanwy toys with the idea of blending her maiden name with that of her husband's surname in a double barrel: like a vintage Jack Daniels whisky, slowly maturing in its keg some distance from the public gaze - until the red letter day when it is gloriously unveiled. But "Myfanwy Propotamous-Esquelle" would be a touch extreme, even for a lady such as herself (with the blue blood of high culture coursing through her veins). So, instead, she has taken a leaf out of Mrs Thatcher's book, and is currently undergoing hormone replacement therapy. Ah, well, – whatever tickles her progesterone! Myfanwy, soliloquising, explains *herself to herself* thus:

'My emotions are all over the place, and there is no easy continuity between them. I suppose I am like Beethoven.' Her husband muses: 'But there is a difference. Beethoven was great.'

Myfanwy is an unfulfilled lover, - owing to her husband's extreme lack of responsiveness to her, – but she is a fulfilled lover of the fine arts; and the low arts too, - for she finds the advertising channels on television curiously soothing. Indeed, she has gifted to Pilate his motto for life, courtesy of John Milton (who was alluding to the attitude of Satan): "Better to reign in hell than serve in heaven". Her husband says, 'Myfanwy is steeped in philosophy, and yet she is the least philosophical person I know.'

And how did a man, wanting in talent and in Mammon, who is lumbered, by nature, with a lethal concoction of vanity and skulduggery, come upon the ownership of a relatively large software house? Sometimes, the very idea seems just too wonderful: like a pipe-dream, or an elaborate hallucination. He married a woman blessed by inheritance. And, on this account, he is controlled by her to a far greater degree than he would care to admit. She need only withdraw her cash, and the implosion of the entire enterprise would follow. Indeed, he has exhausted such a large proportion of his wife's bequests, that she occasionally resorts to purchasing second-hand clothing from the local charity store. This allows her remaining funds to go further, although it may also be true that she likes what is available there.

And she manifests other strange behaviours. On her way to the charity shop, Myfanwy stops every so often to examine the pavement; and thereupon fixes her eyes upon some grubby little object, lying supine before her shoes. She stoops to pick it up, and lovingly dusts it down. 'What is it?' I hear you ask. Why, it is only a used receipt, which she fastidiously wraps inside her handkerchief and places in an empty pocket, - ready to be reproduced later as a tax-deductible expense. Oh, greed, where is thy sting?

'I shall dust it down, and have it pressed like a tuxedo to remove the crinkles. After all,' she reasons, 'someone else did not make use of it, and to leave it on the pavement is an opportunity missed.' This is a strange attitude, indeed, for someone who claims to be "of the moneyed classes". She will say, 'I am rich because I am frugal'. Like every fortunate human being, she gives herself full credit for her circumstances. But, dear reader, you and I know better.

Suddenly, she espies a homeless person crouched over his collection bowl, and pauses to establish eye contact with him. For a while, neither of them flinch. And then she makes her move,

'Is your enterprise listed on the stock exchange? May I buy shares in it?' The indigent male simply stares back at her with a vacant look in his eyes.

Neither husband nor wife is prepossessing. Both are rotund; and the wife has a dowager's hump, and wears thick, horn-rimmed spectacles. To make matters worse, Mr Propotamous works on the principle of every red-blooded male: that a woman well-endowed is his entitlement, irrespective of the physical specimen that he, himself, may be. Yet he did want to find someone with money – anyone – who would enable him to realise his dream of man management. And Myfanwy is relieved to have ensnared someone – anyone - for her conjugal union, for she cannot bear the thought of growing old alone. Indeed, she would drive potential suitors away with her explosive temper, which requires only the slightest provocation to be fully detonated. "Pilate with Myfanwy" may not be a match made in heaven – but, rather, one set alight in hell.

'Oh, my dear! My dear, wasted youth!' opines the husband. 'If only I had done national service for a while, and trained as a bomb disposal expert. Why then, I could defuse - or redirect - this vital spark of yours, before its tyranny is despatched, and the target of its malice decimated.' His wife is not amused; or maybe she doesn't understand the joke.

'My chuck! The estates of my relatives are your great good fortune,' she says, turning faintly Elizabethan in a moment of sentiment.

'*Our* great good fortune, dear. *Our* ... '

'No. *Yours*. This boon would not even be *partly* yours, but for me; yet it would be *entirely* mine, but for you.'

'We shall not depend upon your legacy for long, my darling. Soon, my foray into the world of business will add to that fortune. So, let us be a little cosier with each other now, and become more than the sum of all our parts. In fact, from this day forward, we shall see our glass not as half-empty but as half-full, and (with algebraic elegance) have all our double minuses transmuted into pluses!' She is still not amused.

'Don't talk to me like that!' she exclaims brusquely. He, sensing the trembling of an emotional fault line of geological immensity, agrees:

'You are quite right, of course. I will not talk to you like that.' She flashes her eyes at him.

'I vow,' he murmurs, and then, quietly and seditiously, finishes what he has to say under the radar.

******

Once, when they were on holiday together, Pilate insisted they should set their hearts ablaze with something fresh and exciting.

'Perhaps it will spruce up our love life?' he opined.

'What do you have in mind?'

Pilate explained his idea to her, and she responded,

'But Pilate, dear, you don't normally go in for dangerous sports.' Finally, after much prevarication, he hired a sledge for her, and she flew down a snow-capped mountainside at breakneck speed. She had expected him to climb in beside her; but, at the final moment, he reneged – and, with a homicidal push, set the sledge on its way. When she arrived at the foot of the slope, she was incandescent with rage. He explained that he had just bought a camera with an exceptionally fast shutter speed, and wanted to test it out by photographing her while she was in transit.

'I'll make it up to you,' he promised. 'I will join you on the next descent.'

'There won't *be* any more descents!' she retorted. But he formulated a persuasive argument: that she could keep the camera, and acquire for herself a new artistic hobby (on condition that the photographs he had already taken must remain for his eyes only). She perked up, even ceding to his wish for her to sit in front of him.

'This sport can be dangerous at high speeds,' he thought, 'and, in the event of a collision, she will act as my airbag.'

******

And what of Myfanwy's relatives, who (coincidentally) all met their deaths in unusual circumstances?

'So direful! Genuinely awful!' she exclaims, and beats her chest symbolically, causing a ripple to travel over the surface of her ample bosoms.

'The wheel of fortune first ran amok over my grandfather. He inhabited an old Victorian mansion, with dangerous plumbing problems. Then one day he was blown up ... so the forensic team said, by the *ignition of sewage gas*. But it is my loss-ah. Not yours. Mine! You never knew most of my family. Ah!' Myfanwy likes to emphasise her point; and to finish on a solemn cadence: 'They always invested such sweetness in their manner, and in their mannerisms.'

'Yes. I once had an aunt like that. She made a right royal fuss of me. I never quite got over it when she died. And she was rich, too.' The fierce female eyes light up again, and this time with a spark of competition. He qualifies the remark, 'But not *very* rich; she had but a faint whiff of opulence.' He lowers his hand, and moves it around in a barely perceptible flourish. 'Actually, to be frank and fair, her death was more heavily expected than ... the passing of these others ... who were familiar to you,' he pauses before the end of this wooden sentence, reaching towards her with his hands, as if to conjure some tools of carpentry out of thin air, - with which to nicely round off the jagged tail end of his plank of words.

And now for the false condiment of saccharine:

'Ah! My poor dear!'

His wife's angst is clearly seen. She has an eating disorder, which surfaces when she is under duress. But her habit is not bulimia, for her brief and hurried acts of gorging are not generally followed by vomiting. Rather, what is consumed goes straight on to her thighs. Armed with this knowledge, the rest of the department can gauge whether her marriage is sailing or sinking, simply by observing her latest dress size. She is very sensitive about her weight, and feels that the acronym for "File Allocation Table" is a direct reference to her figure. As if this is not enough, her husband teases her about her confusion between abstract and corporeal things.

When Mr Propotamous escorts his wife and friends to a fine restaurant, she will order a light dish; and when the fulsome plates of those around her arrive, she will begin to pilfer - with courteous apologies ('May I help myself to a little of your ... Oh! You don't mind, do you?'). Pilate calls this, 'an act of inflated modesty'. The dialogue moves on.

'My dear,' she admonishes him. 'I must insist (as a matter of some urgency) that you fill in the buildings insurance forms for this warehouse, before you develop it any further.'

'My most superior spouse,' he replies. 'You are so anthropomorphic. "Urgent paperwork"? Who ever heard of such a thing? Fancy investing an inanimate object like paperwork with the human quality of urgency?'

******

And now, the director must hear, for the umpteenth time, some more of Myfanwy's tales of familial woe. His face contorts. It is as if he is eating something which he cannot bear to swallow, but which he also dare not spit out. Finally his expression resolves into a smile, but the melodrama has only just begun. He is hoping (against hope) that the funny side of this tragi-comedy might wear off, leaving only the tragedy; and allowing him to respond in the appropriate way. Ironically, it is the tragedy that wears off instead: leaving the impression that he is mining for laughs in a subterranean cavern darker than a coal pit. As a result, his wife flares up like a badly run colliery.

'How dare you? Have you no feeling?' she shrieks.

Actually, Pilate does have feeling. He feels that she has lost her relatives in mightily suspicious circumstances. And, lest he forget, his wife recounts them one by one ...

'There was the strange case of an uncle, who choked to death on a loose filling which escaped from one of his teeth. Another relation – a cousin – passed away whilst calmly surfing the internet. He was as soft-hearted as a marshmallow, and was sitting in a bubble bath at the time. The coroner remarked, "as was his custom, the deceased may have been reading a web page on life insurance and fallen asleep; allowing the portable device on his lap to slide into the soapy water and electrocute him – thus ensuring not his life, but his death." Upon that day, every inhabitant of Mount Olympus wept.'

'Yes, I've got the coroner's speech on tape, and I did consider selling it to The Inquirer,' her husband replies blandly. 'It might have been a good little earner.'

'And I fondly remember my uncle, who liked to experiment with hallucinogens, – until one day, at London Zoo, during a face-off with a lion, he suddenly became frantic, believing himself to be on the wrong side of the iron bars. You will recall that, possessing a body far more nimble than his mind, he climbed into the enclosure and had his head bitten off! Terrible, it was!'

'Yes, dear.'

'And once, you almost caused my own demise, when you persuaded me that I should swim with a dolphin. You neglected to tell me that the "dolphin" was a five-ton killer whale.'

Myfanwy has an enormous fear of death, and nurses that fear like the child she never had. Her national poet, Dylan Thomas, has given her the appropriate words:

Hate and fear be your two loves.
Love me and lift your mask.

A family friend once suggested to Myfanwy about applying for an assistant's role in God-Fearing Funeral Services & Son; and that friend, forthwith, became her enemy. As for her husband, he proffered no assistance in this matter.

In the present moment, he is becoming theatrical again; and is defining her physical shape with his hands …

'Oh! My starry-eyed sphere, and love of my pear-shaped life! We should despatch the remainder of your *living* relatives; at least those who have your name inside their wills. The business needs another cash injection,' he quips. The joke falls upon deaf ears.

'You have already laid your greasy hands upon my dowry. Please do not forget our pre-nuptial agreement: that in the event of a divorce, all of the liquid assets, which you have sunk into this quango of yours, shall return to me.'

'Oh! My little titbit, do not speak of separation!'

'Alright. Enough of this. You have an appointment with the simple hairdresser,' says his wife. She always refers to their Moroccan hairdresser in this way, both because he employs *Simple* hair products, and because she regards him as a simpleton.

'You needn't worry. I have it right here, in my diary.' He is turning the pages quickly, but cannot find it.

'And do not overlook how you once vowed that Ross Perot shall, for evermore, be your sublime role model.'

'Yes, dear. How *could* I forget? Everyone must be clean-shaven. No beards or long hair. I even took the corporate decision to move the company hairdresser on site, in order to implement the dictates of that particular maestro. Mind you, I haven't seen the "hair follicle surgeon" anywhere today. I hope he is in.'

'He's not a surgeon, dear. He doesn't replant hair.'

'Well, to the best of my knowledge, a tree surgeon need not necessarily replant trees; but, like the barber with our follicles, he may *reshape and beautify* their arms (according to the prevailing customs) -'

'He *may*, if he's any good.'

'And I cannot think where the pesky little man has got to. Anyhow, while we are on the subject of appointments, I hope that *you* are still on course for your rendezvous with the optician?'

'And *you*, my sweet, must see a sleep therapist,' Myfanwy intercepts him, determined to have the last word. 'When in the middle of a deep nocturnal slumber, in which you barely seem alive, you have a disconcerting tendency to rise like Lazarus, and walk away from the marital bed. And yet, by an odd coincidence, you only "sleep walk" when I express myself amorously.'

******

The two of them populate their lives with behaviour patterns, as outlandish as forest creatures from Patagonia. Think of these patterns less as "peccadilloes" than "armadillos", - which would be facing extinction, but for the bearers conspiring in some peculiar drive at conservation.

'I wish you could be more relaxed with me – at the witching hour and beyond,' says Myfanwy. Like Madame Bovary, she craves sensual attention. And even during the day, her man is not safe from her. He must flee to his office and lock the door, in order to protect himself from having to supply it. He calls this office his *inner sanctum*, and, once there, he does not wish to be disturbed.

When his lady's wish to be indulged is frustrated, she is subject to "pica". Although she is not a man - much less a military commander, - her taste for the bathroom sponge has, in some circles, won for her the nickname of "General Pica". She often suffers from stomach upsets, and comforts herself by watching YouTube videos of a remarkable Asian, who grounds down a brick and then consumes the resulting crumbs and dust; and she views other films, besides, of animals which eat earth to settle their digestion.

She also has a deep love of canines and of wild creatures, yet bares the scars of many a bad encounter when she has failed to read the signs. Her clientèle has ranged from the wolf dog she petted and hugged one day, who perceived her intimacy as a desire for their two bodies to merge and become one, - to the angry badger who saw her kidnapping one of its children.

One particular dog she rescued became an obsession with her. She was forever talking about its health, and measuring the weight and viscosity of its rear output; until, one day, a police officer interrupted this scatological behaviour – and booked her on a charge of "offending public decency". (Perhaps, in some flight of fantasy, she was sampling a block of in-house documentation?) She pretends to a knowledge of high-brow literature, but despairs at her failure to discover anyone suitable to share it with. And so she turns, like a leaf in Autumn. Gradually, the weirder tendencies of the authors themselves are beginning to bewitch her more than all their wondrous words and classical stories. There is one childhood habit of Flaubert's that she has made her own. She scrapes, with her fingernails, the layer of grit which adheres to polished surfaces (such as banisters) and gobbles up the detritus; gently smacking her lips with satisfaction as she swallows. Is it comparable to the attraction that poor children have to mud, on account of it containing minerals which they are short of in their usual diet? Come on! She ought to have sufficient funds for gourmet dining at the Ritz! Rather, is it not low self-esteem which dictates that she must fill herself with dirt? Notwithstanding her penchant for the unusual in her diet, her palate (like a celestial body) can rise as well as fall. She does enjoy visits to fine restaurants, and to the theatre or opera house. And she keeps up appearances in the company of others, by posing with half-open books on her lap, which she never actually reads.

The director's wife is not computer-literate, but she has an insatiable curiosity about everything her husband is doing. This trait can be forgiven, for everything he does is by virtue of her money. And so she insists on attending most meetings: leastwise, whenever her husband has been unable to schedule them without their coming to her attention.

'It really wouldn't be of any interest to you, darling,' Pilate defends his decision to exclude her.

'But whatever you do is of interest to me. That is the natural state of affairs, in an affair of conjugal bliss.'

'My darling, you wouldn't understand what is being discussed.'

'Oh! You are always so condescending to me! Can you imagine: me, a woman of culture and high bearing, being told by a poor church mouse that she cannot understand!'

'My dear, there is no need to be discourteous. I am only being honest with you.'

'What do you mean – only being honest? And fancy rubbing salt in my sensitive wounds by telling me I have no aptitude for courtesy!'

'I wasn't talking about your aptitude.'

'Humph!' she expels some residual air. 'And you've given me no kids to incubate! I feel duty-bound to arrange a visit for you to the local clinic, where you can have the motility of your sperm tested. You know, I have told you before, you must eat more seafood, especially cod roe. It is one of gastronomy's much-vaunted aphrodisiacs.' Her husband laughs, as he muses that his wife would have him increase his fertility, by eating the spunk of others.

'Oh! How I pine to have been of child-bearing age in the good old days of the baby boomers, when the country was filled with infants – after a world war that shed so much blood!'

'Man's inhumanity to man makes countless thousands spawn!' her husband ejaculates. Unfortunately, he doesn't realise that he has just referred to frog spawn rather than to mourning, until he sees his wife's look of thunder at the misquotation of that great line. He tries to cover his tracks:

'My tongue slipped, dear. I just don't know what came over it.'

'Clearly, it was oiled by a frivolous or inattentive mind!'

'Yes, dear.'

A Memorable Telephone Call

At last, the director is rescued from the haranguing of his lady wife, by the need to make a telephone call. He picks up the receiver and starts to dial, signalling to his wife (like a traffic warden to the vehicles of sound) that she may resume her assault and battery only after he has completed the enquiry which he is about to make.

'These damned answer phone messages, each leading aimlessly on to the next ... onwards and onwards ... but never ultimately upwards ... like the steps in an M.C. Escher art-work: layer upon layer of nothingness!' he moans. 'Just to *hear* these messages turns me into a nihilist! Oh! Apathy and emptiness! Apathy and emptiness! The dark arts wield their most fearsome power, when handling feeble weaponry.'

'What is he going on about?' says his wife, while facing the other way. It is as if she is invoking some unseen spirit for an answer. Eventually, her husband reaches a recipient on the other end of the telephone line, only to realise (some way into the conversation) that it is the wrong person. This dud is then succeeded by another dud.

'Why must I be consigned to squander more, and still more, of my precious life's breath?' he asks. Finally, someone knowledgeable puts him out of his misery. He hears a friendly voice from the north of England. And to alter the familiar shape of things, the ensuing dialogue shall be recorded in dramatic form:

DIRECTOR: I wonder if you can help me? Could you tell me if you offer some method of expunging information from a disk? I am reliably informed that data is easier to backup than to remove.

PROPRIETOR OF SHOP: Well, of course. It is always sensible to backup, as you might need the information at a later date.

DIRECTOR: But I want to get rid of it.

PROPRIETOR: Have you tried deleting?

DIRECTOR: Of course I've tried deleting. It goes to the recycle bin.

PROPRIETOR: But you can remove it from the bin.

DIRECTOR: Yes, thank you for stating the obvious. But has it *really* been expunged? I mean, *permanently* and *irretrievably*?

PROPRIETOR: You could try "imaging software".

DIRECTOR: How does that work?

PROPRIETOR: It takes a snapshot of your entire disk at a particular moment in time.

DIRECTOR: OK. And if I restore that snapshot in a month's time, I erase all of the junk I have acquired in the interim; and I am back to the safe place where I want to be?

PROPRIETOR: Supposedly.

DIRECTOR: And is that the only solution?

PROPRIETOR: You might also consider a "data cleanse" or a "disk wipe" ... possibly.

DIRECTOR: They sound like household detergents. What are my other options?

PROPRIETOR: Have you attempted a disk copy, sir? It will transfer the content of every byte on your hard drive to your backup media. But the latter must be exactly the same size as your source media.

DIRECTOR: And I will overwrite every byte on my hard drive when I restore it?

PROPRIETOR: Allegedly ...

DIRECTOR: Only *allegedly*? [Silence ensues.] Could I get a name here?

PROPRIETOR: "Imaging Software" or "Disk Copy".

DIRECTOR: Well, Mr Imaging-Software-or-Disk-Copy, you are beginning to worry me.

PROPRIETOR [With voice assuming a different timbre]: Just call me "Otis". And I am actually a lady.

DIRECTOR [mumbling imperceptibly to himself]: I thought Otis was a bloke's name ... Oh, never mind.

PROPRIETOR: Will that be all, sir?

DIRECTOR: Of course it won't be all! Otis, I trade in certainties.

PROPRIETOR: Sir, certainty is a specialised and highly sought-after commodity [she pauses]. You see, it is generally possible to retrieve deleted files, because some trace of what was initially there remains: which is very useful when you remove information by mistake.

DIRECTOR [thinking of his recent interaction with Foolish Boy]: I have deleted a file or two which I might wish to restore. But, for the moment, I am focussing upon files which I which I have deliberately zapped.

PROPRIETOR: You may be able to retrieve all of them if you want to.

DIRECTOR: But I don't want to retrieve all of them!

PROPRIETOR: Then why did you upload them onto your hard drive in the first place?

DIRECTOR [beginning to lose patience]: Let's say you share a computer, - or give your old machine to a neighbour, or sell it on? There might be credit card details on there. You don't want to pass them on as well, do you? And the hard drive could be carrying other sensitive information: client data, say, which I am contractually obliged to protect.

PROPRIETOR: You might change your mind.

DIRECTOR: Why would I change my mind? The client's not going to change *his*!

PROPRIETOR: Um. Tricky.

DIRECTOR: There. Now you see the problem. So ... what to do about it? Isn't there some software product which overwrites every byte on the disk with zeroes. You must know the one?

PROPRIETOR: It'll cost you. And the shop still cannot give you any guarantee of its efficacy. Some variants of this kind of software are free, and great claims are made for them. Mind you, if you are duped by a hoax, you could end up downloading a virus. Then you will have to buy something else to get rid of the virus. Worst of all, your machine could be infected with spyware, with an alien watching what you are doing.

DIRECTOR: The computer is protected.

PROPRIETOR: Anti-viruses are not foolproof.

DIRECTOR: And what if mine is?

PROPRIETOR: No matter. The server is the greatest spy of all. It will keep a record of all the websites you have visited.

DIRECTOR: If only I could delete the contents of its lists.

PROPRIETOR: Sir. This is not a jousting match which you can win. [She pauses.] Here's what I think. It's just a theory – but imagine you are a geologist, examining tertiary rock formations. Systems architecture has progressed with each decade, through 8-bit, 16-bit, 32-bit and 64-bit processors: and each advance adds a new layer of topsoil above the old [the speaker clears her throat] or an addition to the fossil record. The larger the byte, the deeper and richer each mouthful of data. No? [She smacks her lips and puts her tongue into her cheek.] Just think, a curious scientist could dig so deep, as to unearth a human skeleton or two ...

DIRECTOR: What if I reinstall the operating system?

PROPRIETOR: No. That is not enough.

DIRECTOR: I could always reformat the hard drive first.

PROPRIETOR: There would still be a degree of uncertainty. Some traces of unwanted material might remain.

[The Director takes a deep breath, and emits something like the last sigh of a living being before it turns into a cadaver. Then, just as the expulsion of air is in mid-flow, he changes his mind and decides to stay alive.]

PROPRIETOR: Such is the wonder of new technology, that data can even be retrieved from a disk that has been smashed or burned.

DIRECTOR: Oh, dear. But I might ... want to free up space on the computer ... by getting rid of data in certain sectors.

PROPRIETOR: You can always buy a bigger disk. But, hey! Any erased bytes will be reusable, because the control mechanism no longer points at them. [Now it is the Proprietor's turn to sigh, and a considerable volume of wind passes her lips. In fact, it could have been indigestion.] Well, if you *genuinely* want to delete ...

DIRECTOR [nodding vigorously, although Otis cannot see him]: Yes?

PROPRIETOR: If you actually ... truly ...

DIRECTOR: Yes?

PROPRIETOR: ... want to delete ...

DIRECTOR: Yes? Yes?

PROPRIETOR: Perhaps magnets would help.

DIRECTOR: Magnets?

PROPRIETOR: Or – better solution – get the forensic scientists on board. If you have journeyed into the dark web, they really *will* sort you out. They might even incriminate you ... Sorry, just kidding.

DIRECTOR: Can I buy their software for my own personal use?

PROPRIETOR: Well, you *can* ... but you would need a special license for it.

DIRECTOR: How would I get that license?

PROPRIETOR: Oh, Good heavens! I haven't the faintest idea. [The director shuffles his feet. He finds that he must do this to release the tension on the telephone line. It is extraordinary how electricity passes naturally though organic and inorganic mediums.]

DIRECTOR: But ... but ... If I *could* purchase the license ...

PROPRIETOR: Yes.

DIRECTOR: And obtain the software ...?

PROPRIETOR: Yes ... assuming you could, your problems should be solved ... but the very fact that you were asking about this software might make the process implausible. After all, it would raise suspicions in the vendor.

DIRECTOR: Who is this bloody vendor, anyway?

PROPRIETOR: Presumably the state government.

DIRECTOR: Well. Perhaps you can act as a distributor on behalf of the state? My motives are perfectly wholesome. So let's get on with the vending process, otherwise we'll be here all day. Do you want my card details?

PROPRIETOR: First of all, who is the person on the card?

DIRECTOR [with enthusiasm]: It's me ...

PROPRIETOR: And you are?

DIRECTOR: Pilate Henry Propotamous.

PROPRIETOR: How are you spelling the last name?

DIRECTOR [with smug satisfaction]: Just as I always have: Pea-Arrgh-Oh-Pea-Oh-Tea-Ay-Em-Oh-You-Ess.

PROPRIETOR: You *ass*?

DIRECTOR: That's right.

PROPRIETOR: So, just to clarify, that's ... P for Punctilious, R for Rambling, O for Ostentatious, P for Procrastination, O for Onanism, T for Pterodactyl -

DIRECTOR: I must interrupt you there. Pterodactyl is spelt with a "P".

PROPRIETOR: You don't say? T for Tripe, then. A for Antidisestablishmentarianism -

DIRECTOR: Anti-what?

PROPRIETOR [continuing without explanation]: M and O stand for More Onanism, U is for Unbearable, and S is for Software ... Of course, I may not be able to sell you the software.

DIRECTOR: Couldn't you have found that out earlier, before you engaged me in this tedious exchange?

PROPRIETOR: Arrrrr, possibly ...

DIRECTOR: You meant to take all of my personal details, and then disappoint me? You sound like one of those dreadful travel agents, who agrees a hotel room with you, and, as you dictate your private data to him, encodes it with a long-winded acronym. By the time he has finished reciting the accursed acronym back to you, the desired room has been taken, - and you have to start all over again!

PROPRIETOR: Is there anything else I can help you with today, sir?

DIRECTOR: We haven't finished doing this yet.

PROPRIETOR [audibly tapping his receiver on his desk, as if he needs to empty out the dross he is getting from it]: You couldn't afford the software anyway.

DIRECTOR: What a cheek ...! [He tuts angrily] OK. But if I could afford it ... How much would it be?

PROPRIETOR: So many questions! It's enough to render a perfectly good brain with a headache.

DIRECTOR: How much?

PROPRIETER: About £65,000.

DIRECTOR: Six-ty *five* ... six-ty five ... six-ty five *thou-sand greenbacks* ...! [The Director winces] Oh, my poor head! That's nearly what I charged my last client for minor textual modifications. [Then, as an aside.] There were a lot of them, though. In fact, we positively encouraged them! [Pilate returns to his mantra] Sixty five thousand green backs...! That's out-*rageous*!

PROPRIETOR: Yes. I am afraid so. Now, if you haven't any more questions, I really must get on. Listening to you endlessly repeat that figure back to me is sure to unhinge my sanity. And that's assuming said hinge has not already been corroded by the rest of this here colloquy. [He hangs up.]

******

After this verbal exchange, the director is trembling with exasperation ... but all is not lost, for he has an idea. He intends to bring it up at the next team meeting. The notion relates to the retrieval of computers and discarded storage systems from rubbish tips, for the benefit of gaining invaluable information about their owners. Meanwhile, his wife has been listening to the conversation, and watching him intently.

'Surely, you don't really want to delete your data?' she asks him.

'Who do you think you're talking to - a woman who says "No", when she, in fact, means "Yes"?' he responds.

'I *beg* your pardon?' she raises her voice.

'Why beg? Thou art no mendicant.' He enjoys repartee, but realises he has gone a step too far. So he quickly *reverse engineers* his logic.

'My dearest Myfanwy, you know your mind, but I have problems with knowing mine.' She calms down, and a moment later Mr Propotamous has another brainwave. He could purchase the expensive suite of programs alluded to by Otis, and begin to offer a special service, renting it out at thousands of pounds a time to anyone who has tied himself up in knots;

or, with software in hand, he could act as a purifier of tainted drives: like Jesus (when faced with the possessed) who exorcised unclean spirits.

'But,' he ponders, few would want such a specialist service ... unless ... unless ...' Suddenly, the obverse side of the coin presents itself to his mind, - 'unless we could strategically plant special viruses in their computers whenever they visit unspeakable places online. You know the kind I mean,' he continues, addressing imaginary others in the room (although there is no need, as his fleshy wife is nodding her agreement) - '... places which show you how to make your own bomb, with home–made recipes supplied; or sites of the salacious kind, which offer the chance for some juicy self-gratification. On the whole, the latter is pretty harmless, but potentially embarrassing if the wife finds out,' his mouth waters and Myfanwy is nodding again, for she does not equate this particular wife with herself. 'And finally - *le grand coup* – we would offer to send out the lifeboat (and take away the infection) before they drown. In fact', he is thinking aloud, 'we could facilitate the process (for God helps those who help themselves), by arranging for an impromptu visit from the police, who shall be happy to press for a search warrant. The occupant will fear he has done something illegal ... and willingly pay an astronomical fee for our service of "deep cleansing". For I know how a clear moral complexion is sought after by all, and by none more earnestly than those who least do merit it. Never confuse what a man claims he *may* do, out of a sense of theatre and in order to curry favour, with what he *will* do in order to survive.'

'Well spoken!' intercepts Myfanwy, just as her husband is forgetting she's there. Myfanwy has been repressing her excitement, and now feels the need for some displacement activity. She scrapes the dead skin from the inside of her earlobe and swallows it. Then she returns her hands to her lap, as if nothing has happened. 'We could even diversify, offering face creams to our clients, in order to plump up their complexions, just as they begin to crease with anxiety. Ah!' Both husband and wife are smiling now. Rarely have they appeared so well-matched, or so convivial. And Pilate adds,

'We may *gild the lily* (forgive me, sweet William, for borrowing the petals of your fine words, to sweetly scent a poisoned chalice!), and subcontract out the *whole job* to the forces of law and order, or to some other protectionist agency ... just think ... our *very own virus* with *matching anti-virus*, - unique to the market. Oh, joy! The police will relish the scenario, if they are in the business of ensnaring their prey; and are not above paying rich dividends to informers.'

Another Bout of Eccentricity

Two technical maestros are having a conversation.

MAESTRO ONE: You must never reinvent the wheel.

MAESTRO TWO: Are you serious? How else may we roll on to pastures new? In our industry, the re-invention of wheels is common practice!

MAESTRO ONE: It is?

MAESTRO TWO: But of course. We throw away whole systems, be they partially, or (in some cases) wholly functioning, – along with hundreds of pages of documentation ... all because some fresh technology has been released. And, jovially, do we proclaim: "That's another one for the skip! Old wine into new wineskins!" We are like Hollywood buffs. Every few years, we need a new star to fall in love with.

MAESTRO ONE: I suppose the code generator will curtail this widespread waste?

MAESTRO TWO: It is certainly intended to simplify development.

MAESTRO ONE: Yep. So they say. You answer a detailed series of questions; and then it writes the software for you. Apparently, you never have to *get your hands dirty*. Foolish Boy is using the latest release of this generator, even as we speak. Pilate calls it our "In-House Saviour". By the time that lad is through, he might have another name for it! [Looking in the boy's direction] In fact, he has got up from his desk and is coming over to us.'

FOOLISH BOY: I have just replied to the 186th question put to me – and then the "Q and A" session went black.

MAESTRO ONE: So - you're all done, then?

FOOLISH BOY: No. I had at least another fifty questions to go. I don't know what's happened. Last time, the screen froze. This time it just vanished ... *Oh, no!*

This exclamation is issued in response to an almost ubiquitous boss, who is always standing *behind* you when he is least wanted, and never *in front* of you when he is really needed. In fact, the young trainee can hear Pilate over his shoulder, as the boss passes by on his way to the conference room:

'For the love of apostrophes and ampersands! What is it *now?*'

Another (Minor) "Telephone Exchange"

Pilate is called by someone named Julia, who leaves a message with her telephone number and a promise to get back to him later. He does not know anyone by the name of Julia. He rings her, and leaves a message to the effect that she has dialled an incorrect number. This takes two attempts, as he is slightly stressed, and at first he accidentally calls his sister. After a short while, Julia calls and leaves another message – reporting that she has received his communication, but that it was scrambled: and hence she will keep trying to get hold of him, until she is successful. Pilate sighs (with resignation) that he will never get rid of her. He then receives a call from his sister. She is just returning the call that he made to her earlier. He explains that it was by mistake. And she asks,

'You *have* taken your medication today, haven't you?'

'Yes,' he replies – but he is lying.

A Late-Comer

Outside, in the street, the last employee to arrive is nearing the front entrance. The old (sacked) cleaner, Freddie, has turned up in his scruffiest attire, and homes in on his unsuspecting prey. Freddie is mostly interested in what is not his business, and assumes that everyone else must be the same. He opens as if already in mid-sentence, for he knows the window of opportunity is small:

'... and *do you know* I am usually so dapper? I wear a suit and tie whenever I can: for work, for weddings and funerals, for religious observances, including holy days of obligation, - and for all Sunday lunches involving turkeys; but – and this is a secret which has been spooled to me on good authority – this tie I wear, and which I was given, is really a ribbon from out of an Xmas cracker. And nobody has realised! What a story to tell ... Eh?'

'Maybe they are too polite to say?'

'Rarely, are people too polite ... for they are dissimilar to the squiggles of a paisley tie, and follow a contemporary pattern ...'

'Freddie, I have got to go.'

'It's impossible. I *yaffled* two Cornish pasties down earlier, just so that I would have the staying power to remain here until you arrived.' Freddie is from the West Country, and so is familiar with the patois.

'What's impossible ...?'

'That you should be like all the others.'

At this point, the staff member disappears through the front door - and hastens in the direction of the meeting room.

PART THE SECOND: A MEETING OF MINDS

As our Great Leader switches on the lights in the boardroom, he is attended by a photic sneeze. He then completes the evacuation of his nostrils with a "trumpet voluntary".

'Contractors are as disposable as Kleenex tissues,' he remarks – whilst wiping his nose with one of them.

He is entering the only room, apart from his private quarters, which has been developed beyond its primal state. (Sad to say, Myfanwy feels her money has been spent frivolously.) It also has a rare feature: a window admitting natural light. And it is the venue for a multiplicity of pointless meetings, providing succour to those on the treadmill, who benefit from vitamin D.

The décor is worth noting. Luxurious under foot, is a new Wilton carpet; and near the stylish sash window are expensive vases, each sporting an array of cut flowers - recently in full bloom. Just in front of the flowers are several neatly-potted bonsai trees, landscaped in a setting of stones or grasses; and so, as the first lady is wont to point out, 'they may be referred to as *penjing trees*'. Dominating the centre of the room, is the latest Home Hub advert from British Telecom, bearing a mural from the brush of some street painter in Florence, – and here felicitously employed as the protective covering for a long table made out of cherry wood, and varnished to a rich gloss. Sometimes, the table is overlaid with a velvety green cloth: for in times of leisure it doubles up as a pool table.

The aforesaid mural bears an illusion of three dimensions, tempting an impressionable person to try and fall into it - and never return. Meanwhile, enclosed within two dimensions, are padded antimacassars, draped over the backs of chairs. On the window-sill is a respectful nod to the pagan gods: of Triton, the messenger of the sea, and of Venus, who is known to all. The latter is adorned in gold, and glinting beneath a fluorescent tube hanging from the ceiling - for the blinds are drawn, and nature's light is waiting to be invited in. On the wall is a plaque, sporting a tax rebate from the Inland Revenue. It is so rare and so special a thing, that it deserves pride of place – even though the amount indicated is only six pence.

There is a raised platform at the end of the room, grandly referred to as "the rostrum", which the director occasionally stands upon, when he wishes to make a public announcement (or when the rabble require "knocking into shape"). And the most recent addition to this Speaker's Corner is a pulpit, on loan from the local church. How this transaction was effected, no one can say.

Just as he is shuffling his papers around, and preparing mentally for what is to come, Pilate is disturbed by the telephone ringing. He lifts the receiver.

'Yes?'

'Hail, you! May I spick wit Meeeester Propota-mouse, pleassss?'

'Yes.'

'My name is Joan Broon.' (For a moment, there is just a trace of a Scottish accent.) 'May I speak with Meeeester Propota-mouse?'

'Don't you mean John Brown?' Some crackling is heard on the line. It is like the sound of bacon rashers being fried.

'Is that Meeeester Propota-? '

'Who is this?'

'-mouse! Hail, you! Is that ...'

Pilate hears some more crackling.

'We are not ceiling anything. We wish for you to participate in a pie-lot survey. May I just confirm your fool name ... and it eeeeze ... Pie-lot ...'

'Stop pursuing me. Remove me from your list of contacts – or I will report you as a stalker!' Pilate slams down the receiver. Meanwhile, the market researcher, ensconced in his remote office thousands of miles away in Pakistan, navigates to the appropriate screen in his computer system, and sets a "due date" for the next round of his annoying pursuit. But let us not be too severe in our judgement of him. After all, he is only following orders. The Indian softly abuses the director, who can no longer hear him. The director has been called many names in his life. He tolerates this on the grounds that he is all things to all men.

Now ... at last! He switches off the overhead light, and opens the blinds.

For The love of Material (over Spirit)

Soon, a preprandial meeting is in session, and a post-graduate (of some unnamed discipline) is being called upon to make tea and coffee. He is upset, because he believes himself to be a higher order of being than a caterer. He was employed to produce sophisticated software. He has a PhD and is referred to as "Pinhead Dope" by jealous detractors. On the blackboard is a remnant of some previous meeting, voicing the all-important issue of the day ... "What is a customer?" (A more constructive question might have been, "Who are our customers?" or, "Which businesses should we target?" - but, for the time being, preference is given to the world of metaphysics.) Beneath the question, a *Smart Alec* has drawn a rough sketch of a thin face - tinged with a trace of wickedness and a Hitlerian moustache. Herein, does he pander to the gripes of (peevish and powerless) programmers everywhere: that a customer is someone whose pool of empathy is shallow, whose demands are without bounds, and whose personality is imperious.

Foolish Boy

The persons attending the meeting are predominantly mature professionals, but there is one attendee who is a mere stripling – a beneficiary of a youth training scheme, in fact, – who occasionally sticks his foot in it. You have met him more than once already. Hereinafter, he shall retain the title of "Foolish Boy". The reader may be assured that he has not missed much of the meeting (the reader, that is; not Foolish Boy, who misses the greater part of most meetings because his mind is elsewhere). The mature gents are still scuffing their shoes in an agitated way, having sat through a brief introduction (but, alas, not brief enough), and because they are apprehensive of the principle agenda still to come. But hold on. The young lad is talking energetically. Perhaps the agenda is about to change, or to acquire a certain *frisson* ...

'Earlier today, an exciting banner scudded across my screen (like a cloud in the sky). It told me to install this facility called ABC Quick-scan – and, what's more, the service is absolutely free.'

'What does it do?' asks the director, opening the portal of his mouth still further (after the words have come out) in order to release a substantial yawn.

'Well. It freely scans the computer and tells you whether or not you are protected.' The director adjusts his underpants, having just been reminded of something which the boy is not talking about.

'You mean it tells you whether you are free of any viruses, worms or other malware?' he asks.

'Er, no. Not exactly.'

'Oh ... what then ...?'

'It tells you whether you've got the ABC anti-virus installed, and (if you haven't) it points you to a web page where you can download it. What a lifesaver! And absolutely free! I heard you normally have to pay for it.' A silence ensues, in which nothing can be heard except for the youth's excited intake and expulsion of breath.

'You *do* have to pay for it.' This peremptory remark is met with a few more moments of silence, in which the youth attempts to stifle his surprise. 'The only thing that's free is the advert.'

'Still, I suppose that's ... something ...' the sound of innocence tapers off into the ether; but still, the *ebb* of oxygen and the *flow* of carbon dioxide continues as predictably as the tide. In his embarrassment, Foolish Boy feels the need for some displacement activity. He sips from a mug of tea. Unfortunately, it is not his tea, but the director's.

'The tea was not mine ...? Oh ....!' The voice of youth fades again; and the following words of the Director do not relate to the depreciation of his tea, although the miscalculated sip may have been the provocation that led to them:

'Is this the same member of staff who attempted to reinstall his broken Windows *out of Windows* – so that a brand new product, *Windows within Windows*, could be born! When I once spoke of this software house giving birth to an unusual child, that was not what I had in mind.' Everyone simpers, while the boy gulps a large mouthful of his own tea and goes quite red. Mind you, it has only just been made and is boiling hot. He is remarkably self-possessed in directing the fluid down his gullet (rather than out through the portal of his mouth), given that the soft tissues of his tongue and pallet are presently undergoing second degree burns. Heartened by this triumph of mind over scalded matter, he is determined to rectify his predicament, and will wait until an opportunity arises. Little does he realise, he already resembles a creature which has taken the life-terminating decision to cannibalise itself; and every time he speaks, there is a strong anticipation that he is about to consume the last morsel of what little dignity he has left. The conversation turns to a difficulty experienced in retrieving lost files, and he seizes his chance.

'I, too, have had difficulty in retrieving lost files,' he proclaims, hoping to curry favour, by manifesting his empathy with the dispossessed. Sadly, any favour is improbable because it was he who lost them. And they are files he should not have had access to; although, admittedly, he *was* assisted by the main man.

'Didn't you back them up?'

'I tried. But the disk I used for that purpose was drive E – and the computer won't talk to drive E, because it thinks it is drive F.'

'Ah! A personality disorder, then? Poor E! What a cruel fate hath befallen it! And after so many years of honest, active service,' is the sarcastic reply. Then the director leans towards the boy and issues a false whisper in his ear. It is as if he wishes to enjoy a harmless *tête-à-tête*, or to impart some fatherly advice to a daughter (of the kind that has volume enough for public intercourse, and yet is dressed in words fit for a boudoir). In fact, he is mocking the boy ... and – oh, dear! – there are smiles on the other faces in the board room to prove it. Someone in the room makes an impolite reference to the public school behaviour known as "fagging", and an instruction is issued:

'Well! I think our young friend should say nothing more until he has made us all a fresh pot of tea.' Foolish Boy obediently retires to the kitchen – where he is free to open his mouth wide (like a whale shark), in order to examine his scar tissue in the face of a pocket-sized mirror.

'There are no onions in existence which can cleanse the arteries of his judgement,' remarks Dmitri (who is fond of allium vegetables). Meanwhile, Pinhead Dope sighs with relief as his petty duties, along with the director's tea, are swallowed by someone else.

The director resumes his serious discourse, with the following contentious remark:

'You must all work harder in order to make me richer.' He glances around the room, hoping for corroboration, but he meets with nothing but open-mouthed astonishment.

'Ah! You think I am joking, but I speak from the heart – a heart which holds precious to its very core the greater good of the economy: for as I and others of my ilk accumulate wealth, so every strata of society must slowly benefit.' At this point, the speaker notices an advertisement from a homeless charity. It is sitting on the desk in front of Dmitri. On it there is a photograph of a young homeless male called Mark. The words on the leaflet are, "Mark is used to being ignored".

'So he won't mind then ...?' says Mr Propotamous. The director scratches his nose. His underlings express their solidarity with him by scratching their noses also. He crosses his legs and, inadvertently, so does everyone else; except, that is, for the ones who are too fat to cross them, and who exacerbate the sores in their crotches by rubbing their legs together, before giving up the posture as unattainable. All of this is known as "going through the motions". Mr Propotamous feels like *Herr Fuehrer* after the collapse of the Weimar Republic, for he has complete control. And the time has come for him to make a speech:

'I would like to remind you all of a most excellent justification for the uneven distribution of wealth in human societies: that being, the concept of money trickling down from the richest people to the poorest, and *en route* to everyone in between. This magical transfer of Mammon flows through the benefaction of the rich in charitable causes; through employment of the poor, as the rich bolster their corporate enterprises; and, finally, through the willingness of the rich to spend freely, and so aid one of the key elements of the economy, which is cash flow.' Dmitri has other ideas, and philosophises:

'But the majority now realise that it is the poorest citizens who improve cash flow through the economy: spending their money with abandon ... living from hand to mouth. They are paid on Friday – and skint by Monday. Economists and

Thatcherites – both - are critical of such feckless behaviour, and yet they should be thankful that poor fools do not live within their means. By contrast, the rich, already possessing what they need, will hoard their splendid excesses; and squirrel much of what they have away in havens where there are no returns, whatsoever, for the society they live in, not even via the maligned but age-old principle of taxation. And they have no compunction about it.'

'Never mind about all that,' says Pilate. He recites some words in a philosophical tract which he prepared earlier:

'It has been suggested by some revolutionary factions that capitalists should, *themselves*, be subject to the principles of capitalism: and allowed to go bust. But these factions are made up of Communists. If there are any *Communists* present in this room, will they please leave now.' The director has a very selective attention span, and focusses on the mimicry shown in the postures of his staff, as symptomatic of a bull market for the acceptance of his ideas. But his challenger is determined to play the bear:

'If it were true that wealth is disseminated ever more efficiently, the smaller the number of individuals it is concentrated among, - then why not take the principle to its logical conclusion? That is to say, let one person, alone, seize control of everything – which is to say, all of the land, the property, food, water, pounds, shillings and pence, and all of the mineral resources to boot ... which, hitherto, have been spread amongst all the peoples of the earth; and, by this extravagance, shall universal justice be restored.'

'What an ingenious idea!' replies the director. 'But with my perspicacity of mind, I must confess that I see one obvious and chilling defect in this argument.' He then mouths the following words so as to render them discernible to no one but a lip reader, 'Suppose it were not me?' Of course, the observers on the floor can no more read lips, than extract ore from iron, or (by dint of sortilege) divine the future from a display of tarot cards. So they can only guess at whether he is being wistful or rude.

The Name of the Venture, and a Mission Statement

'Now, the first scheduled issue of the day must be addressed. And not before time, for the progress of my meeting has been delayed by a mild course of disagreement,' the venerable director clears his throat. 'It leaves a bad taste in my mouth, much as a course of Aspirin, Kaolin or Andrews Salts is prone to do – but, unlike those substances, it offers no relief from aches in the head, nor from upsets in the bowel.' The blood rushes to Dmitri's cheeks, as his boss revolves his head in a semi-circle (after the fashion of an Eastern diplomat), and – serpent-like - touches his septum with his long tongue. It is rare that he has sniffed the White Lady, but he likes to reassure himself that she has not made off with any part of his nose.

'You will remember that we wrestled with various names for this new enterprise of mine; and we eventually settled upon, The Perfect Launchpad Limited. Software is the engine that drives any successful business these days. With the right computer programs in place, every planned-for success shall follow. Hence, what better than to suggest that an entrepreneur may launch himself, with our assistance, to newly-imagined horizons. The hours and expense taken to arrive at this name were astronomical – but of minimal concern to ourselves, since we shall simply pass the cost on to our clients (and call it a *sales tax*, as Adam Smith might have done). We would focus upon those we know in local government, where the honey pot is said to be shallow when it is actually profound. It is the opposite of a mirage.'

'Let us all fly heavenwards, to the very pin-prick of sublimity!' comments a technical Irishman, who is swept up by a tide of exhilaration, and who believes the sublime to be a discrete place of limited issue. He receives a warm endorsement:

'I couldn't have put it better myself. And I must impress upon you all, how lucky you are to be working here in these exciting times. Private industry is so much more fruitful than the public sector. But this software house is poised to milk the benefits of both.

My friends, we have embarked upon a famous journey; and one tiny port of call has caught my eye. I have grown to love our corporate name so dearly, that I wonder if a precedent has been set. Have we not acquired a certain proficiency in the art of naming things, that may be applied more widely within the field of computer science? Might we not even consider farming out this new-found talent to other companies, who are breaking new ground but struggling with this most unusual of art-forms?'

'So we are moving away from developing software?' someone suggests.

'I confess, the "art of nomenclature" is not allied to the "art of software". But still it is, shall we say, *soft* rather than *hard*?'

Oh, Foolish Boy!

An especially hungry Foolish Boy tears open a cellophane bag, and rustles some crisps he has stored there. He might have waited, for catering has been accounted for; but he has done it under the table, and considers this to be sufficient discretion. Having no handkerchief available, he wipes his greasy fingers in the doughy white bread of a pre-prepared sandwich, and looks up to check no one has noticed. After swallowing a few crisps, his confidence rises like the Morning Star; and so he begins to munch upon a bag of Smarties. The corners of his open mouth turn brown with chocolate, as he smacks his lips with satisfaction. Dmitri, who sits opposite, cannot escape his eyes, nor the churning of the sweets – which are tossed around like clothes inside a washing machine.

'Have you quite finished?' Dmitri asks.

'Wot? I never said nothink,' replies Foolish Boy.

But hush! The Director is about to make a formal announcement:

'As a rule, I would not say this so early in a meeting – but like a five-year-old faced with a plate of pungent vegetables, I feel compelled to dispatch the unpleasantness sooner rather than later. So, here goes. One of my chiefs of staff, Charles, will soon be altering his identity: but not in a significant way, of course. Oh, no! He has been absent for a while, and shall resume his duties one or two mornings a week, applying his superior brand of consultancy, just as before. He is still our captain of user acceptance, in the area of personal presentation. He is our on-site hairdresser, no less. So, then, my brothers in arms, how will he be different?' Pilate likes to pose a question, and then answer it himself. Over long years of practice, such performances of unchallenged egotism have wrought a strange effect upon him. He has grown into an actor – who, by performing all of the stage parts on his own, renders the other players useless.

'The difference, my dear friends, is that Charles is about to change his *gender*, and will henceforth be known as "Charlene". It is somewhat distressing to me that he is not the first in our department to be "altered" in this way ...'

'Really? Who else is there?' someone asks, in all innocence.

'Mary.'

'Mary? No. Who was he *before* he swapped the vital elements of his scrotum - for a squirt of oestrogen?'

'He was Mary - also.'

'So his vitals had not changed? He was really just a cross-dresser?'

'No. He was an Italian.' There is a moment of silence, before the respondent catches his boss's train of thought. It is just as well he is on board. Without this insight, he might otherwise have been waiting at the station for some time.

Mr Propotamous resumes,

'Anyhow, back to the small issue of Charlene... Specifically, my characterful hairdresser is beginning to develop a trace of a mammary gland or two; and so, for a brief time only, he will feature in your imaginations as a hermaphrodite. In his own words, and like a sophomore student at college, the doubtful man (who is our barber) says, "I'm only just beginning my induction course". Notwithstanding - when nature calls, he will occupy a cubicle in the ladies' department; and not, as it hath previously been, the *gents'*.'

Now, Foolish Boy has been fast asleep during this news release, and he has woken up just in time to pick up a tiny morsel of data from the final words. He has pencil and notepad at the ready, and scribbles down some irrelevancy - imagining that the director has announced the venue for the next meeting.

'Which cubicle?' he asks innocently.

'Don't worry. You won't have to share it with him.' The director raises one palm to his mouth, as if a quantum of smog has escaped (if smutty humour may be so described) and he is applying a cloth to protect his lungs from its re-entry. The youth realises that a joke is afoot, and that it is on him; and he makes the situation worse by protesting ...

'Here I am, sat here, just doing my best, and everyone keeps picking on me!' He says, in a fit of self-pity which would be insipid if manifest in anyone else, but is oddly endearing in him. Certain fellows cruelly curl their lips, and the cruellest of them all begins to convulse behind his handkerchief.

'You are not *sat* here,' the principal corrects him.

'I am. I am, I say.'

'You are *sitting* here, just doing your best.'

'S'wat I said.'

'Young sir. S'not what you said,' says the director, blowing his nose and chuckling gaily at his own cleverness. Polite laughter gives way to guffaws.

'Watch out! It is catching. You are spooling your malapropisms into the pure, liquid eloquence of our breath.' All who are present glance every way possible (to avoid the gaze of either the youngster, or the older man who is chastising him), and each is mindful that he (or she) should not breathe in the miasma arising from Foolish Boy, and become infected.

'Is your aunt called Mrs Malaprop?'

'I don't have an aunt,' replies the wounded youth.

'Dear all, I could weep for the growth of poor expression (especially among the aunt-less) – for this growth is not benign, you know,' says Pilate, in an entrée of sweet speech, prior to an offering full of carcinogens. I trust our *documentation* shall have "perfect phrasing", even if our tongues do not?'

'Perhaps we should send it to the Royal College of Music – where it can learn perfect pitch as well?' suggests Dmitri, with his tongue literally in his cheek.

'Perfect pitch cannot be learned,' says Foolish Boy. 'It is God-given. Even *I* know that.'

'Well. We shall have to submit that opinion to the consideration of the Canon, for he is the local authority on all things divine.'

Apologies From Absentees – and a Whirlwind of Bad Health

'Gentlemen, I must now convey to you sincere apologies ... from Demeter, our Database Administrator, who (most peculiarly) bears the name of the Greek female goddess of agriculture - although he is a bloke. He was removed to hospital several days ago, complaining of an excruciating headache. Tragically, he suffered a brain haemorrhage when he was resizing his database.' A wicked smile flickers across the director's lips, as if he is about to make a joke and has thought better of it. 'We honour him for his commitment to duty in the face of failing health ... for staying up to midnight and beyond ... always beavering away ... you get the picture.' He points to a tiny pyramid in the middle of the table, around which they are all sitting. Identical photographs of the stroke victim adorn the three sides of this object, and are framed in black – giving it the appearance of a tiny mausoleum (as if the poor man had already died); whilst, beneath each reproduction, the name, "Demeter", has been decoratively displayed, employing the finest implements of calligraphy. (It must have been purchased from a gift shop, for there has been insufficient time for anyone present to have designed it.) The face shown has a large, square cranium, which, of late, might be imagined to have ballooned in size during the course of his employment, on account of all of the thoughts which filled it. More incredibly, the weight of his oversized head rests upon a single finger, reminiscent of Salvador Dali's depiction of sleep.

'I must also convey apologies from the sacked and the injured.' The director says this as if it was their fault, but his words scarcely raise a heartbeat. His troops are becoming inured to the unusual paths via which they are lead into new subject areas. 'From the legions of the sacked, there is Benjamin Disrami, otherwise known as "Einstein". Of course, whether he really *is* apologetic for not attending this meeting of minds, we shall never know, – since he has been banned from ever setting foot in this building again. We also have a previous employee suing for damages over a broken leg, a calamitous accident born out of the usual contingency of too many wires spread around the legs of his desk. Why, oh why, this gentleman is attempting to indict me, when it was clearly *his own* "spaghetti junction" which brought about his downfall, only the good Lord knoweth.' The speaker is about to add, 'It is a pity his leg did not snap right off, for then he would have had a rudder by which to steer his proverbial boat into the abyss'; but, at the eleventh millisecond, the Speaker of the House takes a diplomatic course of action, and deletes the offending article from off the tip of his tongue. 'I had to sack him, and I do believe that what he rails (so bitterly) against, is this clean break in the continuity of his employment, more than the cracking of his femur or any sleight upon his good name. Am I right? We shall never know. It is a deep and insoluble mystery. But we must move on.'

But before he can move on, health, or the want of it, continues to rear its ugly head. One employee is worried about repetitive strain injury. The director is told,

'Repeat, but do not strain.' Another is concerned about hair loss, arising from emissions of radiation. The hair-loss candidate strikes his bald pate, and there is great pathos in his movement.

'Be assured, my man, that computers primarily leak radiation from their rear end or undercarriage, and not from the liquid crystal screen itself,' Mr Propotamous defends the good name of his equipment. In response, the irradiated sole trader (nicknamed "the hairless hound") protests:

'So what! Most purveyors of public services, - a London bus, a taxi ... etcetera, etcetera - have their exhaust pipes protruding from their backsides. Even humans are designed in this way! And yet that offers you scant protection from the fallout!' The director listens with an implausible attentiveness: that is to say, the inclination of his upper body implies attentiveness, but he has a sceptical squint in his eyes which belies it. And this is in spite of the fact that the speaker wears a silk shirt which, at this very moment, is so affected by static that it sticks to his body, as if subject to a gentle implosion.

'So long as the laptop is not resting upon your *lap's top*, - in which case you may reduce your sperm count through exposure to thermal radiation – you should be just fine ...'

'Ah! So it's true, then?' says the complainant.
******
Next, is the turn of a young Asian secretary, who is pregnant:

'I, too, am concerned about radiation; and I am worried I might have a miscarriage.'

'Now, look here!' exclaims the director. 'I've had quite enough of this. The phenomenon of radiation is all around you anyway! There is *good* radiation, and there is *bad* radiation. Animal bodies emit radiation. Even your wife will give you a dose when you are close to her.'

'I don't have a wife. *Wife*, indeed! What do you take me for?' replies the Asian lady sharply.

'No! *My* wife. *Anybody's* wife.'

'No wonder he's avoiding Myfanwy. That wife of his is making him sick!' someone else quips.

'There is a familiar understanding between the members of the unwell, in which the healthy are never invited to participate,' another meditatively suggests. And then, there is a sudden outburst from the member of staff who is rapidly balding:

'Proof? You want proof? I'll give you proof!' He seizes a clump of his remaining hair, wrenches it out of his scalp, and tosses it, bloody roots and all, onto the long executive table: whereupon it slides across the "BT tablecloth" for a second or two, like the Lion King performing upon ice, before arriving beside the director's mug of tea.

'You know, *toupées* can be fixed in place more securely these days, if you want them to be,' replies Mr Propotamous. 'A cheap adhesive from any general store will suffice ... even sellotape or liquid gel. Now, just calm down and put that hair-cluster straight back onto your head where it belongs.' The boss is trying to appear unflappable, but his lower lip is quivering with ire. If he doesn't have this condition seen to, he might end up with a tic.

'It's not a toupée!'

'So be it. Do you want some sellotape ...? Moving on at long last ...'

'And to think, I used to have the most marvellous head of glossy, black hair,' the balding man remarks sadly.

'So much for hair loss. What about mobile telephones and brain cancer?' asks another young lady.

'The research is inconclusive,' replies the director. 'Anyhow, can't you just amplify the signal, and then hold the receiver further away from your ear?'

'But what *is* the signal?' she remonstrates. 'The signal *is* the radiation. Can you save yourself from being shot by standing further away from a rifle as the trigger is pulled, if you have also amplified the killing range of the firearm?'

'Well. What do you want me to do about it?' The director has begun to squirm, and yet his two legs lie strangely still. It is as if they have become trapped in quicksand, while the upper half of his body is frantically trying to escape. (For many a long year he has hardly used his lower body – and so his legs are in a quandary. They hardly know what to do.)

'I'm sorry, but we really must get a move on. We have covered stroke, broken leg, repetitive strain injury, hair loss and loss of baby. If we stray towards other ailments, we will surely never finish; or, alternatively, we shall all be well and truly spent!' The director is beginning to feel like his precious meeting has been sabotaged.

Seizing Control

'Next issue. Deadlines. You must, you simply *must*, meet your deadlines. Otherwise I will have *to let you go.*' This is a thinly veiled threat, and shall be extrapolated upon elsewhere. Insurrection is in the air, but the following words shall quash it. 'I secrete a couple of colleagues (I call them my *henchmen*) in a private room. Their purpose it is to offer moral support to me when I say "good bye" to one of you - or words to that effect. If necessary, they will escort the disposed person off the site. I once saw an obsessive compulsive disorder arise in one of my staff. This person was relentlessly checking the same piece of code. He was also spending far too long in the lavatory, because he was obsessively washing his hands. Eventually, he developed a skin condition, for which he took time off work. To be fair, the culprit may have been our choice of toiletries. The public convenience is amply stocked with carbolic soap, the scent of which is both nauseating to the young, and comforting to the very old (as it reminds them of their childhood). Anyway, he, himself, was young – and he had to leave. And my henchmen made sure he went.' The director pauses to fill his lungs.

'Next on the agenda is: the general din from the tape units, the humidifiers and the air conditioning systems. Admittedly, it is all rather old technology, and the whirring sounds might put you off your stroke, but -'

'The warm air can be moistened with a bowl of evaporating water, so the humidifiers can go. As for the air conditioning, can't we just open the windows?' is the complaint from the floor.

'The machinery has to be maintained at a constant temperature. You should know this by now.'

'In that case, couldn't these items of equipment be kept in a separate, hermetically-sealed room. That way, they will operate in an environment that suits them; and we will have one which suits us.'

'No, that would cost too much. And, also, keeping the windows shut reduces the heating bill. Really, you must try to be at one with the resident technologies.'

'But how may I be at one with them? I am not a tape unit. I am a human being!' is the loud and soulful reply. It almost calls to mind the 1960s television drama, "The Prisoner": except that here, Homo Sapiens has not lost his humanity in a number, but in a machine. Mr Propotamous, after the fashion of all good warlords, knows that a battle must first be started, or escalated, before it can be won.

'Yes – you – are.' The big man spreads out these three little words over a number of seconds, and they are succeeded by utter silence.

'Yes - I - *am*?' It was possible to hear a pin drop. For some reason, both parties have risen to their feet, and the great leader now stands eyeball to eyeball with his questioner. Then, he does something entirely unexpected – for he knows that an element of surprise can throw an adversary off balance. He rolls his eyes independently but in perfect unison - as if they were celestial satellites attempting to encircle his brain (or some other exotic sun), but lacked the courage to complete a full orbit. It was a little trick he learned at school. On one occasion, it had elicited a yelp from a young female teacher; and it was something which he thought worth perfecting under the tutelage of that oddball, "Einstein".

'When you are in my employ, you will be whatever I say you are.' The employee makes no attempt at a reply. He simply scuttles out of the boardroom, like a tiny insect escaping from the sticky tongue of some predatory lizard. The director sums up,

'The air conditioner is to be preferred to an open window, which allows the sounds of the street to enter the office and become a source of distraction. Do I sense a trend arising? The windows of coaches are sealed nowadays, as if they were coffins. After all, if the journey is long, a passenger may lose patience and wish to jump out. And bathrooms, separated from perimeter walls, rely on extractor fans to freshen them up. These fans are the lungs of the future! Really, open windows are so passé! In fact, the whole of civilization is rather like a hermetically-sealed unit. Picture a London Underground train: on the Northern Line, perhaps. Or a Tupperware box full of meat. You dare not let in fresh air, because everything will spoil.'

Matters Arising: Dress Code, Technologies and Acronyms

Even though he ambles into the former warehouse each day in a scruffy pair of jeans full of holes, and a grubby old T-shirt covering his upper body, the director emphasizes a strict dress code, in order to create the right impression in front of visiting clients. He freely admits to his own lack of style – but impresses upon others that he is not the one being hired out to the client; and that when he meets anyone in an official capacity, he will dress for the occasion. Then he remembers his last meeting with a client when he forgot to be smart, and he explains: 'That was the exception which proves the rule. Of course, no exception can really do this. It can only be too weak to disprove it. Anyhow, we have established that appearances are important for visitors. And the right look is closely associated with productivity. So, while we are on the subject, – remember, remember, the clear desk policy.' He smiles, as Guy Fawkes flashes across his mind. Then he gulps some hot tea, freshly poured, and wonders if his peace of mind might once more be broken: by a personage whom he is scheduled to receive later that day ... one who will apply his magnifying lens to the sticky area of tax evasion.

'Such a shame the Inland Revenue is not one of our clients. In that scenario, I am sure they would be susceptible to a little twisting of the arm,' he thinks.

******

The door opens to admit a new professional.

'Ah, Mr Scripting-Lang! Your lateness was scheduled, and so it has my toleration.'

'I am most grateful,' he replies. Mr Scripting-Lang is German by birth, but has been saturated by the culture of the Eastern Seaboard of America. He has a gravelly accent (which still sounds more German than American) and, unusually, a dearth of Yankee confidence – except when the subject of American "high tech" enters the mix. He can be a sycophant when he wants something. Latterly, he has been responsible for sourcing some old Dell laptops, procured in a shady deal with a middle aged Chinese lady, said to be his girlfriend and employed by the sales department of Dell Computers. (Rest assured, we will meet her later.) Prior to his software life, Mr Scripting-Lang was employed by the US Air Force. His neck has been greatly enhanced by G forces, and has grown to be a fine match for his square jaw. He has also been a policeman in the Vice Squad. Currently, he is the Chief of Quality Assurance – capitalized, according to his wishes.

'Gentlemen, let me bestow some well-earned praise – and draw your attention to a member of staff who has not been with us long, but who has already made an impact: Mr Scripting-Lang.' The owner of this name nods his head, and with his left arm signifies something approximating to a Nazi salute.

'Mr Scripting-Lang,' he repeats the name for effect, 'is the most ardent supporter of certain policies which I have instigated: that of being immaculately turned out, and of having a well-organised desk. And it is he who maintains our Error Reporting System, by assigning fresh tickets for new problems, and closing each ticket after the attendant problem has been fixed – or has gone away.' The recipient of this confidence wears a smile which shines as bright as the summer sun. 'Of course, we forgive the fact that he does not resolve very much himself,' the praise is qualified, and the man of the moment shrugs dispassionately. 'But ...' and here the director cups his right hand and raises it to his right ear, 'there is news on the grapevine (a virtual and superabundant tree) that he has been shredding vital documents in order to keep his desk tidy. Shall we indict him?'

'I most certainly have not!' he protests. (But he has.) And the director believes him. (More fool, he!) Or is Mr Propotamous afraid of certain transcendent powers which have, on occasion, been imputed to this quiet man?

Now, it is a strange irony that Mr Scripting-Lang suffers from a misnomer. This is not as serious as a *miscarriage*, which is the contingency a certain Indian colleague is most apprehensive of, but his *name* is a miscarriage of justice nonetheless. For the man has only a passing acquaintance with scripting languages, such as Java, PHP, Perl (those readers with technical know-how may extend the list). English and German are all he really knows, and (needless to say) the computer doesn't understand *them*.

'However, the grapevine also tells me that you have completed some documentation recently assigned to you. Please God, these grapes are not tainted as well?'

'I have, and they are not,' says the German-American, warming to this U-turn in the conversation. Mr Scripting-Lang loves acronyms and technical writing, and positively embraces the unspecified task of planning novel approaches to the marketplace. He is normally withdrawn, and finds in such tasks a palliative of sorts. The director explains,

'I refer to the document, Financial Accounting and Commercial Undertaking. But you may replace the word "undertaking" with "usury", if we decide to lend the system out to competitors at extortionate rates of interest. Anyhow, to cut your output (like a circumcised organ) down to its essentials, it is FACU.'

'And SODUTOO,' replies the man of German extraction. His voice retains the utmost gravity.

'And what is that short for?' asks the director, showing an air of concern; but only a slight air, for he has confidence in the Teutonic ability to supply a wholesome meaning.

'Systems of Divergence Undertaken Towards Other Organisations,' his opposite number replies, without batting an eyelid (or a cricket ball).

'I was a bit slow off the mark there, I think?' the director remarks affectionately.

'It comprises various methods of persuading others to jettison their own systems and buy ours,' the explanatory words come thick and fast.

'A noble cause. And I hope you will stop at nothing - not even extortion - in your efforts to fulfil it.'

Some people consider the arena of acronyms to be a subset of verbal diarrhoea, or "VD". But VD is a language that both the director and Mr Scripting-Lang can understand, and one which they employ to baffle others.

'Sadly, Mr Scripting-Lang has not limited himself to compiling documents. He has also been inserting notes into the code, and forgetting to apply the important marks which tell the machine that the additions are "free text" rather than "commands",' remarks Dmitri. He considers the German-American to be insidious – and a "servile flatterer".

'It vaz an honest mistake,' Mr Scripting-Lang parries.

'You mean you sincerely meant to do it?'

'No! It vaz an *honest* mistake,' the accused replies, using the power of emphasis to protest his innocence.

'You mean it was an accident?'

'Yes. Zat's right. An honest accident.'

'An instance of *friendly fire* – but easily corrected,' the director interposes. 'We'll let that one go.' He glances at the colleague who has been receiving flak, and he - appreciating the military reference – winks back at him.

During these proceedings, certain rivals for the boss's affection are wondering whether the "teacher's pet" spends his time closing tickets assigned to himself - that should still be open; or foisting his own open tickets upon unsuspecting victims. Mercifully (for his colleagues) it tends to be the former. When a customer has not responded within 48 hours, the matter is considered *passé* and marked "Resolved". In the words of the director,

'If the user wishes to pursue the problem, he must open a brand new ticket and submit the entire history of the fault again. The hope is, that a mood of complete exasperation will prevail, and that the customer will simply give up on the issue: thereby liberating our resources, and enabling us to retain our 100% record in resolving problems. Indeed, you may even elect to intensify this plan of attack upon a client *who doth protest too much*, by purposefully placing a bug into his system; and then requiring that he raise a ticket for its removal! Once the code is corrected, you might tell his overlord that the error was a figment of the complainant's imagination, and gently hint that it would be advantageous to us all if he "went".'

And now it is time to hear another complaint:

'My test data has been stolen. A thief is trying to better himself at my expense.'

'*Himself?* How do you know it's not a woman?' asks the director.

'I only work with men.'

'You prefer men, do you? Are you revealing something about yourself?'

'I ... er .... that was the team you placed me with.' The skin of the speaker is burning, and he has acquired the colour of Parma ham.

'Well. It's a very serious accusation that is being made. Mr Scripting-Lang? Will you investigate?'

'With pleasure, sir.'

The victim who has just spoken out was already seething, and now that his private life has been impugned as well, he is unable to withhold the following outburst.

'It's him!' he points at the German-American. His oval face has now assumed the aspect of a plum tomato. He is about make another serious accusation, but the director once again comes to the rescue of his foreign ally.

'Yes. *It is he* who documents and explores new working methods, so that we may achieve my favourite kind of system: one that is user-friendly, water-tight and feature-rich. He is occupying his rightful place within the Milky Way.' The director projects his arms outwards, as if to engulf the whole of interstellar space, before he is rudely contradicted.

'No. That is not what I am saying.'

'Well! It is what *I am saying*. Anyway, we should reduce the volume of testing we do. Let users be our guinea pigs. They will soon tell us if anything is awry. And please remember: if we cannot fix it ... then it's not a bug. It's a *feature*.'

Timescales (Again)

'Now, then,' says the director, rubbing his palms together with the greasy balm of satisfaction. Perhaps this is a throwback to the symbolic ablutions of Pontius Pilate? The present day Pilate then takes one of his shoes off, along with the concurrent sock, to examine a corn on his big toe. He begins to finger that callosity; but we must not dwell upon his unsightly fingering. 'Did I mention the importance of timescales? My memory is not what it used to be,' he excuses himself, 'and nor is the adherence of this House to its timescales. We must ... we simply must,' he says, addressing everyone except himself, 'meet our deadlines.' He contemplates his next move. 'I have tried (God knows how I have tried) to see why it is so difficult to bring in a project on time ...' In the distance, the sound of manual labourers can be heard. They are digging up the road and laying subterranean cables. It is as if reality is impinging upon a dream.

'After all, if they can complete on time,' he points his chin towards the window and beyond, 'then why can't you lot do the same?'

Quiet protest hums through the room, to the effect that logical processes are more difficult to bring to fruition than physical ones, because they have repercussions which are harder to predict.

'In summary, we, the murmuring protesters, draw a parallel with the game of chess. How may we know whether two opponents will play all of their moves within one finite session – or whether they will need extra time? Ours is not the realm of the soothsayer!'

Dmitri elects to speak:

'Quite apart from this, rarely – rarely, I say, - do the builders of tangible things ever bring in their projects on time.' The software developers are with him on this point. 'Why, three months ago I was chatting to one of those workmen whom we now hear,' Dmitri nods in the general direction of the disturbance. 'That man told me (and these were his very words), "The giant crevice you see before you will only be here for another week or so, gov". I have to tell you, it is still there. I nearly fell into it the other day! And compare the labourers' predicament with our own. The invention of a computer system has been likened to a voyage of discovery. It is not a straightforward execution of a predefined set of rules ... Therefore, it is nearly impossible to test the code which underpins it fully, or to weigh up the different potential outcomes in combination. Five things to check soon become five factorial!'

'How do you find a needle in a haystack?' retorts the director. 'Why, you line up five hungry ponies and wait for one of them to choke.'

'*Qu'est-ce que ça veut dire?*' asks Dmitri, although the imagery invoked has quickly embedded itself in his mind's eye.

'In other words … modularise it, link test it, and wait for one part within the composite whole to fall over! It is better to have five ponies feeding in moderation, than a lone shire horse processing an entire feast. That way, when you isolate the one that chokes, you will have only one set of entrails to rummage through in the post mortem!' What follows is an act of solidarity: evinced by a nodding of heads, a murmuring of mouths and a raising of eyebrows. For the moment at least, the incongruous ruler has the team back on his side.

******

Next on the agenda, is the entity model for their flagship system – the beneficiary of which is a local electricity supplier.

'I don't see myself anywhere here,' says Mr Propotamous. He is hoping to strike fear into the mind of the designer, in much the same way as Henry VIII may have done, when he seized upon the manuscript of "Greensleeves" and claimed it for his own - most likely assisted by the composer himself, strenuously rescinding his copyright for fear of losing his head.

'You see yourself as part of the abstract rather than the physical world, do you?' Dmitri ventures, for, whilst others might ask questions of the great leader, he alone has the status to make him look foolish and get away with it. The director scratches his head … and then responds in kind:

'But to ask, Where am I? - is, perhaps, to miss the point. I need only be faintly sketched into the schema as a token of respect – like a ghostly watermark asserting ownership, and known in the trade as a "legend", - since my genius imbues all that we do. I am immanent in all things. I am the alpha and the omega. Without my presiding spirit, how can you achieve anything?' Thus does the director account for himself, when – merciful heaven! - he hears a voice pervade the room:

'Even the humble worm leaves a cast within the sand, and yet I cast only shadows! Let the flesh substantiate the shadows!'

Our anti-hero looks quizzically up, and wonders where the voice has come from – although no one has moved his lips. Having spoken of himself in Godly terms, the boss wonders if God has taken it upon Himself to verbalize some inner doubt that he might harbour. But do not worry. It is only the author blowing some words into the mix, and gently stirring the concoction within the cauldron. Authors can do this if they wish. They have special permissions assigned to them, for all manner of insert, update, view and delete functions within their narratives.

If Music be the Food of Love ...

We have reached the point in our tale where the meeting must be delayed - yet again! Swing is in the air. Nat King Cole is singing, "Mad about the Boy"; and he is followed by a smooth touch of Mantovani. And then, for the *finale*, - with the volume raised in order to drown out any objections, - ladies and gentlemen, will you please make way for the great Giuseppe Verdi himself, who, according to an Italian poet, wept and loved for all of us. A diva is belting out the libretto, before an impending act of doom: a suicide, perhaps? And if the office staff strain their ears, another voice can just about be heard. It comes and goes, by turns. Yes, there it is again! Myfanwy, herself, is singing. It was only a minor embellishment at first; but now, she is going at it full throttle.

Eventually, our venerable chief of ceremonies calls a halt to a new subject of debate – Who is your favourite composer? - which, by the way, is an extracurricular item. He has been swaying, not with the rhythm, but in between the beats, for he wants their pounding to cease. He has just risen, and is moving towards the door. His stiff joints are creaking like some instrument of percussion. He speaks the same parting words as were selected by Captain Oates, in that doomed expedition to Everest in 1912, 'I am just going outside and may be some time'. Then he closes the door sharply behind him. He is talking to himself, as the sound of his footsteps disappear down the corridor ...

'I told her ... How many *times* have I told her? I *keep* telling her (but she never listens) ... not to switch up her bloody music when I'm having a meeting!' He is, of course, referring to his estranged, and most unlovely, lovelorn wife, who craves attention, especially of the romantic kind, and receives it through the verbal ejaculations of her favourite divas – and most especially of all, when Giuseppe Verdi is "giving it to her".

The music falls silent. The office workers in the meeting room are all agog. Somewhere, in another place, a *fortissimo* argument has ensued. It is as if the whole thing has been choreographed. (Contemporary operas can have a lot of dialogue in them.) The extraordinary thing is, that only the wife can be heard, except for one brief line ...

'Good grief, woman! What's that coming out of your head? Surely, your eardrum can't have burst?' The fracas dies down, but this bodily fluid is not the solution Pilate was looking for.

'How unfortunate am I,' he muses silently, 'to be a male who is alive in an age of feminism: to be confronted by the emergence of dominant women, after centuries of their oppression?'

The director returns to the conference room, feeling like a battered cod. No one asks about the outcome of the dispute, nor does anyone requisition a progress report on the state of his marriage. Shortly afterwards, his mobile phone rings. His wife is on the line. In a moment or two, he cedes to her expressed wish (which is as heart-felt as the arias of her tragic heroines), to sit in on the meeting and be by his side. Ah! His one and only Myfanwy! She is not at all technical, and will have nothing constructive to say, but she would like to be included in the general body count. Her husband accepts his fate, as his wife enters the room and settles down. She complains of a spinning sensation and mild tinnitus, whilst dabbing her ear with cotton wool.

'Are you sitting comfortably?' he asks. To his alarm, his wife is sitting too comfortably. She is in between her husband and Dmitri, and, to provoke the former, is whispering sweet nothings to Dmitri. She snuggles up to that technician, before nodding her assent. 'Then I shall continue.'

Devotion to Duty

The director parries the wordless wave of atmosphere that has accumulated during the minutes of his absence, by erecting breakers before the wave reaches the metaphorical shore. He achieves this by waxing lyrical about dedication to the job.

'I want to praise one highly intelligent practitioner, who will be returning shortly from his trip to the dentist. He has suffered – oh, how he has suffered – from the ravages of halitosis. Sad – how sad! - are his unspoken thoughts; and glad – oh, so glad! - are the atoms that escape from his oral gas chamber, and touch us with the piquancy of his genius. The humans who have been breathed upon by him (or who are nearby when he is breathing out) have likened the assault on their nasal passages to that of a sewer at high tide, or an industrial processing plant handling food waste. But enough of that. I want to tell you about how we should strive consciously, all the days of our lives, to emulate this man. Stay with me on this one, and you will see why.' Now, there is a wild vein of hypocrisy at work here, for the Speaker of the House (the software house, that is) has been puzzling for some time over how he could go about removing this individual, within the confines of existing employment legislation. This is a challenge, because his level of proficiency with respect to technical matters means that the usual *force majeure* could not be actioned upon grounds of incompetence.

'And your point is?' Dmitri asks. He sounds irritated.

'My point is that, due to a tiny oversight on his part, he has not brushed his teeth for six months.'

'And *that* is your point? replies Dmitri with astonishment.

'Ummm. Sounds like a *large* oversight to me,' whispers someone else, who is just out of earshot and so cannot be identified.

'My point, gentlemen, if you would let me finish, is that he was so wrapped up in his work, that he was not able to set aside the time for brushing, or simply did not notice the stench. Ah! If you had any poetry in your aortas, the beating of your hearts would quicken; and if there were poetry in your minds, you would wax lyrical about such diligence ... such love of an honourable vocation. My fine crew upon this ship of progress - look further than your olfactory bulbs! There is immense self-sacrifice evinced in his personal neglect, if mortals could but see it: a sacrifice which may be reckoned as old-fashioned in these capitalist days. This man should be hero-worshipped!' Mr Propotamous turns his eyes up to heaven, as if he is communicating with the god of slave labour, dressed in all the finery which money-laundering can buy, and surrounded by opulent splendour: a scene pulsating with the sauciest of angels whom the inward eye could conjure, - each moving (as if in some Busby Berkeley musical) upon her treadmill, in perfect unison with the others; as she generates electricity for the national grid. But as soon as the vision has unfolded, it dissolves, like the after-image of a pop-up on a dumb terminal. The director sighs with resignation, lowers his eyes towards his dullards, - and then, trapped in the confines of a mere mortal day, performs an abbreviated spin upon his swivel-chair.

The Worker Bee returns from his Dentist

The one whose praises are so richly sung, opens the door and enters the room. He is holding his lower jaw, as if it is loosely suspended from hinges and might (at any second) disconnect itself from his face and fall to the floor. He has been nibbling on some pages of program documentation, - scribbled down on rice paper to serve as a snack when he is hungry (and when the information it bears is out of date). He has a twinkle in his eye as he thinks,

'There, now. Like Satan in the Goya painting, I have ingested one of my own children!'

This strange behaviour has become habit-forming, and unfortunately some rice paper was lodged under a tooth and had begun to rot, - prompting his dentist to perform an extraction with a pair of pliers. So much for the "hair of the dog that bit him". But now he is armed with a sharp little fish bone, which shall be employed like dental floss should the need arise.

'Wice wiper,' he whispers as he settles down. The director affords him a generous nod and a warm smile, before casting his eyes over the agenda of the meeting once more. Regrettably, the boss cannot persevere in this for long, as he is distracted by the new arrival's speech impediment (which others are referring to as his *verbal impedimenta*). The problem becomes acute when the director asks him, 'How was your visit to the dentist?'

'Well, just to chlorify, - after mar ingestion of wice wiper, I 'ad to leaf. Somethin' to do with nah bruffin' mah teef, and insuffithion mou' waff.'

'So you never got treated then?'

'Oh, well. Ne'er mine. It woth 'ave been fan, but de man is a vorn-again athieth, an thar boffers me.'

'A born-again atheist, you say? Our parish priest, Fr Bertrand, is very concerned about the proliferation of evangelical atheists. He says they are propagating with the speed of termites; and, last I heard, the venerable Canon was developing a pharmaceutical spray which good men may employ as a repellent against them. I'm not sure if he's joking.' A couple of those present now smile, but Dmitri appears unsettled. Momentarily, he has made the mistake of breathing in when the previous speaker was exhaling. Ironically, this is the very situation which he has given warning of to others - although the noxious gases which have been released are only a speck of the issue. The "Worker Bee" is particularly unprepossessing. He has a warty complexion, which bears some resemblance to that of a barnacled sea lion ... snoozing in the sun. His skin hangs loosely about his face, and his substantial tongue has escaped from the cavern of his mouth and unfolded itself over his chin, after the fashion of a sweaty blood hound. As a rule, the tongue glistens - like one of those fat slugs you see in the Welsh mountains, after incessant mist or showers; but today, it is not wearing the correct livery for polite society. Rather, it is dressed in a sallow coat, and has begun to stiffen and to point outwards (as if it was an erect penis) in the general direction of Mr Propotamous - who tries desperately to redirect his gaze to *every* location where the tongue is not. He is rapidly falling out of love with the "Worker Bee"; and feels, due to the sulphurous compounds in the air, that a warning should be issued about the danger of lighting a match. Pilate composes some blank verse in his head, the sweetness of which might work a kind of magic to reverse the actual meaning which is conveyed,

'E'en the bluebottle in me is not well pleased!
Shall particulates in polluted breath
Act like spanners inside my wheel of health?'

'Well, think on it,' he muses. 'In time, even romantic love must lose its lustre and its lusty home-made lubricants.' He wonders if the display of the tongue is a bold expression of rebellion; but - no – the tongue is still recovering from the effects of an oral anaesthetic, necessary for the root canal treatment: which, in the end, did not happen. 'Ah! Root nerves … bloody root nerves … nature's mistakes, that's what I call 'em!' he murmurs. Eventually, our great leader can restrain himself no longer:

'Sir, will you please put that thing away? I shall not ask you twice.'

With some difficulty, the man uses both hands to cram his enormous tongue back into his mouth. The dentist's jab has, indeed, had a catastrophic effect, for his emotions only register on one side of his face - as if he has been affected by a cerebral embolism. Noticing this, everyone is careful not to foment too much excitement, in case a lopsided grin should upset the director's presence of mind. Extensive dental work has been, in part, necessitated by the patient's relationship with his metal rollerball pen: for oft, in the throes of logical creation, he places the end of it in his mouth and bites hard, like a horse chomping at the bit. Once, he was so overcome by a eureka moment that he cracked a couple of his teeth.

'Dentists are so enterprising,' says Mr Propotamous.

'The word on the street is that his molars were chipped, and the dental hygienist applied the finishing touches – with the full force of the drill!' a rebel observes. 'And now, the crooked establishment has won further employment by having to fix them.'

'The skilled practitioner is always on the lookout for new sources of income,' replies the director.

'My point exactly,' agrees the rebel.

'Sir, if you are arguing with me, how can your point be exactly my point?'

But, in this New Age of Logic, the same line of reasoning may be variously engaged to stand for different values. (Indeed, there are times in Parliament when a bizarre concurrence of opinion on opposite sides of the House goes one step further, - and accusations are made relating to who has the copyright on a policy, and who is guilty of pilfering it.)'

'Well, this is a prominent example of capitalism poisoning health care,' the rebel blurts out.

'Come, now! Every craftsman is worthy of his hire. Gentlemen, please! Have a heart.'

The Unorthodox Trial of Myfanwy Esquelle

Shortly afterwards, the "Worker Bee" leaves the room, complaining of toothache.

Mr Scripting-Lang has lain low for a while, but now he speaks softly to the director, as if sharing a secret plan. And the languorous sight, and soporific sound, of Mr Scripting-Lang sends the big man into an altered state.

Yet Mr Scripting-Lang is strangely coy, even when no inhibition is called for. His hand always flies over his mouth just as he is about to hold forth, as if every attempt at outspokenness is accompanied by a wish to attenuate, or, at least, to edit the words which follow. Perhaps he must say them, but little minds if they are not heard? Nevertheless, some noise does escape through his mouth, and the attempt at speech is too strong to pass without acknowledgement.

Myfanwy would like to break up the cosy relationship that Mr Scripting-Lang enjoys with her husband. This is especially so, as Mr Scripting-Lang wishes to impugn her reputation. He knows the pair do not get on well, and he likes to spread rumours about them. He is also jealous of Myfanwy's money, and the power she has over her husband. And jealousy is closely allied to spite. One might say, jealousy is the motivator - and spite, the emissary. Meanwhile the wife is thinking, 'Attack is the best form of defence'. So she confronts him.

'And what about the easy access to firearms in America? Even children use them in target practice,' says Myfanwy. Mr Scripting-Lang has thought of this.

'But a key principle has been laid down by ze American firearms lobby.'

'And, prey, what principle is that?'

'Why, of course, ze one which establishes that it is permissible for ze very young to participate in a high risk or fringe activity, so long as they do it with an adult ... and with lashings of relish!' He cannot resist rounding off his statement with this wanton turn of phrase.

'Pah! Adult supervision? And never mind a little carnage here and there!' Myfanwy is getting hot under the collar.

'Vell, I hear zat you may have misfired yourself von day, when you and your man had a cadet to stay,' the German-American grows more Germanic in his excitement.

'What's that? Oh, the student,' interjects Pilate. 'But really, Mr Scripting-Lang, there must be crossed wires in your head. We don't keep firearms in our house. Ahem! You really need a glass cabinet to display them properly; and Myfanwy cracked the last one we owned by falling against it.'

'I vas using a metaphor,' replies his adversary. 'Anyhow, regarding ze student from France whom your wife tutored ... the supply chain of pupils vas not broken on account of a questionable access to firearms, but because of something that happened between ze student and your wife.'

'Whatever could it be?' wonders Pilate.

'Did she abuse him?' asks someone else.

'Now, don't let's leap to conclusions,' Pilate objects. 'Or else I shall be compelled to put up my dukes, roll them like cogs in a bicycle wheel, and grease up the command chain!' (He is shaking his podgy fists.)

'The lad had difficulty with his *AAARRRs*,' Myfanwy intercepts. 'In order to assist, again and again, I threw back my head and showed him my tongue. And then – for some reason – he became upset and decided go to home early.'

'In modern parlance, she was *totally abusive*,' says Mr Scripting-Lang.

'What else did she do?' someone throws paraffin on the fire.

'Tell us! Do, please ...' another stokes the fire.

'She,' he is biting hard on his bottom lip, '*she* ...' (that little pronoun again) 'was somewhat free and easy in the adjectival department ... *She* ...' (he takes a deep breath) 'passed comment upon a certain feature of her student's physical appearance ... saying that he was ... beautiful.'

'A mask of beauty offers no reassurance against foul habits. The dragonfly is a case in point: for it is both ravishing to the eye – and breathes through its butt-hole.' No one knows from whence these words arise; although most suspect a would-be philosopher at the back of the room. As heads turn, the suspect adds:

'Oh, but of course, - a cad! And the other, an *unfortunate cad*!' He gestures first to the wife, and then to an imaginary pupil whom he has conjured out of thin air.

'To refer to my pupil by his proper title, he was a *cadet*. And he did not mind my choice of adjective at all!' Myfanwy defends herself.

'He did not mind reporting you, either,' comments Mr Scripting-Lang dryly. He then turns to her husband. 'And she made a song and dance about him with her mouth.'

'Hoy, there! Be careful, now,' objects her husband.

'Nowadays, you do, indeed, have to be careful. A woman,' the German-American nods towards Myfanwy, 'recently struck up a conversation with a boy in WH Smith about ze length and girth of his mechanical pencil, how comfortably it can be held in ze hand, how soft and regular are its refills, and whether its output has a tendency to smudge. She is now being investigated by ze Crown Prosecution Service under Operation Yew tree.'

'Well, that certainly wasn't me!' pleads Myfanwy.

'I feel a drama coming on,' says Mr Propotamous quietly. And so it is – with the spoken words now taking the form of a play.

MR SCRIPTING-LANG [behaving like an interrogator]: And how may one expunge the offence given by this verbal misuse of a common implement?

MYFANWY: You mean the pencil? [Condescending, and making full use of her superior age] Just as *you* would, yourself. I would lift the cap off its backside, and use a rubber on the page, boy!

PILATE [to his wife]: Darling, you're speaking to an American. Their rubbers are different from ours. [And then to Mr Scripting-Lang] She means an eraser. And she is - in no way - referring to a pageboy.

MR SCRIPTING-LANG: I'm glad to hear it.

DMITRI [utterly unflappable]: Well, if you're glad then so am I glad. We are all glad. And so it is time for us to move on; and, collectively, we are glad of that, too.

MR SCRIPTING-LANG: And what of ze need to mark a key moment with grand sentiments?

A FELLOW PROFESSIONAL [passing comment]: Properly speaking, her deed was an abomination without precedent.

ANOTHER VOICE: Upon this day, the world hath changed forever.

MYFANWY [deciding to lighten the atmosphere which has soured, with some lines of her poetry]:

He tantalized me with his sweets:
Lapis Lazuli were his eyes;
His hair was soft as eiderdown;
His skin, like satin, toyed with light.
My lips were decked with luscious rouge.
They lured him once, then once again.
The lovely sculpture of his cheeks
Bears two bright lithographs as proof!'

MR SCRIPTING-LANG: So you admit it, then? You kissed him!'

MYFANWY: Never!

MR SCRIPTING-LANG: So you deny it, then?

MYFANWY: Absolutely. Red just isn't my colour, babe! But the word, "rouge", scans well inside my composition.

PILATE: Darling, this is serious. [He turns to Mr Scripting-Lang, who has assumed the role of prosecutor] All of this doesn't mean anything at all. She just loves poetic word-plays. A very cultured person ... is my wife.'

MYFANWY: You don't have to explain my behaviour to *him*. *He* can't do anything. *He* has no authority, except that which you assign to him.

MR SCRIPTING-LANG [stripped of all authority, but pressing on with his interrogation]: And what else passed between ze two of you?

[Myfanwy fidgets with the loose threads hanging from the sleeve of her pullover. And then her husband hears the following strange words.]

FROM AN UNKNOWN SOURCE:
Her "period" was the period of his dreams
Until he once inhaled some airborne thrush
(Named, by its owner, as "My Fetish Cheese")
Which, reeking, wafted all his dreams away!

MR SCRIPTING-LANG: Ze yeast did not make his bread rise!

MYFANWY: What of it? It ain't my fault if the thrush was guilty of cottage cheese-like emissions, - which, incidentally, was a condition that I first discovered behind the closed door of the kitchen.

MR SCRIPTING-LANG: That's an imaginative metaphor.

MYFANWY: It's the literal truth.

MR SCRIPTING-LANG: And, I suppose for your next venture into ze realm of fantasy, you will suggest that a bird of that name appeared incarnate, flew in through ze kitchen vindow, extracted a slice of Hovis, and, thereupon, excreted its foul matter onto the dough?

PILATE [responding, and yet it feels as if some other is speaking for him]:

If all is true, then I shall lose my patience.
If not, then truth itself has become poorly,
And all your words, like vectors, make it so.

[And here is a snippet of conversation, as Pilate is roused from his reverie ...]

DMITRI [seizing his superior by the shoulders, and giving him a good shake]: Mr Propotamous? Pilate ...! Henry ...! Are you quite sure that everything is alright?

PILATE: How apt that I should be asked. As a matter of fact ... I do confess ... I have not been feeling myself of late.

DMITRI: Sir, your head has been resting on the desk, and you have been whispering as if in a trance.

PILATE [stirring himself]: Nothing bad, I hope?

******

It is said that all great men have moments of weakness, but it is in their aptitude for recovery that they show their mettle. And so with Pilate, who simply dusts himself down (as if the aforesaid trial were nothing more than a cobweb) and continues to chair his meeting. He knows the best antidote to embarrassment is to behave as if nothing has happened.

The drama has passed, but Mr Propotamous is hampered by fear. The German-American, aka "Fraud Squad" - for all of his shyness – may have hidden powers which Myfanwy (the real Myfanwy, and not the inhabitant of the above fantasy) knows nothing about. He is well-organised and good at following orders. He very rarely has a part to play in people's dreams! And yet his *alter ego* warmed very nicely to the role of prosecutor. For a few moments, Pilate is trying to formulate his next strategy; and then, at last, he finds his tongue.

'My dear brethren, to facilitate you in hitting your deadlines we must move with the times. The beauty of online systems is that the client can access his information from anywhere. And, remember, open source software is absolutely free.' As the director is a cheapskate, this is certainly a winning argument. Even Dmitri says,

'This announcement is a welcome one. But we should have moved our systems online ages ago.' The great leader raises the palm of his hand, - like *Herr Fuehrer* when he was in a Bavarian *Bierhaus*, and summoning a silence after an extended period of applause. He proceeds,

'We flirted with ORACLE for a while, but it was so expensive. I felt like I was signing a series of blank cheques! And we are only made of flesh and blood and bone – and not of money. Clearly, Open Source is the way to go.' Like a dictator, he waits for further congratulation. The seconds tick by. A couple of heads nod. 'And we do not need to have our own server. There are many hosting outfits which can assist.' Truth be known, the director is a Luddite who struggles with new technology. No sooner does he adopt it, than he starts to complain. In fact, he is complaining already:

'At this juncture I should say ... there is a slight issue with online response times: because the data travels, perhaps two hundred miles, down the line to a remote server, before certain results are construed, and those results make the two hundred mile return trip back to the screen in front of you. It is similar to the tortuous journeys of home-grown foods, which must sojourn abroad, before finally wending their way to the shelves of the local supermarket a mile or so down the road.

Gone are the days when everything happens *inside* your personal computer and *in front* of your very eyes.'

'That is true,' concedes Dmitri. 'But advancement always brings problems of one kind or another. What about the Dr Watson Errors we have been subject to in the past ... apparently, when another facility running under Windows Explorer fails - the tool itself automatically crashes in sympathy.'

'Is that like when you see a pile-up on the M1, and experience an overwhelming urge to drive straight into it?' asks Myfanwy.

'Quite so. And all good fun, I say!' Of course, the director is able to say this, because he does not have to clean up the mess afterwards - unless he volunteers to, that is. He then dons an expression of the utmost solemnity as he says,

'Data is the soul of an organisation. Where would we be without it?'

The Transmigration of Souls

'Gentlemen, the time has come for us to inaugurate a mass migration. Since a man is no more than the data which is held about him, or which is contained within his cognition, I imagine this movement to be like the diaspora out of Israel and into Egypt several millennia ago – and hardly less significant.' The director likes to paint his canvases with broad brush strokes. You may have noticed.

'Where are we migrating to?' asks a certain junior member of staff. The director waves his hand to indicate that all inferior beings should be seen and not heard.

'Yes. We are shortly to move the data we hold within Excel spreadsheets, into our brand, spanking new, online area.' He pauses for effect. 'It is ridiculously passé to retain a large database on spreadsheets. Too static by far. We need to be dynamic! Let anyone who does not feel dynamic leave our meeting this very instant.' His eyes circumnavigate the room, and nobody flinches. Several programmers groan inwardly, knowing the subtext of all this is that they will receive scores of unformatted files (many purchased, at regular intervals, from a local syndicate), and be required to undertake a tedious data mapping exercise stretching far into the future. Worse still - the boss prohibits the use of any tool which might aid in this process.

'Alas! It cannot be helped, my friends. Everything must be done in the most laborious way, and every action documented in the most acute detail, – for only then can I properly oversee what you do.' A deep melancholy pervades the faces around him. It is as if there has been a bereavement – and, in a way, there has. For nothing is so close to his employees' hearts as time ... spare time for hobbies ... time for love ... time left in their lifespans ... time, in all its speculative forms, which shall soon be poached as if they were tiny fish - by a cetacean with a little intelligence and a very great deal of blubber.

'Perhaps I can be of some assistance?' the director ventures. 'I once was a programmer, myself. And the memory of that trauma is passing into the distant history of my life. Where is it said that all the pain of child-bearing turns to joy at the first sight of the newborn child?' No one replies. Maybe they just want the meeting to finish. 'It is, of course, in the Good Book.'

Some Hot New Hardware

And thence to a new subject ...

'I have recently purchased some refurbished computers for our department. They are cheap, and they are wonderful. One of these is sitting on the table, plugged in and ready to go.' Several pairs of eyes examine it, and when it is suggested that Mr Propotamous should have bought the most up to date equipment, he says:

'The lower processing capacity needn't be a problem. These machines can be used as training vehicles for new staff. And for my wife to play around on. She needs something to keep herself occupied ... you know what I mean.' He smiles at her, while she is stony-faced. 'My wife could work on descriptors in certain modules. We always require more documentation.'

'Humph! Descriptor? *Description*!' she exclaims. 'Why is it people cannot speak English properly any more.' Dmitri looks unhappy, and supports her linguistic cause:

'Too much foreign investment in our speech patterns, I'll warrant. The investors' tongues are exotic, and their pockets are shallow. Hence, all of our best clients are local.' Mr Propotamous continues,

'As I was about to say, the more recent hardware productions are not made to last. They do not need to be. The advertisers want us to run with the latest software, which is very disk and processor-hungry! And the general PC-owning public obediently upgrade every couple of years. So the manufacturers prosper. But,' he stretches out an arm and lifts a forefinger, thus invading the aerospace of his nearest neighbours, 'change is in the air. The market in refurbished machines has grown into a flourishing sector. The consumers have been granted an alternative, and, in future, may be buying new stock less often. What can I say? With the stockpile of disposed goods being recycled, at least this gorgeous planet of ours will last a little longer. Furthermore, I know that you will be glad to hear that our refurbished laptops will have wide screens. That is now the industry standard. And we don't want to be Luddites, do we?'

'Well! I tend to think that the old-fashioned displays, which were square rather than wide, are more practical for those doing serious work - entailing the *vertical* examination of many lines of code. Wide screens are for watching videos,' Dmitri contradicts him. This time, it is the director's turn to be silent. He fully intends to watch videos – especially when his foot soldiers are hard at work. And it is true that certain videos have deposited the odd virus or two, which proved to be remarkably resistant to the "household detergents" (mentioned in an earlier conversation with Otis, from the computer shop).

'What make is it?' Dmitri points to the portable machine on the table.

'It's a DELL,' answers the director proudly. The Indian employee misconstrues. She is relatively new to the team, and is slowly growing familiar with the names of her colleagues. She wants to show off her knowledge of them.

'Adele ... ? There is no one of that name here.'

'No. *Dell*, you idiot! Not AAAAAAAdele. *Dell*' Everyone is shocked that he should speak so unchivalrously to a woman, and yet they say nothing.

'You know around 400 of these were returned to the factory a few years ago, because they were deemed to be a fire hazard?' warns Dmitri.

'Nonsense! It's a great little lappy!'

'You are *quite sure* that everything is safe?'

'Yessssssssssss, quite ssssssure! Shhhhhhhhhhhh!' the director is clearing his throat while he speaks. He sounds as if he is imitating that evil character, Gollum, from The Lord of The Rings.

'Shall we check the battery?' asks Dmitri.

'Later. Layyyyy-ter. For now, we should lay some more plans, and revel in them, – like so many engineers balancing on tiptoe across a scaffold near the summit of an unfinished tower block!' This remark does not inspire confidence; and everyone remains poker-faced, but the director persists. He would like to win over public opinion by tickling its funny bone. He really would.

'Hmm. Returned to the factory ... It was the Sony battery wot done it,' says the director, imagining his use of a common malapropism to be highly amusing – although (oddly enough) no one is laughing. Instead, they are thinking about the fire hazard.

The computer was actually switched on before the meeting, and has, rather foolishly, been placed on top of somebody's pullover, thereby blocking the air vents and causing both the machine and the item of clothing to become very hot indeed.

'I think I could save on my heating bill with this,' the director comments flippantly, as he removes the piping-hot item of clothing.

Foolish Boy is instructed to recover a bag of ice cubes from the fridge in the office kitchen. The scope of the young man's responsibility is on the rise. (Hitherto, he dealt only in hot beverages.) A moment later, the lad returns with the requisite bag.

'Well, I never! How extraordinary that an ice pack should be available just when you need one,' says his great leader, with all the innocence of a child. Meanwhile, the attendees whisper to each other about the saucy rumour that his wife has secretly employed ice for sadomasochistic sessions. Indeed, impressions of her rear end have occasionally been observed in the largest of the crisp, translucent blocks. (The Society of Engravers would be so proud of her). Her husband is an old-fashioned man who rarely has cause to enter the kitchen. And, as it is for all men, an unfamiliar kitchen is like a foreign country. If he did venture there, he would never find what he was looking for. For her part, Myfanwy shudders. She rues her determination to sit in on the meeting, - and the imprinting of her buttocks in the ice.

Lateral Thinking is the Way Forward

'In order to survive in today's marketplace, we must be innovative. And there is one outfit which swims into my mind, that perfectly exemplifies the innovation of the human heart: Google. They are developing a miraculous resource. I refer, of course, to their charitable intention to take all published works throughout the ages, - without respect either to copyright or to the authors' wishes, - and make them available, in the modern era, to all nations.' At this, there is one collective, awe-inspired sigh, similar to what issues forth from a bevy of teenage girls when they have spotted a good-looking boy at the bus stop. The director completes his speech with a quiet caveat, 'But while the service is free to Google, it is unlikely to be free to Google's customers.'

'And this isn't theft?' asks one intrepid programmer.

'No. Not at all. It's *enterprise*. Of course, we could have offered our opinion on the feasibility of such a project, but we were never asked,' the director wears a crestfallen semblance, which is removed as easily as the pullover from the table. 'We can, instead, offer a service assessing the feasibility *of various feasibility studies*: revealing whether the *studies* are cost-effective or not. And we can access the credentials of those who conduct them. After all, these people should be morally upright, or at least well-trusted. That is to say ... they must be ... either above the law, or not too far below it. Believe me, you cannot throw caution to the wind in this matter.' His audience is wondering what he is driving at, but his flight path is already pointing to another latitude. 'You know, I simply cannot pass by the amount of money there is in anti-virus software.'

Dmitri enters the frame:

'Yes ... and it is so hard to ascertain what is really going on. The Christian Right might be responsible for creating viruses to combat pornography. Who knows? They cannot infect the perpetrators with AIDS; but they may infect their machines, instead. And then a freak who has been touched by genius has to contrive some kind of solution. The same process on the field of battle is already well-documented by stand-up comedians. The west destroys the infrastructure of some downtrodden enemy ... and then it gets first refusal on the contracts to build it up again.'

'That's it! We could generate a software malaise (the like of which has never been seen before), and then make a mint by selling the antidote. No one would be able to compete with us, because we alone would understand the inner workings of the virus. Now that's what I call lateral thinking.' Pilate shakes his head in wonderment, and the jelly of his grey matter becomes tremulous with anticipation.

'I wasn't recommending ...'

'Now, Dmitri ... there's no need for modesty.'

'I am less concerned with modesty than with propriety.'

'Nonsense! (Propriety is a form of modesty.) I don't know how to thank you enough! You have all the morality of the creative spirit! Ah! You look confused.' And then, speaking more loudly, he proclaims, 'Your fresh ideas are the product of a superior mind, - and your willingness to embrace these ideas is the very embodiment of your morality.' Dmitri screws up his face and thinks of Nietzsche.

'You know, sometimes I do not know when you are being serious, and when you are joking,' says Dmitri, wondering how to steer the conversation back on to the straight and narrow path. The director, meanwhile, has a smile on his face. He likes to apply a simple psychological method ... firstly, he raises a sensitive issue in an ebullient or humorous way, and then he watches to see if anyone else is on his wavelength. If the answer is affirmative, he will allow that person to carry the banner for him. And if an idea tests negative, then he may decide that he no longer likes it himself!

(Pilate may be a sociopath, for he does not know the psychological state of others - and must experiment to find out. But, reader, be light in your criticism of this weakness, for having once embraced the zeitgeist he will not let it go – until he has wrung from it every last drop of usefulness. And afterwards? It will be like an erstwhile friend whom he denies all knowledge of.)

'Dmitri, I do believe that you have stumbled upon some interesting facts on the web recently. Would you like to share them with us?'

Dmitri pulls out of his pocket a folded piece of A4 stationary, upon which he has printed several paragraphs. He holds it aloft, and reads,

'In 2003 two MIT students purchased 158 used disk drives from various locations; and (on those drives) they found more than 5,000 credit card numbers, medical reports, detailed personal and corporate financial information, and several gigabytes worth of private emails and pornography ...'

'Were they phishing?' asks the director.

'Fishing?' asks Myfanwy. Her husband ignores her:

'Herein, do I recognise a cheap source of valuable information, - a veritable treasure-trove, no less, – undiscovered and not yet coveted (much less patented). It is a means by which one human being may gain incalculable power over another, although the two may be strangers who have never even met.' There is electricity in the air. 'And what of the exponential increase in surveillance? I say, let us welcome the drones!' He pauses for breath. 'Why, an individual looking on Google Maps may soon be able to watch a second person, a thousand miles away, also looking on Google Maps, observing his own observer – and all in real time. The day is fast approaching when bosses of the world shall cooperate in monitoring each other's staff for the common good. Everyone on the planet will be able to spy upon - or *be* spied upon *by* - everyone else (just as the fancy takes them, or the Fates provide for); and with supremely accurate heat sensors, even the brick walls of the office or the home will offer no sanctuary. Then will you need to be a paragon of virtue, as you will not know, at any given moment, who is recording your every move! Be vigilant, for you do not know when that day is coming.' The venerable speaker has some wisdom of Jesus stored in the back of his mind, - which he has reconstituted for his own ends. 'But do not be afraid: for the inception of this new life shall be celebrated, just as Independence Day in America is now. And yet – ironically and wonderfully - from that day forth, everyone's independence will have been compromised forever. No longer will any man or woman be able to misbehave. No, never again will you take a newspaper into the lavatory to read for half an hour, when you should be at your desk. Or, if you do, you will not escape prosecution. That'll be the day! The day when the human race will have achieved the complete democratisation of espionage!'

Coffee Time – and (almost) Time to Round Up

The bell is rung, as in a boxing contest. It is time for a well-earned rest, and several packets of croissants, cashew nuts and crisps are transported to the table on a platter, along with pots of freshly brewed tea and coffee. There are even coffee beans on the tray, in order that the consumers should lay witness to the genuine article. And there is a bottle of the ever popular, effervescent, brown-as-a-peat-mire, coin-cleaning fluid, which is to be found in the food halls of most supermarkets. (I shan't be more specific that this, for fear of litigation.) The director believes that he leads a good Christian life, and one way he fulfils the dictates of this life is through the provision of refreshments at meetings. He has also accepted two individuals on work placement, supposedly from the war-torn Middle East: and introduces them with this assumption. I say "supposedly", for one of them is protesting as vociferously as his shy nature will allow.

'We reject the accusation about M.E.,' says he.

'M.E.?'

'We don't actually come from the Middle East,' he explains scornfully.

'Shhhhh! Don't tell 'im that. You'll give the game away!' admonishes the other, under his breath. But the speaker has the bit between his teeth,

'We never socialise upon aircraft these days, for suspicions are easily aroused. Speaking for myself, I have always enjoyed entirely positive experiences. Happily, once when I was travelling to some romantic, far-away land, with two stop-offs *en route*, I was informed by some kindly gentleman that he, or any other member of his race, would tell me "where to get off". And when he accidentally tore my tunic, he issued the most devout promise that he would "stitch me up". But a neighbour of mine was less fortunate. On one occasion, whilst cruising at an altitude of thirty thousand feet, he sympathised with the Air Stewardess, "You must be feeling tired, what with being on your feet all day." With this harmless remark, the sensitivities of the passengers in the fuselage were aroused, as they speculated upon the man's forlorn attempt at intimacy ... "could he be propositioning the young lady?" "Perhaps he wants her to sit on his lap, and make any turbulence more pleasurable?" And so, at a rate of knots, the poor man was whisked away - and strip-searched in the cockpit.'

Pilate Propotamous claims that he habitually acts out of the kindness of his heart. But his heart is a questionable source of kindness. In truth, the director has been counting down the days to that longed-for moment when he may legitimately bid his temporary recruits 'farewell'; and, in the mean time, he comforts himself with the thought of a sizeable government subsidy for training them in the use of office printers. One of these newbies now sallies forth with a verbal flourish,

'Oh! I do so love the bizarre, but the bazaar does not love me! I once received a mild infection inside my rear end from a river snake who was employed at the famous square in Marrakesh.'

'That's a strange place for him to work,' someone pipes up.

'He's a member of the largest family of the serpentine brotherhood: the colubrids,' Pilate elaborates. 'And how, prey, did this misfortune come about?'

'I deemed the creature to be a bandanna, tightly rolled up, and sat on it by mistake.'

The two additions to the team have long, thick beards, and are approaching their late fifties. The boss has booked appointments for them with the barber, and is distressed to see that they have forgotten to go. It has been proposed by some that they are of normal intelligence, yet hampered by some indefinable quality which makes it difficult for them to secure employment. The reader, who *is* of normal intelligence, may judge for himself. Mr Propotamous asks,

'And what potato crisps would you both like? We have them in four varieties: the very old-fashioned style, familiar to our grandparents, with the salt in a tiny blue sachet; we have Ready Salted; there is also Hand Crafted; and, bringing up the rear ... Foot Salted.'

The two exotic gentlemen look baffled, but one of them hides his puzzlement and bites the "snack bullet". He knows he must not delay, for his stomach is rumbling.

'I will have Foot Salted, please.'

'He's just showing off. He doesn't even know the difference,' says his compatriot.

'Yeth, I do! Yeth, I do! It'th … it'th …' In his excitement, the speaker has suddenly acquired a lisp. In fact, some hard particles of nut are resting on the end of his tongue, and he is being careful not to eject them from his mouth. Unfortunately, he makes matters worse by burping violently into his fruit cordial. Meanwhile, his friend, who doubts the wisdom of his choice, makes impatient clicking sounds by placing his tongue onto the roof of his mouth and then releasing it. It is like a rifle despatching the contents of its magazine – and has the effect of spraying a mouthful of coffee (not yet swallowed) onto his neatly pressed suit.

'Oh, excuse *you*!' the director intercepts these gassy outbursts. 'Foot Salted … mmmmm … Allow me to inform you. It means the poor people who used to prepare crisps by hand, have subsequently lost the use of their hands and found gainful employment as foot artists.'

'And their new (artistic) endeavour involves the preparation of potato crisps with their feet?' asks Myfanwy. 'Ouch! That's just *too* weird.' Time passes, while the denizens of the software house absorb these surprising revelations. The absorption completed, our newcomers begin to call out their latest liquid orders:

'Me first. Some of the yellowy orange stuff, pleath.' The speaker elicits a pineapple juice.

'And my turn, now,' adds his colleague. 'I'll have a cup of the piping hot, brown fluid, currently residing inside the coffee pot.' They are both somewhat demure, and find it hard to refer directly to what they want.

'You'th life a cuff of coffee?' clarifies the other, and at last swallows the residue of nut particles on his tongue. Without answering, the one who is speaking normally imagines that a substantial meal is on its way,

'And for the *hors-d'oeuvre*, I'll have a bowl of mulligatawny soup.' The director looks confused.

'Is that the carton of blancmange on the kitchen table, beside the milk which has been left to congeal?' asks Foolish Boy Incarnate. The director is none the wiser, although FBI is only trying to be helpful.

'Mulligatawny ...? As I recall, it is made of curry,' explains Dmitri.

'And I,' the verbally-challenged newcomer enlarges upon his order, rejoicing that he has now lost his lisp, 'will have a bowl of camel hump stock, with a teaspoon of lemon juice. Or, failing that, posssssssss-ibly "Cream of Pneumonia".'

'He means "tapioca and lemon curd",' explains Myfanwy, who knows all about the contents of the kitchen.

'Well, you can both ask away, but you're not getting *any* of it!' says the director. Dmitri contradicts him,

'In that respect, sir, I am afraid you are mistaken. They stored it all in the refrigerator earlier on.' The director looks irritable, and his crow's feet are tip-toeing from his eyes up to his crumpled brow - as he launches into another theme:

'Visualise for a moment (if you would) the white "electronic cloth", which so often covers the television screen just after you have switched on. It is fresh from the ironing board – and so consummately pressed, that one is surprised not to see steam seeping out of it! Summon up, in your mind's eye, the unwanted message on the dratted cloth, "New DVB service found! Press OK to start Auto-Setup". And if you wish to watch a programme without changing channels, you must first exit "the life of the cloth". Now, I appreciate that this might sound like a nod in favour of the secular over the religious life, but it is not.' The boss makes a grandiose gesture with his hands. 'Relive the frustration you felt when it last appeared ... *Are* you feeling irked? Well, in this irksome state resides an essential truth. Always remember,' proclaims the speaker, holding one digit aloft, - and allowing his fingernail to catch the light, and shine like a wax taper sporting a tiny Olympic flame, - 'never give the user the default he needs. Quite the contrary, in fact! Always give him the default that *you want him to have*.' All who are present nod their assent, whilst simultaneously munching peanuts and slurping coffee. Meanwhile, the chief shuffles the papers on his desk, and checks his watch.

'I want to round off today's meeting by emphasizing the most important points: hitting your deadlines and turning in excellent work. And the third protocol is,' he pauses while he tries to remember, 'that you must ... must ...' He is like a shaman with his mantra, but the mantra has been broken by forgetfulness. The foot soldiers are thinking, 'Thank God! The ordeal is almost over. It will soon be time to go back to our desks.' Meanwhile, the director feels as if his mind is being transported to another place, as he hears,

'Ah! The sunny isles of productivity, lapped by the south seas of a boss's smiles.'

'Did I just hear somebody say that? Yet no mouth opened and shaped the words,' he thinks. 'Did I unwittingly say it myself? And yet I felt no expulsion of breath pass betwixt my lips. Did I imagine it? And yet no loquacious farmer, sitting upon a tractor of his dreams, tilled the soil of my mind and sowed his seed in its furrows. Must I suspend belief? Am I Macbeth, faced with a dagger of the mind, suspended in thin air, and not yet soaked in blood - but dripping with anticipation? Was ever the spoken word so mystifying?' No one reacts, except for a certain youth, who chuckles, 'I thought there were only two protocols?'

'Foolish Boy! Wipe that smirk off your laughing gear!' he barks. Foolish Boy straightens his face. Mr Propotamous puts the auditory hallucination behind him, and returns to the business of haranguing his staff,

'If there is a failure of productivity amongst my programmers, I will begin to remove them one by one.' The director scratches his head, as his memory returns to him. 'And the third protocol is, that you must document everything you do. Not a single stone is to be left undocumented.'

'May I just ask,' one of the programmers offers gingerly, 'whether the documentation could be left until after we have met our development deadlines?'

'Why, certainly not! How dare you have the effrontery to ask if you can ask? I must stress the importance of typing out each descriptor – ahem, *description* - even as you create the the corresponding function. If you leave the documentation until later, it will slide into neglect. Always remember the three (equally) important things: fast turnover of work, excellent standards maintained throughout, - and readable, accurate notes, to be completed in real time. We must generate an ocean of notes, a veritable symphony,' he frowns deviously, 'so if the client wonders what unearth we have been doing for so long ... a large output may be shown for the greater glory of our profit.' He pauses ...

'And there is good news. Help is on its way. Upon occasion, many of you will have observed me picking over the code.' He winces, as the image of a vulture enters his mind. 'With respect to this, I would like to make an official announcement: forthwith, I shall become one of you.' (He makes it sound as if he is a divinity who has suddenly assumed human form: as in the Second Coming, perhaps?) 'And I will not stand for any personal feuds or petty jealousies, unless such unpleasantness exhorts you all to attain perfection. And I want economic, efficient code ... Ah! The joys of removing defunct code from a system. It is like silicon, originally inserted with difficulty into a lady's bosom; and afterwards, requiring an operation, equally large, for its removal. How ridiculous is that?' He pauses for breath. 'Furthermore, forever and a day, always remember the *four* most important things: speed of output, accurate notes ...'

'I thought that documentation was the *third* protocol ... and I don't remember you mentioning a fourth?' comments his right-hand man, Dmitri.

'*Yes. Yes.* I *can* count, you know! High productivity, flawless skill, quality assurance, and – er - spontaneous combustion! Ha! Ha!'

Any Other Business

Our venerable leader now holds forth on a subject dear to everyone's heart. Yet he does so with false sympathy.

'There are moments when I feel somewhat like a pastor. My brothers in coding, I know that some of you are still waiting to get paid, owing to a cash flow problem. But never fear. What you have rightfully earned shall soon be yours. My wife and I like to think of this enterprise as a family business – and you are all members of that family.' His wife nods her approval, whilst one or two of the power-dressers privately believe this business of his to be more of a dystopia.

'I shall soon be moving the contractors off their hourly rate, and on to a flat daily rate.' He does not add - 'so that I can extort an unlimited number of hours out of them each day, without having to pay any more'. He is, after all, a man of refinement - and a diplomat.

'If you are undertaking a critical task at the end of the day, then the task must be finished before you go home ... or else your head will be served upon a platter in the morning! (Perhaps Gladys will spit-roast it – and afterwards put an apple in your mouth, just as a Medieval king might have done to one of his pigs.) In some cases, you may need to stay late. But there will be handsome bonuses at Christmas time for those hardy souls who can stick it out.' A young man named Henry is smiling like a Cheshire cat. He is newly married, and has a baby in his wife's pipeline. And he could do with a handsome bonus.

'How much, sir?' he asks.

'That is for me to know, and for you to find out. If I sate your curiosity now, then how shall I whet your motivation later, when the chips are down?' (Myfanwy licks her lips.)

The chairman has heard rumours that people might be leaving, and his aim is to make them work like dogs until Christmas, and then give to each of those members of staff he wishes to retain just one Marks and Spencer £20 voucher; and to those whom he wishes to dispel - an "excremental handshake". This is to be contrasted with the "golden handshake", which he *neglected* to give his staff when they arrived. There will be no severance pay, and wages for the final month of employment may be withheld due to weak performance. Mr Propotamous is wondering how he might build a valid case against those he has ear-marked for departure ... it is, to coin a well-worn phrase, "work in progress".

'Now, then. Is there anything else that concerns you?'

One employee complains of a tiny crack in the screen of his laptop.

Another says, 'There is a thin line of dead pixels bisecting my slender Visual Display Unit.'

'Think of such flaws as birthmarks,' is the unhelpful reply. 'Imagine if you were a young mother, whose neonate was confused with someone else's. If your own dear one has a feature by which it may be identified, then the ward where you gave birth will not be able to dispossess you. And the parallel is especially germane - when you consider that so much of who you are is contained within the hard drive of your computer. And, also, when you remember that no laptop is capable of standing out from the others by crying for its mother's teats; although, with artificial intelligence, we may one day create one.'

Another staff member (who suffers from a rationing of true love) now seizes his chance ...

'We are not praised often enough,' he complains. His mind is put at ease with pure logic:

'If others will not praise you, you must compensate by praising yourself.'

'But that's not quite the same thing, is it?'

'No. Of course it is not the same thing.' (Here, there is a brief pause for reflection.) 'It is a far, far better thing. It is more sincere, and it can take exactly the form you want. Be on your guard against praise from all sources other than yourself. Be aware of the inferior quality of every encomium which is issued by those around you; and of how rare – rarer than a Texan steak – true praise is, in all its forms ...! What is more – in professional life, the praise you have is frequently so well disguised, that you need a special kind of antenna to register its presence.'

PART THE THIRD: AFTER THE MEETING

With the main business of the day now done, there is a generous delivery of toasted sandwiches from the local suppliers, "Sarnieland"; which, at the very least, will serve as a wonderful *hors d'oeuvre*. (Hopefully, this term applies; and a sufficiency of the main course is still untouched.) After consuming these victuals, the general and his troops ramble off to a local pub known as "The Space Bar", where they celebrate the near-completion of the first phase of their project for the local Electricity Generating Board, with ample drinks and even more sandwiches. No one alludes to the fact that this client is not really theirs at all, but somebody else's. (More of that later.) Mr Propotamous is in a jocund mood, and takes civic pride in his generosity. At the bar, he orders his favourite beverage. It has been christened the "Eschatology Cocktail", and is composed of three strata. On the surface, there is "Heaven", a white and creamy spirit, laced with coconut oil and shredded ice, glittering under the dim lights of the ceiling (just above the head of the tall waitress); in the middle, there is "Purgatory" – a warm, indefinable, solution of whisky and black treacle, which could be confused for a poisonous, brown mud; and, at rock bottom, there is "Hell", a boiling sediment of coffee beans, clinging to the glass. It is, in point of fact, an over-indulgent Irish coffee, in which the first two layers are delicious, and hell is just an afterthought.

'Cheers!' says Mr Propotamous. 'So which of the three strata am I destined for, then?' Dmitri, who is standing beside him, perceives this to be a loaded question, and does not answer. His boss continues, 'It is good to be here. When we try wine-ing and dining in the office, Gladys forgets to do the catering. And so there arises a proportional increase in whining ... of the alternative kind.'

'What vintage?' asks Dmitri.

'A very poor one. The "liquid notes" give you a headache.'

For a while, they break off from their parley, and are entertained by the words which surround them:

'... So there I was, utterly flummoxed by the message, "error in your SQL syntax" ... and I'd put so much effort into making my syntax *nonpareil* ..."

'The aforesaid code did not work then?'

'No. It works just fine – which is to say, it achieves what it is supposed to achieve, but it still spools out this message ... Really, I am reminded of a scene in Monty Python's "Search for the Holy Grail", where the peasants must be slapped as they receive the basic necessities of life!'

'Tough love,' replies the listener.

The buffet tables have been neatly set out, with fresh linen cloths, and plates or bowls all full of tasty things; and now they are declared as "ready". Suddenly, there is a mad scramble towards the food, with the inevitable collapse of the artless and the clumsy as they trip over their feet and send a couple of the salad bowls flying. Two elderly office workers are fighting over a slice of salami. There are spillages of white crumbs and gravy upon suits; and various concoctions of wine and tartar sauce are curdling together, like lovers, on the lino floor (which has been especially laid on for accidents). Never mind. The German, Mr Scripting-Lang, will supply a running commentary:

'Ah! I zee ze great English tradition prevails ... von or two coffees vurst; zen cake; and zen, to round it all off, the main sandwich or savoury course. It is highly illogical.'

The *un*savoury behaviour quickly subsides. Very soon, everyone has eaten and drunk more than they should have. Even Mr Scripting-Lang becomes so relaxed that he lapses completely into his German vernacular - and is barely lucid, as he expatiates upon the romantic nature of his uncle:

'You know zat I am zigzag drunk. Alzough I must zay ... You vill zink him shy, and zyet in the cowse of huz brief life, he hoz dated many vermin. Yet alvays ze last vos ze best. Indeedy, he vonce annotated how he messed his ox. He was truly uxorious – and he voz a laboratory scientist too: he would dezcribe to me how, ven hungry brats are stored in a cage and females introduced, they vould fight and eat each other.'

Some of Pilate's employees have private enterprises which they must pursue in their spare time (in order to supplement their income from him, since it is so little). One mentions a conventional shoe repair shop, and the empty premises which lie beside it. Another thinks laterally,

'Perhaps I could inaugurate an "Unconventional Shoe Repair" business beside your conventional one, eh? And back up my durability guarantees with research conducted on previous buyers. Hmm, I think I will promise that the repair shall last for a set period of months ... depending upon "miles covered", of course.'

'How can you make such an outrageous claim,' says the other, fearful for the solidarity of his own business plan.

'Why, I'll fix a GPS tracker inside the heel of every shoe I mend. It will be so discreet that no one will notice. And as the Tracker passes information back to my computer regarding journeys made, my software will calculate distances covered by interacting with Google Maps. When the Tracking Device indicates that the shoes have lain unused for a predetermined period of time - then I shall assume that they have reached the end of their natural life, and have been dumped in the skip (or "knacker's yard", as I like to call it), thenceforth to become landfill. After a while, I'll have gathered enough data to start making predictions.'

At that moment, a couple of utensils fall from somebody's plate; and Mr Propotamous is ready with a witticism he prepared earlier,

'Now that's what I call, "the entirely culpable tendency of most knives and forks, to slip from a plate of greasy food straight onto our laps – always timed to coincide with the very afternoon when we have taken our Sunday Best out of the Airing Cupboard, and donned it for effect!' The greasy *human* culprit is, indeed, wearing a tuxedo. And hereupon, an unknown voice replies to Pilate:

'Well, you may *call* it that.' He examines the face of Mr Scripting-Lang, who has suddenly appeared beside him. But that man's face gives nothing away as he informs the director,

'A composite of soil and decaying plant matter has been found on a tray in ze kitchen, labelled "hummus". *Humus* is, in fact, what ve have!'

'Ah! A culinary misunderstanding, then?'

'And, zir ... I am zorry to have to tell you,' Mr Scripting-Lang raises his voice ever so slightly, 'that traces of Corsodyl 'ave bin found in zome black pudding, which is beside ze aforesaid tray.'

'Corsodyl ... the toothpaste for people who spit blood when they brush their teeth, I believe?' clarifies Pilate.

'I understand that your vife has a penchant for inedible substances?'

Pilate wonders if she has had a hand in the preparation of the food on display around him, and he cannot help observing comically to his right-hand man: 'After an excess of self-congratulation and champagne, one or two rear ends are beginning to quack like ducks!' And he defends his other half by adding, 'So much for the alcohol. Did she get the black pudding from here? Or from Gladys, perhaps?'

Mr Scripting-Lang ignores the question and continues,

'And now, zere is a zmall problem with zee soup. Zeveral consumers, a few minutes ago in zis wery establishment, have discovered foreign bodies, including human hair and nutshells; and, in von instance (ze instance of Myfanwy's own soup), a dark blue oven glove 'as been spotted, - preserved in its entirety. Your poor vife vas lost vor words. Still, never mind. She did have a little giggle vith us, before she fished it out and put it into her sandvich bag, to conzume later.'

Much to the speaker's chagrin, Pilate has suddenly stopped listening. He is concerned that he has heard voices.

The Sackings

The title of this section could pass for a quaint English place name, or a series of deprivations. We are going with the second interpretation.

The director is entertaining a very receptive pussy on his lap. He strokes her ticked fur in a mesmerising way. Like an aircraft, pussy is transported. And she expresses her gratefulness by leaking through her undercarriage. As his hand moves up and down, he reflects upon the concept of normalisation - the process by which data is streamlined, - and he applies this concept more generally. He imagines the totality of knowledge to be a confluence of streams, flowing in one great river obediently towards him. He thinks about the erasure of "duplicates", the term he uses for those who perform the same duties as others. And he realises that if you do not hire anyone for very long, then you are not obliged to give severance pay. And so he hatches a plot to fire everyone before they have completed two years of employment with him. Dmitri would be the last to fall foul of this policy, as he is the least dispensable employee; and, to facilitate the whole backstabbing exercise, staff would report to him on the failings of each other - just before he wields the axe.

'Waste not, want not,' says Pilate.

And what if, when he is in the throes of *force majeure*, his victim "doth protest too much"? Why, for that special purpose, the Grand Master has two henchmen on his payroll (bouncers whom he recruited from a local nightclub), who may be summoned at short notice to frighten the protester into submission, before escorting him off the site. There are even a couple of police uniforms, stashed away in a cupboard somewhere, to add a certain piquancy to the fear: although these might need to be washed first, since rumour has it that the First Lady of The Launchpad has employed them for sadomasochistic sessions. (Ah! Capacious Rumour has her eye on everything these days, and there is no one brave enough to de-prize her of her dark gifts!) But the suits cannot have been used very often, for they have acquired mothballs.

The director moves into a private office, and sends out a request on the intercom for his first victim to come through. With the victim *in situ*, his opening gambit is as follows:

'You know, Hubert, - it is Hubert, isn't it? - we have an issue to discuss.'

'It's Henry, sir.'

'Excellent! A man after my own middle name. I won't say, "after my own heart", for no man can be after that, - or, if he is, he cannot have it. Henry, my dear fellow, one afternoon last week you wilfully changed an old warehousing program ... and instantly became one of life's losers.'

'Yes, sir.'

'You invoked the much-maligned "COBOL ALTER" command. (Thank God, it is the only module left which is still written in the original COBOL.) At that moment, you were effectively attempting to rewrite history. Only certain individuals are allowed to alter history, and you are not one of them! History is written by the winners, such as myself. You know, Henry, the very idea of code dynamically altering itself can never work. It smacks too much of anarchy. It is a strange largess to a computer programmer. On the one hand, the compiler has given him a facility possessing such raw power as to be irresistible to his instinctive love of control; while on the other, he is told by his superior that he must refrain from using it. It's a hard life.'

'Yes, sir,' Henry answers. He sounds deadpan.

'One is reminded,' continues his manager, 'of the wilful concupiscence of the teenager, and the oppression of law. Or, to give another example, the right to peaceful protest officially supported by every civilized nation, but only until the freedom is most needed, at which point it is quashed on the grounds of inciting violence. Or – another fall guy which comes into my fertile mind - *Habeas Corpus* ... but, then again, you are not my captive ... I am not pressurising you to stay here; rather, to leave ... Ha, ha!' he pauses to let his words sink in. 'Henry, Henry ... Did you not study history when you were in school?'

'Oh, God! Put me out of my misery!' Henry whimpers.

'You are put out of it, Henry. You are free to go. I trust you will do so quickly, and without provocation - or the need to be accosted.'

******

The second sacking involves a very unfortunate case indeed. A member of staff had booked a week off work, and, at the very point when he was about to return, his mother died. He telephoned in to explain the situation, and was granted a further week of compassionate leave. This is his first day back, and he has been summoned by the venerable director into what, in common parlance, has come to be known as "the Oval Office". In fact, the motherless wretch has moved stealthily into the office while I have been completing the last two sentences. He is now sitting before his Great Leader, who pops the question:

'The work is just not getting done, is it?'

'But I have been away ... with your blessing ...'

'I know. I know. But still, the unmet time scales flash before mine eyes. They are like a mass of concrete, laid by Corbusier. They simply cannot move.'

'We have had a great loss in the family, sir.'

'I do sympathise. Parents are irreplaceable things. But you cannot always think of yourself. Your colleagues have been put under enormous pressure by your absence. While you have been bearing your loss, they have, like a funeral cortège, been carrying the dead weight of your inactivity; and even for some time, I might add, before said sad period blighted the horizon. And so, at last, I am forced to lay your payroll number to rest.' The speaker touches four points upon his person: his forehead, the largess that is his heart, and each of his fleshy shoulders. It is a performance known as "making the sign of the cross".

'Sir, I am engaged; and my wife-to-be and I recently took on a large mortgage. At the inception of this new epoch of my life, I really need a safe job and a steady income.' This is a soulful plea which an ordinary mortal would find hard to resist. But Mr Propotamous is *no ordinary mortal* (especially when reading "Beyond Good and Evil", by Frederick Neitzche).

'Young man, it is a harsh world. And there are no extenuating circumstances.'

'But ... but ...'

'No provisos. You really must learn to live within your means. *I will have to let you go.*'

Now, all ye who hail from the land of reality, – please reflect for a moment upon what a lovely, gentle turn of phrase this is. It implies that a humble soul has politely requested to leave the firm, and that permission has been graciously given: a "gentleman's agreement", you might say? Perhaps Stalin could have touched as delicately upon this consideration, before slaughtering a few thousand of his people? Let us imagine his words:

'Rather than have fate inflict another thirty or forty years of miserable life upon all of you poor wretches - within the confines of this small, blue planet of ours, that we are slowly putting to death, - We (the Royal We, that is; well, actually it is I, acting via the Red Guard) have settled upon a dispensation, allowing you to take leave of all that melancholia right now. Would you please just step this way, and line up over there against the whitewashed wall. A sterile background has been sympathetically chosen, so as not to foment strong feelings; and to enable the marksmen in my employ to see clearly what they are aiming at. They shall make no mistakes: for they are humanists to a man ... or woman. (I am an equal opportunities employer.) In the hail of their capable bullets, you will feel nothing – for you are in safe hands now. And, in a few minutes time, you will slump upon your haunches ... which shall proclaim, like a trumpet, that the goodly task is done.'

And then, perhaps, the soon-to-be-slaughtered crowd would gratefully respond: 'Hail, Caesar! What a rare act of clemency is under way! What wisdom is herein manifest! How benevolent is our leader!' And, at the count of three, they might burst into song, 'For he's a jolly good fell-ow ... For he's a jolly good fe-hell-oooooooooooooooowah! And so say all of us!'

'My self-knowledge is blossoming,' thinks Pilate.

Anyhow, enough of all that. On to sacking number three: the one you have all been waiting for.

******

It is said that osmium and iridium, in their purest forms, are the most dense of all elements, although the compiler of the periodic table may have overlooked systems documentation: which has a meaning not easily permeated by the light of daily understanding. In fact, Foolish Boy is puzzling, even as I write, over some delightfully abstruse documents; and the outcome of his confusion is here included, for the edifying instruction and entertainment of the reader:

'I was adding days to a date and I got: "Call to a member function modify on a non-object". What is a *non-object*? I was trying to get some help from the manual, which proposed turning fatal errors, generated from calls to a non-object, into E_RECOVERABLE_ERRORS. And then I started reading a scientific-cum-philosophical paper which poses the questions, "Are there more non-objects than objects?" and "If I construct a non-object, what is its object status?" My friends have occasionally referred to *me* as a non-object, because I don't have a girlfriend. But I know more about the anatomy of the female reproductive system than they do, and I can aver (with all honesty) that it resembles the head and horns of a ram.' Midway through his soliloquy, he stops, having realised that he is in close proximity to several mature professionals who are laughing at him.

'So ...' the youngster tries to explain everything in his own words, and then tails off. 'Alright. *You* tell me what it all means ...?' A third technician joins the fray. He is an emissary from the general manager, and he tells Foolish Boy that he must report to the "Oval Office" immediately. The youth picks up his folder, and makes his way to the place where dreams are brewed up like steaming cups of tea, and evaporate in sour vapours. It is curious how events inside that office may elicit

naïve astonishment, or the shock of fear, or sheer delight, –
and all depending upon a few choice words.

In a matter of seconds, Foolish Boy has taken the place of
the motherless, soul-searching young man, and he now sits
before his principal. The latter is just about to "pull the
trigger". The lad feels cowed, but he is attempting to appear
cocky. They face each other across a desk, which is the only
solid object traversing a current of misunderstanding – and
which has, on occasion, been called the "Bridge of Sighs", after
an iconic place in Venice, noted in folklore for hosting
terminations of a more permanent kind (such as a parting
view of the beautiful city afforded to convicts, before their final
imprisonment).

'Like other novices, you were supplied with a manual. But
you haven't *read* the manual, have you?'

'Well, normally I would not be arsed ...'

'Young man, you just *have* been asked ... or were you
annotating your lack of a posterior – which appears to me to
be both round and well?'

'Sir! All weekend, I am laying on the settee, studying the
manual that I am so kindly provided with.'

'No. You are not.

'Yes, I am. I have it on my desk right now.'

'No. You are lying.'

'I am not lying.'

'No, that's true. You *were* lying ... on the settee, that is. You
are now *sitting* before me in my private space, and gobbling up
my precious seconds like a hamster with its cheeks full of
nuts.' The Boy puckers his face; and turns his cheerful lips
from a "U-bend" into an "n".

Having got over the preliminaries, the director refers to an
episode reported to him, in which Foolish Boy was told to peer
at a revolving disk, at the very moment when files were being
fetched.

'Was it like this? Did they say ... "Look! Look verrrrrrrr-ry
closely, and con-cen-trate." Were you being hypnotised? Were
your eyes misting up? "Keep looking verrrrrrrr-ry closely ...
and you might *just* make out the datasets rising through the
mist."' The boy is embarrassed.

'You do realize, of course, that datasets are not visible at
all? Their potency is immanent in the meaning which they

convey, or in the information they contain; and not in the possession of any physical substance?'

'Yes,' the boy gulps.

'When you listen to your favourite LP, do you see the notes leaping, like salmon, out of a sea of vinyl, into the sharp point of a stylus?'

'What? No. No, I can't say I do.'

Suddenly, the director's fist comes crashing down on the table. Now, this is a surprise, as he is known for his misanthropic nature but not for his violence. And he is as much affected by surprise as the boy (indeed, as much as the author, himself) – when he sees everything around his fist jump as well. The boy levitates above his seat and lands safely upon his rump; the table (resting upon a thick-piled carpet - acting as a trampoline) sinks, and rises modestly once more; and a delicate finger of fluff upon the shelves of manuals is suddenly airborne and, like a ballerina, performs a pirouette one centimetre above its station, before gently coming to rest ... precisely two centimetres due east from the spot from whence it was launched. Even a huge beetle, who has been tempted onto the windowsill by the light, takes off and lands somewhere just outside the compass of the narrator's sight. So he will have to be formerly introduced later on.

'And you believed the one who was teasing you ...? Have you ever worked with computers before?'

'No. I told you that when you hired me.'

'Noooooooooooo, you did not.'

'Yesssssssssssssssss.'

'No. You could not have done. I would never have hired such a person. You must have fibbed on your curriculum vitae.'

'No. I know ... I know what you mean. But ... no.'

'It is a crying shame that I must be singed in the furnace of all your "KNOWs" and "NOs".'

'I know.'

'Perhaps we may stitch all of your "knows" into a fabric of true wisdom. Or shall we – instead - weave your words, like threads, into a rope! Take care not to hang yourself!'

'At the outset, I only said I had a friend working in the industry, and that my conversations with him planted a seed of interest in me; and, also, that he gave me his old computer.'

'Well, there you are then. Misleading information. You lied by omission.' The director is "on a roll", as they say. 'I want to tell you about another person, whom I once had the misfortune of hiring; and who, through the deployment of copious cooking foil, almost wiped out the kitchen. Inside our microwave oven was a bowl of effervescent fluid which boiled and bubbled furiously until, at last, it acquired the properties of an incendiary device – blowing open the door, and flinging the bowl and its contents (in tandem) across the parquet floor. It was quite a show, and I would have appreciated it if I was a circus manager employing a clown. Well, anyhow, after that incident I just *had to let him go*. But, trust me, the worst acts of foolishness are at the coal face.'

'Let me reassure you, sir. There haven't been any problems in the kitchen while I've been here. I've always used the microwave oven with due care and attention.'

'I speak in riddles. It's not the oven I'm worried about.' The boy looks confused, and so the director amplifies his voice: 'I don't want you blowing up the system! For now and evermore - I prey you, take your leave.'

More Jobs on the Line

At the end of this encounter, the boy is very happy to leave; and the boss's accountant-come-financial advisor walks in through the door, and manoeuvres himself into the hot seat. He is a slightly built man, except for a paunch; and he has a primitive, inbred look about him; yet he speaks with perfect diction. He is taking his rain mackintosh off, and wants to describe a little escapade he has been on:

'The wet weather came so suddenly! But I am happy and excited. I have just returned from giving a seminar to a firm of solicitors, entitled "The Mechanisms of Length and Interest".'

'Really? What was the seminar about, then?'

'I was exploring ways in which the process of conveyancing may be protracted, allowing the solicitor to make a mint prior to "completion", through the judicious investment of client funds.'

'Well, I must say that sounds most interesting! Ha, ha! And you are an excellent gentleman, for nurturing the enterprise of legal practitioners.'

The scrawny accountant leans forward, as a radical idea swims - like a spermatozoa - into the ovum of his consciousness. It has a short period of gestation; and, with the lower buttons of his shirt undone and his stomach exposed, it seems as if he is attempting to give birth straight into the director's lap. For this accountant, bucking the rules is a guilty pleasure. And his one concession to good health is a head of thick, black, greasy hair, with a quiff at the front - which so irritates his eyes that he now extends his lower lip and blows upwards. He is like a scuba diver, who releases used oxygen before breathing in again.

'The Inspector of Taxes will be here soon,' he informs the director, whilst glancing nervously about him and fluttering his eyelids in an effeminate way. 'But never fear! You are in safe hands.' He exposes his grubby palms in a show of honesty. 'I have put your accounts in order and, through earnest endeavour, I have brought a greater clarity to your affairs.'

'But you can't do that. The Inspector will realise what we're up to!'

'Oh, ye of little faith!' exclaims the accountant.

The director has sometimes questioned the verity and usefulness of this man, and now he doubts it more and more each time he looks at him. But at least he's cheap.

'Pilate, you must beware,' he lowers his voice. 'Your business has been registered as a charity for tax breaks – due to promises you made to supply labour to the unemployed, and training for those who are without hope. Whatever would the man from the Inland Revenue do, if he suspected that your promises were purely strategic ... in other words, that you are motivated not by charity but by Mammon?'

'Yes. I freely admit - I did it to reduce my tax bill. Who wouldn't wish to reduce his tax bill?'

'Your openness is commendable. But I take it you acted for the other reasons, also?'

'What other reasons?' Now ensues a long pause, as the respondent scratches his head. He reflects upon the sandwiches his staff are treated to, and the promised bonuses at Christmas time; and remembers the praise that he has heaped upon certain employees. Finally, he puts his head into his hands and sighs, 'But we're very charitable at The Perfect Launchpad. We *really* are ...'

The accountant opens his eyes wide with doubt; and the director perversely squints, before continuing,

'Well. I have already spent longer in this tiny office today than I intended, and I still have things to do. I am scheduled to meet someone who has travelled one hundred miles for an interview. In fact, if it pleases me to do so, I may pick his brains with no intention of employing him.' As he speaks, there is a knock at the door. It is an Australian - a new recruit; and the director uses his intercom to issue an instruction to his secretary,

'Upon his arrival, please usher the interviewee into the waiting room. I will be with him shortly.'

'Hello, sir. I hope I am not disturbing you,' says the Australian. 'You wanted me to stop by for five minutes.' The accountant departs, and Mr Propotamous embarks upon a description of how the organisation works, and of the visitor's place within it. Following this exposé, the big man asks,

'And exactly how long is your tenure here?'

The respondent has a look of concern on his face, as if to say, 'Surely, you must know? You are the one who hired me!' In fact, the director told the agency to draw up an agreement for whatever length of time would please "our mutual friend", and so procure his services. The newcomer *is* needed – but who can say for how long? As a safeguard, the director pretends ignorance of the contract length; and, when the contractor has outworn his use, he will be removed through an invocation of *force majeure*. That way, everyone is happy ... everyone who matters, that is.

'It is six months,' says the recruit from the antipodes. The director scratches his knee through a hole in his jeans.

'Oh. That long, huh? Most of our contracts are only for *three* months.'

The boss leaves the room, and takes his visitor (who is now rather glum) on a brief walking tour of the building. He opens with an apology,

'Please excuse me. I should have shown you around on the day you arrived. It is quite remiss of me.' When they come to the room full of tape units, one of the staff is bemoaning a "Mount error on Unit 8". The boss explains, 'There will be no more errors if everyone will only work a little harder.' And then he castigates this staff member for his lack of punctuality ...

PILATE: And what have you to say for yourself?

STAFF MEMBER [late for work]: I was due to catch the 9.10am train. At 9.10, the expected time of arrival was 9.15am. At 9.15, the train was expected at 9.18. At 9.18, the train was expected at -

PILATE: By the Hare and the Tortoise, will you please stop, man! You are making me dizzy!

STAFF MEMBER: I wasn't in The Hare and the Tortoise. I am not a patron of that establishment – and, besides, I never drink early in the morning.

PILATE: Perhaps not – but you *are* proposing that British Rail has based its timetable around a fable by Aesop?

STAFF MEMBER: Not *my* proposal.

PILATE: You have been late every day this week. And your excuse? The trains cannot run on time because of graffiti!

STAFF MEMBER: *Not my excuse, either.* It was the reason the train company gave. And, not only that ... Freddie, the old cleaner, held me up.

PILATE: I forbade you to speak with him!

STAFF MEMBER: But is it *my fault* if he blocks my path to the front door?

PILATE: It would appear that nothing is actually yours (not even your culpability), and that everything is merely on loan to you! My good man, the aforementioned excuse was *proffered* by you. Therefore, by association, it *becomes* yours – and it is preposterous. Can a man not walk if he is covered in tattoos? But, alas! 'Tis worse: for although the man might be recumbent on the grounds that he is still sore from the piercings of the needle - such a defence cannot be made for the sluggish railway carriage, which hides no nerve-endings behind its metal-plated skin.

STAFF MEMBER: But it's all true.

PILATE: Yet I am turning it around and around, through the galaxy of my mind, as if 'twere a planet in an orrery. And I find it to be insupportable. You have five seconds (and counting) to provide a better defence for your lateness ...

five … four … three … two … one. Your time is up and you must leave upon the instant.

******

Pilate's attitude now becomes distant. Once again, he is thinking about the auditory hallucinations he has experienced. He knows there is a variant of mental illness in his family, and comforts himself by thinking, 'A coffee will restore my faculties to their equilibrium.' Meanwhile, the interviewee from a hundred miles away cancels his appointment … and Pilate reaches into his draw, to his most private records. He is about to enjoy some personal wealth therapy: mulling over his pension funds, his investments and his bank statements, with a loving care that only Ebenezer Scrooge would understand.

Time to Assess A New Accountant

Pilate has recently been examining some specimen documents that were drawn up by his accountant for the preceding tax year. They include micro-payments he had hoped would be overlooked, and the fact that they were not is an oversight in his eyes. He is irked by his accountant calling for greater transparency in his records. Is it time to replace him?

A "round, brown man" (Pilate's own choice of words) has been selected as a possible alternative, although Pilate finds that it is he who is being interviewed. The name of the significant other is Shangri-La Gupta, of Excelsior Mammon Services Ltd, and he is addressed by Pilate in the following terms,

'You could join my existing accountant – and, together, operate as a team. Furthermore, for your mutual delectation (and my peace of mind), you might perform a series of checks and balances upon each other.' Mr Gupta becomes fidgety. Indeed, he creates anything but an excelsior impression. When he has stopped fidgeting, he speaks volumes for the professionalism of his practice:

'We are here for you. Every bit of your financial indigestion is soluble in our hands: whether it relates to auditing company accounts, or inheritance tax … You name it. There is nothing we cannot handle.' Pilate's suspicions are aroused, for the man appears to be speaking from the heart (and openness is not what he is looking for).

'You wouldn't believe what some big businesses get up to. Personally, I am all for the little man. But, just before we leave the subject, let me tell you one of the *larger man's* trade secrets: the principle of "Stacking and Backhanders".'

'Stacking, hey?' Pilate stifles a yawn.

'If the natural price for a job in a residential building is £25,000 – then you get the building company to sign it off for £50,000, and present this bill to the residents. Meanwhile, you reach an understanding with the contractor: that the difference between the two sums shall be shared out between your management company and the builders.' Pilate nods politely, and the accountant smiles triumphantly, heartened by the reaction of his listener. 'There. You see how much I have already taught you? Most people do not know about this.'

'Sir, they know well enough – but they can do nothing about it!'

As the conversation augments, Mr Gupta resists Pilate's every attempt to redirect his attention to the *raison d'etre* of the meeting – which is, how suitable an accountant would he be for The Perfect Launchpad; and, instead, the visitor rambles on interminably about his early life in Asia Minor.

'The wonders of Anatolia!' he exclaims. 'Have you ever been?'

'And yet you were not tempted to stay there?' Pilate ignores his remark, and counters it with a question of his own.

'I am no longer a child – and a man must make a living,' Mr Gupta replies, glancing around furtively, as if an officer from the Department of Immigration and Customs might be standing on the other side of the closed door, with his ear pressed hard against the keyhole. Shangri-La then relaxes, and continues with his armchair travel. After an hour or so of "foreign tales", he proclaims that he has been in Britain for more than forty years, and may be more British than Pilate himself is. He then asks some very pointed questions, which (like the rest of his prattling) have nothing whatsoever to do with accounting:

'Now then, Mr ....? Tell me something of yourself. Are you married? And for how long? And ... you say there are no children. Why is that?' And, finally, 'May I see your passport, please?' Mr Propotamous checks his watch. Shangri-La resumes,

'I must have proof that you reside in this country legitimately, otherwise I am afraid I cannot do business with you.'

'Sir, I, unlike you, have resided in this country ever since I was a flame in my father's eye.'

'Ahem!' the accountant clears his throat.

'He had only one functioning eye – having damaged the other in a boating accident, in which he struck it with a loose oar whilst paddling over-enthusiastically,' explains Pilate. May I now take the liberty of asking *you* for *your* passport?' He addresses Mr Gupta, who winces - before once again launching into a description of his unique homeland in Turkey. And again, Pilate looks at his watch. Things begin to get heated. We haven't the space here to describe the meeting in full; but, suffice it to say that Mr Gupta refers to his visitor as "Pontius", and Pilate responds sharply, 'I will not be partaking of your services – for they offer no "Shangri-La" to me! You must depart now, and never darken my door again.'

Mr Propotamous keeps the episode from his existing accountant – who, like many men who perform discrete (and discreet) functions within society, shall remain anonymous.

Conversations in the Corridor: Too Many Cooks

During the course of The Sackings, several unscheduled visitors have arrived; and Mr Propotamous is forced to change out of casual wear, and into one of his "power suits". He does this in a hurry, for the visitors include representatives of: his main client (the Local Electricity Generating Board), a recruitment agency, and a primary software house which he is beholden to, called, appropriately, "First Software". In a nutshell, the end user hires the agency, and the agency employs First Software – which outsources particular requirements to The Perfect Launchpad. With respect to this software challenge, the Perfect Launchpad has, in the words of its misanthropic leader, 'dedicated several of its brightest stars, to consume the debris of some grave, old problems, - and shine forth with the beacon of a new solution'. (Who needs substantive actions, when we have words like these?) So here they all are – not the stars, but the three nuts aforesaid, loosed from their shells, thrashing out the spoils and manifesting all the quirks of avarice and suspicion - and any other trappings of power which you can think of. Close by, Gladys, the cleaner, is attending to the dusty floor with her besom, formed out of the sprigs which she has lately (and criminally) sourced from an area of protected woodland (near her home). She bides her time, indulging herself with a little eavesdropping. The vibes she gives out are harmless enough, and the businessmen are unperturbed by her presence.

The client is trying to identify the reasons for his enormous bills, and Mr Propotamous (who is the party mostly responsible) is looking to allay any fears of overcharging. Initially, our man is playing for time, and (like a senior statesman) he begins to introduce a trio of "significant others" who have just that moment joined them – but to what avail? For they have already met.

'I am humbled by the arrival of three representatives of Her Majesty's Government. And how do you do, Mr Numbskull?' he seizes the hand of the person furthest away from him, leaning across the others in order to reach him. He pauses for an acknowledgement, but receives none - except for the sight of "the Numbskull" wiping his affected hand on a napkin which he keeps in his waistcoat pocket. The speaker recommences his introduction:

'And to my left, we (the Royal We, that is) have Mr Trip, the Health and Safety Officer; to *his* left, Mr Drainaway, the Inspector of Taxes; and to *his* left, the right, honourable Mr Numbskull, - a private investigator for the Inland Revenue, I presume?' Gladys nods, as if the show of words is purely for her benefit. Meanwhile, the one who has been named "Numbskull" is reddening with ire.

'You are, indeed, presumptuous!' he expostulates. 'I am told that Mr Numbskull is away on leave.' He nods in the direction of the Tax Inspector, whose colleague they are referring to. 'I am Mr Failingham, the Recruitment Consultant.' This is a sharp rebuke, - and, hereupon, the originator of this book passes a resolution to relegate every one of the aforementioned back into the ranks of the nameless. For the author giveth and the author taketh away. And he acteth in respect to their disrespect, and out of sympathy for his anti-hero. Now, the reader may have been faintly bemused by this sudden inclination to christen such "human irrelevancies", anyway. And yet your truly wishes for this tale to mirror life, where it is so often those who are least important who make a name for themselves.

'Dear me!' says the client. 'There are so many links in the chain. I am a little concerned about the overall cost.'

'Please don't be. Not on my account, at least,' says Mr Propotamous, and nods symbolically towards the others, whilst maintaining an expression of the utmost innocence and idealism.

'And certainly not on my account, either,' says the agent; who, in his turn, nods towards the spokesperson for First Software.

'Nor mine,' says that spokesperson. He looks a little lost – for he has no one else to nod to. It is as if he is at the end of a Mexican Wave. Mr Propotamous, believing himself to be a good Christian, and a team player *par excellence*, eases the friction with a little "Oil of Ulay", as he likes to call it, – or, to refer to it by the popular phrase, "tact and discretion".

'Gentlemen! Gentlemen! *Please*. We can be civilized about this. After all, we have a common objective.'

'We do?' ask the others, simultaneously.

'Why, of course. It is clear that our goodly client is in receipt of a generous allowance every year, to splash out on his information technology needs; and, if he does not use it up, his budget is cut the following year, on the grounds that he no longer needs it. We are an agency and two software houses which should join forces in helping him to spend it. This, naturally, benefits us, and benefits him also. With our backing, he can insist upon his full and fair apportionment of funding, year after year.' The speaker is just getting into his stride; but at this very moment Foolish Boy appears. The boy has not yet collected his goods and chattels, for his dismissal has come down upon him like a thunderbolt, and for some time he has been wandering around in a daze. Fickle Fortune has him "just passing by" at this most sensitive of moments, and the mere mention of large sums of money changing hands makes him prick up his ears. There is an alteration in his demeanour and, for the first time since his unfortunate meeting in the Oval Office, he smiles. Then he steps forward, ready to rejoin the ranks of social humanity.

'Do you have a direct contract?' he boldly asks. It is unclear whom he is addressing, and there is just a hint of mischief about him - as if he knows the answer already.

'This is a most objectionable young fellow,' states the director. 'His mind is quiescent when it might be actuated by diligent study; and polemical, when it should be a vessel of obedience.' Mr Propotamous is about to give the lad his marching orders, but the process of "seeming merciful" (a constituent element in the much-touted Oil of Ulay) forbids him. Anyhow, the end user has already raised his index finger; and, as he does so, he personifies a deity who ranks even higher than the director, himself.

'Oh, not at all! I am sure he is *most* agreeable,' the higher deity humours the boy. 'Indeed, the contract is direct between the client – who is myself - and the recruitment agency.' Seeing that "moneybags" has condescended to engage with the lad, the others are prepared to condescend as well.

'Yes. My contract is direct with the client,' confirms the recruitment consultant. 'And I must take this opportunity to emphasize how I would have involved a second recruitment agency but, acting out of sympathy to the client purse, proceeded to throttle and drown this idea as soon as it swam into my consciousness. And *his* contract,' he adds, opening his greasy palm towards the man from First Software, 'is a direct one with me.'

'And I, *too*, would like to take this opportunity,' adds the man from First Software (whilst opening his own palm at the same angle), 'to reassure the client that whilst I might been introduced to The Perfect Launchpad by another software house, - I, nevertheless, in one inspired move, shook hands with Mr Propotamous, and saved you *oceans* of dosh.' And hereupon, he literally shakes the hand of our anti-hero – in an entirely superfluous gesture.

'And you, sir? What have *you* saved me?' the client asks of the final player in this carousel of offerings. Mr Propotamous stumbles over his words,

'Well. I ... er ... would like to take this opportunity ... um ...' (Foolish Boy wonders to himself, 'How may the very same "value of opportunity" repeatedly be *taken away*, whilst still remaining intact for *the next subtraction*? It simply doesn't follow the rules of algebra.')

'I must say, the process seems highly convoluted. I have an agreement with the agent, but as for the rest ...' the voice of the client slowly fades away. Then, finally, Mr Propotamous grasps the nettle:

'I was tempted to outsource some of the most challenging software development to a third party - or is that a *fourth* party? Or even a *fifth column*? - who lives at home with his mother.' (At this second, Foolish Boy thinks, 'That must have been me.' Ah! The vanity of youth.) 'But I, sir, have run a tight ship by keeping all of my development work "in house".' And then, as if he were making a presidential address, the director clears his throat and continues:

'To clarify, the situation *could* have turned out as follows: a contract between you' (he faces the client) 'and your agency; a contract between your agency and another agency; a contract between the second agency and First Software; a contract between First Software and The Perfect Launchpad, with possibly a third software house mediating; and, finally, a contract between The Perfect Launchpad and – er – a technical wizard who lives at home with his mother. Think what a fortune in pounds sterling, and in obfuscation, that we, collectively, have saved you by *not* going down that route.' For once, all of the service providers are in agreement – and even the client is coming round to their point of view.

Pleased with the royalties he might secure from this transaction, the host ushers the agent and the representative of First Software towards the back door, and out through it. He then slams the door in their faces, and heaves a huge sigh of relief. Finally, he steers the client towards the front of the building, and, after some cheerful small talk, issues a brief valediction as he leads him out of the main entrance. Before the client departs, the director proceeds to lock up - whilst wiping his brow with his handkerchief. By now, Foolish Boy has, very sensibly, made himself scarce.

'Steady on, old fellow,' protests the client, 'you haven't shown me around your premises yet.' The director lets him in again, and accedes to this reasonable request. The lucky client is then hurriedly introduced to the programming team, before being forced out through the nearest exit.

Now, the president of The Perfect Launchpad is once more the only deity in the building. But as one danger passes, two more are approaching. They take the forms of the Tax Inspector, and of a man from the Health and Safety Department. The latter has been promising to pay a surprise visit for some time. So, within minutes, here they both are: two Frenchmen (with usually scant trace of a foreign accent) in the safe hands of the accountant. Monsieur Health and Safety is concerned about the "spaghetti junction" beside every desk which has equipment on it; and the Inland Revenue representative is thinking about tax fraud. For a few seconds, just sit back and bear witness to the following conversation which Pilate has with Monsieur Inland Revenue – during the course of which, Monsieur forgets *entirely* about fraud. And how does he lose the thread? Pilate is responding to a challenge which Dmitri once made to him, 'to tear down the temple of good will and rebuild it in three days'; and Pilate is on record for saying that he would achieve satisfaction in just three minutes ... to which Dmitri responded, 'Faster than Jesus, then?'

'And you are ... Mr Propotamous? How pleased am I to make your acquaintance?' is the civil approach from *Le Monsieur* who handles taxation.

'How should I know?' answers a stroppy Pilate. The words which come back are bi-lingual.

'*Pardon* ...?' (This is issued in a French accent.) 'Sorry?'

'You were asking me a question?'

'No. I think I was stating a fact ... albeit in the form of a question.'

'You are sorry to be disguising a fact as a question?'

'Now you are asking me a question, and it is you who should be sorry.'

'And what, pray, should be the wellsprings of my sorrow?' Pilate's query goes unanswered, and *Monsieur* looks distinctly uncomfortable. So here is Pilate's summing up (levied against Dmitri's challenge), by which he hopes to reprise the man's good will ...

'My dear fellow, we should neither of us be the least bit apologetic. No. Quite the contrary. You are to be complimented: for the art of disguise is the new honesty!' And hereupon, *Monsieur does smile*, but it is a simper to cover his discomfort ... for he is a man cast – like clay - in the acerbic words of the present moment. Having turned the dry-as-dust official around, first with antagonism, and then with sprightly praise, our anti-hero is feeling rather pleased with himself. (He is, indeed, a *control freak*.) He embraces Monsieur Inland Revenue warmly, and it truly seems like the assassin has become putty in his hands. But all the while *Monsieur* is cringing. And still, he somehow opens up a little ...

'You know, my personal cash flow is appalling at the moment!' Mr Inland Revenue has espied a most unusual cardigan, which was woven for the benefit of the Right Honourable Propotamous himself. It has the logo of a large financial institution, and its wearer now seizes his advantage:

'I am a privileged account holder.' Pilate points to the garment he is wearing, knitted with the slogan, "Take more interest in your account". 'This is a free textile from my bank,' he explains.

'Well - my own bank never clothes me, and hardly pays any interest at all: just 0.01% when last I checked,' the tax man remarks woefully. 'At first, I was promised that the best rate on offer would always be 6%, and that my rate *was* currently the best; although this was mere chicanery. Having persuaded me to liquidate as many of my assets as possible, and to pour the resulting capital into their high interest account, the bank then surreptitiously reduced the rate for that account down to 0.01%; whilst simultaneously setting up another savings vehicle - which paid the old rate of 6%, and which I had no money in, - so as to make good on their promise.'

'Well. Let me tell you: with my help you might - you just might - get *two whole hundredths of one percent* interest on your deposits. That's one hundred percent more than your current annual rate. My dear man, how can you refuse?'

'All I can say is that, once, I opened an account paying 0.030% interest and incurring 0.030% bank charges. On the occasion of my next trip to the till, I remarked to the cashier, "Please, be a good man and just allow both figures to cancel each other out. It will save me the infernal paperwork for the Revenue Services – of which I form a humble part" ... to which the cashier replied, "I couldn't possibly do that. What you have is an interest-bearing asset. How would *you* like to be deprived of *your* raison d'etre?" And I pointed out, "The account is not an animate being. It will not bite us in revenge for its privation!"'

******

Mr Propotamous now turns his attention to the Health and Safety Inspector, who is concerned about a series of damp patches which he has observed near some exposed live wires. Monsieur Health and Safety comments on the danger of combining water spillages and electricity. Then he goes down on all fours, and places his face against the liquid residue on the carpet. He sniffs once, raises his nose a few inches; then lowers it and sniffs again. His nostrils are flared and he moves his hands laterally, as if they are the fins of a fish. And all the while he parleys with himself, like a holy man deep in contemplation:

'Umm. Breathe in deeply! Umm. Not water ... No! Not at all ... nor Flat White nor Earl Gray ... but ammonia! Ooooooh!' He rises, with a quizzical look on his face as if he was Doctor Watson, - and the in-house accountant reacts, after the fashion of Sherlock Holmes:

'Pia, my dear sir. Pia, the cat; latterly known as "Puddles" - and brought to us, ironically, by the cleaner. We tolerate our cleaner, on the grounds that the presence of her feline - and that of her winsome daughters (who will sometimes follow her into the building) - have a calming effect upon the office staff: for the staff, you see, are subject to unreasonable pressure from their team captains. No one has the heart to put her down, for she is unhealthy only with respect to her incontinence ... That's the cat I am referring to ... not the cleaner.' (And this is quite unlike the software house she inhabits, which is unhealthy in *every* respect.) Suddenly, the cat appears. She is seen rubbing up against the legs of the director, and purring with unfettered joy at ... who knows what?

'As fond of each other as we appear to be - she is pushing her luck,' mutters Mr Propotamous. He addresses his accountant,

'Can you look after my guests while I fetch a cup of tea?'

He is delighted with the chance to delegate. 'You know your way around by now, I trust? And as you visit the Portakabins, you will doubtless explain my turnover and cash flow to our mutual friend' (he signals to the tax inspector) 'better than I ever could myself.' (He then nods to the other professional, before fixing the accountant with his gaze.) 'And I believe you also, perchance, know a thing or two about ergonomics – which you can share with the expert.' As the Health and Safety professional turns away, Pilate winks at the accountant, signifying that he should be complicit in a little deception.

'Of course I will,' is the faithful reply.

'And I shall join you later.'

At that moment, the director notices Myfanwy approaching. She is sampling the air like an Irish Wolfhound, and has a scowl on her face. She is not fond of Pia, and much prefers dogs. For once, the chief of staff is quite pleased to see her. He is sure that, in her bullying presence, these unwelcome personages will have no chance to ask awkward questions. As he retires to consider his situation, the accountant leads the visitors away; and Myfanwy joins them for the tour, for she has nothing else to do. Before long, Monsieur Health and Safety is speaking,

'Concerns have been raised about the poor health of the staff brought on by overwork, and about various injuries sustained by tripping over wires.'

'I blame the sarnie lady for using out-of-date produce,' says the accountant, loyal to his master. 'She surely induced this spate of illness, - and, you know, ill men have a poor sense of balance.'

'Well. Perhaps we should pay her a visit, too?'

A Sad, Sad History

At this juncture, Myfanwy will (again) raise one of her favourite emotive subjects: how her relatives have died. She needs an audience, and so she sets about detaining the three dapper gentlemen by obstinately standing in front of them.

'Ah! My unfortunate relatives ... how tragically were their lives cut short ...? You would never believe me if I told you ... No, you would not! The first, she choked to death on an ancient threepenny piece, baked into her birthday cake in a moment of misguided kindness. The second? She was murdered by the family dentist. Can you imagine?' The three men, all in silky-smooth suits from Savile Row, elegantly embroidered with tartan patterns, and fronted by the ever-popular white shirts and paisley ties, exclaim:

'Oh! How could we?' (They all, to a man, think, 'We will play along with her antics for a while. After all, she is the spouse of the chief.')

'Yes. I am afraid she swallowed a loose filling, which had been fitted without due care and attention by the practitioner - a *foreign* dentist, I'll have you know.' She lays great emphasis upon the adjective, thereby making it a pejorative term. 'Yes,' she acquiesced with her own sentiment, as if the sentiment comprised some other personality. 'And I had an aunt who was slain by her painter and decorator.'

'Ooooh! How unutterably terrible,' utter the three professionals, all of them speaking the declamation at once, like a choreographed team in a West End musical just before the romantic lead breaks into a song: although God, alone, knows what the lyric would be. Then they expostulate - 'How tragical!' - with slit eyes, and they suck their cheeks in until their lips form the shape of a painful "O".

'Was the decorator not happy with her remuneration for his services?' asks Health and Safety.

'Or was she so damning of his achievements – as to make him react violently?' inquires Monsieur Inland Revenue.

'Perhaps he broke off from the job too early,' suggests the accountant, 'causing a terminal conflict to occur?'

'At any rate, he could not have been happy with her unhappiness,' opines Health and Safety.

'I think it is time for us to go,' stipulates Monsieur Inland Revenue. He must be reading from a different script, because everyone ignores him.

'No,' says the director's wife. 'It was none of those things. The fellow was doing some exterior decorations, known in the trade as *pointing*.'

'Painting?'

'No. Pointing. But, yes, he was painting as well as pointing. And, for his painting, he liked to keep his bucket full. Well, it just so happened that he was standing astride the top of a remarkably tall ladder, - and, as he was leaning back in order to assess his handiwork, my aunt walked underneath the ladder. Now, her passing beneath him went without incident. But, being of a suspicious nature, she had a change of heart.

She retraced her steps under the fateful ladder, so as not to provoke Lady Luck. But Alas! Lady Luck was already agitated – and at the very moment when my aunt was passing through, the decorator let loose his bucket. It came crashing down – a heavy metal object with an ultra-sharp edge, mind, – and struck her head *bang* in the centre, splitting it like a coconut sacrificed to the blade of an axe. One half of her skull collapsed upon each shoulder, and the exposed bone gleamed white as the settled snow in winter ... then she fell to her knees, as if about to recite the Lord's Prayer. Unfortunately, the *Corpus Callosum* and other commissures were not spared the bisection; and so her cerebral hemispheres could not communicate sufficiently in her dying moments to make a recital possible. Imagine the two half-brains, as they lay on their sides like speechless twins ... and the cerebrospinal fluid raining upon her Moccasins as she fell. Meanwhile, the resident squirrels climbed down from the branches of overhanging trees, and licked it up as if 'twere coconut milk flavoured with raspberry jam. Picture it! And all the assassin could do was flee the scene of his crime ...' There was an astonished silence.

'It sounds suspiciously like an accident,' one of her audience ventures. She glares at him. All three gentlemen now wonder if this is their cue to leave. Indeed, a single act of *carpe diem* would have yielded a sweet sense of relief. But they do not seize the moment, or anything else for that matter, and the near-monologue continues:

'Yes. And *both* of my cousins came croppers to misfortune. And how awful were their deaths?' The three suited gentlemen look askance at her, as if to say, 'How awful were they?'

'One of the cousins so loved her nineteenth century opera, that she gave her only life for it. She was attending a tiny Conservatoire of Music, near to some exotic coast that (as a rule) is bathed in warmer climes. And at the end of the performance ... she drowned.' The three professionals, who all regard themselves as exponents of logic and good sense in their various fields, scratch their heads.

'You mean, she drowned in her tears ...? How romantic.'

'There was a tropical storm.'

'Ah. Flooding, then.'

'No. There was no flooding!' she cuts short their speculations with a sting in her tongue. 'And, even while she was dying, another cousin whom she had planned to lodge with overnight ... was crushed in the vicinity of his own (domestic) conservatory. He had just built it as well, so it was doubly tragic. Such a waste of solid masonry and fine glass.'

'I think we should go,' speaks the same voice who aired this sentiment a few minutes earlier.

'He was in the living room when it happened,' she continues. (Why should she grace the rude interruption with a reply?)

'I thought he was in the conservatory?'

'You're not listening,' she retorts neurotically. 'The second cousin was *underneath* the conservatory, but he was *inside* his living room.'

'How is that even possible?' This question is like a lighted match to a sulphurous compound. She is angry now.

'Well! It is, when the conservatory is lifted up by a visiting typhoon – with its foundations, like nerve endings, still clinging to the bottom of it, - and (look you) deposited right on top of him whilst he was seated and watching television in his living room!'

'And I suppose the academy of music, the "conservatoire", along with everyone inside, was spirited away and dumped into the sea?' Can Myfanwy detect a note of sarcasm? Evidently not.

'How absolutely extraordinary. So you know the story, then?' she sounds crestfallen, and realises that if the surprise element has spent itself, then it is time to crank up the emotion. 'Oh! How dreadful it was. They never found the bodies, you know. Nor the original instruments and musical scores.'

'Nor even the entire orchestra, I suppose?' one respondent ventures.

'We really must be on our way,' adds another.

'The world hath no tears, like those that gush from a woman's lachrymal gland. Ah!'

'Umm. Sad. We're off now,' is the decisive reply. And with that, they hurriedly take their leave of the director's wife, - but they are still in the building, and available to cause trouble.

Idle Hands and Wagging Tongues

Ms Myfanwy Esquelle has been nicknamed "Open Source", owing to rumours of her free and easy sexual favours. She even has the sobriquet knitted into her pullover: although, for her, it is only an expression of her allegiance to Pilate, her prince charming, – who often uses the term – and not an indication that she has knowledge of the online world.

If only he paid her more attention, she would be faithful to him. She really *would*. Meanwhile, she is receiving assistance from a well-known sex therapist, Madame Splatterpuss. At present, Myfanwy is learning about a special technique which is socially responsible and hygienic … known to her as "frictionless trade" (but more widely referred to as "frottage"). (We wish Myfanwy good luck; having been dumped by a previous therapist, Sappho Sextophileye, - who now devotes her time to the composition of pornographic sonnets.)

******

Two contractors are talking in one of the Portakabins …

CONTRACTOR ONE: You know, Myfanwy has become famous for her ability to draw hermit crabs out of their shells. Apparently, she has a generous spirit, and a tendency to say "Yes" when she means "No". In fact, she won an award as a teenager, for making the most outstanding social contribution to school life.

CONTRACTOR TWO: Yes. I heard she got pregnant seven times.

CONTRACTOR ONE: Well, the official line is - they were all phantom pregnancies.

CONTRACTOR TWO: So she was a wise owl, and made sure of taking remedial action against the consequences of her "outstanding contribution". Or did she have an "In-Out Referendum"?

CONTRACTOR ONE: Imagine if news of her exploits ever travelled back to her? Her reaction would be like a fault line, terrible to behold and widening any cracks in our peace of mind. Her personality can be very sweet, but it has indigestible bits, - like a thickly-cut marmalade.

******

As the two contractors are having their conversation, the director's wife is socializing with Foolish Boy in the machine room. They are away from prying eyes, and she is in one of her "sweet" moods. With her voice almost masked by the soporific whirring of the tape units, she praises the lad's achievement in landing a "solid, safe job" during a recession. The boy begins to remonstrate. He is trying to explain that her husband has just got rid of him, but she is hearing none of it ...

'I am no longer wanted -'

'Don't contradict me. You should learn to accept flattery with good grace, and be proud of your station in life.

'But I -'

'Your mother must be beaming with pride, and boasting to her neighbours about her brilliant son. And yet ... you are so slim. Are you feeding yourself properly? You need to be sufficiently nourished in order to master your new role.'

'I'm alright,' he says quietly.

'Have you had lunch today? You can eat half of mine if you want? I apologise for the absence of *escargot*.' She retrieves from her voluminous handbag a Tupperware box, filled with spinach and blue cheese - in a poisonous compound of diced garden snails and olive oil (some of which has leaked onto her sleeve). She leans towards him, and he shrinks from her, as a rodent might from a ravenous Boa constrictor. Myfanwy is building a bridge of trust, although the innocent on the other side of the bridge wonders if she is laying the foundations for a full-scale invasion. She has shed all of her previous embarrassment, relating to any impressions which her anatomy has made upon the ice stored in the freezer, and she is ready to say or do virtually anything to win her prize. Faced with a formidable assailant, Foolish Boy is starting to feel dazed once more.

'I'm fifty nine years old. Would you ever guess it?'

'Uh. No,' replies the youth, finding the perfect little word in this tricky situation.

Now she is adjusting her massive bra, and tip-toeing across the bridge - so to speak; whilst forming, in her head, the words that will serve as a preliminary chat up line in this romantic comedy. Suddenly, the moment has arrived for its press release.

'You might not guess it, but I still bleed you know.' She issues the line in hushed tones. The boy is nonplussed. He is frantically referencing the database of his short life for assistance, but he can find nothing of any use. Perhaps he has applied the wrong search criteria? Or maybe the database is inadequately indexed?

'Yes. I bleed. I really do. The motions creep up on me when I am least prepared for them.' She walks her fingers over his breast, as if they were the legs of a tarantula. The surface underneath the imaginary arachnid's feet is firm and smooth, allowing the fabulous conceit to proceed swiftly to first base, which is a faintly swollen nipple - some three inches or so above a beating heart. 'And when I am so affected, there is no antidote.' The boy is silent, as she runs her hands through his hair, and suddenly clamps them around his neck. 'The red stains on the kitchen table are mine. At least, I think they are – although a recently chopped tomato may be the culprit. (To be sure, you can check the area for tomato seeds.) But the blood stains on the bread bin? Have no fear. They are *definitely* mine ... as well as those curdling within the ice in the freezer ... and the ones dotted liberally around the stairwell. And my spittle is in the kitchen, for my periods are emotionally and physically enervating.' (Yet here's a thing. Some of that saliva could belong to Foolish Boy! For, little does Myfanwy realise, her beloved has adopted a revolting habit, which among his contemporaries passes for a sport, and goes by the name of "spit bombing": the targets being those tiny silver fish, who colonise our sinks and draining boards.)

'And, often-times, my tampon lets me down – which giveth unto me the pen name, "Lady Beaverbrook", although news of this phenomenon shall not travel far and wide (for no national newspaper would carry it). You do not mind my dribbling, do you?' And without waiting for a reply, she answers, 'I see that you do not.' She adjusts her underpants. 'And listen to this, my darling. I become most sanguinary when my appetite is pricked by a winsome sight.'

Suddenly, the boy has conceived of a response - and just in time, too. Thank heavens!

'That blood you spoke of ... is it the stigmata?' he asks gingerly. This is sure to invoke a passionate reply. (The passion has not become mutual, has it?)

'What a wonderful comparison!' she exclaims. 'You have poetry in your soul. Never, never lose it! Promise me you will not change.' Her eyes are half-closed, and her lower jaw has dropped open. Meanwhile, he is a claustrophobe gasping for air. 'Do not mind our differences, dear one! Beautiful relationships are like beautiful places, and often have fault-lines embedded in them. Think of California.'

'What are *you* doing here? I thought I told you to leave!' the director has suddenly appeared. But do not feel sorry for the naïve young actor in our unfolding drama: for these two sentences provide the means by which he can escape.

******

Let us cut to another of the Portakabins. Therein, reside a couple of contract programmers who love to play with words – and whose acquaintance you have briefly made. The common conception is that they are mismatched to their profession, and are more interested in literature than in procedural logic. In fact, this scurrilous attack is unfounded. The targets are renaissance men, who are good at everything they turn their minds to. I am sure they would like to meet my readers, for they are also gregarious beings (as the following dialogue shall reveal). But don't get your hopes up. They probably won't be available. Of all their loves, they are most deeply devoted to Mammon; and, when the hour is late, are often to be found sharpening their grey matter into a point more prickly than a church spire, with the ignoble objective of wounding the economy and bleeding it into their piggy banks. And they follow the time-honoured tradition of wise men and troublemakers alike, in conversing about other people's business rather than their own. One of them is speaking now. Let's listen in, and see if there are any jewels that we, ourselves, may steel (or borrow) for the employment of our very own waggling tongues.

CONTRACTOR ONE: You know, a menstruating woman who knows her time is running out, is like a flower which saves its richest aroma until dusk.
CONTRACTOR TWO: Funny you should mention her.
CONTRACTOR ONE: And while we are on the subject, let us reflect upon the director's chief of technical staff as well.

CONTRACTOR TWO: Yes. Apparently Dmitri is subject to an obscure psychological condition – some rare strain of erotic desire, possibly more common in Mediterranean areas like the south of Italy, than in colder climes north of the equator.

CONTRACTOR ONE [tongue in cheek]: Oh? Whatever could that be?

CONTRACTOR TWO: Well, I have it on vague authority that he is, most especially, drawn to hirsute, fat ladies who are just passing through the menopause.

CONTRACTOR ONE [muttering to himself, in a dreamy fashion]: Just passing through, hey? [And then, straightening himself in his chair] Good heavens! That *is* unusual. Generally, those who have left the (apparent) age and dimensions of Aphrodite as far behind as the female who presently occupies the mind's eye, tend to make better companions, - because they have mellowed, somewhat, like the Autumn sun. They certainly do not shout as much, not even when you make their two legs of old mutton tremulous at midnight.

CONTRACTOR TWO: So much blubber wobbling like jelly! Old Myfanwy covers the "inner tube" of her anxiety with a spare tire, girded by a belt that leaves its tread. But the hymen is still open for business ... and what a tease it is ... for Old Father Time [the speaker touches first his crotch, and then his mouth] forgot to decommission her labial lips as he loosened her facial tongue.

CONTRACTOR ONE: I say, old fellow, does either his condition or hers have a name? It isn't catching, is it?

CONTRACTOR TWO: Well. I have spoken to the psychiatrist who is treating our most esteemed technician for his peculiar orientation. In point of fact, he is my psychiatrist as well. Ahem! My conversations with him are always entirely confidential -

CONTRACTOR ONE: Oh, naturally. They would have to be.

CONTRACTOR TWO: And I was reassured that this condition is so rare, that science has not yet graced it with a name.

CONTRACTOR ONE: I find that hard to believe! But perhaps we can think of one anyway. And if *you* are the first to identify something, you may anoint it with your own name, and so (at once) confer immortality upon both the newly identified thing *and* upon yourself: for example, Humboldt's Woolly Monkey.

CONTRACTOR TWO: Now, there's a creature who has a slight tendency to put on the pounds, and is subject to the growth of bodily hair in unwomanly places, but – and here's the rub – the woollies are reputed to be delicate, susceptible to colds, and – mark you - relatively docile.

CONTRACTOR ONE: So, clearly, she cannot be one of *them.*

Back to the Corridor

The director has moved further up the corridor and is talking to Gladys, the diminutive cleaner, who has all of her five children by her side, including two girls who are about eighteen or nineteen years old. Gladys is only five feet tall (one foot for each child, perhaps?), and, as the boss looks at her, he is puzzled by an issue of logistics. 'How,' he wonders, 'can such a tiny oven bake so many buns? And now, she is pregnant with a sixth!'

'How are you today, Gladys?'

'Oh, I do feel most put upon, sir. I'm always being asked to do things.'

'And have you done them?'

'Always, sir. I am always doing 'em. Even though Freddie is no longer 'ere to 'elp me. Why, just the other day I grabbed a handful of disks and was busy scrubbing 'em clean, until they acquired the reflective quality of marble – or until I was interrupted by a startled Software Engineer. I can't remember which.'

'Well, now you mention it, I do remember some inordinately shiny CDs,' says Mr Propotamous (Gladys nods proudly), 'and a crisis over lost or corrupted data. *These objects are not coasters!*' For this final sentence, his voice rises in both volume and pitch. But such subtleties are lost on Gladys, who is out to impress with her work ethic.

'Provenance is a wonderful thing, sir. I once owned two antique dishes from the Stoke-on-Trent potteries. I bet – over the years - they've contained a porridge or two!'

'*Listen*, you daft woman! I'm talking about *data*! You've probably damaged those disks permanently.'

Sir, you may rest assured. There is no such issue. I speak the truth. My heart is pure. I swear upon my mother's knitting needles! And I could countenance this oath with a wound which I sustained from an unlucky occasion ... when she used them to jab at me after a tantrum on my eighth birthday.'

Pilate groans inwardly. Gladys continues:

'I do the work of two people, sir. I am the cleaner and the caterer; but I am only paid for being the cleaner.'

'Yes, I remember now. The cleaner-cum-cook,' he mutters. 'My name for you has a certain ring about it.' And, simultaneously, he is simplifying this nickname for her in order to imply an entirely different role, "the cum cook". Sometimes, he can be quite coarse.

'I need you to supply extra sandwiches, and to put aside some salad as well. The troops will be working late tonight.'

'And ... and ...' says Gladys disconsolately. The director is lost for words at her impertinence. 'I have a large family of youngsters,' says she, 'and I'm bringing them all up on my own, you know.'

'But you didn't *produce* them on your own, did you? There is a significant other who was implicated in the process, is there not? Or did they all come out of a test tube? Perhaps they were immaculate conceptions? Eh? What are they doing here, anyway? Do they know about computers? Eh? Can we use them as software developers? They might as well serve *some* useful function. Eh?'

'They left school early today. They had a project to finish off; and they were told that, once they were through with it, they could go home.'

'Well! *This* isn't their home, is it? Eh? Eh?' he says, nodding his head and twitching his cheeks like a maniac. Unfortunately, he has been so upset by the loitering of Foolish Boy, that he appears to have given himself a temporary tic. Finally, addressing the youngest of the children, he says, 'Do you know how to make a sandwich?' Without waiting for an answer, he continues, 'Gladys will introduce you to the dark arts of the kitchen – and the servant's quarters.' (Gladys looks quizzical.) 'I suppose you *do have* a kitchen at home? Eh? Well, this one's much the same.' (And to Gladys): 'There, now. No need for an employment tribunal. With your children preparing the food, *you* can get on with your cleaning.'

'It's not fair, sir. Not fay-air.'

'Madam, it is a remarkable feat of dyslexia and dissection, that a word blessed with only one syllable at its inception may be split in two by the faltering of human breath.' He pauses. 'And it is infinitely worse than splitting the infinitive – since, as any mathematician knows, you may carve up infinity as often as you like, and yet each part shall (of itself) remain infinite.'

'I'm just a poor little downtrodden Mrs Mopp,' she says. As a matter of fact, during this conversation she has exchanged her besom for a mop, and (for several minutes) has been clumsily swishing it back and forth over his polished shoes – but only now have both of them noticed.

'Gladys! My shoes are sopping wet. What are you doing, Gladys? Eh?'

'Sir! So sorry, sir.'

The director passes out of earshot. He harbours grave suspicions about his rebellious cleaner. Is she collecting welfare whilst in his employ? Indeed, he has a general disdain for all of those who have sought help from the state at one time or another: the unemployed, the poor, the dispossessed, and those who have contracted diseases during the pursuit of alternative lifestyles.

'In fact, I find them distasteful,' he says to himself. 'There are no poor people alive any more; there are sufficient jobs for everyone; and if you hanker for an alternative lifestyle, go seek it in an alternative place. But at least the cleaner's two elder daughters are here. They are nubile and in fine fettle. If their sandwiches are good, I might give them a free work placement. They will have something to put on their *résumés*, and I shall receive gratification - as the daughters are *objets d'arts*. Ah! To feast my lascivious eyes, and break the monotony of another day of marriage.'

******

There is a rumour – although our venerable director would call it a "fact" – that several of his staff take time off from their desk duties in order to read for pleasure in the lavatory. Let us examine the evidence. It is true that some of them are nowhere to be seen for long periods each day; and, often-times, in the gentlemen's room, the rustling of paper can be heard. Now, you might say this is perfectly "kosher" when they are acting as "grooms of their own stools"; but, dear reader, it is *not* – not when the sound produced is nearer to the crunching of dry leaves under foot, than to the soft *swishing* of toilet tissue; and most especially not, when accompanied by the audible vocalisation of the odd news item or two from the daily press. So, in order to capture some data, the director has installed a recording device – including a video-camera and timer - in "the Gentlemen's doorway". Armed with these instruments, he can access the time incurred by each person performing his ablutions – and deduct the concurrent amount in money from that individual's wages.

'I have lost enough man hours already,' he opines. 'The moment has arrived when I must take action.'

Earlier on, Larry, the engineer, had been busy setting up the new equipment. Whilst he was perched upon a wobbly stool provided by the director, they had conversed about the value of surveillance. The precision of the apparatus was called into question, and Larry satisfied the doubter's curiosity on all counts. Now, the director is on his way to see Larry once again, this time to examine his handiwork. Can we imagine the chief's surprise when he turns a corner in the corridor and finds the engineer sprawled across the floor, near the door of the Gents Lavatory, with his zip undone and the ladder dismantled by his side. There is a large pool of what appears to be blood on the floor – but how can this be? Several people have gathered, including Gladys, who will have to clean up after him. For the moment, she has seized a chair and taken the weight off her feet – in lieu of her forthcoming exertions. With the arrival of the director, there is an air of hope that "the great Propotamous" will say or do something humanitarian for once ... sullied by a warped air of expectation that (in point of fact) he won't.

'*Mon Dieu!* What has happened?' he exclaims. He is not feigning his reaction. He is *actually* in a state of shock. Gladys takes it on herself to explain:

'Sir, I was just passing by, and I stopped to ask Larry how he was, and – being of an affable disposition, - he obliged and spoke to me. Then, as I was leaving, his eyes followed me, and, as a result, he lost his balance and fell off the ladder.'

'So you distracted him?'

'No. Begging your pardon, sir, I did nothing of the sort!'

'Good grief! There's blood everywhere! His clothes and his hair are soaking with it!' Even some distance from the fallen figure, the floor is bespattered with huge droplets, that shine like cherry apples fresh from the orchard trees. The director's mouth waters faintly, for he has not eaten all day: even though he has altruistically laid on food for others. (Indeed, he is tending to sup later and later; although this is through force of habit rather than hard work.)

'God's Mercy be upon us! Blood is seeping out of his head. Gladys, this is diabolical! What have you to say for yourself?'

'Nothing, sir.'

'Nothing? What do you mean, "Nothing"! You were a witness and (if I am not mistaken) an instigator of this atrocity; and, as I am a man of few words, we (for your purposes, it is the *Royal* We) shall hold your womanhood in contempt.'

'Oh, sir! Please, no!'

'Is he alive?'

'He has a pulse, sir.' The director stoops down, and puts his fingers against the nostrils of the damaged goods, and proclaims happily: 'He is still breathing. Pass me a soft platform for the seat of his consciousness to recline upon.' Gladys hands over a sumptuous cushion – which she has cut with a pair of scissors from the upholstery of an antique chair (purchased from Harrods Department Store by a friend of hers: suffice to say, they are no longer on speaking terms), - and Pilate gasps as he lays it ever so gently beneath the broken head.

'Gladys, call an ambulance.'

'Yes, sir.'

'And with God's speed!'

'I'll try, sir.'

'Fit a tourniquet.'

'Yes, sir.'

'However, I do perceive he might need it around his jugular, and then I shall have to accuse you of strangling him ... Poor fellow! He was an honest, practical and useful man. Sorry ... *is* ... *is* ...' He has to correct the tense, for Gladys's lower lip is quivering and she may be about to shriek. Indeed, she has imbibed a lungful of air and is already preparing for that very action. Pilate holds up his hand to stop her, and the following words issue forth,

'Sir, this is the most stressful moment of my life; or, leastwise, the most stressful moment since one traumatic day at school, when I broke down after being told I had an "add-on".'

'An *add-on*?'

'Yes, sir. I was told I had a bump on the end of my nose: brought on not by accident, but inheritance, - or (worse) by Darwinian design!'

'Gladys. Listen to me. You haven't *got* a bump on the end of your nose!'

'Sir, with all rightful respect (which I have owing to you), that is of secondary importance. The crux of the matter is, I was *teased* for having one!'

'Just like my wife,' he thinks. 'So irrational.' And then he fantasizes about the effect of a warm emotional outburst upon the jet stream: whether it arises from Gladys or from Myfanwy. 'Perhaps, like butterfly wings in the "law of unintended consequences", it would bring us one step nearer to a tropical storm in Asia?' He has descended to his knees and wears the heart of sympathy on his sleeve. He even plays with the man's blood-strewn hair for a while, and hums a lullaby he learnt at nursery school; whilst wearing a profoundly doleful expression on his corpulent face. Self-awareness is a sign of high intellect, and he is fully aware of his own religiosity. Would a psalm be appropriate? Or should he hold off until the engineer breathes his last? There are even tears in his eyes (although this could be the effect of a rather fierce air conditioning unit in the vicinity). He turns to Gladys. 'He is a fighter. He will survive ... Is he conscious?' She does not answer. He adds wistfully: 'You know, this is the worst thing that has happened to me all year.'

'I dare say it is, sir.'

Mr Propotamous leans forward, and then, ever so gently, he lifts the injured man's head towards his mouth, for his words are for Larry's ears only. Larry moans softly as the director says, 'You are awake ...? Thank God!' Then he drops his voice to a whisper, 'You know, Larry, this just isn't good enough. I'll have to let you go.' After issuing his dismissal, he addresses Gladys.

'Well. Don't just stand there. Look sharp, woman! You've got some mopping up to do! And I want this bloody object removed to hospital, before the Health and Safety Inspector arrives.' With one hand she seizes her best scourer - a composite of barbed wire and the dead roots of a sycamore tree, - whilst with the other hand she reaches for a bottle of bleach, with its cap unscrewed and ready for action.

'What is that cleaning fluid you have? It's making my eyes water,' Mr Propotamous complains. But all the woman can do is mutter,

'Poor Larry! *Poor* Larry! Oh! Aren't I just so heavily put upon?'

******

Now it transpires that a certain toxic duo are still in the building, led by the accountant. They are, if you remember, the two Inspectors: of *Health and Safety*, and of *Her Majesty's Inland Revenue Services*. And the director is rushing down the corridor towards them. He catches their eyes and signals to them, before – most peculiarly – performing a pirouette. After this balletic movement (who would have thought him capable of it?) he speedily retraces his steps, whilst turning his head and issuing directives over his shoulder to his associate, who is skilled in handling the almighty pounds sterling.

'Please ... If you do not mind ... I have a staff member who has just collapsed. Kindly show these gentlemen the premises.'

'I've already done it,' says the accountant.

'Well ... keep doing it!' he pauses for breath. 'You are familiar with my tight adherence to Health and Safety Regulations, and you may apprise *him* of the same' (he points with his chin to the man who oversees such things); and, of course, you are aware of my high moral stance towards taxation' (he nods towards the Inspector of Taxes). 'Leastwise, you are the one who files all my tax returns for me, and who bears complete responsibility for them. I have my hands full at the moment.' The accountant shudders, and then he grabs the sleeves of the officials as if they were the wings of diseased pigeons (or some other species of flying vermin), and leads them roughly away in the direction opposite to the bleeding body. Meanwhile, Mr Propotamous returns to the ill-fated engineer, – leaving the trail of an uncomfortable conversation in his wake.

The boss is a thoroughgoing capitalist: from the brown mess in his belly, right up to the purest oxygen of his breezy thoughts. As he arrives at the bloody scene, the last of his feelings are verbalised thus,

'This is a right royal pickle. Thank God I laid down linoleum two months ago. The original underlay was far too absorbent.'

The Marketplace and Classified Ads

My focus must now pass to a couple of part-time documenters, who have just got wind of the firing of our characterful youth. As they are the leader's "henchmen", they believe their positions within the organization are safe. Like most men of their ilk, they are tall and heavily built. When not engaged in the shady practice of "bouncing", they are hired for light data processing tasks. Mr Propotamous is fond of this frightening pair, on account of the warm sensation in his gut that comes from having them around. But in spite of the jagged edges in their personalities, they are not without some refinement. Generally, a conversation between them will be instigated with sonorous ideas - and end in depravity. Herein, one may act as a guide - and the other, as his trusting dog. They have a talent for political debate. At present, the subject under the spotlight is the economy. And why not? After all, it is their coffee break. The term "monetarism" rears its head. One asks the other what it means, and his colleague respectfully gives a formal definition.

'It is all to do with the supply of money in the economy being the chief determinant of production, employment and price levels.'

'So – a byword for Capitalism, then? Or common sense?'

'Perhaps. But we should appreciate the perfectly rational desire to be creative that resides in uncreative people, to the extent that they must apply unusual terms to describe what is commonplace. After all, in the light of their limitations, what else can they do?'

'Yes. The flow of money is a phenomenon to behold. Some say, "It is terrible that we are all in debt"; and others reply that "debt is, nevertheless, the oxygen of the economy".'

'My Lord! What a state of affairs, that we may only subsist on what we least do want!'

'So it must be. And so it must remain. But it is really not so bad. Let us say country A owes country B 1 billion pounds sterling; and country B owes country C 1 billion pounds; and country C owes country A 1 billion. It is a matter of the most arcane mystery as to *who* really owes money to *whom*; how much is owed; and whether, in point of fact, *who* owes *whom* anything at all. If we broke the chain of interdependency, so much of world debt could be cancelled, – but, of course, this would not be politic.'

'And what of the machinations of this software house of ours?

'Where do I even begin?' says the guide. 'Foolish Boy has been dismissed, and there is some talk about his being reimbursed for lost earnings.'

'Pilate won't be happy.'

'Oh, he won't mind. The boy didn't earn anything!'

'And what else ...?'

'Let us examine the subject of documentation. One folder points to another folder, which, in turn, points to another folder, which' (the speaker pauses for breath) 'points to yet another ... which is *missing* ... Hang on! Is this it? No, this one points back to the first folder – or to a place of infinite mystery! The last sacked contractor must have taken one of the files away with him! And, occasionally, proper pointers are replaced with false ones ... so all we have are pointers to pointers ... and no *actual* documentation at all. We can only hope the end user will be far too lackadaisical to notice.'

'Are there no standards in place?'

'Oh! Don't get me started on standards. Methinks they are an excuse to switch off the power of human judgement. Upon the scales of truest value, an anagram weighs not a gram – nor even a feather. There is ISO9000 (Idealistic, Subtle Overviews they are not); and there is BS5750. Ah! The famous *BS*.'

'In that case, we have had a *power failure* for some time.'

'Were the company to function like a human brain, the electroencephalogram would be flat.'

'Methinks the client will not be happy! Does he know about these problems yet?'

'Even the manager doesn't know!'

'All of our procedures seem so convoluted. What's the cost?'

'Well, that's just it. The boss is totally in favour of as much documentation as possible, since the more paperwork he hands over, the more he can charge. And he can be quite passionate on the subject.'

'An angry mouth conveys a weak argument.'

'Yea. The mug is hot, but the liquid it proffers is only temperate. Clever, eh? After all, no client will protest that little was done for him, in the face of so many folders of notes!'

'He will, if they contain nothing but pointers.'

'I exaggerate for effect. Truthfully, the organization did generate some useful paperwork – when it ditched an outdated version of ORACLE for the cheaper option of *online programming*. With the latter, the code is interpreted one line at a time, – rather than the whole lot being compiled in one go. And we now provide the client with a very rough outline of what each module does, which is all he will want to read anyway. After all, who has ever read the entire user guide for his washing machine, gas oven or refrigerator? And yet who, among us, would accept delivery of an appliance without a user guide to go with it?'

'The ancient language of COBOL is mentioned here as well!' says the other, turning the leaves of an official statement, as if it were papyrus decorated in hieroglyphs. 'It sounds to me like the boss can't make up his mind about which technology he favours. Perhaps he needs shaking up?'

'We can't do that. It's not in our contract ...' (Their eyes meet.) 'Yea, shame though. A small dose of electro-convulsive therapy might be just what the doctor ordered. Nothing is bloody working. Not since *you know who* embarked upon an ambitious attempt at software engineering himself. Good heavens! We have been *reverse engineering* ever since. My wife has the same sensation when, as a seamstress, she pulls upon a loose thread in an intricately woven garment, and sees the entire textile come apart before her eyes. Each time we uncovered an error, we would correct it and dig a little deeper; and then - blow me down if we didn't find another error; and, beneath that, another ... and so on.'

'Like Thomas Aquinas, did you eventually get back to God?'

'In a way ... Yes, mate ...'

'In a way?'

'Well, our Great Leader and pseudo-programmer was unwittingly behind it all! In each case, the rotten core of the apple was an erroneous seed, planted by "God's" fair hand. It could be as insignificant as a misplaced comma or apostrophe; anything, really. On one occasion, he generated a Cartesian product because he failed to identify a date range for his output. On and on the program ran: greedily consuming space and processing power, like a rocket *en route* to some unknown galaxy.'

'Oh! So that was *his* doing, was it? You know Foolish Boy got the blame for it?'

'Like an upturned oil tanker in a wildlife sanctuary, our leader's mistakes poison everything!'

'Oh, dear. You have to be so careful. Many years ago, a programmer working for the Ministry of Defence typed a hyphen in the wrong place. The bug cost 15 million pounds to fix! That would have been a fortune at the time.'

'It's a fortune now!'

'Well. Our own Project was costing the client a cool £100,000 per annum – and everything was going smoothly.'

'I bet that's changed now?'

'Not half! The latest estimate is £200,000.'

'Our energy-supplying customer will never pay up. I hear he is even considering litigation.'

'Ha! Except that the contract both parties have signed, designates the client as the guinea-pig. He must test everything and raise a log number within a preordained period of time. If he exceeds that period – and he has - then "God" will charge him for the repair; even though we will still only deliver what was originally promised! The longer the delay in error reporting, the higher the fee. It is rather like the financial crisis. Everyone owes money to those who are most culpable. Or – another parallel – it is as if a burglar has broken into your home, ransacked everything, stolen your valuables, and left your household economy in tatters; and then emails you a week later, to say that his gain from the heist was less than he had been hoping for, and that he will issue a legal writ stating that you owe him the difference.'

'How far we are from whence we came! Now, we cannot move for documentation requests – even though much of what is written is soon lost. Before, we could not move for testing.

Back in the day, we employed something hugely time-consuming and fatuous called "the grid" – with an x axis comprising all of the programs in the system; and a y axis, representing all of the scenarios to be tested against each program. Every issue solved would reduce the possibility of system failure. We were forced to collate statistics and apply mind-blowing actuarial formulas, to arrive at the likelihood of user satisfaction, as measured against a "happiness index" employing the famous 5% probability level. In the end, we just fabricated the data. The boss didn't mind - so long as our corruption of his perverse methodology did not become our guiding principle; and provided we were able to *convince the users of their own happiness.*'

'This boss of ours needs a good kicking.'

'Yea. If only the Kray twins were alive. They would have sorted him out.'

'Anyhow, have you ordered those women for tonight? You know my predilection.'

'I know you like my sister. I have to say, she's not my cup of tea.'

'But I know what you *do* like,' replies the other, passing over the last inappropriate remark.

'Yea. Early exotics ... "never knowingly underage".'

'You once uttered some wisdom on them. How does it go?'

Hereupon, they both speak the following words in unison,

'If they're old enough to *BLOW YOU UP*, they're old enough to fffff- '

They stop in their tracks, for one of them has been making large gestures with his hands, and has knocked his mug of coffee flying from its resting place. But it is an accident of good fortune – sacrificing the carpet in place of the reader's delicate ears.

******

Near by, a colleague is reading super-bike magazines. He is not on his coffee break, and he may be in cahoots with the director. At the merest hint that he is lazy, he will alert the critic to the key verb displayed across his terminal ... the one bearing witness to some obscure, and deeply entrenched, process: "Working ...". He will then explain that even whilst he, himself, is in the throes of idleness, his steely workhorse is a paragon of diligence. He reasons thus,

'There is no incentive for me to work any harder, because I know I will simply be given something else to do. No matter what my productivity level is, I will never go home early. In fact, tonight I'll be lucky if I go home at all!' As he speaks this last sentence, he is holding a new manual in his hands. This is not another super-bike magazine. At least, we hope it isn't.

Attitudes to Our Noble Leader

The two colleagues whom we met earlier, engrossed in the throes of word play about Myfanwy, are at play again: with their rare combination of *base bully* and *high literacy*. It is unknown which of these features emerged first; or whether, like a couple of mismatched orphans on a bicycle, they evolved in tandem. This time, the two ruffians turn their attention to the "Great Propotamous" ...

THE FIRST: He saves the most extravagant gestures of altruism for those situations where his offer is sure to be forgotten, or sure to be refused. I'd say it was a clever little ruse, if I did not mind my tongue! Ah! To be impelled by the force of Christian virtue, and saved from the hassle of a follow through: like a tennis opponent who falters just as he is about to make contact with the ball.

THE SECOND: Except that in this case, the falterer wins the spoils – and succeeds in keeping his largess.

THE FIRST: He is very loquacious, and holds his listeners in the palm of his hand, quite spellbound, as he personally offends them: for a surprise element leaves them speechless. He operates on a guiding principle, which is the inverse of that employed by reasonable men. He will tirelessly search for the most irritating or provocative thing which may be said ... and then, having discovered what it is, – he will just keep on (and on) repeating it, until the listener becomes giddy, and will say *anything* to make him stop. I do confess, he has a certain verbal dexterity; and, as I say, he can be mesmerising. But when he seizes your attention and shakes you up, you feel like an antelope in the mouth of a crocodile. He has not *the gift of the gab* but *the gift of the gob*. And, on occasion, he ceases to be master of his own verbiage, - and his snowy white complexion is swallowed whole by a most bloody and unfortunate malapropism.

THE SECOND: Bloody?

THE FIRST: Well, I'll warrant that all of the blood which hitherto resided in the nether regions of his corpulence, has suddenly fled north, like a voluminous migration of cheap labour into the promised land of England.

THE SECOND: Where the climate makes the complexion go white again?

THE FIRST (somewhat ruefully): Ah! The metaphor has fallen down.

******

And here is a parley between three persons of mixed gender who dislike their leader greatly. They are not dressed in frocks, although such attire would be appropriate. One of them *may* be named Michael, but I cannot say for sure, since the informal name by which he is addressed is incidental; nor can I give their whereabouts, for that would be telling. Anyhow, as I write this, one of them is holding forth ...

'Shall we form a pact and leave this place together? Upon completion of our dastardly deeds, what further need have we to stay? Let me allude to the deeds like so ... we shall tempt him with a cup of ... Whatever shall it be ...? And watch as Micky Finn finishes him off, at least for the nonce - and perhaps forever. But let us pause a while. Has the final unravelling of the plot already come to pass? No? Then it is yet to be - but when, oh *when*? And where, oh *where*? Such details cannot be revealed.'

Led by young "Micky" (is that his real name?), the cabal pretend to be the personae of the three witches in Macbeth, stirring an imaginary pot-pourri of elements that are not normally miscible, and declaring, as one:

Double, double, toil and trouble
Fire burn, and cauldron bubble

Plotting and Scheming

Day turns into night. Pilate is at his desk in the Oval Office, musing upon everything except the proper running of his business. And the accountant, who appeared (like a Jack in a

Box) just when he was needed to be a foil for awkward guests, has gone home - as have the guests themselves. At last, Pilate is free to explore his plans to defraud the Inland Revenue. He would half favour the disposing of his wife as well, but he doesn't want the hassle. So, instead, he settles for another pleasure, as dark and bitter-sweet as a bar of high cocoa-content chocolate brought to him by one of his minions. In a mild act of sadism, he will keep the office open all night.

'I'm really doing everyone a favour,' he thinks, 'for they don't want to go home to their wives anyway. The long hours are so often a voluntary smokescreen. And as for myself, I can sleep on the divan in my office, - when I am not watching videos, that is. Although, of late, I have rolled up my sleeves for some hard graft.' And I am sure the reader wishes him every success. But just before the boss re-enters the technical sea, and waddles out of his depth into the sunset, his wife shows up. She has an idea which she is excited to share with him.

'It keeps coming back to me like a boomerang,' she says. 'But first, there is a small duty to be addressed. Pilate, dear, isn't it time you attended confession? You know you haven't been for some time. Now, don't look at me like that. If I fail to remind you, you'll never go.' She is always pestering him on this issue.

'But why should I? There's nothing wrong with me,' he replies, as if he were in remission from a disease, and the Canon were in the business of fixing bodies rather than souls.

'Preventative medicine, my dear,' replies his wife. Absolution before sin: with the glorious boon that you can do whatever you want afterwards, because you've already been forgiven for it. It's the religious equivalent of the law on double jeopardy.'

'Gosh! Are you quite sure of that? Was there ever such freedom under the open sky? It sounds highly implausible.' And then he adds, 'But the Canon can do anything. I have heard that he is setting up an internet chat room on the dark web, where a sinner can go and commune with his local priest: admitting his misdemeanours before absolution is sent to his inbox. The site is called:
"sin-ye-no-more@confessional.com".

Apparently, one of my men has been *moonlighting* – and this is his love-child. I don't know who the culprit is. Yet I will say this: he has broken his contractual promise to work only for me (and not for anyone else – not even himself), and he should admit this sin of his *own* online. Perhaps a hacker can find out his name for me?'

'And I have heard that you needn't even confess to your local pastor,' his wife agrees.

'That's right ... It could be any priest. Just select a *diocese* from the list of values, and a *misdemeanour* from another list; and get the automated instructions for your penance, calculated for you by a clever algorithm. Dear me! Imagine if someone *does* hack into it, and corrupts the priestly verdict. You might have to say five hundred *HAIL MARYs* or a thousand *GLORY BEs*, when all you've done is put the bin bag out for collection on the wrong day!'

'Well – that's hardly a sin anyway, is it?'

'It is, if you contaminate the local environment with household waste!'

She ignores him, and introduces a new theme,

'You know, I have an inspiration which refuses to leave me. Why don't we get this software house blessed by our affectionate pastor – especially as he is only next door.' For once, they are in agreement.

'My dear, you are so right. It strikes me as prudent from three angles. Firstly, the growth of an honest enterprise would benefit from some help from above. Secondly, the building, prior to its conversion from a warehouse, was declared unfit for human habitation, owing to a series of infiltrations from insect colonies; and, in spite of hiring the services of Rentokill, there was some doubt as to whether it would pass the next Health and Safety Inspection. But never fear! The capabilities of our Lord surpasses those of Rentokill. And thirdly, the Inland Revenue would never believe that an organisation blessed by the church would fail to pay its taxes. On the other hand, I have heard that Fr Bertrand Tyson has errant leanings, that distract him from the purity of his calling.'

'Don't mince your words. Fr Bertrand has *artistic* leanings. And jolly fine leanings they are too! Did it ever occur to you that he could paint a picture of this limited company? I can see it now ... you would be standing at the front door, with all of your "foot soldiers" (as you call them) in tow; and the nearby building site as a backdrop. The venerable father would render the scene in such an attractive way, that the local newspapers will be unable to resist publishing his artwork with a caption – which he could write, for he is especially eloquent when helping friends. Just think. You would have free publicity.'

'Yes, our parish priest has many gifts. And he's definitely someone with a history. He used to practise wrestling; and afterwards became an officer in the armed forces; and then, back in "civvy street", he was a professional weightlifter for a while; and now he's a Canon, *a bouncer for the "Backward Dog"*, as I like to say.'

This *faux pas* passes unnoticed by Myfanwy, and the husband smiles wistfully, before continuing.

'Fr Bertrand runs his parish in an unusual way, and is not above introducing competition in the arena of grace and redemption. Once a year, he institutes a "prayer-athon". With the aid of Close Circuit Television, he assesses which parishioners have grovelled on their knees for the longest period of time, and he intercedes on their behalf. But how (you may ask) are their prayers made known to him? Well, the contestants have written them down on tiny pieces of paper ... and then transported these notes to the most poorly maintained wall of the church (next to the East Transept, I believe); before keeping faith with the Jewish tradition at Temple Mount, and delicately inserting them into the cracks.'

'"Grovels" is a bad choice of word. You should pay more respect,' complains Myfanwy.

Pilate has an unusual relationship with Fr Tyson. He has, in the past, accepted pills from his parish priest that will "enable him to remain upright". It is not "something for the weekend" (since both of them are opposed to the "spurious twinning of general behaviours to specific days").

'I *could* take my friendship with the clergyman a little further. Perhaps I ought to purchase the chapel with its private grounds, and declare it all as a branch of my personal enterprise?' murmurs the big man.

By chance, his accountant has suddenly returned, and his wife departs – leaving the two men alone together. Pilate floats this latest idea while his companion listens intently. The accountant clearly feels that he is onto something.

'But I am wondering how the Inland Revenue would view this acquisition?' Pilate looks to his visitor for guidance.

'Give me a moment ... Let's think about it ... How about this for a sterling concept: when declaring the income on your tax return, you would simply put *Offertory* for what is collected in the plate, and Foreign Missions for sales of your software abroad.' Having won the appreciation of a familiar expert, Pilate is "on a roll".

'You are so right,' he ventures. 'It's high time I organized my finances. I've done enough for others. I hire them. I fill their Christmas stockings (so to speak) with bonuses. I enrich their minds through training schemes, and through hopes of promotion (never mind whether these are ever fulfilled). And that is to mention just three facets of their great good fortune. On rare occasions, I will even take them to the pub for a little free sustenance and liquid refreshment. Were I their shepherd and they my sheep, I could not treat them more lovingly.'

'You are to be congratulated,' the accountant concedes. (He will concede anything for a peaceful life.) 'But you have a wife by your side. You can afford the luxury of gushing in your charity to others, in the sure knowledge that, should you fall upon hard times, the mainstay of your life – which is her dowry, - will still support you; and should you fall sick, she shall nurse you. But I,' he sighs sorrowfully, 'have only myself to rely upon. If I deplete my nest egg of its yolk, who shall replenish it?'

******

The accountant retires, and the principal switches his attention to a form and an accompanying brochure on his desk, entitled "The Enterprise and Initiative scheme". This handy booklet offers methods by which the captains of industry can gain generous grants and save on their tax bill. Mr Propotamous already receives government handouts for his employment of school leavers, and of the dispossessed. Now - a peculiarly Swiss idea occurs to him. He has a number of rubbish bins outside his premises. He could employ a couple of these in the usual way – and then padlock the others, with the aim of renting them out for profit. (After all, green issues are at the forefront of public consciousness these days.) At times like this, when his thoughts are flowing effortlessly, he grows irate if anyone impedes him. That is to say, anyone except his wife, - for she is capable, at the slightest provocation, of achieving a state of high dudgeon: which is difficult to cope with, and even harder to explain. She is also fiercely proud of her mixed nationhood, as the following words of hers will verify ...

'When you advertise your services, you can mention how your wife's genes perfectly fuse Italian reliability and Welsh engineering.' (Little does she know, these qualities are easily disbanded by a wet wind inside a green valley.) The response is soft and almost apologetic:

'But, darling, no one will know what you're talking about.'

Husbandly and Wifely Devotions

Pilate and Myfanwy are not above the sharing of a little humour. Here they are, discussing Freddie the Cleaner ...

PILATE: He has given up nothing for Lent, and is finding it very challenging.

MYFANWY: Sorry? I don't quite follow.

PILATE: Well. His conversation infuriates all of his acquaintances, because it is empty of content: *a dose of nothing* as I like to call it. And so he has made a solemn promise only to speak sentences that are edifying for his listeners - throughout the forthcoming period of Lent.

MYFANWY: Has he really? Does he not realise, it is a sin to make promises you cannot deliver on! [She chuckles]

PILATE: In fact, in a roundabout way, he more than delivers on his promise: for if you cease listening when he is in full flight, he becomes so upset that he vows never to speak to you again. And this is far better than a promise made just for Lent.

******

It must have been observed by many an amateur philosopher, that loneliness (or the lack of a listening ear) is the foundation for soliloquies. So it is, that at this very moment, Freddie may be found outside the front entrance of the building – talking to himself. He is repeating an idea relayed to him by Foolish Boy earlier in the day, and (clearly) he is still smarting from the words,

"Tis said that people grow less sensitive with age, less "touchy", - but 'tis not so. Their feelings are more easily hurt; and so their frailty is emotional as well as physical.' He is holding his chest, as if his heart has been spiked by a rapier, and he is drooling ... as he reminisces and falls upon a metaphorical sword: 'The wisdom brought on by age is not philosophical, nor is it born out of empathy or tolerance. It is simply self-knowledge. That is to say: you do not understand or tolerate others more, but only yourself. You are more certain of your own likes and dislikes - and less inclined to have them compromised. When I was a youth, I would shake my arms and gyrate my hips in time to music which I could not easily tolerate, simply to blend in with a crowd with whom I had little in common.'

******

Myfanwy has an occasional lilt couched within her speech. It tends to make an appearance at the end of her warmest effusions, - and finds expression in a sudden release of air, 'Ahhhhh'. The following examples may serve as illustrations: 'What more can I do for you than I have already done, ahhhhh?' or 'You have-ah no respect for me. Ahhhhh!' She is full of unhappiness and fatty tissues: the former gives rise to the latter through comfort eating; and, in an act of symbiosis, the extra inches on her waistline make her even more unhappy. Mind you, her predilection to gorge herself has a favourable effect upon her complexion. It plumps up her skin and melts her worry lines.

Her neurosis is counterbalanced by the wearing of expensive jewellery, and by the bright colours which show off her nails to spectacular effect. For, as she is apt to remind others, 'when you see colour, you turn away from gloom'. She is a sybarite. Even as I write this, she has her nail varnish in one hand, and a large box of soft Belgian chocolates in the other. She fully intends to eat everything in the box, but the feast is an imprecise art, - for the nail varnish keeps dripping onto her chocolates and staining them purple; and, even more distressing for her, some of the fine, soft chocolate is melting all over her hands and nails. She licks them greedily, and then simply carries on eating and varnishing, - until the sight of her becomes almost hypnotic. (This is a woman with strange tastes. Whenever she treats her cracked heels with an abrasive device such as an emery-board, she proceeds to collect the yellow dust that falls from them, and sprinkle it - as if 'twere a condiment - upon her *Chicken Jalfrezi*, whilst perpetually muttering, 'Parmesan, anyone ...? Anyone for Parmesan cheese?')

After consuming her chocolates, she downs one phial of nail varnish. Even for "General Pico", this is a moment of thoughtlessness. (Dear reader, please do not follow her lead. Such a beverage is surely poisonous?) But our heroine is feeling positive about herself - and romantically inclined. Then she peers into the mirror at an enormous figure (the *bête noire* that is her reflection), and her spirits sink. She reaches for a box of toffees - and starts her next binge. Very soon, she arrives at that point in her bulimic cycle wherein she will vomit into the sink. And yet, in spite of everything, she *does* have a health plan. She recently joined a "leisure centre": which is a great misnomer for a place dedicated to exercise. Bless her! Will she use the facilities? Only time will tell - and Father Time is already shaking his hoary head. So far, Myfanwy, on the occasion of her only visit to the centre, grew tired of rescuing drowned insects from the outdoor pool; and was dissuaded from entering the water by a human torpedo, who performed the common crawl as if he was splitting the Red Sea for Moses. But to her, even the acquisition of a membership card is a momentous step towards vitality.

Once, a large sponge sandwich with honey and cream disappeared - just minutes before the arrival of a delegation of officials, who were the intended consumers. And later, the guilty party was seen wiping the residual crumbs from her plump lips. Apparently, she had devoured it in one sitting. But she would never have a spoonful of sugar in her coffee. Now that *would* be excessive!

Occasionally, she suffers from a fit of "pica", a displacement activity most likely caused (in her case) by being insufficiently loved. Often-times, her husband has seen her emerging from the shower with her cheeks bulging, and her teeth clenching a bar of soap. One day, she may be done in by her oral secretions; but, in the mean time, her husband has to be on his guard to keep the bathroom well-stocked. She has a voracious appetite, and is consuming inedible items as fast as he can buy them. Once, she was caught red-handed by a staff member, whilst in the process of unravelling an enormous bathroom sponge from her mouth, which was caked in scum. And she was reputedly eating conventional food at the time, as well. The observer of her exploits was later sacked, in order to stem the embarrassment at source: for the stream of dialogue possesses self-regulating powers. Having spat your two penneth into it, there is no telling where it might go.

Mr Propotamous thinks to himself, 'If only I had stuck to the smaller toiletries, her behaviour might have escaped detection. Yet in spite of her ability to eat for England in private, her diet in public has the modesty of a sparrow's. And oddly enough, when I broach the subject of these strange urges, she is (for a change) able to take herself lightly.'

His wife is his senior by ten years. She was never attractive, not even as a young lady. To aid her figure, she makes extensive use of cookery books, and, like many persons of her culture and her age, she is overly concerned with how pretty a meal looks on the plate. She also professes to love animals, and to be a strict vegetarian. Hence, on the blackboard in the meeting room, a mischievous employee has written,

'Is veganism a moral cap, doomed to be donned by fat people who eat cake? Discuss.' And someone has added, 'Is soap composed of animal fat? If so, how does she wash?' (For everyone knows to whom "she" refers.) Finally, there is a third (highly erudite) analysis, 'The manufacture of soap can swing both ways. At the lower end, it may involve tallow or lard; and at the higher end, - olive, coconut or palm oil.'

Mr Propotamous cannot resist pontificating on health and sickness:

'Exercise and diet! These are the twin pillars of life. You reap what you sow.' He applies both pillars to his fat wife, and neither pillar to his fat self.

'What else is there?' he adds. 'Unless our figures (slim or portly) are the product of our genes or of our stars – rather than our lifestyles? And neither the apologists for *strings of DNA or stars* on the one hand, nor those for *lifestyle choices* on the other, can ever quite prove their point to the satisfaction of the opposite camp. Yet the inescapable truth is that people were less fat two generations ago than they are now; and if this is not the result of lifestyle choices (produced by idleness and by the easy availability of food), but of a new biological inheritance, then except for a general aberration of nature ...' (here he pauses for breath) '... which would take a period of time measurable not in generations but in geological time ...' (he pauses again) '... our portliness must be the result of immigration altering the gene pool. Really, the nation's DNA is like a database, and anything new should be vetted in order to prevent contamination.'

Myfanwy has a different theory, and through it she manifests a rare moment of rationality:

'I am never able to become full up ... I wonder if the food manufacturers are adding a cocktail of ingredients which block the satiety mechanisms in my brain?'

In spite of her dips in self-worth, Myfanwy has flights of optimism. She is on one at the moment, and wants her husband to supply the thermal winds of flattery. She is familiar with the painter, Hieronymous Bosch, - and refers to herself as 'The Garden of Earthly Delights'.

'Whatever pleases you,' is all her husband has to say.

That night, Pilate has a dream. In this dream, his wife is standing, naked, inside a hospital ward: naked, that is, except for her shoes, a big bowler hat on her head, and two placards. One of these is attached below her naval and directly in front of her saucy region. It reads,

'Dirty utility room. Please keep this door closed.' Meanwhile, the other notice covering her rear end is equally explicit:

'Garbage disposal area. Back Office Specialist required.'

His wife sits down in front of him and leans forward, so that her huge breasts are hanging down, and almost overshadowing his knees. She then begins to sway from side to side, slapping one appendage against the other. Pilate is mesmerized. She is wielding each mammary gland like a shiny watch on the end of a chain, which in folklore has long been the favourite tool of the hypnotist. Next, she holds up a sign: 'Please remain seated while the bust is in motion.'

Pilate has an electronic tablet on his lap, displaying a menu with magical powers and a virtual keyboard. He touches View, and his wife suddenly appears like Eve in all her pre-serpentine glory. Then he touches Delete; and her pimples, sunspots and stretch marks all disappear. Thirdly, he selects Update, and - wonder of wonders! - she is transformed into the kind of woman he would like to have married. Finally, he pokes the Insert button, and she signals for him to 'Come hither'. She is now wearing an apron, with the words knitted into the fabric, 'Fanny Exit or Ramona Remain? How should we best trade our wares? Do you really want to leave our sacred union.' She speaks to him with words he might hear on a journey with British Rail,

'You must pay the full price before you touch in.' He is aroused, but realises he hasn't brought any money with him.

'Can I pay later?' he asks humbly. With a sober look upon her countenance, she shakes her head ... and then yells at the top of her lungs,

'Fanny Exit-er!'

He stirs. Never before has a figment of his own imagination awoken him! Even his dreams cannot eventuate as they once would have done. Until the imaginary Myfanwy raised her voice, his dream had seemed like the balmy air on a Spring morning in the Highlands of Scotland: full of promise, and yet ... such a deceitful temptress! For a moment, he had no longer been frigid. Clearly, if Myfanwy could be different - then he could be different too.

Meanwhile, the real Myfanwy is beside him, fast asleep and snoring.

'Shhhhh!' he exclaims. She slowly stirs.

'Don't tell me to shush!' she murmurs.

'I didn't! What you heard was the whirring sound of the kettle boiling water for my next coffee.' There is, indeed, a coffee pot - along with sachets of tea and coffee – on top of his bedside cabinet. He is lying about the kettle. He thinks she won't notice, but she is awake now.

'Why are you making coffee at this time of the morning?'

'I can't sleep.'

'I'm not surprised - drinking coffee.'

'Cause and effect confused, darling. Cause and effect confused.' She grunts, and begins to breathe deeply again.

Now he is thinking about money.

'I could hire my wife as a secretary. She would then be on my payroll as a tax-deductible expense.' He remembers one morning over breakfast in bed, when he asked her what she thought ...

'I will only agree to this arrangement if you make my cup of happiness full,' she replies. She is in a playful mood. 'What aspect of me would you like to praise?'

A long and embarrassing silence ensues.

'Well?'

'I'm still thinking ...'

'What do you mean, "You're still thinking?"'

'I mean, where do I start?'

'And while you are pondering where to begin your generous account of my numerous and exemplary qualities, here's something else to consider. You will have to insure that warehouse. What happens if it is destroyed by fire?'

'It's funny you should say that. I am, as it happens, searching for the best deal online -' he stops reminiscing, for at this very second his accountant enters the bedroom.

'What the deuce are you doing here!'

'I couldn't help overhearing. I have a specialist knowledge of the insurance market.'

'The devil's gift is my astonishment!'

'Oh! Is this not an opportune moment? Shall I call by later?' The director realises he is dreaming again. His wife rises from the marital bed, and dons her dressing gown as she speaks her parting words,

'I'm just going to set his accounts to music. A little Puccini in the background would make them sound so much better. I'll come back this evening, after you've had your haircut.'

'Yes, dear. You do that.'

Playing God

Pilate is awake again, and staring at the ceiling. He wants to get some kip before the long night ahead. He sits up in bed, and sips a glass of water before settling down. Soon after, he is a willing participant in another unusual dream. It is the south coast of England. He is in a sailing boat, and moving soundlessly over the waters like the God of Genesis. There is a voice-over in the background, - and the whole setting feels like an old Hollywood feature film directed by Cecil B. DeMille.

"In the beginning Pilate created the heavens and the earth. The earth was without form and void, and darkness was upon the face of the deep. And Pilate said, 'Let there be light', and there was light. And Pilate saw that the light was good; and Pilate separated the light from the darkness. Pilate called the light Day, and the darkness he called Night." And then Pilate wakes up. His wife has switched on the ancillary light in the bedroom, and she is sitting in front of the dressing table with one foot on her knee, painting her toenails.

'Cometh the age, cometh the neck,' she whispers. On the table before her is a bottle of "Ageless Throat", which she has been rigorously applying while Pilate was asleep. Her neck is positively gleaming. It is also oscillating in and out - like the body of a python in time-lapse photography, after overcoming a hapless creature wider than its girth. Why is this? It is because she has been swallowing chocolate laced with nuts, and a portion of this delicious mixture has got stuck. To make matters worse, she is also in the middle of an impassioned soliloquy,

'How may others love me, when I cannot love myself?' Here, she pauses. 'Well, naturally they must have the devotion of two people, in order to compensate for the love which I lack.'

Some of her cosmetics have lain unopened for many years, since she always thought it was a shame to disturb the florid packaging. But heat and light are the enemies of cosmetics! And so their time has come. Be that as it may, - why, oh why, does she store her perfumes beside her enema? She whispers,

'When shall I employ thee? Oh, great one!' As Myfanwy addresses the small phial of perfume which she has placed on her dressing table, she continues to paint layer upon layer of glossy varnish onto her toenails.

Pilate cogitates ruefully, 'Mankind has subjugated womankind to his overburdening will for millennia – and, for the most part, no one complained. It is just my rotten luck that the historical epoch into which fate has placed me (to live and have my being), is the very one which sees the pussy turn into a bulldog!'

Myfanwy shuffles her legs around and grasps another toe; then pauses to wash down the chocolate and nuts in her gullet with some water, before reciting a famous nursery rhyme,

This little piggy went to market,
This little piggy stayed home

'You know, you really shouldn't delegate tasks in that way –
leastwise, not unless you intend to dismember your toes,' says
Pilate. Myfanwy flushes red hot, although she says nothing.
She raises her hand to her chest, and gulps awkwardly.

'Are you alright, my dearest?' asks her husband. Myfanwy
spreads her free hand out and waves it, as if hailing a taxi (or
attempting a karate chop). Evidently, she is not alright.
Suddenly she begins to cough, and showers her mirror with a
sweet, brown mucus. It is not a gentle cough, as might be
practised by the queen of England to convey uncertainty or
distaste. No! It is more like an explosion of artillery fire. And,
once begun, her coughing will not stop.

'There's-a-nut-in-my-airways!' she blurts out in broken
English. For once, she is not referring to her spouse. The
coughing gets louder.

'Help me!' she rasps.

'Shall I bring you a glass of water?' is his humble offering.
She slices the air with her open hand again. Pilate has not
moved. He is still comfortably tucked up under his blankets,
and strongly resents what he will have to do.

'Dar-bling! Kelp me!' she gasps. Pilate will have to leave his
warm bed. He tries to remain dignified as he walks over to his
wife and pats her on the back. In between her coughs, she
gives him detailed instructions. (She is good at multi-tasking.)

'No. Not there. Ah! Down a bit. No. Ah! Up a bit – and
across. Harder! Harder! Ah! Really give it to me! Ahhhh!' Pilate
is beating her now with his fist. Alas! His fist is too weak. This
is good news for his computer, but not for his wife.

'Bang me!' she shouts. Pilate obeys, but he secretly reserves
one hand for opening a particular drawer in the dressing table.
He slowly rummages around for a certain expensive artefact,
hidden there for emergencies. It is a gilt-edged hammer from
his distant youth. The hammer is top-heavy, and has been
fitted with an especially large metal head. His fingers freeze
around its handle.

'This will finish the job off – once and for all,' he thinks. For
a moment he feels a remarkable affinity with Sharon Stone
(aficionados of Hollywood movies will know what I mean); and
then he shudders, and withdraws his hand with celerity as his
wife shrieks,

'What are you doing? Stop that!'

'My hand is not strong enough,' he apologises meekly, 'and so I was looking for assistance.' Frankly, he is awestruck at how easily peace may dovetail into chaos.

'Harder! Bang me harder! Ahhhh ...!' she demands. He has given up on the gilt-edged solution, and is pummelling her with both fists now. Whatever will the neighbours think? Finally, Myfanwy expels the offending article from her windpipe - and grimaces. In point of fact, it is not a nut but a tiny piece of rubber; and, following a smooth trajectory from her mouth, it has reached the mirror and affixed itself to the phlegm which arrived there earlier (and which is still hanging from her reflection like a cobweb).

'Now see what you've made me do? With all of that exertion, I've strained my back. And all because you didn't respond fast enough when I asked you to come over to me.'

Pilate digs his fingers into her fatty tissues, in order to ease the pain. He finds that this also relieves his own stress.

'No. Not there. Up a bit.' He adjusts his kneading.

'No. Down a bit – and across. Aaaaarrrrrgh!' she coughs, and two droplets of reconstituted soup fly out of her mouth. Then, from under her flimsy chemise, there arises an audible sound of gurgling.

'Would you like me to administer some medicine?' asks Pilate, who has not the faintest idea what chemical relief is required. His wife throws back her head and opens her jaws as far as they will go, whilst signalling for Pilate to peer down her throat. And there, in that dark recess, largely hidden behind her tonsils, is the fingertip of a blue oven glove ....

'Are you alright?' he asks for the second time, whilst massaging her double chin.

'No, don't do *that*! Get a pair of forceps!' she screams.

'Oh! Lord, take pity on me,' says Pilate.

******

With his wife's breathing apparatus restored to normality, the Fates decide to squeeze in another quick dream. This time, the boss finds himself in a café. He asks the proprietor,

'Do you serve phials of rat poison?'

'Why, funny you should ask that, sir. The latest order of that particular stock item has just arrived this morning. And shall I prepare for you your usual - an Americano - laced with one shot or two?'

'Two – extra strength. I want to be sure.'

'Oh, sir! That will do for you, most certainly ... And the damage to your wallet shall be ... £10.50.'

'Pilot rummages around in his old school satchel: after the fashion of an elderly lady seeking an ever-disappearing purse in her multi-departmental handbag.'

'Paying with card today are we, sir?'

'No, with Mammon.' The dreamer revives himself before taking his own life.

Faithful in Head and Heart, if not in Private Part
(*An apposite epigram for Pilate, perhaps?*)

Mr Propotamous is still at home. The forceps have served their purpose, and his partner has been brought back from the brink. She depicts herself as a damsel in distress, and is rushing into the arms of a close neighbour. Once there, she intends to receive sympathy in abundance - and free lodging for the night. Her husband is clearly hopeful of her success in this venture. In fact, he is so confident of it that he has even requested the help of certain specialist services which must remain unspecified; although their existence is actually a matter of public record. Put simply, he orders a girl from an agency which goes by the esoteric name, "The Romanian Special Branch". Many have been called, but only one is chosen. Whether she is on the straight and narrow in business or in private affairs (which in her case are the same thing) we soon shall see. Pilate, being an honest man, has made ample payment in advance of services rendered. (In fact, his candid visitor insisted upon it). He has even tried "sweet talking" her, through the inclusion of an exception:

'You know, I tend to feel – present company excepted - that humans of a certain ilk are like dolls made from a composite of rubber and plastic.'

Since the present author has the rest of his story to tell, he is (apart from this peculiar comment) only recording the last few minutes of this most sequestered of all transactions: but he is confident in his ability to transport his readers, convincingly, to a place of his creating; and he feels that, once there, they will get the drift ...

Skilled in the equestrian arts, the service provider is riding her client like a horse, and digging her spurs into his love-handles, whilst eliciting from him the most porcine of grunts. Finally, she slides off (aided by the lubricant of mutual sweat), as if suddenly bored with a lack of responsiveness from her "stallion".

'Kiss me,' says Pilate. She plants a dry kiss on his cheek - that leaves a remnant of poisonous dye, yet bears not the fruit of pleasure. It is like a tulip bulb in the tundra, doomed to perish without rain or compost.

'No. On the lips.'

'I cannot. It is not possible,' she says solemnly.

'You know, my dear ... I feel this is in no way wrong ... for the closer we become, the more readily shall the taint of sinfulness which opened up our sexual congress, be wiped clean by wholesome affection.'

Pilate touches her rear end. She pushes his hand away. Pilate touches her there again.

'No, baby.'

Pilate touches her front end.

'No, not there either.' Pilate sighs, and reaches down to tickle her foot – and her foot gives him short shrift.

Pilate manoeuvres her torso on top of his, and she *wiggles* her toes, inducing nervous excitement in the sensitive organ of his skin which they brush against; and then, once more, she *wriggles* off him with ease. She explains to him,

'I cannot do these things, baby.' He touches her behind again.

'No, baby. No.'

'Well – what then?'

'Just *norrrrrrrrrrrmal*, baby.'

He is upset that he didn't read the "contract of employment" before embarking upon the task at hand, and he is upset that there even *could* be a contract of employment.

Eventually, they settle into a groove. Some light music is arranged by the host; and as the disk is caressed in ever-decreasing circles by the spindle, she plays with him – until her wrist begins to suffer from repetitive strain injury. Then she stops.

'I am not a robot,' she protests.

'Yes. A robot is what you are. You are my Romanian robot.'

'I am doing a course in interior decorating, and I have been typing all day,' she excuses her lacklustre persona and her limp wrist. Then she tries a different approach.

'I'm thirsty. Have you got anything to drink? A cola, perhaps?'

'I've got milk.' He looks sheepishly at her. Pilate would like to do some interior decorating of his own. He readies two digits of one hand just prior to insertion; and then stirs in a circular fashion, as if he is whipping double cream.

'Na. I don't like fingers. Something else.' (Pilate thinks to himself: 'What? My whole fist then?' But it is only a thought.) There is a pause. 'Tell me what you *really* want. Whisper your dream,' She murmurs. For a moment, they are like two naughty schoolchildren about to share a dirty secret in the playground. And then, before Pilate has time to answer, she pre-empts him, 'I haven't been trained in your special needs.' She holds his attention with her gaze, and tilts her face as she says this. And then, quite suddenly, she sits on the side of the bed and begins rolling her tights up.

'You're not going *already?*'

She switches on the ceiling light, made incandescent by the want of a lampshade.

'Switch off that light immediately! Have some respect while I'm still in my birthday suit!'

'I've had enough.'

'What do you mean: You've had enough? This isn't about what *you* want. It's about *me!*'

Mr Propotamous has booked the girl for an hour. So far, she has only proffered 35 minutes of service – and he feels short changed.

'She must have subtracted the time it took her to get here!' he thinks to himself. Meanwhile, she has become fully clothed and is on her way out.

'Hey! Don't turn your back on me when I'm talking to you. Turn around and face me this instant! You can't fool me that you've fulfilled the terms and conditions of your contract.'

She flees. Given the choice of two biological mechanisms, fight or flight, she has always preferred *flight*. In fact, the girl is receding from him so fast that it seems to him, if only for a moment, that she belongs to the past tense. And thus does Pilate speak unto the whore:

'Fly back into your cage, little birdie, – or there will be consequences!' The flabby and undressed Mr Propotamous sets off in hot pursuit, beckoning and calling out to her,

'I'm warning you … turn back now, or I'm reporting you to the ombudsman.' She has run across the landing and is approaching the foot of the stairs, pursued by the words: 'What did you say your name was? You can't pull the wool over my eyes. I *know* who you are. You're *Romanian*. And you won't get away with this!'

Labouring Towards the wee small hours

The director is back in the office again, having found it impossible to sleep. He is still in dire need of some catharsis, but life has offered him no respite. He imagines he is climbing to the summit of Mount Everest, but always sliding down to the foothills before he can reach first base.

The programmers are sustained by a diet of spaghetti code and stale pieces of bread. Some employees will stay in their Portakabins all night, although they are only paid a daily rate; and – like meerkats - each may take turns to sleep in snatches, whilst a colleague acts as sentinel. The long working day is a contingency Mr Propotamous is well pleased with. But he regrets his decision to participate personally in the systems development. Naturally, he is too proud to admit that he cannot cope, and he has done his kudos no favours by once being discovered sleep-walking in the middle of the night, as his staff sat in their Portakabins sniggering to themselves. They were grateful for some light entertainment after a long day in the sweat shop. Indeed, the word on the ground is,

'Just think, if we spiked his drink we'd send that deranged behaviour into overdrive.'

The director was a programmer in his former professional life. He murmurs to himself,

'I must have forgotten at what cost.'

He has, however, discovered how to handle apostrophes successfully, and feels like he has split the atom. The golden rule is, "Thou shalt not encompass a character string with any character which the string already contains - else the computer shall not know where said string ends."

Soon, he is running a program. He watches a little disc revolving, with almost schizophrenic absorption. He thinks, 'How like an exercise bike it is – for, in both cases, the wheels are turning even though you're not going anywhere.' He receives the message, "Estimated Time to completion: 3 minutes". He stares at the clock for a while, and then at the screen. Now he is told, "Estimated time to completion: 2 minutes". Soon after, he is joyfully informed, "Estimated time to completion: 1 minute". His heart fills with anticipation. Small things bring him great happiness. Outside, darkness is falling. But there is light at the end of this particular tunnel.

'Almost there,' he sighs. Again, he looks up to the clock on the wall, then back to the screen; and then up to the clock, where his eyes rest for a while, delaying the moment of fulfilment: like someone on his honeymoon, sublimating the consummation of a vow ... so that when it comes, it will be savoured even more. Finally, he can avert his eyes no longer, and glances screen-wards to be informed, "Estimated time to completion: 3 minutes."

He wonders if he is seeing things, and is reminded of British Rail's waiting times for the next train. He shuts his eyes, and opens them again ... only to see, "Estimated time to completion: 5 minutes."

He decides to while away the time by checking out some freeware report generator from the internet. He looks sceptically at the handsome claims of the advertisers. Apparently, it can produce results in every conceivable format: long lists with totals, graphs, bar charts, pie charts and, apparently, doughnuts ('whatever the hell they might be,' he grumbles to himself). He decides to click on pie charts – and gets the message, "Bake delicious pastries. Download hundreds of free recipes right now!"

Having made extensive use of his built-in mouse, Pilate is beset by windows from the operating system, entitled, "Can I help with anything?" And "Would you like to bake a cake?" And Pilate responds verbally,

'If I were in a less virtual world, I would, with so many windows being cast at me, be surrounded by dangerous fragments of glass.'

Next, our forlorn user searches for the HTML command to "throw a line". And, inadvertently, he summons up: "North

Water Tow Lines & Throw Lines", and a link to "Paddle Floats & Re-entry Aids". He alters his criteria, only to arrive at a webpage on "the lines and dimensions of a basketball court". Pilate continues to surf online, and reads,

'"Cortana is your digital agent. She'll help you get things done" ... *She* ...?' Oh, good heavens!'

'Tell me a strange place to visit,' insists Cortana – before adding, 'Did the dinosaurs have feathers?'

Pilate closes the webpage and grimaces. He opens up "Task Manager", and deletes the Cortana process. Upon the instant, "she" reappears. He tries once more, and once again she stubbornly returns. Then he remembers recent attempts to remove this feature altogether. Alas! Even "major surgery" has proved unsuccessful. At last, his own program finishes running with an error message. He is struggling again, and bombards his key member of staff with questions.

'Dmitri?' he calls. Dmitri enters.

'Yes.'

'Incorrect parameters in the call to native function concat.' His opposite number issues a world-weary sigh.

'I have bugs of my own at the moment ... and I have a "list of values" to create. Can we revisit your code later?' The director wears the face of a disappointed toddler. 'It's just syntax,' says Dmitri. 'Really no big deal. Examine what you are concatenating. It should all be alphanumeric.'

The director opens another conversation about a condition never being satisfied. Dmitri peers over his shoulder.

'It's never satisfied because you have typed "if (x = y)".'

'What's wrong with that?'

'A single equals sign will cause the condition to become an assignment. Therefore, x will be made equal to y. And as for any commands which follow, they will be performed anyway ... because the interpreter does not realize you have popped the question.' The director appears shell-shocked. He is wondering what he has got himself into. And thus does he formulate his defence,

'Really? Suppose I was in a restaurant, and was asked by a French waiter if I had enjoyed my meal, or if I would like to eat anything else; and I mistook his heavily-accented words? Would I not ask for clarification? Or would I simply spool the entire contents of my stomach onto the table cloth; and indicate that, despite entering his establishment like a "teacup pig", I would (without this expurgation) walk out like a "well-endowed, pregnant sow"?'

Dmitri feigns a snore, and rests one cheek upon the palm of his left hand ... before suddenly shaking his head and pretending to "come to" with a snort.

'And yet, amidst the flaws, there are marvels to behold ... witness, the preternatural power of a Virtual Private Server – whereby an alteration to its internal settings, causes all sent emails to cease displaying pictures they originally contained. What avian mother is this, who controls her young even after they have flown the nest?'

'I wasn't going to mention this,' says Dmitri, ignoring the outrageous comparisons, 'but as I am talking to you about bugs ... there is an error I found in the Accounting Routine ... the module you assigned to me the other day to approve, and hand over to the "live" area when I was done with it.' Dmitri describes the error.

'No, that certainly is not a bug. It's a *feature*,' says the director.

'I think not.'

'No. It all works. I should know. I programmed it myself,' is the rejoinder. 'We simply cannot afford to expend any more time on this module.'

'But ...'

'Just put it to bed. The client will do the testing for us. Having paid through the nose, you can depend on it!'

There is concern on Dmitri's face, as he remembers how the last person to correctly raise an issue like this got fired. But his face soon relaxes in contemplation, as he arrives at the following opinion: 'Pilate cannot afford to lose me'. Then he says,

'I have a very good manual on my desk. I wrote it myself. I have never had it officially published, so it is a little on the rough side, but it covers many issues you are encountering. You may borrow it if you wish.'

'I know that manual. I've seen it. And – no, I don't want to borrow it. It's gigantic, poorly punctuated and inscrutable ... a dreadful example of clerical abuse. Wading through it, I felt I was inside a medium more dense than custard.'

'It is the unabridged version – that is true. But you are working with a feature-rich language, which gives you a hundred and one ways of doing everything.'

'Yes - and none of them work!'

'Not so! Just surf the internet forums. Like a water-diviner, your stick is bound to go down on *something* useful, that will illuminate what is, at present, shrouded in darkness. Anyhow, we are all under pressure right now.'

'Don't worry, Dmitri. Your job is safe.'

'But is yours?'

Pilate stares at him in silence for a few seconds.

'What unearth do you mean by that?'

'Well, if everyone – spontaneously - were to arise and leave of their own volition ... what then?'

The boss trembles slightly, and disguises his tremor as a mild fit of the shivers.

'I say, it's a bit draughty in here. Is the heating on?'

******

On this particular evening, Dmitri is up to his eyebrows in onerous duties. He takes no respite - until the hour of nine is struck on a grandfather clock in a certain private room, and he requests leave to rest there for thirty minutes. This area is a retreat, and has been supplied for exhausted staff to rejuvenate themselves with a power nap. Permission is granted, and very soon he is thrust into an eccentric dream. He finds himself amongst an live audience readying themselves for an impressive lecture. He does not recognise the interior, and is sure that it forms no part of the warehouse in which he works; but, at a glance, he sees a handful of colleagues from The Perfect Launchpad. Then, upon closer inspection, the whole scene is revealed as fantastical. The physical bodies of those around him – like the loaves and fishes of the parable - have been cloned hundreds of times, such that a few faces are seen throughout the auditorium. He is holding a flyer in one hand, with his boss's face on the front - beneath which is the caption,

'We had to make up the numbers somehow; and I do not want you to be distracted by the presence of too many people. I command you, now, to gather data: all that you can eat. Read on, to discover our new methods in the field of creative accounting.' The director is standing on a rostrum. He has a lectern in front of him, supporting a loose-leaf manuscript which he is reading from. He is like a priest in his pulpit, who is facing his congregation in the most imperious way. Behind him, his image has been projected onto a vast screen, which magnifies every slight contraction of his facial muscles. He is delivering a speech on the subject of "the enemy within".

'And who, prey, *is* this enemy? Can any man or woman who is suitably informed provide an answer?' Dmitri puts up his hand, although he hardly knows why. It is as if he has been impelled by a tacit understanding that he *ought* to know what the answer is, - in spite of the fact that he does not, and despite a fear arising as a result of his impulse, causing him to cower even as he raises his arm. But he needn't have worried. No spotlight picks him out, nor does any young lady rush over to him with a speaker phone. And the director just carries on regardless.

'They are persistent. They are omnipresent. They are insidious.' Hereupon, the speaker begins to sound like a senior statesman, with an accent similar to that of Winston Churchill. 'They are stalwart, and yet we British are made of stronger stuff than they. Surely, I need not ask again, "Who are they?" - for you will have guessed by now. They are the bugs in our software. Mmmm.' Here, there is a crescendo on the word "software" just to ensure that no one falls asleep. And then he launches into some fine rhetoric, reminiscent of a much earlier (national) crisis:

'We shall fight them offline, on the intranet.
We shall fight them online, with the Lord of Hosts:
for the server shall be our staunch ally. Mmmm.
We shall fight on the beaches,
we shall fight on the landing grounds,
we shall fight in the fields and in the streets,
we shall fight in the hills;

we shall never surrender, and even if, which I do not for a moment believe, this Island or a large part of it were subjugated and starving, - then our noble friend, Dmitri, armed and guarded by the British Fleet, would carry on the struggle, until, in God's own good time, this menace is expunged from my software house forever.'

******

At that moment, there is a tap, tap, tap upon the door of the retreat, and Dmitri is awoken from his dream. It is the director, asking for help again.

'Good grief. Has half an hour gone by already?' asks Dmitri, rubbing his eyes and moving clumsily across the room to meet the principal. Pilate and Dmitri walk back to the open plan area from whence they came. All of a sudden, Pilate stops. Nearby, an Australian is typing rhythmically and crooning about a love that was never reciprocated. Two tears have stained his orange cheeks (brought on by the excessive consumption of carrots), and the keyboard is being caressed like a piano. His eyes are as red as raspberries, and a pathetic simper is settling upon his fish-thin lips.

'That fellow is always homesick,' says the director. 'He's been away from his family and friends for too long.'

'And – to think – the longed-for damsel is far away in Sydney. The poor fellow,' replies Dmitri.

The Australian begins to hum "Waltzing Matilda". He seems frozen in time; except that he is keeping the metre by cracking the joints in his fingers. With each cracking sound, the director frowns a little more sternly; and upon the sixth crack, the rhythm and blues are drowned out by the chiming of the grandfather clock, which has been conditioned to sound every thirty minutes.

'He must be driven by loyalty to the organisation – an attribute you value highly, I believe,' remarks Dmitri. The Australian varies his solo act, now whistling the melody through pouting lips, as if they formed an open hatch at the end of a hen coup – through which a dying bird might creep. (Perhaps the very "bird" he is serenading?)

'That infernal tune is getting on my nerves!' exclaims the director. 'If he feels so forlorn, why doesn't he just go home?'

'You recently extended his contract.'

'Did I? Oh, yes. So I did.' Pilate pauses for a second, and then continues, 'Well, if the issue should arise - I hope this Matilda woman is refused asylum. What is she? An economic migrant? We don't want any *terrorists*! ... Anyway, Dmitri, there's this database record ... you know the one.' (Dmitri does not know, but he can guess.) 'Do you recommend I update it?'

'If you like.' A few moments pass, during which the director sits down and applies himself to the task at hand, and Dmitri says, tentatively, 'I really must get on. I still have so much to do.' He turns and is on his way through the door - when his boss calls, almost apologetically, after him: 'Dmitri?' But Dmitri is gone. And so the director attempts to win back the attention of the chief programmer with a little intrigue:

'You'll never believe this, but I just tried to update the record – and it's disappeared.' An authoritative voice is heard from the next room:

'That'll probably be because the presentation of the record is contingent upon a field which you have just zapped!' Shortly afterwards, the director starts to protest at the computer rather loudly. Dmitri returns, wondering what all the fuss is about.

'Look! An HTTP 500 error.'

'Gosh! Don't ask me to diagnose that. It could mean practically anything,' responds the weary programmer. In an adjacent room, the tape units and humidifiers are humming like so many bee hives, and the technician (mindful of "super foods") momentarily wishes they really *were* hives – and full of honey.

'Look, I can't help you any more! I've already broken down a block of your code into two formats. One of these is "ready to go", and the other shall be supplied with essential values when it is run. At the moment of execution, you may imagine the passage of time has been reversed: with discrete sections of "Humpty Dumpty" drawn together into one functional unit, and given life in abundance. Of course, the situation must be differentiated from a real-life execution, when the spirit separates from the body ... never to communicate again.'

Pilate massages his temples.

'You know, Dmitri, earlier on I was told that my query is empty. How can a question be empty? Now, I understand that a reply may be vacuous, but ... then again, perhaps my very question is deemed unworthy of a reply?'

'There might be a stack overflow,' explains Dmitri. Pilate thinks of Sainsbury's, and puzzles over how a shelf can be both empty and overflowing at the same time.

'You misnamed the cursor,' says Dmitri. He emits a "passive aggressive" yawn. 'The *buffer* is overflowing, but the name you have specified for it is wrong.' Pilate stares into space for a couple of minutes, trying to grasp what he has been told, until his virtuous assistant explains:

'Your instruction is pointing to the wrong place. In fact, it is pointing to sweet F.A.!' The director seizes his sore head with both hands, and holds on to it tightly in order to prevent it from spinning upon its axis of multiple chins - and launching itself into the atmosphere.

Dmitri leaves, to apply himself once more to his own outstanding tasks, whilst the director continues his unremitting struggle. Every so often, his connection to the internet is lost.

'Pop!' says the computer unsociably, after disconnecting from the router for the third time. The noise is similar to what is produced by a kindergarten child, who presses his curved forefinger hard against the inner hollow of his cheek, before withdrawing it with great speed through tightly pursed lips.

'Oh! I do wish it wouldn't do that.' He clicks on the option to reconnect.

'Pop!' says the computer, again, after pausing for a few seconds to shake hands with the router.

'Great! It's back again.' Dmitri is listening to the fiasco from a safe distance, and shakes his head. Worse is to come. A little later, the connection is lost yet again. This time, the director is not merely querulous. He is angry. Nay, vengeful. He raps the keyboard with his knuckles, and then thumps the screen. Fortunately, this particular model is an old-fashioned desktop, and, in the course of its short life with Mr Propotamous, it has proved itself able to survive grievous bodily harm on more than one occasion. And now the screen is frozen. So the director applies his usual method. He switches the machine off, waits for 30 seconds, and then powers it up again. Shortly afterwards, he smiles.

'Ah, Success!' he says.

The Death of a Feline

Suddenly, the lower regions of the old warehouse are enlivened by mortal terror. There is a blood-curdling scream, issued at a pitch that may crack glasses as well as eardrums (assuming the old wives' tale to be correct).

'Oh, my God! Pia! Pia!' The source of this Edvoard Munch-like emission has attracted the attentions of both Mr Propotamous and his wife. Others can hear the distress signals, but they prefer to stay out of trouble. To Dmitri, the cry (whatever its cause) signifies the onset of a brief period of freedom. The misanthropist and his lady wife are on their feet and making haste to the source of the commotion; and the wind from the boss's corpulent frame disturbs the programmer's paperwork as the frame waddles swiftly by. The husband and wife have emerged from separate corners of the building, although they arrive at the appointed place almost simultaneously.

'She's been poisoned!' yells Gladys, holding the head of her beloved cat above an unsightly pool of vomit. 'Someone called me and I came as soon as I was able. Oh, God!' Gladys is suffering from hysteria, and her sorrow resolves itself into what might have been a perpetual wail - except that all things must come to an end.

Mr Propotamous would like to be presidential in his address, but somehow his words do not come out right:

'Surely not ... er ... why? Gladys, what is this vile mess which your animal has left on the carpet? Oh, too much ... too much. First Larry, and now this. I feel an urge augmenting within me, to call upon all of the Old Testament prophets, from Isaiah onwards.' He amplifies his voice for effect: 'How much more can a man *take*?' Then, speaking in the third person, he adds, 'And how come, when poor Larry's head was cracked upon the parquet floor, she never serenaded the event with this cacophony!'

Next, Myfanwy sallies forth with the words,

'You must crack a few eggs in order to make an omelette.' She cannot hear her husband, for two of her stubby little fingers have been inserted into her ears, in order to prevent them from being damaged by Gladys, whose wail is persisting right to the final atoms of her breath. At last, the dreadful noise subsides, and Myfanwy is able to remove her ear-waxy fingertips, and wipe them on her slacks. Both husband and wife are in denial.

'It was not *I*. Ah!' says Myfanwy.

'Well, it definitely wasn't *me*,' adds her husband.

'If not *I* nor *thou*, then whom could it have been?' rejoins Myfanwy.

'And, my dearest, if 'twas not *me* nor *yow*, then whom would you suggest?' (For no observable reason, the dialogue has become somewhat Elizabethan.)

Gladys is whimpering. Did they collaborate in this dastardly deed? Eventually, husband and wife come to a truce, which involves pointing a finger either at the grieving party or the dead party: wherever the blame most appropriately shall sit. First up, is the grieving party.

'Gladys, how well did you care for your cat?' asks Myfanwy.

'What?'

'You know, Gladys never took it out in the open air,' Myfanwy turns to her husband.

'What is that thick brown goo dripping from its mouth?' asks the director. 'A cat, unlike a canine or a capybara, is not ordinarily given to the impulses of the dung beetle.'

'It was force-fed chocolate,' protests Gladys. Her bottom lip is quivering.

'It committed suicide,' Mr Propotamous corrects her, passing all of the blame in the direction of the deceased. 'The evidence is indisputable.'

'Yes. Cats do not enjoy the taste of chocolate!' agrees Myfanwy. 'It must have known what it was doing.'

'It was *force-fed*, I tell you!'

'Don't raise your voice to my husband!' Myfanwy ejaculates.

'Nor to my wife!' adds her loyal partner. He pauses, and then his attitude softens.

'Gladys has had a hard time,' he concedes.

'Mmmm,' half-confirms Myfanwy.

After listening to Gladys for a little while longer, the couple manifest a complete change of heart. They begin to comfort her by stroking her back, and running their hands through her hair, before leaving her to her sorrows. What is their exit strategy? The boss takes the lead,

'Dear Gladys, so great is our sympathy for you, that our hearts will burst if we stay a moment longer. Perhaps there is yet some life left in the poor creature. Take her home with you. But first, I shall go and fetch my stethoscope. If you see Dmitri, be sure to tell him I shall be back later.'

******

The married couple depart at great speed before Gladys can delay them. Myfanwy expresses her relief:

'It's good we're leaving. She was beginning to get stroppy.'

The pair arrive back at their house, just in time for a phone call. Upon picking up the receiver, a text message is relayed from a pest who is selling something that neither of them want.

'Who is it?' asks the wife.

'Well! Would you believe it?' complains Mr Propotamous. 'That message was left three hours ago by a heckler. He even thought he was starting a conversation, "Good afternoon, sire. Joan Smoth wishes to conduct a short survey with you today ..." Honestly! Our species would be more efficient if it went back to hiring carrier pigeons.'

'With a name like Joan, he might be a cross-dresser. Or a hermaphrodite, perhaps?' suggests his wife.

'I think that's highly unlikely, dear. He's from Pakistan.'

'Never mind, darling,' answers Myfanwy in her most comforting voice. 'Let's enjoy a midnight *supper* – a normal repast comprising meat and two veg, followed by a homely *cuppa*.'

******

We must try to understand events from their perspective. They have had an exhausting few hours. To recapitulate, there was the near-choking of Myfanwy by the oven glove - and the period of yelling which ensued; followed by the near-crossing of the River Rubicon by Pilate ... from sociopath to actual murderer, via a gilded hammer; before Pilate finally settled upon the safe side of that fabled river. And there were hard lessons to be learned about the art of computer programming; and, finally, to round it all off, there was the overpowering reaction of Gladys to the death of her feline – which had to be witnessed to be believed. Now, all the pair want is to snuggle up to each other on the sofa, whilst cooing false sighs of gratification; and to watch a recording of their second favourite Reality TV show, "Brand New: Always Blubbering and full of Humbug" - an event which marks the blossoming of our two "Dramatis personae" into the most elaborate flower of their weirdness.

Three hours pass. Pilate is back in the office again, and speaking with Dmitri. The inept boss has grown as weary of asking questions, as Dmitri has of answering them. And so the chief programmer lightens the mood with a few choice words,

'A colleague mentioned Shylock's name to me (just in passing) the other day. He knows you and your wife are a cultured couple: and fond of Shakespeare, I'll warrant. And so he has left an unusual gift for you in the other room.'

Dmitri makes himself scarce and Pilate remembers a conversation he once had with his wife. At the time, she was reading a book about Medieval history, and she proposed that it might be possible to be so absorbed in a book, that its contents become more real than life itself.

'In fact,' she theorised, 'I even wonder if such an absorption may be passed on, so as to invoke a dream-like state in some other who is close to the one who is reading: as if that significant other were a fly caught in a kind of gossamer.'

'Surely not me?' he wonders.

Mr Propotamous begins to "surf the net", and mouths his opinion quietly about "some elaborate conspiracy". He even paraphrases an online request which he has just received:

'We value your privacy. Therefore, will you please comply with our wishes to gather data about you – so that we may bombard you with inappropriate and unwanted advertising? Yes or No.'

Pilate responds with "No" – and, for a while, the computer clams up like a stroppy teenager.

He is beginning to feel drowsy, and commands himself to maintain his wakefulness with strong ground coffee, before murmuring another complaint about "that infernal waltzing song" emanating from the next room. The objects around him appear tremulous, like petals in a breeze, and on his laptop screen he "minimises" the window displaying the code he has been working on. He seeks some light relief from his unsettling state of mind, by clicking on "Now Trending"; and moans softly to himself about technologists poisoning the language. He notices that the "trendiest" video features someone whom he does not like at all (although it may just be an actor in a fantasy). His stomach is churning, as if it were a vat with globules of cottage cheese. The person featured has bright pink hair, and tends to follow his own "path of least resistance". This individual is seen emerging, - with furtive, sensual glances left and right, - from a mortuary; pausing, for a moment, in the video-camera's "line of fire". And then the scene cuts to the front gates of the Clink Prison, with this vilified character reciting a twisted variation of a catch phrase that was formerly a half-rhyme (made famous by a television campaign on road safety many moons ago), 'clunk, clink, every trip'.

'I thought that man was a *goner*,' he mutters.

He moves the space bar down, and there – in the lower right-hand corner – is an unsolicited advertisement.

'Dmitri, I don't feel at all well. Dmitri, I .... Dmitri?' For some reason, Dmitri is no longer at his beck and call; and his dead in-laws are assembling in the online commercial, in readiness for their cameo roles.

'Well, I never!' he exclaims. 'Dmitri, come and have a look at this.'

One of them – a woman - speaks, and the zoom lens of the camera is employed for a closer inspection: 'I had always thought of myself as a healthy individual. And then, one day, I began to feel queasy. I couldn't believe it when I was diagnosed with a death-inducing illness.' Following her lead, each of the other voices are heard, as the camera moves slowly across the row of faces ...

'And I could not believe it, either, when a mercury filling became separated from one of my teeth and lodged itself in my gullet: thereby emptying my cup of life.' The second voice is faintly ironic, and is reinforced by a "special needs smile", which is brightened by polished dentures.

'Nor I, when all activity within my seat of consciousness became a game of two halves,' offers another, whose head has been split open like a coconut.

'Nor I, with ocean water on my lungs.'

'Nor I, when I was crushed by disappointment.' The speaker of this line holds up a photograph of her conservatory, with her mortal remains buried beneath it. 'My body was retrieved ... and, after a fattening period of gaseous decay, I put on my "wooden jacket" and exploded.'

The zoom lens draws back and takes in the whole family of unfortunates once more, as they nod in unison. The commercial now introduces a voice-over: 'One in three people will be affected by death at some point in their lives'.

Finally, the presentation is rounded off with all of the ghoulish players speaking with one voice:

'On our own, we can do nothing.' They join hands and look steadfastly into the camera. (Horror of horrors! Mr Propotamous feels that he is being scrutinised.) 'But if we stand firm, then together we can beat death.' A sickly sweet folk melody is initiated in the background, as the faces slowly turn sallow. Their flesh putrefies into an oozy, semi-liquid state; and drips off their bones like hollandaise sauce mixed with raspberry jelly. Parts of their skulls are exposed, and bluebottles hover close to their lips, - just catching the light in a way that would have been poetic way had they been butterflies, – before those self-same lips curve into a series of lugubrious grins ... and the virtual window closes.

'Thank *dog* for that!' Pilate blurts out, unaware of his choice of deity. But his torment is not over. He feels himself drawn inexorably towards the computer screen, and so he types a "tilde" in the search box, and focusses his eyes on this character in an attempt to retain his hold upon reality. Momentarily, he looks away, and an after-image of that symbol hovers several feet in front of him. Meanwhile, the lyric in the next room has mutated into "Waltzing Tilde"; and the after-image of the tilde metamorphoses into, of all things, a Moroccan belly-dancer. In this shape, he recognises the figure of his exotic hairdresser. He says to him,

'Sir! I implore you. Will you cease that infernal dancing before you make me retch!'

On this occasion, and for the purpose of his dance, the Moroccan, alias "Charlene" (who – you will recall – is in the process of altering his gender), has chosen to dress as a page boy. He wears a pair of shorts that are very short indeed, and that would hardly befit a man outside the walls of his private dwelling (even in the height of Summer). As he summons the boss for a haircut, Pilate rises to his feet - and watches the strange character tip-toe towards the door. Pilate is grasping at straws as he proclaims aloud,

'I knew I was due to have this haircut. Hairdressing often occurs on site at my behest, and this is (it really *is*) the official company barber. And yet I feel most out of sorts. Perhaps a recent offering from the sarnie lady was tinctured with a dose of something ... or, possibly, a foreign body found its way into my teabag?'

'Now, would I do that to you, sir?' asks the hairdresser.

'No. *You* wouldn't.'

In this trance-like state, Pilate feels that the path to sanity lies not in questioning the scenario, however bizarre, but in accommodating it. He dusts himself down, shakes his head, and staggers after his hairdresser, who has exited through the doorway and is bypassing a waiting area laid aside for interviewees. As Pilate moves in his wake, he cannot help noticing a large shadowy pink object, suspended - by a series of hooks - over a little-used desk by the opposite wall. The hooks are on the ends of wires tethered to large nails - that appear to have been hammered into the stippled ceiling with great force. How could such an action have passed unnoticed? And the pink pendant? It is an entire loin of pork, fresh from the butchers and with a note stapled to it. There is blood trickling from the incision made by the staple, which has smeared and elongated some words written in blue ink on the note; and, acting like a natural dye, it has made them purple. And yet they are in capital letters so huge that they cannot fail to grab Pilate's attention, even from a few feet away:

'From all of the software development team ... Your pound of flesh, as requested.'

'That bloody piece of carcass weighs far more than a pound, I'll warrant!' comments Pilate, who derives comfort from verbalizing irrelevancies. He is out of kilter, and attempts to normalize the situation by emulating the body language of his companion. To this end he balances, precariously, upon the ball of one foot (like Marcel Marceau, without a ball), and points with his index finger at the incongruous article, hanging - like a condemned child - from the ceiling. What else can he do? And as he assumes the aspect of a dandy, he poses the following non-technical question,

'Why didn't they just put it in the fridge?'

To this, Charlene obligingly replies,

'Perhaps they confused it for a partridge - and wished to suspend it there until the first infestation of maggots.'

Soon, they arrive at a tiny room adjacent to the Gent's Toilets. It is fed by the same water closet as the public conveniences themselves, even though it has been installed to fulfil a very different function. This tiny room is the official barber's shop, where employees (like it or not) will lose their beards and their locks; and, generally, be groomed to a standard that the acknowledged emperor of software houses, Ross Perot, would approve of.

'Well! As I say - I knew I was having a haircut this afternoon, but I had quite forgotten when, exactly, you were coming.' The barber breezes past this issue, inviting Pilate to make himself comfortable in a swivel chair - and to insert his hind brain into the sink (protected by its cranium, of course). Then the artisan applies his trade.

'Now, sir. What will it be? A wash and trim, perhaps?'

'Well, it's always going to be a trim, isn't it?' is the gruff reply. The main man is starting to feel himself again.

'Why ... sir, if a trim displeases you, I will merely "style" it. However, it is usual to receive an "LTRIM" or an "RTRIM".' The able barber shows him pictures of customers with their hair exclusively on the right or left side of their heads.

'Why would I want my hair cut on one side of my head, and not the other?'

'Why, indeed, sir? For I do keep telling the more – shall we say? – discriminating clients, that an LTRIM or an RTRIM might imply (untruthfully, of course) that half of the underlying head is empty. Tread with caution. That is my rule of thumb: for, like Alice, you never can tell what the looking-glass will report back to you.'

'Ha! Ha! Quite the humorist, aren't you? If I was half empty-headed, my quotient of cognition would leave me unable to make any sense of my own reflection, anyway. Indeed, if I were so poorly endowed, I doubt I would even care,' Pilate philosophises in a matter-of-fact way. 'But you should not make unfounded assumptions.' And here, he attempts to consummate his thoughts with a well-worn phrase: 'Never forget, grass will not grow on a busy street.'

'Ah. But what happens underneath the street? For the seat of your consciousness is, after all, beneath your skin – and not above it. Furthermore,' he clears his throat with a sudden rasp, 'were you aware that the Paris sewers, in their Machiavellian twists and turns, reflect to the last iota (or so I am told) the infrastructure of the thoroughfares above ... but, of course, your brain is utterly unlike the Paris sewers.' The barber notices that Pilate's complexion has grown as flushed as the skewered slab of meat hitherto described.

'And your point is ....?' he asks.

'My point is, that there is not the remotest positive correlation between your cognition and your crown of hair. And so, I wonder, – could there be an inverse correlation? Then, in order to retain your capacious mind, you must needs be accepting of a bald pate: in which case you will want a "TRUNC" (or truncation), removing *all* of your hair.' The speaker touches himself between his legs. He is noticeably effeminate, and loves the art of innuendo.

'I hope that *sir* is putting a little aside in his time of plenty? Of late, I have come by an investment vehicle, perfectly designed for my *passive* income in those "twilight years",' he says with a twinkle in his eye. Pilate notices he is wearing a T-shirt, with the following motif stitched into it, "Additional plug-ins are required for this page". And, as if that is not enough, the page boy lookalike points to it now and gives the director a saucy wink.

'What *are* you on about, you clown?'

His companion pauses to consider ...

'You know, the tiny brooks of human difference are flowing into each other. Soon, every fish shall occupy the main stream.'

The boss's companion imagines himself as part of a cartoon. He points to his head and, in one fluid gesture, draws a speech bubble in the air, and (within it) the following words:

'All camaraderie is gratefully received. But a plug-in is required to display this content.'

The director wishes that once this catamite has finished with his hair, he would lose all power of expression and disintegrate back into the tilde from whence he came. Just as Pilate entertains this thought, he notices the hairdresser staring listlessly at him.

'Don't look at me like that,' says Pilate. 'I am not supplying any plug-ins, be it for you or for anyone else. I am simply paying you for washing, cutting and dressing my "oozy locks" ... to quote Milton. And that, my good man, is that.' (But in a moment, a fiendish idea will occur to him.)

'And when I have shaved your hair off,' pursues the hairdresser, 'would you like me to pad it out for you. You know you have a meeting to attend, and it is important that you look your best.' (The director creases his forehead into a frown.) 'Perhaps I should set you up with an L-PAD - or will it be an RRRRRRR-PAD?'

'Don't growl at me!' the director responds with ire. 'And how can you add volume to my hair after removing it? You daft ape.'

'Well ...'

'Well?'

'I could re-fashion the removed follicles into a *toupée* – which would be professionally blow-waved to achieve the effect of padding.'

'And Lord knows what the point of *that* would be! Look. I'll have a *semi-trim* with *no padding* ... and I'll have it in double quick time – before you complete your transfiguration into Charlene. Is that clear enough for you? Just throw the old hair into the trash can! Good heavens, the thin and speechless air has more substance than your verbal offerings. Now, just get on with my humble wash and cut.' Then, quite without precedent, our anti-hero becomes friendlier (and more sly):

'You know, my wife wears a very unusual perfume these days.'

'Yea?'

'Yes. She does. It might be just your cup of tea. In fact, you might even like *her* as well.' The hairdresser interposes,

'Now, then. I just have to explain something to you, before I get underway. The only characters you stand to lose in the cutting process are rooted in your scalp, and, as such, will be randomly selected and have no substantive life once separated from it.'

'Really! This peculiar man is getting off on personifying the individual strands of my hair, - as if they are sentient beings. Whatever will he think of next? Hair follicle heaven, perhaps?' Pilate is like an actor in a restoration comedy, addressing some alter-ego or an imaginary audience. (But I suppose my readers are his audience, and I would hope you are not imaginary.)

'Sir, just remember. We are qualified to trim leading or trailing spaces.'

'Only spaces? So you are not actually *qualified* to give me a haircut at all?'

'Shhhh! Don't *spread it around*! My reputation will be compromised. Now you are *in situ*, just relax. I can do the business without having letters after my name!' The man sets about washing the director's hair. A short while later, as he is cutting it, he opens the dialogue again:

'Computers are such powerful devices.'

'Yes, and it would be marvellous to know what goes on inside them,' concedes the director. 'Personally, I haven't the faintest idea. But keep that one under your hat. I can't have my underlings believing that I know less than they do.'

'So, we have each shared a secret today. Our weaknesses are revealed. And you never know your luck. Maybe you are about to discover something about these mysterious devices?' The director nods his assent, and considers his next move. A few minutes pass, with no sound except that of the hair-clippers. After this, a towel slips from his shoulders; his head and neck are rubbed down to remove any residual strands of hair; and his locks are swiftly spruced up with an aromatic gel. At last! The customer rises, and service has been rendered. He says,

'As you have given me a service that I was in need of, I shall return your kindness in equal measure and supply *you* with something that you lack.' Contemplating the message on the hairdresser's clothing, he guides his oddball companion to an electrical appliance at the bottom of the wall - a standard three-aperture socket, in fact, - which is ready for the next plug-in. He nods, as the innocently-led party simply points and stares at it – like a figure from the Elgin Marbles ... or someone near Vesuvius in AD79, identifying the source of his doom, and frozen in time by solidified lava.

'Oh, my sincerest thanks,' is the unwitting reply. 'I must say, I *am* starting to flag a little. When you go, I may well recharge my batteries. But, just before we part, may I interest you with another service we have on offer today?' After a moment's hesitation, the speaker behaves like all good salesmen, and assumes silence to indicate agreement. 'You know, I have a beautician in my practice who also has surgical skills. She can perform a "nip and tuck", and I have another employee who can pull teeth.'

'You have? Good grief, that is decidedly odd.'

'Not at all ... barber-surgeons were common in the middle ages. Anyway, where was I? Ah, yes. The beautician refers to this other service as her *LPAD and RPAD mammaries*. She'll plump up, with silicon, the left and right breasts of your woe-man,' he explains, expressing the noun with all of the emphasis and sensitivity which a Negro might give to it. 'In fact, the appendages could be enlarged with silicon-filled letters. Then, when a horny man such as yourself feels it is time, he can tear her bra off and *read the writing on the wall* - so to speak. In fact, if you have the letters filled with hot air instead of silicon, your lovely wife may, at some later date (and at her own convenience), employ an LTRIM and an RTRIM to shrink them back to their former sizes.'

'Well. Fancy that? Anyway, thanks very much - but my wife's bosoms are big enough already.'

PART THE FOURTH: THE USURPER

A Second Meeting

The director leaves the in-house hair salon and moves slowly and cautiously to the board room. As he approaches, he notices the rise and fall of human voices.

'I am surprised I scheduled another meeting so soon. It is most atypical of me! And I am irked that it has commenced in my absence.' He takes a draught of air into his lungs, and opens the door. What a great surprise – nay, horror, - awaits him! Someone else is sitting in his place. It is the well-tempered, fatigued and heavily put-upon technical maestro, whom he has a habit of pestering. And what is more, the man is dressed in the finery of a Roman Caesar – with a laurel crown upon his head, and full regalia. Such a sight must give one pause. Even stranger than this, Dmitri (for it is he) is utterly absorbed by a notebook, - the contents of which elicit a range of expressions upon his countenance, like light and shade rolling through a volatile landscape. Meanwhile, his face is being heavily applied with make-up by two assistants in front of a small, hand-held mirror. Pilate watches him, as his lips move quickly and silently for effect; whilst seated all around are enthusiastic minions, waiting upon tenterhooks to hear "their master's voice". And yet it is not *this* voice which they eventually do hear – but rather the voice of Pilate's accountant, who is reading from some loose leaves of a printed manuscript.

The *Master of Ceremonies* has a bucket beside him, labelled "spittoon", into which he frequently coughs and spits – whenever he wishes to "raise an exception" to what he hears. Prior to each green emission, Dmitri takes a sip from a glass of water, and swills it around his mouth. It is as if the sole purpose of sipping is not to clear his pallet but to sample some new wine – which he must never swallow. There are Dulux paint stains on the outside of the bucket, indicating that it has seen nobler days. Pilate is reminded of the disgusting habit adopted by the ancient Romans of eating too much, and then vomiting to make room in their stomachs for the next course. Indeed, the illustrious technician is masticating vigorously after every line that is read aloud by the accountant. As he does so, he holds aloft his notebook (containing a transcript of the spoken words). With the approach of his visitor, the make-up *artistes* move away – and he orchestrates a break in the sequence of events.

'Good afternoon, Mr Propotamous. We have been waiting for you; although, I must confess, I was beginning to wonder if you would ever show up. I am the President of this corporation, and known as "the Interpreter". We are garnered here, today, like precious grain, to hold the chaff of your programs up to the purest light of scrutiny.' The shadows around the director's eyes darken, but Dmitri is undeterred and sharpens his tongue,

'I must chastise you for being late. How very *dare* you! And (unless I should forget) this may be the last time I refer to you formerly as "Mr Propotamous".' His voice softens. 'For the time being, I feel bound to proceed with a modicum of politeness. Yet, as the day draws on, my mood may change. Now, then, what is next up ...?' A colleague furnishes him with some information:

'Article 1.1 of the case for the prosecution – that the accused creates unreasonable in-house coding and documentation standards for everyone else to follow, and then fails to follow them himself. In fact, he is forever going off at a tangent. He should swallow his conceit, and attend to the formalities of senior management. Or is that article 2.1?'

Mr Scripting-Lang comes to the assistance:

'No. Article 2.1 is zat he charges his clients var too much and pays his staff var too little.'

'And what has the accountant-come-financial advisor to say for himself ... having achieved nothing remarkable, except for inveigling his odd self into his master's affections?' Dmitri is seething, and softly pats the portly stomach of that gentleman, adding: 'I hardly know how to address you. Shall I call you "Pork Belly" as a mark of irony – for, I cannot help observing, the pampered upper half of your anatomy (which your greedy appetite has been increasing) looks unwieldy, perched upon the streamlined lower half. Do I behold a pig or a stick insect? Or the strangest cross within nature, incorporating both?' The target of his attack smiles broadly, feeling that to complain would be to invite more insults. Sadly, he invites them anyway, for his persecutor feels obliged to add,

'This "object" we behold has a face which is somewhat atavistic. Its unwholesome features may be likened to those of "Java Man" - which is another suitable name for him, don't you think?'

The accountant shrugs feebly, while the director puts his head in his hands and asks, 'What is happening to me?' - and then says plaintively, 'My mind is poisoned.'

'Must be,' replies a flat, dull echo, though he knows not from whence it comes. He has heard of hypnagogic dreams, and wonders if the words he hears do not come from the fantastical place where he presently finds himself; but, rather, from the *ordinary* place from whence he came.

'Excuse me. May I just interrupt your train of thought, and, after you alight upon the platform of reality, relegate you to making the coffee?' asks Dmitri. Pilate points to himself and wears a question upon his crinkled brow.

'Oh! How far has this man fallen? From the zenith to the nadir!' speaks the voice with no source.

'I'll have some waffle with my coffee,' says Dmitri. He sees Pilate stutter (in a failed attempt to hold forth), and he adds, 'In fact, I do believe that our very own Propotamous is, at this moment, about to whip up some waffle for us with his mischievous tongue.'

Pilate casts his eyes around him. All of the office staff are present, with their children. Curiously, the cleaner, Gladys, is there too. She has brought her daughters - including the tinniest one who is called Dot. What are they doing in a rarefied meeting held for I.T. specialists? The littlest girl has been sitting motionless, but now makes reference to her favourite board game:

'Mis-ter Pro-pot-a-mous cannot climb society's ladder any more, and so he must slide down the snake. Hissssssssssss!'

'Why don't you go and pleasure yourself for a while,' says Gladys – unaware of her *faux pas*. Dot was actually deriving pleasure from speaking her choice words prior to her mother's intervention; and now she stomps out of the room in an infantile temper, slamming the door behind her. Dmitri raises his nose into the air and sniffs. Then, like an heir elect, he turns to his fallen emperor.

'Now, where is my promised coffee? I am not picking up the scent. My tongue is thwarted by sparse employment, and is straining at the leash … whilst my dry throat is rasping, and my thirst is far from slaked.' For a while Pilate has been frightened into submission; but at last he speaks up with words very similar to those of that memorable tyrant, Saddam Hussein, when, at the moment of being accused of crimes against humanity, confronted the prosecution thus:

'You speak of a legal case, and of articles. This is nothing but a kangaroo court. I do not accept its judicial authority. Where is the *jury*? And my *defence* – where are *they*?'

'You foolish man,' Dmitri reprimands him. 'Do you not realise that, formerly, in a court of the assizes, the magistrate presided over the vast majority of cases, without either of these adjuncts? And, even today, in the Youth or Magistrate's Court, there is no jury. A little humility would not go amiss. Nor a little awareness of our shared history!'

Dmitri curls his lips seditiously - like an alpaca, readying itself to spray a mouthful of virulent saliva in whatever direction it pleases. But at the point of critical mass, he restrains himself and swallows.

With trembling hand, Pilate scoops two spoonfuls from a tin of "real coffee" (prepared earlier) into an attendant beaker, labelled *Cafetière*, and hot water is applied from an adjacent pot. He stirs; and Myfanwy (who is here too) gazes longingly - as he works the plunger with a firm hand. When the process is complete, Pilate decants the steaming beverage, and peers into his own cup. He adds cream to the mixture, and watches it curl round and round - as if outlining the details of some far-off galaxy.

'What a medley of delicious colours!' Pilate exclaims, in an attempt to lighten the atmosphere.

'Not so. It is either black or white – or possibly brown. To refer to it as being "coloured" is disrespectful,' states one of his mixed-race employees.

'Its appearance has been elevated by a thick, white cream,' Pilate defends himself.

'Yes, but it has received its flavour – nay, its very essence, – from those rich, dark beans which I was recently grinding for you!'

The final argument is persuasive, and Pilate falls silent.

Dmitri cracks a dry joke, and the oppressed masses titter faintly. The subjects know only to laugh when their "sovereign" laughs; and, generally, to calibrate their responses so as to be a mirror image of his own – much as they would have done in empire days, or in the reign of Pilate before he was (apparently) deposed.

Dmitri introduces a new topic, as if reading from a dossier, 'Article 3.1. The persecution of the powerless.'

'Isn't that Article 3.2?' asks the German, Mr Scripting-Lang.

'Shhhhhh! Shut it!' Dmitri exclaims. 'Article 3.1. And the first plaintiff for this case is Gladys, who has lately lost her cat, murdered by some foul hand. But was this feline not observed earlier, kipping in the kitchen sink beside the sunniest window in the building?'

'Oh!' says Gladys. 'If only it were so, t'would be marvellous in our eyes.'

******

An index appears, taking the form of a conventional Edwardian city gent, in tuxedo and bowler hat.

'What about me, then?'

'What *about* you?' asks Dmitri.

'I am an index, and – properly honed – I can expedite your fact finding; so if ensconced within a legal database, you may have all of the articles for prosecution immediately to hand.'

'Indexes are only for dictionaries and encyclopedias!' says Myfanwy.

'Oh! I think not.'

Once more, Pilate glances around him. He is full of dismay. Everything has lost its point of reference. Besides himself, the persons in the room are purely representational. They are standing in for characters on the keyboard, or for various programmatic functions. Even a certain invalid who has, in the past, assisted Gladys in the staff canteen, - appears with her usual deformity greatly exaggerated. Her body has been twisted into the shape of a triangle, and part of her spine is sticking out of her back, - thereby emulating the *less than* sign, which is sometimes used to cordon off little sections of obscure code. And in those cases where the purpose to be manifest is too challenging for either the known forces of nature – or, indeed, the supernatural - to invest with a physical form, the characters wear jerseys, embroidered with identifying marks like advertising logos. These include a chevron, a hash, a dollar, an apostrophe, a colon and a space bar. And yet, in other respects, many of those present are apparelled in their "Sunday best", as if in readiness for a ball.

'I could introduce you to *all* of the characters around you, one by one,' says Dmitri, considerately. 'But, in reality, they are already known to you. And so ... to the apologies. Chief among these is one I have received from our new Technical Support Person, of whom I have this to report ... After long hours of work and training, and all at great cost to his social life, he became forlorn and depressed. He saw his doctor, who referred him to the locum consultant in genetics – so that he might receive some useful tests. Perhaps this bout of neuroticism was not down to nurture, but nature? Then it would be nothing more than a birth defect. After a long battery of tests, the clinician said there was nothing he could do. This patient shares 44% of his genes with *drosophila*, the famous fruit fly; and a high-flown consultant can think of better ways in which to spend his days, than improving the lot of some jumped-up fruit fly! Now, this software labourer is a man of pride, a man who exults in the far reaches of the human intellect. Can you even conceive of the impact that such a shocking revelation will have had upon him? I tell you, you cannot. He became so crestfallen, that he made an attempt on his own life; but he was rescued just in the nick of time – and thank heaven for it, since his attempt is commonly known in the trade as "a cry for help". So a termination of his life would have been a most unfortunate outcome.'

'Exponents in the art of suicide are such time-wasters!' Pilate thinks to himself, as Dmitri continues,

'Thenceforth, he was prevailed upon by friends to seek a second opinion. Now, this second expert put his mind at rest. He informed him that when *he* had had his *own* genome analysed, it also shared 44% of its genetic material with *drosophila*; and (worse still) about half of its genetic heritage with a banana.'

Several persons in the room begin to discuss the matter among themselves, and one of them wishes to ask, 'Is that just any banana, or a particular one?' but he is drowned out by another voice ...

'How utterly tragic! It is shame – I say, a *crying shame* - that the first practitioner did not reveal that we *all* share the same percentages of our genes with that fly, and with said fruit.'

'Yes. And I have it on good authority that the family is suing the doctor for, and I quote, "a general breach of his responsibilities, involving an extreme lack of sensitivity in the department of emotive information, - which was released too swiftly to be assimilated, without the functional breakdown of the assimilator occurring as a direct consequence ..."'

All who are in the room nod glumly, and remark upon how awesome - how truly awesome - must have been the depression which their colleague was suffering from; whilst Pilate is considering how odd - how truly odd - is the situation that he finds himself in, and how far beyond all precedent is this conversation. Indeed, he is wondering if he has been thrust, head first, into a cartoon; for everyone he knows within the organisation is here, and yet ... altered somewhat.

'Please note these curvaceous cuties,' says Dmitri, diverting Pilate's attention to the two older daughters of Gladys. 'I think you have been introduced already. No?' The two dance into the centre of the room, like athletic gymnasts. They are under-developed for their age in height and build, but over-developed in suppleness. As such, they are able to twist themselves into any shape, - and have chosen the shape of curly brackets, which, in modern computer languages, mark the beginning and end of commands to be executed upon the fulfilment of a condition. They explain ...

'We were working through a demanding routine earlier this afternoon, when suddenly we contorted ourselves into the oddest of objects. Upon achieving the wished-for conformation, we discovered that our bodies had belligerently packed up, and refused to return to their original shapes.'

'And there is no cure for this problem?' asks Pilate, barely believing what he has just heard; to which the cook and cleaner (and mother of the two) replies,

'Not so fast ... there is a minor palliative ... if they get sick and depressed ... I have plans to bake the sweetest of cakes, infused with garlic and linctus and evening primrose oil, to stave off the forthcoming winter blues – along with the germs which shall cling to them during the months of cold and shadows.'

'But they haven't caught the flu,' says Pilate.

'And who else do we have?' asks Dmitri theatrically, opening his hands and gesturing to the floor. 'Ah! We have your wife ...' Myfanwy nods. She is dressed rather frumpishly in a thick woollen jumper and a colourful 1950s hat, both tailored for a windy day by the sea; combined with a pair of thick, horn-rimmed glasses perched on the end of her supersized nose (enlarged, perhaps, by a tendency to sniff out technicalities which are way beyond her ken). She also has high-heeled shoes upon her feet – which are a fashion statement in stuffy offices; and wrapped tightly around her private quarters is a very short and racy mini-skirt, which she wore as a teenager at her first discotheque, and which barely fitted her even then.

'And we have our COBOL compiler.' Dmitri points at the compiler directly, with his index finger just two inches from the man's nose. 'Now, don't be shy. Say "Hello" to him.' Pilate's eyes alight upon an ageing man with "salt and pepper" hair, and a distressed look on his face. The fellow is seated by himself, counting his pennies like Bob Cratchet in A Christmas Carol. He is rueing the fact that he has been laid off work ... and that he can no longer support his family.

'Shortly after I came of age, everyone wanted to use me. Now, nobody cares! Oh, my! Oh, my! My very creditable services, replaced by this bunch of weirdos!' he exclaims.

'Well, I know I've let a few people go, but – I must say - I wasn't aware that I had ever axed a compiler ... or recruited one for that matter,' says Pilate.

'Oh! But you have – albeit some time ago.'

******

It is clear that everyone is experiencing a fear of unemployment. The German, Mr Scripting-Lang, has a fetching look of sadness on his face. His physique has also been strangely exaggerated. With his prominent jaw, his rectangular head, and his broad and muscular neck, he refers to himself, in a self-deprecating way, as "Square Brackets".

'Ah! See how he pines away,' says Dmitri.

'Ze last director took such good care of me, but Dmitri is utterly ruthless.'

'Nonsense!' says Dmitri. 'You are alive, and you are still here, are you not?'

'He has no appreciation. If there ist not zom recourse to justice, I shall 'av to remove my services altogezer!'

'Well. Remove them then. See if I care.'

'You ze what I mean?' Mr Scripting-Lang explains. 'A stance of zavage indifference, is vaht I call it!'

Dmitri points skywards, as if the Almighty will be his judge; and he argues,

'This is a democracy. It is all about supply and demand; and, I'm sorry to say, your services (whilst they remain in supply) are no longer in demand.' "Square Brackets" begins to cry.

'Mind how you go, or you vill all be unemployed soon,' he blubbers through a mixture of tears and saliva. 'You see vat happened to me, transferred to ze scrapheap before I have had ze pleasure of rendering maximum performance; or zhese others' (he spreads forth his hands) 'ze pleasure of receiving it!' He turns to Pilate, who is hoping for camaraderie (since he is feeling like an outcast himself); and Pilate pats him reassuringly on the shoulder, whilst issuing those anodyne words of solace which have been used, time immemorial, in moments of terrible privation (but never with any appreciable effect), 'There, there. Never mind.'

'Hey, you! If your sympathy had a practical bent, then you would brew us all a cuppa,' says the compiler, addressing Pilate.

'What kind of insolence is this?' growls Pilate. For the moment he is keeping his voice down, because he doesn't feel confident enough to shout. He then pours himself a hot drink, but pours nothing for anyone else. Thankfully, the one who has usurped his position seems not to notice. Dmitri is preoccupied with introducing his new computer manual, which, he says, 'is written by my own fair hand and, having been compiled over a course of months, contains exactly what all of you will need to grow into functional members of the team.' All nod in scholarly assent.

'My daughter, Alice, is very fond of computers (a chip off the old block, you see). So, I decided to name my book after her.'

At this, Pilate wonders, 'He has a daughter? Clearly, she is well-favoured, and yet he has never mentioned her.' The girl who has been named enters the room with a graceful deportment. She is blessed with cool blue eyes, a perfect oval face, and a fair complexion. And everyone is wondering, 'How can *she* be *his*? Perhaps his wife is a pretty, blind girl.' Dmitri introduces her thus:

'This is my beloved thirteen and three-quarter year old daughter, in whom I am well pleased.' Miraculously, a white dove flies into the centre of the room and perches on her shoulder, whilst merrily cooing to itself. 'Yes,' continues Dmitri, 'I downloaded her to my woe-man thirteen years ago. Not everything I download turns out so well.' There is a hum of expectancy in the room, as if the "Great Leader" will renege upon his claim of siring a young beauty – and, instead, admit to fostering an orphan. But, alas! He will not. He merely rambles on,

'And I am under the influence ... under the *happy* influence ... of this most glorious being ...' his right hand hovers above her head, and then over a copy of his fat manual. Thereupon, his fingers curl as if he were of royal blood and seizing a bottle of vintage Merlot – in order to smash it upon the manual, before the latter sets sail upon its maiden voyage into the uncharted waters of minds more turbid than his own. And now he grasps his masterpiece and proclaims: 'I name this book ... "Alice in Wonderland for the Computer Industry"'. Dmitri raises his voice as he delivers these words, which everyone else in the room takes to be a cue for applause. The applause is duly delivered; and after several minutes of sweet praise, such as the mouths of kings would drool over, Dmitri invokes a respectful silence by slowly waving his unoccupied hand up and down with a limp wrist. He conceives it as a grand gesture, but he looks like a window-cleaner with an arthritic arm.

Mr Propotamous, who has remained quite motionless during these proceedings, can contain himself no longer. He lunges at Dmitri with the words, 'Cad! That's my seat you were sitting upon!' But, upon the instant, the door opens and two cherished henchmen rush into the room to restrain him with ropes and handcuffs. He parries, but to no effect. Yes, they are the self-same thugs as those he formerly would have summoned, to escort challenging and unwanted personnel from the site. And now they are being deployed against him! Meanwhile, Myfanwy instructs Foolish Boy (who is also present) to go to the shower unit adjacent to the public conveniences, and retrieve the largest bathroom sponge which he can find. He is only too happy to oblige, and returns with the sponge - which he hands over to her. She thence proceeds to assault her husband by forcing the sponge into his mouth. She is a little short of empathy, and fails to realise that this is not his idea of food or fun - but only hers! Having made repeated attempts at entry, only to be resisted by tongue, teeth, lips and hands, – she finally desists. And the violent male duo take her sponge, and hold him down.

'Oh, heavy hour! King Arthur's sword is turned against him!' exclaims the victim, just before a soft object normally employed for ablutions attenuates his speech. His Shakespearean outburst is ignored, and Alice, delighting in the helplessness of her father's adversary, lightens the atmosphere by satirizing Pilate's vein attempts at computer programming:

'Pil-ate Pro-pot-amous attempts to enter The Magic Circle that is the world of coding. An obsolete row in a look-up table is deleted, but the obsolete description still appears where the code is referenced. How can this be? The code now points to something which no longer exists! It is like an after-image produced by a brilliant colour, or a disc of light encircling the moon in an eclipse! Ooooooo! It must be a phantom!' The teenager moves her hands around in a haunting way, as if she is defining the contours of an apparition.

'Yes. That bug is still a mystery to me,' admits the subject of her taunting, who has narrowly missed being stuffed with a bar of soap smelling of Dettol, but has now ceased struggling and accepted his fate. He cuts a pathetic figure. He is affixed to his chair, and the ligature applied to his neck is so tight that his cheeks are red and bloated – since his flesh has nowhere else to go. He resembles a puffer fish depleted of its poison. Then the soap, along with the bathroom sponge, are applied, and his nostrils flare like those of a horse.

'Anyway. Back to the book,' says Dmitri, who is mildly irritated at being upstaged by his own progeny. But the youngster isn't through yet:

'I once saw a ghost. I couldn't sleep for ages, until mummy finally gave me barbiturates. Then, months later, when I stopped taking the pills, I had a paradoxical sleep rebound. It should have been profoundly disturbing – but I actually found the nightmares quite exciting!'

Another character, on stilts and with 'OR' stitched into his clothing, complains, 'I don't like this girl. She's too clever by half. She needs to be taken down a peg or two.' He is ignored, however, for the articulate girl has won the approbation of almost everyone else.

'Anyhow ... The book! The book!' ejaculates Dmitri. 'It is divided into two sections. The first is technical. The second is full of helpful suggestions for a programmer who wishes to relax after a hard day in the office. With my daughter in mind, I was going to call it, "Alice in Wonderland: How to do Everything" ... but was advised against it.' He turns to Pilate, and is able to muster an ounce of sympathy -

'I might read some of it aloud to you: perhaps one of the longer paragraphs, ideal for oratory. Shall I call my declamation, "Listen with Father"? It may help to pass the time while you are tied up.'

Horror is Conveyed on the Airwaves

Just as the meeting is about to adjourn for a "hot drink break", there emerges, quite suddenly, a series of blood-curdling screams from somewhere else within the four walls of the building ... and the director – or should I say the *former director* - remembers his session with the hairdresser, and imagines the poor man must have clasped one of his hands around the live part of the plug whilst inserting it into the wall. If so, he is now full of mains electricity-inducing spasms, and is unable to release it.

'Ah, shame,' says Pilate. The screams continue, unabated.

'Will you untie me?' Pilate asks. No one moves, and he salves his conscience with the thought, 'Well, I cannot assist the barber while my limbs are fastened to this chair. And I'd say that absolves me of all responsibility.'

'Goodness gracious! Will that man *never* cease making such a racket?' wails Dmitri. 'He is just *so* inconsiderate.' Finally, a mood of calm prevails.

'Silence is golden,' says Dmitri.

'It sounded to us like the person was on the premises. Should someone see if he needs any help?' several people whisper. A period of "Copper-plated Reflection" ensues, replacing the brief period of "Golden Silence" which has just come to the end of its tenure. Life moves on; and the passing moments - like cabbage leaves filled with pitted olives - simply become stuffed with something else.

'No. That is hardly necessary. We will not be disturbed by him again. My antenna tells me so,' answers the chairperson. And everyone bears the semblance of an angel and thinks, 'Oh, well. At least the thought was there. Our willingness to rescue him deserves a commendation.'

The meeting continues, but, over the forthcoming twenty minutes or so, a strange scent of cooking imbues in the air, and yet there is nothing being prepared in the kitchen: either on the stove, or in the fan-assisted oven. Has some half-digested morsel of food repeated upon someone? The collective consciousness returns to the deceased.

'Who could he have been ... this poor unfortunate?' asks one of the newest recruits.

'He worked in a salon ... most recently, for me,' answers Pilate, wriggling like a jelly until the cushion behind his back becomes more comfortable. 'He was also a belly-dancer (briefly) ... and prior to that, a tilde above the hash sign on my keyboard.'

'And now, sadly, expunged from the database of life,' sighs Dmitri; who thinks that if he offers a small token of sympathy, he will be able draw a line under the subject and move on. 'Someone should write a memorial for him.'

'Yes. That would be apposite,' all nod their respectful assent.

'Did anyone know him intimately?' asks Dmitri. No one answers. They are not quite sure what he means. 'Ah! Hairdressers lead such colourful lives. Perhaps we should all keep a moment's silence out of respect for the dearly departed: and, with devout religiosity, package up a mouthful of prayers in a zip file, before posting it in a shuttle service up to *you know who*.' Obediently, no one says a word for a whole minute (although one or two individuals do check their watches).

It is ironic that, during the course of their brief tribute, no one thinks to switch off the mains electricity and disconnect the young man, now presumed dead, from the fatal plug. And so he continues to fry ... and to sizzle and steam and crackle ... as if he were a hog reared for the butcher's knife. And the rich scent, which permeates the air where he "put himself to sleep", grows steadily more pungent, until it becomes redolent of his weight in rashers of bacon; and the airborne humours, like rumours, travel further and further afield.

Larry is Also Remembered

To his great relief, Mr Propotamous is unshackled. At the same moment, the Health and Safety Inspector enters the room, linking arms with the injured engineer's mother. They sit down, and the official begins to take notes, - whilst allowing his chin to rest upon his chest, and grumbling the following mantra under his breath, 'Improper health and safety ... health and safety ... improper health and safety ...'

'My son, Larry, should be uppermost in our thoughts today,' his anxious mother blurts out.

'Why? He hasn't died as well, has he?' barks Pilate, who has now had any toiletries removed from his mouth, and ropes or handcuffs separated from his wrists, by his attentive wife. The two bullies leave the room, and he would be busy "licking his wounds", - if these were not more emotional than physical. Larry's mother sees that he is preoccupied, and adds sternly,

'You will not get rid of him. He will never, ever leave you.'

'And how do you arrive at that conclusion?' asks Pilate.

'The recent fall which he sustained has damaged the ability of his brain to consolidate short term memories: so, even if his contract of employment is terminated, he will continue to arrive for work each morning as if nothing has happened – and any warning to the contrary will simply be forgotten. In fact, even as we speak, he may be signing himself out of the Severe Head Trauma Unit in the local hospital, with the intention of coming here and completing his day's work.'

'It was an inauspicious fall which cracked his hazel nut, and uncorked a litre of his vintage claret,' Pilate remarks sympathetically. 'And to show such devotion to duty, even after the umbilical cord of duty has been severed!'

The distressed mother does not reply, for she has other tales of woe to relate:

'Oh, Lord! My poor boy's damaged head is so injurious to my peace of mind. Yet as if that is not enough' (she stares at Pilate, as he tuts to himself) 'I am faced with this monster! Is there no mercy in heaven? And all of this – at a time when my installation of a new kitchen is beset with more difficulties than I can enumerate. I hired a Polish team from the Fatherland. The carpenter took advantage of me. He came late. I was forced to the floor by his collapsing handiwork, and I had to *suck* him - before he finished off. The electrician arrived late from the fucktory. He abused me. Sparks flew. I was electrified, and – forthwith – I had no alternative but to *suck* him also, right on the very spot of his tainted employment. Finally, the plumber's pipes leaked all over me, and I made sure I sucked him too.'

Myfanwy responds with alacrity: 'But, madam, you are not here today to give evidence about your – er – sackings ... are you?'

Much to Pilate's consternation, Dmitri is holding open his rival's very private diary, as he finally resumes, 'There are, and I quote, "no apologies from the disgraced engineer, who destroyed a stepladder, and who has since been fired for the subsequent non-performance of his duties". Sorry – I am simply reading from the notes of you know who. Don't shoot the messenger.' Larry's mother wants to give Pilate a piece of her mind. Presumably this is not the same piece which, latterly, went missing from her son's hippocampus. There is a visible fury in her face, which the new boss placates by taking her side in the matter:

'Apparently, your son was fixing a timer and a video camera over the toilet door, which would have enabled this unconscionable man (whom we have lately restrained with *force majeure*) to measure the time spent by overwrought staff in relieving themselves, - before the unfortunate son fell off a wobbly (and poorly maintained) ladder, bashing his head on the parquet floor. Naturally, his family is considering legal action ... and the action would be double-pronged ...'

Now that Pilate is free of his constraints, he wishes to generate a familiar occidental gesture in the direction of the one who has all but assassinated him. This involves opening the backsides of the two longest fingers of his writing hand, and moving them up and down; whilst wearing an unpalatable look upon his frazzled face. It is a symbol of his *new spirit* (which, in point of fact, is remarkably like his *old spirit*).

'I shall ignore that foul invitation,' responds Dmitri, and retaliates by wielding his own forefinger like an *épée* in a fencing match. 'The first prong raised against the defendant is that, in dismissing the injured party from gainful employment, he has unfairly discriminated against someone who is crippled.'

'But I was going to let him go anyway,' Pilate defends his decision.

'The second prong,' continues Dmitri, undeterred by the audible objection to the first prong, 'is that a faulty ladder, not fit for function, was, with malice aforethought, supplied by the director, himself, for the instalment of the video camera and the timing device.'

'What do you mean *with malice aforethought* ... ?'

The Health and Safety Inspector is lowering his mouth down to his notebook - as if its paper leaves were ears that hung upon his every word. As he does so, he murmurs,

'The case against the accused is mounting ... the case is mounting ...' His nose is now just one inch from the paper. He may be extremely short-sighted. Or is he just shy or retiring in his manner?

Dmitri adds more weight to the prosecution:

'The accused has, on occasion, complained of "spaghetti code"; but what about the "spaghetti junction" beside every desk in the office. He didn't mind about *that*, did he?'

'Nor about the ladder, unfit for function,' adds the disaffected mother.

'Look. That bloody man is not coming back here to work, and that's an end of it,' says Pilate.

'Mind your tongue!' the mother responds sharply.

'Silence, you fiend!' Dmitri countenances her.

'Madam, I was speaking literally. I mean – how *can* he come back? He is probably still bleeding.'

'Mr Preposterous -'

'Propotamous -'

'Mr Prop – I am concerned not only regarding the ex-ter-nal effects of my son's injury. The effect upon his cog-ni-tion, generally, has been dis-ast-rous. I am considering my next move; and may sue on the grounds of diminished adherence to health and safety regulations. Do I make myself clee-air?'

'Health and safety ... health and safety,' repeats the inspector who is handling these areas of etiquette. His nose is now pressing hard against his notepad, and the words which come out of his mouth are sounding more and more nasal.

'Indeed!' the mother agrees, and then, with an odd intonation spiced with alliteration, she says, 'My mind has come to an outcome ... I fully intend to attend the bar, and thence to seek out an efficient liar who will countenance my case against this careless crackpot. How could his own *matka* do less, in the absence of his dordoi: Adalbert Wiskobitch.' (She's Polish, and doubly upset because her poor son is fatherless and she has had to rear him on her own. Stress has caused her to slip into her familiar vernacular. We must hope that fortune shall supply her with a truthful lawyer.) Then, with more than a touch of melancholy in her voice, she explains (and, for easy communication, her speech is henceforth rendered into conventional English) ...

'My son was too polite to demand a new ladder ... He was always such a coy child,' she reminisces. 'When he was growing up, I used to re-produce him everywhere I went, in the hope that, by rubbing up against others, he might shrug off his pupa - and emerge like a Red Admiral in full bloom. And yet, despite his reticence, he was a salubrious boy. When I came to fetch him earlier on (and was asked to leave him for the time being), he remembered his rude health, and commented upon how the passage of time saddened him. He also noted that my ageing skin – which was once so soft and so becoming of a comely maid – seemed, to his delicate touch, to have lost its moisture and its elasticity ... while still retaining some indefinable quality of youth. I thanked him for revoking a previous consideration of his, that my beloved skin resembles a hard-boiled egg, which is cracked in various places on account of it being overdone. But my appreciation appears to have gone to his head, since he has (from his hospital bed) been attempting to contact our local building society.'

'Your local *building society*?' inquires Dmitri.

'Yes. And when the nurses asked him what he was up to, he said he wanted to re-mortgage the family home, in order to raise the requisite funds for an egg-timer from Fortnum and Mason. He thinks that by marking tiny movements in the passage of time, he can better appreciate the look and feel of his *matka*; and, perchance, even *stop* time in its tracks. Bless him!'

Acts of Treachery

'Well. That is a sad story. Allow me to introduce another topic, which also has legal consequences. I am thinking, naturally, of the thorny issue of tax evasion.' All of those listening hold their breath for a few seconds, before breathing a collective sigh of relief as they realise that it is not their *own* tax evasion which is under scrutiny. 'Pilate's accountant, who, from this day forward, shall be known as "Pork Belly", has assisted in a criminal investigation, by providing incriminating documents, and by bringing with him a senior officer from Her Majesty's Tax Office. Er – where is he?'

'He's just outside. Shall I go and fetch him?' asks the accountant meekly.

'And now I am stabbed in the back by my personal friend and financial advisor,' rues Pilate. 'Have I not always been faithful to you?' he looks forlorn, as he addresses "the little man of numbers". He cannot help noticing that the atavistic attributes of this particular turncoat have become greatly exaggerated. The stomach is even more distended than usual, and the legs even more like scrags. Even the accountant's face has assumed certain ape-like qualities, such as a flatter nose and an extremely hairy chin.

By this time the Inland Revenue officer has grown tired of standing outside, and is twitching with impatience. He has a thought on the tip of his tongue, which is poised for action like an Olympian on a diving board; and he (the tax inspector, that is, - and not the Olympian) is afraid that if he dallies much longer, his nerves will make him misfire and crack the nose of his opening salvo on the way down. But upon entering the room, he dives straight in:

'Excuse me. If I may just intercede at this juncture ... the despised gentleman (who is the subject of our discontent) stands accused of, amongst other things, -'

'Many other things,' comes the echo from the floor ...'

The Tax Inspector clears his throat ...

'If I may be permitted to continue ... the accused, that is to say, the former director who sits before us today, produced a "mount error" on one of his tape units; and, having overcome this setback, instigated a further problem just at the point of inception, "Inserted value too large for column". I therefore propose, ladies and gentlemen of the jury, that the plaintiff, known previously as "the director", did cruelly affect the pre-natal development of the latest child of this poorly, this most pathetic of creatures.' Hereupon, he waves a young woman forward, who has been waiting patiently for her moment to arrive. Pilate instantly recognises her as Gladys, although no one refers to her by her real name.

'In the final analysis, Pilate's code caused this pregnancy to terminate with an abnormal condition. He wrecked the life of an innocent young woman, - a "pretty sweeting", to quote Shakespeare!'

'Thank you for your sympathy,' says Gladys.

'What? This is most unfair!' exclaims Pilate. 'Excuse *me* while I just butt in! The speaker is grossly exceeding his jurisdiction. He's a tax inspector. What would *he* know about mount errors, or about a value being too large for insertion?'

'Now, now. There's no need to be bitchy! Or I'll summon the VAT man – and you won't like *him* very much. He's a tiger; whereas, by comparison, I'm just a harmless pussy.' He attempts to crouch down on all fours and emit such mewing sounds as would befit a small feline (or George Galloway); and then suddenly desists, on the basis that it would be unseemly for a grown man to do this.

'Begging your pardon, sir. When my process aborted, I thought that I would never be the same person again,' says Gladys. She clutches her womb tightly as she speaks; but Pilate interrupts,

'Woman, you've had five children already. You cannot want any more – for that would be nothing but greed! Pure greed!'

'Oh! How can he?' whines Gladys.

'Myfanwy and I have had *only none*,' Pilate continues his tirade.

'One?' asks Dmitri.

'*None*,' replies Pilate.

'You never wanted any!' wails Myfanwy. She has tears in her eyes, like rain before thunder. (God preserve us from two electric storms!)

'That is beside the point,' says Pilate. Anyhow, this man ... he knows nothing about tape units at all! His only function in being here, is to accuse me of tax evasion. Indeed, his very presence will aggrandize the perceived problem into something far bigger than it really is. I would like to say that everything in my accounts – apart from one or two fraudulent mishaps, - is perfectly fine. I know how concerned for me you all are. But you can relax.' Instantly, the bizarre characters in the room, having pricked up their ears at the impending drama, slump back into their familiar postures. Pilate thinks his quick-witted defence has worked, and heaves a huge sigh of relief: 'Phew! That was a close call.' Whereas, in fact, he has unwittingly indicted himself.

'One or two fraudulent mishaps?' asks the tax inspector.

'Yes. Just a couple of minor errors. I paid no VAT at all last year. But you knew about that ... didn't you?' For quite a few seconds, no answer was the kind reply. And then, finally, the accountant clarifies the situation:

'He always pays less tax than he should ... and I ought to know ... I do his tax returns for him.'

'You're meant to be helping me, you apostate! Now you are acting as a witness for the prosecution! When we are alone, I'll give you a *dressing down*, I will.' The accountant smiles wistfully. His hearing is not the best, and he does need a *dressing gown*.

'Oh, for God's sake! Stop squabbling,' says Dmitri. 'Now, then. On with the principle reason for our convening – the reading. Yet ... I am a little vexed ... where were we, before our late and errant guest, the felon who stands before us, broke the mellifluous flow of our concentration?'

'Dmitri? Why are you speaking in that lofty manner. Normally, only my husband can do that,' says Myfanwy to him, ever so softly. 'You are the proud owner of an orator's tongue.'

******

Noticing that Gladys is still unhappy, Dmitri comforts her with his newly-defined tongue:

'They say that when an infant dies suddenly, he will go straight to heaven, and be filled with every grace and blessing. He shall look upon the face of God ... but only if he's been baptized, of course.' The pain Gladys feels was beginning to ease - until this last clause.

'And what if he has not?' Her lips are quivering: a bad sign, if experience is anything to go by.

'Then, my dear, he shall go to Limbo. You know Limbo?'

'Not personally, no. Is it a tourist resort?' replies Gladys. She is not joking.

'Limbo – according to the poet, Dante, - is one of the seven regions of outer hell.'

'Oh! I should not like him to go there,' says Gladys.

'No, indeed. The Estate Agents are even attempting to reclassify the area, because land and property there is just not selling like it used to. However, it may become "spiritually gentrified" - with young mothers moving in to be re-united with their infants.' During this solemn speech, a certain young man has been examining his naval, and then his box of magic tricks (which is a present he received for his last birthday).

'Foolish Boy Incarnate! Approach me within arm's length, and I shall have no compunction in smacking you!' exclaims Dmitri. But his anger does not endure, and he soon resumes his normal tone,

'Pork Belly is reading for us today, and I am interpreting.' The skinny little man with a portly midriff, whose facial resemblance to some missing link is growing more exaggerated by the hour, lifts a manuscript from the desk - comprising numerous instructions printed on graphical note paper. He then takes a bow, like an impresario at a performance of light operatic arias, straightens his torso, and purses his lips.

'Well, then. Let's have it. We haven't got all day.'

Pork Belly, alias Java Man, and formerly Pilate's corrupt accountant, begins to read; and, despite his ungainly appearance, projects his voice with volume and with perfect diction - as if he was a medieval town crier, addressing his fellow citizens in their market square.

'Well, Pork Belly is not a very flattering soubriquet for you, but if you are going to play the part of Judas, I am damned if I'll defend your good name,' Pilate is seething with anger, as the accountant leans towards him and delivers an explanation for his treachery.

'I didn't have any choice. They forced me into it,' he whispers, and then (to appease Dmitri) takes another bow.

'Hey, Pork Belly. Cheer us all up. Sing us a line in the key of C Sharp,' the interpreter calls over to the partially-evolved man; meanwhile tilting his head, as if he were addressing a dog. The respondent reads, in flat monotones:

'EXEC SQL SELECT salary INTO :sal FROM employees WHERE name = 'Diablo, Pax'.'

Dmitri looks disappointed, as well he might, since (and someone has to say it),

'That's no singing voice at all! More to the point, it's not C Sharp! In fact, it's not even C. It's *Pro/C*!' Dmitri bellows out his analysis (like a rutting heifer) to the rafters. One of the audience whistles something in C Sharp, and two daughters of Gladys rouse themselves into a few smooth moves.

'This reading is like a performance of an eighteenth century opera, with little interruptions composed of music and ballet known as *divertissements*,' Pilate's wife explains proudly. Dmitri nods his approval.

The little man begins to read some "Hypertext Markup Language". After a few words, he pauses and says, 'I can't concentrate while that man is watching me.' He shoots a nervous glance over at Mr Propotamous, for it is an extract from one of the director's own computer programs. He shudders right to the core of his being, and then holds up his hand half-heartedly (with the manuscript still in it) in order to attract attention. He resembles an old lady using her handkerchief to flag down a bus.

'I've got to ... you know ...' he explains nervously, and then scurries off for a toilet break.

'Me, too,' adds Dmitri – and he disappears after him.

While the Cat is Away ... A new Role for Myfanwy;
and some Advice on the subject of Marriage

For a while, everyone can relax. Everyone, that is, except Myfanwy. She seems to be utterly self-absorbed. She stands first on one leg, and then on the other: as if she were a gymnast before the commencement of an athletic performance.

Of course, her figure precludes this as a possibility, and we can only wonder at why she groans with discomfort. She is concerned about the folds of blubber on her stomach, and about their "profound cracks", as she unflatteringly calls them. She introduces a new persona for the benefit of the confused masses ...

'Myfanwy Esquelle is my name. I am known in the trade as M-y-s-q-l, or Mysequel. I am the door to the Data Repository.' She turns to her husband. 'I'm not yours exclusively. Not any more. Everything I have is open source now, honey. Anyone can use me. I'm like the Health Service - free at the point of use!' she concludes with a crescendo, and raises her eyebrows in a highly suggestive fashion. Having been largely overlooked in the unfolding circus of events, Myfanwy will now perform an act which, in most situations (present company excepted) would surely catapult her towards the epicentre of the public gaze.

'I am experiencing hot flushes,' she says, and promptly does a handstand against the wall, as she delivers the following words in her best Welsh accent,

'I must open up the cracks and air the valleys!'

Her dress falls over her head, and what is exposed is so diabolical as to require its very own hyperbole. Petticoats, layered after the Georgian fashion, surround her torso. Below them are turquoise pantaloons and an old pair of sawn-off leggings. And now the folds of her stomach fat are falling over each other, like the waves of a mudslide.

'What unearth is she up to?' someone whispers. She murmurs softly. Could she be revealing a classified secret?

'Is she about to lay an egg?' asks Foolish Boy. 'Earlier in the day, someone mentioned there were no eggs in the fridge for an omelette. I just wondered.' And yet, beyond issuing these remarks, no one is fazed by her antics. The First Lady of The Perfect Launchpad is disappointed with the prevailing apathy - and so she must take matters further. How much further can she take them? She touches, first her crotch and then her two breasts in a symbolic motion, whilst informing the party who are gathered, 'I think it is high time for an official address.' (In another room, both Dmitri and the accountant-come-reader are sweating; whilst in present company, Foolish Boy wears a big smirk on his face, for he imagines she has said, 'I think it is time for an official to undress.') She pauses, giving her words time to sink in, before continuing,

'After all, I am the meat and two veg of the whole operation.' She raises her eyes up towards heaven and proclaims, 'No one may come to the database, except by me. All these others are just a bunch of props!'

'You see that woman over there,' says the director. 'That's my wife.' Is there a sense of burgeoning pride in his voice? Perhaps he feels that he will reprise the common boundaries, and the familiar nature of things, by stating the obvious? He will not. However, he has nothing to fear from embarrassment, for his wife is still largely overlooked. The persons in the room have, for too long, inhabited a male-dominated profession, where womanly problems never seem to arise. However, Myfanwy's exploits suddenly remind them of "the elephant in the room"; and two colleagues embark upon a brief discussion about marriage. One of them, the young man recently dismissed, is intending to "tie the knot" in the near future, and seems to be afflicted with self-doubts, which he anticipates will be partly dispelled by a little harmless banter. A second voice helps him out, with a third providing encouragement; and the present author shall render the entire result in a form employed by masters of the dramatic art through time immemorial.

THE BETROTHED [otherwise known as Henry]: I am so nervous. But I can hardly call the wedding off. I *do* love her ... kind of ... but ...

SECOND VOICE: You should stop all this marriage nonsense, and just buy yourself a puppy. It is much less expensive than a wife – and exhibits an unbridled amount of positive energy. In fact, pound for pound (measured with a pair of scales or a bank account), the puppy offers a higher quality of companionship in every observable category.

THIRD VOICE: I so much appreciate why dogs are kept: there is loyalty, affection and obedience. But I struggle to understand why humans would *ever* wish to associate with *each other*.

THE BETROTHED [attempting to speak in a rich baritone voice, in order to make an adjustment for his nerves]: I truly want to get married. I really do ... Anyhow, while we are on the subject, what "make" do you recommend?

SECOND VOICE [in broken English]: Dog ...? Pure mongrel is best. Wife ...? These days – also – mongrel is best. Actually - better idea – why not buy a virtual pet, or virtual wife? Won't cost a penny to maintain. And, unlike wife or dog, it won't bite the hand that forgets to feed it ... but, rather, will just conveniently die.

THE BETROTHED: Funny you should mention that. My fiancé did bite me once, when I was unable to feed *her*. I remember it vividly. I'd done a hard day's work in the office; and, that evening, I went to the gym for a workout. Once at home, I prepared her a makeshift meal: a creamy-grey liquid refreshment from you know where. It was just a tablespoon-full: super-calorific, fishy-fresh and hotplate-ready, - to be ladled from my manly tureen into her womanly soup bowl ... What else can a man do ...? What more could a woman want ...? Yet it was insufficient for her ... and now my spheroids were dry as a bone ... too enervated by half. She accused me of being lacklustre. And then she *bit* me!

THIRD VOICE: That might be a sign she wanted more!

SECOND VOICE: I had a dog once. I left it in kennels for too long when we went away.

THE BETROTHED: I suppose the separation anxiety caused it to return to factory settings?

SECOND VOICE: Oh, no! It remembered me alright. But it had lost some of its health and vigour – and about sixty percent of its body weight. Apparently, half way through my holiday, the proprietor of the kennels ran out of food.

THE BETROTHED: Is that the same dog that was on heat, and was observed (on one occasion) pacing this depot after it had been rescued?

SECOND VOICE: Why, yes. The so-called "Panda Dog". How clever of you to remember. And the director's wife – *Ah, the director's wife!* She has such a way with animals; or, at least, she did have, prior to her present incarnation as an engine behind online programming. [Mr Propotamous pricks up his ears.]

THE BETROTHED: So what did she do?

SECOND VOICE: Well, she applied some special technique to bring the bitch out of season. She never discusses it with anyone; but, after "the laying on of hands", the dog was wagging its tail whenever it saw her. [The others look towards the speaker, somewhat dubiously. This is with the exception of the person who is implicated; for she is totally preoccupied with her yoga.] Yes. Apparently, the technique is foolproof.

THE BETROTHED [as the mandatory expression of mild shock gives way to the optional feeling of curiosity]: No, surely not ...? really?

SECOND VOICE: I think it's something to do with her thumb and forefinger. [Speaking as an apologist] But don't worry. After all, they're both consenting adults. Ha, Ha!

PILATE: Hold your tongue! That's a very serious accusation. [And then, his mood slips from anger into the muted voice of one who is ailing and has no remedy to hand.] What are you accusing my wife of? [A pause ensues.] My wife wouldn't do that ... would she? [The question is completed on a note of uncertainty. Oh, dear! The reply to that question is loud and clear and universal: and takes the form of a lacklustre and ponderous nod of assent.]

The Marketplace (in a Virtual World)

PILATE [attempting to switch the focus of conversation away from his wife]: Dmitri has been away for a while. [Chuckling to himself] I can't imagine what the surveillance equipment is picking up!

SECOND VOICE [ignoring Pilate, and addressing Henry]: In the light of your forthcoming wedlock – is your financial situation healthy?

THE BETROTHED: Dear me! My phone bill has been rather high, of late.

FIRST VOICE: Oh? Why is that?

THE BETROTHED: Well, the telephone company which presides over the service has taken to supplying hardware ... and on one occasion the device supplied registered a call lasting three days. Yes ... it's hard to believe, I know ... but the duration of a dialogue is not logged correctly by the receiver, unless said receiver is replaced *very* carefully. If it is not – then there is no end in sight! You will have heard of intelligent software; but now we have devious hardware! [His voice wavers.] And I am grossly overcharged for my own electricity too – on account of "estimates" taken, in the absence of meter readings. An estimate, based upon reasonable intelligence, stands a 50-50 chance of being accurate. It is a strange "estimate", indeed, which is *never* accurate and *always* exorbitant. *And* it is *underhand*, for the estimator never consults with me for a second opinion.

SECOND VOICE [with sarcasm]: Well, perhaps you are charged more, because your dialogues have little intrinsic value for the bored eavesdroppers on the telephone exchange? [Pausing, and with a veil of reverence] Henry, are you doing anything exciting for your honeymoon?

THE BETROTHED: We may have a cruise, priced per person, or seek out a fixed abode somewhere in the sun. I was looking at a "large studio flat - sleeps ten"! [He grins as he cites the advertisement.] Really, I ask you! I am not purchasing nine people to share with. I already have one, and that's quite enough! I am renting a ship's cabin. Now, if the persons proffered for sharing could also match my specification ... and if I were not engaged to be married ... but we won't go there ...

THIRD VOICE: In Malaysia, twenty-one people have just crammed themselves into a mini cooper; but, so far as I am aware, they are not intending to live there.

SECOND VOICE: And, young Henry, do you have your marital abode planned – and a car to boot?

THE BETROTHED [joyfully]: Yes. And the car is so cheap! But I cannot drive it off the forecourt.

SECOND VOICE: No?

THE BETROTHED: Unfortunately not. I bought it from Argos and I am in a quandary. The vehicle is flat-packed. One must depart the garage with hessian sacks of auto-mobile parts. They do give you a wheelbarrow to aid with transportation, though.

SECOND VOICE: Ah! The celebrated Argos, creature of legend, who has one hundred eyes and yet ... imperfect foresight. He's bloody good at starting jobs, is Argos, but always leaves it to the client to finish 'em off. Still, at least your house is not pre-fabricated. And how does it measure up? The last time I asked, you gave me oblique measurements.

THE BETROTHED: Well, all I know is that it's a forty-five footer. That's how the surveyor described it, when he recorded the distance from one corner of the building to the other. Good heavens! They measure everything diagonally these days. My television is a thirty-two incher. The liquid crystal screen on my laptop is a fifteen incher. God knows why they cannot measure from top to bottom, and left to right. (They lack the right instrument, I suppose: *the instrument of common sense!*) For a while, my surveyor was advising me to set up a home cinema system; but my lounge is not 100 feet wide, so I thought I'd leave it. Then he mentioned "Quad Core".

SECOND VOICE: Ah-ha! Four bedrooms, then?

THE BETROTHED: Yes. And double-fronted like *his wife*. [He nods in the direction of Pilate, and draws Myfanwy's bosoms in the air.] Some would say that's overkill, but it depends upon what tasks have to be performed. Mostly, you only need one processor - but it's so much better, with in-laws visiting, if four sleepers are accommodated at once.

SECOND VOICE: And what about the décor?

THE BETROTHED: It will be off-white.

SECOND VOICE: Like *this one's* skin? [He reaches out and strokes the right cheek of an exotic colleague; and, whilst this is a cheek, a *downright cheek*, - it is performed with gallantry.] A lovelier shade of auburn ... man hast never known ... And the *cost* of this home?

THE BETROTHED: The estate agent referred me to a newspaper article. You've got the newspaper in your hand.

SECOND VOICE: Ah, yes. Here's the article. There's some small print. Myopia forbids me! Alice, get a magnifying glass, would you? [Alice obliges.] What does it say?

ALICE: It says ... it says ... I need a higher magnification.

SECOND VOICE: Why would it say that?

ALICE: No! That's not I mean. I *said* what *I* meant. Article writ upon crinkly paper did not say it. [Alice fetches another lens to better magnify the well-worn page, and then reads out loud.] There's an asterisk referencing a proviso. And the proviso says ... it says ... the price may vary depending upon circumstances ... specifically upon the number of those who are purchasing ...

THE BETROTHED: Well. That is most peculiar. Let's get to the essentials. Hurry up – before Dmitri returns.

ALICE [tapping on the computer keys]: I'm in the website now. Apparently, there's an algorithm calculating the cost of the property you wish to buy.

THE BETROTHED [with lips quivering, for he can sense what is coming]: Well, I was given a figure of £200,000.

SECOND VOICE [gazing into the computer screen]: You have to answer some questions, and then you will learn what the price is.

THE BETROTHED [his voice has begun shaking, in concord with his lips]: I do?

SECOND VOICE [pushing Alice out of the way, in a flurry of excitement]: I'll read it! Here goes ... [He alters his tone, delivering the short clauses in a staid and fatalistic fashion, as if he is a Dalek.] Do you have a wife? Does your wife work? Do you have a brother? Does your brother work? Do you have a sister? Does your sister work? Do you have a son? Does your son work? Do you have a daughter? Does your daughter work? We assume you have a father. Is your papa working? Yay? Nay? We assume you have a mother. Is she only kitchen fodder, or does she work? Sorry – I just made that last one up!

THE BETROTHED: My wife works, but I don't ... not any more. [He glances at the man who sacked him. Meanwhile, Mr Propotamous looks the other way.]

SECOND VOICE: With two contributors, the price is £200,000.

THE BETROTHED: And with one?

SECOND VOICE [After entering the question on his keyboard]: Then it is £400,000.

THE BETROTHED: Oh, Lord! I am unemployed. My prospects are not good – and I can only afford a mortgage for half of that! Even my best friend made an official statement to me. He has found himself a woman and he will not be seeing me again, until this fresh relationship ends or is stricken with uncertainty; and not at all, if it prospers.

UNIDENTIFIED VOICE: Found? You mean she was there already, but he just hadn't noticed her? Not very observant, is he? Or did he need a pick and shovel to unearth her? There was no foul play, was there?

SECOND VOICE: Right! Here we are. The revelation is at the foot of the web page – along with the four horsemen of the apocalypse. Sorry, just kidding! Relax ... and hear me out. It says "pp", in conjunction with "BOTPOTS".

THE BETROTHED: Pee pee? BOTPOTS?

SECOND VOICE: *Per person, based on the principle of two sharing.* It's a bit like your holiday, really. By the way, check you are not two persons flying for the price of one. You will be feeling even more crushed than you already are. [He pauses, and sips a glass of water.] Well, think on it ... an entire flight with your lady friend sitting on your lap! She's not heavy, is she? Most of 'em are, these days. [Changing the subject.] And - look! There are brand new cars for a quarter of their normal price: based upon the principle of four sharing. (I'm guessing that's: husband, wife, son and daughter.) And lawnmowers, half-price, – based upon the principle of two sharing. (That'll be husband and wife.) Or just a fiver per user – when numerous neighbours "chip in". (It's part of the "Community Lawnmower Scheme", apparently.) And, blow me down! There's even a special deal on a toilet bowl. Now let me see. Would that be the single-seated norm? Or one of the "back and front" variety, with a seat on either side of the cistern, allowing two bodies to evacuate in synchrony, while their respective heads are facing in opposite directions? Rather like Janus, don't you think? Anyhow, it's half-price: based upon the principle of two backsides sharing! Seriously, though, I do *hope* this will not be at the same time – for that, my gentle sires and ladies all, would be *cottaging*! Ugh! A savage mode of conduct!

ALICE: Funny. I've never seen one of those bowls – not in all my toilet days.

PILATE [mouthing the words, so they cannot be heard]: Oh, God! Get me out of here!

[And hereupon there is a collective uptake of breath, followed by the spouting of a heartfelt sigh of repulsion. It is a sound rarely heard outside of the society of whales. Meanwhile, several listeners complain that this gross nugget of knowledge has caused their food to repeat on them; and so, to avoid choking in polite company, they resort to spitting bits of half-digested biscuits into coffee cups and saucers, thereby creating a flotilla of crumbs. One of them even excuses himself thus: 'You know, when I worked for the Ministry of Agriculture, I was voted the *Messiest Eater in all of Christendom*. And that was including pigs.' Anyway - back to the main dialogue ...]

SECOND VOICE: Such gorgeous deals as I have annotated were never matched, *not ever*, throughout the merry history of human commerce! But there is a surcharge for doing the calculation, which divides the whole sum and gives us the partial "BOTPOTS" price. Such a time-saving act of human kindness deserves a ready purchaser!

PILATE: Ah! The much-maligned "jurisdiction of pee pee": where vendors piss out poor logic through intellectual incontinence.

THE BETROTHED [gulps]: Woe is me!

SECOND VOICE: Bad move. Eschew that woe. Leave it exactly where it was. If the abstract should transmute into the concrete, your burden will become heavier! (Just imagine: your human form reconfigured as a breeze block.) Anyhow, listen up! Here is a marvellous three-piece suit. [The owner of the second voice is revelling in the facts again.] There are three prices for this – as two, three or four persons may wear it (at different times) and pay for the privilege. And I could present other examples within the "jurisdiction of pee pee", from the discrete domains of haberdashery and electronics.

THE BETROTHED [becoming desperate]: I shall renounce the idea of buying a house, in favour of the inexpensive option of a acquiring a log cabin. I am guided by the decree that "A simple log cabin does not generally require planning permission."

SECOND VOICE: Ah-hem! *That* is because it is generally intended for land contiguous to a house – and it therefore, by courtesy of the house, *already has* planning permission. I mean, *really*! For the vendor to boast that what he sells has no requirement for something which would normally be essential, because he presumes the buyer already has it, is like ... it is like ... [The speaker takes a deep breath, and then accelerates, like a sprinter, towards the finishing line.]

... selling a car without wheels to a mechanic who owns his own well-stocked garage, - and then boasting that the merchandise is a vehicle which "does not normally require wheels"!

[The Betrothed rushes out of the room and into a draughty corridor, from whence there arises, in biblical proportions, a great wailing and gnashing of teeth. And whilst he stands there, cutting the most forlorn of figures, he earnestly (Oh, how earnestly!) solicits the sympathy of Melpomene, the Greek goddess of tragedy; and someone inside the meeting room comments, 'If *that's* his girlfriend, then his problems are only just beginning'. A moment later, Dmitri scampers past him – with his midriff bobbing up and down. The self-appointed boss has one hand pressed hard against his stomach, and the other reaching out towards the entrance of the conference room. He is pursued by an obedient "Pork Belly", keeping   a measured distance from him, like a dog on a leash. Dmitri is a bit "puffed", and so self-absorbed that he does not even notice the "wailing wall" of flesh and blood and bone, that longs for a "post-it" on affordable homes: which is just as well, for soliciting outside the entrance of the principle meeting room would normally be a capital offence. Dmitri has been embarrassed by his dilatory bowel movements, which were unusually loud. He enters the room in a flustered state, and proffers the excuse for his long absence that he has been de-installing the video-camera from the toilet door.]

PART THE FIFTH: A DOSE OF SOFTWARE DIALECTIC, AND OTHER DOSES BESIDES

Lesson Number 1: Copying Variables

'And now for some light entertainment after the ponderous issues which have gone before,' announces Dmitri. He has endured a prolonged session of griping and tenesmus, and appears to have lost weight. Enter, those two bearded men, presumed to hail from an unsettled region of the Middle East (although they strenuously deny it).

'Hani Haphazardi,' says one, and bows respectfully.

'Bin Liner,' says the other, and folds himself into an even humbler bow. Dmitri waives any further introductions, excepting his own (on their behalf), which follows,

'I bring you Copyvarfrom and Copyvarto. These gentlemen are, in fact, identical twins, and mimic each other in the most important activities of their day; except when they are away on business ... which is to say, when they are engaged in the execution of a certain copy function. And we are not talking about moving values from one procedure to another, or *parsing* them as we professionals like to say – oh-ho no! - but about the assignment of a value to a field.'

'You mean *passing*?' asks Myfanwy.

"Swot I said. *Parsing*.'

'I see,' replies Mr Propotamous, who is fascinated by the abundance of flowing facial hair on the new arrivals – even though it contravenes his regulations. His standards are dropping, for he is further bewitched by what he calls their "Ali Baba pyjamas", - decked in the loveliest of floral patterns, which would befit a Chinese rug. Pilate comforts himself with the thought that these exotic gentlemen are only the puppets of Morpheus. The whole occasion has more in common with a fancy dress party than an office meeting – and so he thinks to himself, 'I shall treat it accordingly'. We all like to give the impression of being in control of our destiny, even when our authority hardly exceeds the bounds of Disneyland. Readers are invited to supply their own examples from reality, to underpin the bricks and mortar of this metaphor (and they had better do so quickly, before we get subsidence).

'Quite obviously,' remarks Dmitri (whilst assessing the mind of the spent power in the room), 'our two guests have to be from a certain ethnic minority, for a cursory glance at their copy function reveals that it must be read from right to left; and Arabic, as we all know, *is also read backwards*.' Copyvarfrom and Copyvarto begin to nod vigorously. It is as if their heads are no longer supported by their necks, but are sliding around on ball-bearings, with nothing but magnetism to prevent decapitation. And, like a well-oiled mechanism inside an infant's toy, their heads continue to roll backwards and forwards for an indeterminate period of time. Then the penny drops.

'Hold on!' exclaims Copyvarfrom, as their heads abruptly come to a standstill. 'In defence of our copy command, and in support, also, of our most noble language being written and read the *correct* way round (unlike the Queen's English, which is *clearly in reverse gear*), I should like to say that while, for an island nation in Europe, the antipodes might be New Zealand or Oz, - for those who are *over there*, the English would appear to be *under* the earth, and the antipodeans, *over* it. For it all depends upon one's orientation ... ahem! I am sure my twin concurs.' Dmitri and his Caucasian underlings swallow awkwardly.

'Orientation and affiliation!' the other twin announces dreamily. They both nod, so pleased are they that filial sympathy should raise its beloved head. The dreamer then reinforces his brother's point, 'If an Australian, residing upon Her Majesty's soil, were to be hung by his ankles, like a steak from a meat-hook, he would regard himself as being perfectly orientated towards the earth, and would perceive you' (he regards Mr Propotamous sheepishly) 'as being *upside down*.'

'Quite so,' replies Copyvarfrom ... 'and how right the suspended man would be.' Pilate is wondering if this is a preamble to his next punishment. Meanwhile, Copyvarto, realising that his approval is once again being sought, indicates his *dis*approval. He does this as subtly as he is able, by shaking his head so vigorously that a slight but perceptible wind tunnel is generated, that runs laterally - from the wall on his far right to the wall on his far left, and back again.

'My dear twin, you did not wait for me to finish. The hanging man would *perceive* Pilate that way – but he would be wrong.'

'Now, now, gentlemen!' interposes Dmitri, who sees an argument brewing. 'How tempted am I to introduce a discussion on the difference between deductive and inductive reasoning, but I'd better not – otherwise our conventional proceedings will grind to a halt. Allow your tempers to be tempered by a little light refreshment. Who would like something to wet his palate?'

At this suggestion, the synchronised nodding returns, only this time at an accelerated rate. Dmitri is pleased to see that the rift between the twins has been crossed by a viaduct; and Pilate is commanded to pour lemonade, and brew a cup of herbal tea as well. This choice, however, does not sit well with the twins; and Dmitri strains his ears to catch their words, as they begin whispering to one other. He even leans forward, like a newsreader keenly anticipating notice of some international catastrophe.

'They have grown shy - and so someone else must speak for them,' Dmitri motions to Pilate; for he is seated nearer the two subjects.

'If you must know,' says Pilate, 'they are claiming the King of Jordan to be a jolly fine fellow.' (Pilate hears their words, almost, as a babbling brook, and is soothed by them.) 'In fact, they would like to toast his life and work ... with a glass of ... of ... some beverage ending in *i-n-e*.'

'Wine?' asks Dmitri. He sits back in his chair. 'It must be wine.'

'Apparently, no. Urine. The King of Jordan was a great believer in urine as a cordial.'

'We don't have any of that. Will a pineapple juice do?'

The two pairs of Near Eastern eyes scour the table, with its host of beverages, both hot and cold, and then look from Pilate to Dmitri, and down to their crotches, and back to Dmitri again: and then, finally, cast a knowing glance at each other as only identical twins can, - which is to say that what has been requested will soon become available anyway, with or without any help from the acknowledged powers in the room. After all, the example set by the king was that a *home* brew is preferred. But for now, the homely canisters are empty; and so a shadow of disappointment moves across their faces, as they whimper:

'So long as it looks similar, I suppose we can pretend.'

But there is hope on the horizon. One of the exotic pair swallows a full beaker of some disappointing liquid described as "pressed fruit, shaken up with water"; and – within a short while – he protests that he is 'gagging to go somewhere', and that 'there is not a single used crisp bag in sight'. In response to this strange observation, the accountant, alias The Reader, alias Client Server, alias Pork Belly (you get the drift), holds up an explanatory notice:

'Failed to open stream. No suitable wrapper could be found.'

'And while we are on the subject,' adds Dmitri, 'a survey suggests that the fluid under discussion could charge mobile phones.' He is ever the technical enthusiast – although not everyone is convinced.

'Oh, yes!' he adds with boyish enthusiasm, 'apparently, organic matter can be turned directly into electricity. Basically, the mobile exploits the metabolism of living micro-organisms. It's really exciting!' He stops in his tracks, as no one else is excited.

'So, then,' Pilate weighs in with a quaint observation of his own, 'my idea of attaching a video-camera and timer to the toilet door has been vindicated. I could recycle the output (of lazy, leaking personnel) and create heat energy for the propagation of our profligate tea and coffee drinking; or turn that energy to our financial advantage, and sell it to the grid ... or run some surveillance equipment off the piss of those under surveillance! Was man ever so perfectly countenanced by his rival? Such a delicious irony makes even the soft tissues of my mouth want to pass water!'

Dmitri listens with an look of disgust spreading over his face. Then he turns his attention to one of the chief characters who was formerly under Pilate's management. His name is Pascal, and sociability has impelled him to drop by and make small talk. Is he, in fact, a programming language that has assumed bodily form? We shall see.

Lesson Number 2: More Entertainment from the Arcane Vaults

'Ah! "Contactless" has arrived.' A young man is entering the room. He is known to all as "the one who used to work from home". He does, indeed, have a remote connection with Wi-Fi – but there are colleagues who jest that he took it one step further, and controlled the database on the remote server directly through the power of his mind. He strides towards the centre of the room, nodding his head maniacally like the comedian, Michael MacIntyre, or like our hirsute visitors from the Near East, - before taking a respectful bow. He does all of this with complete confidence, even though he is an uninvited guest. Pilate has often complained about Pascal (for it is he), and so Dmitri has long adopted the tactical position that is summarised as "the enemy of my enemy is my friend".

'These days,' declares Pascal ruefully, 'you must *commit* data to a table for the table to be aware of the data's existence. Methinks the table's left hand knoweth not what its right hand doeth,' he says, grabbing Pilate's mug from its coaster. 'Back in olden times, life was so much simpler. As soon as you *pushed* the data in, you knew it was home and dry; and you could *pop* it out again whensoever you pleased. Just push and pop. Push and pop.' As he speaks, he pretends that the hot beverage contained by the mug is fresh data; and, guided by this fantasy, he puts the receptacle down on the table ... then lifts it up, with the moist coaster sticking to its underside just long enough to gather a few drops and make a mess as it falls off. And then he puts the mug down again ... and lifts it up ... and puts its down again ... and brings it up ... and down ... up and down ... again and again. And each time he returns the mug to its former position on the table, he does so with a crack of ceramic upon wood. This is less comforting than the sound of leather upon willow, and poor disenfranchised Pilate cringes at the sight of his expensive chestnut table being wilfully chipped, and then stained with coffee ... chipped and stained ... chipped and stained. He mouths the words, 'I say, would you mind not doing that, please?' But there is no sound coming out. His train of thought continues, 'I could swear I fired that Pascal guy ages ago. And what is the purpose of this ridiculous monologue, anyway? You can't deploy Pascal online

... can you?' And while he is pondering this little conundrum, the grandfather clock chimes in the hour; and this is the cue for Dmitri to embark upon a new subject.

'Um. Yes. Thank you for that,' says Dmitri to Pascal; which, roughly decoded, means, 'That's quite enough. Now shut up.' (Dmitri has shown considerable forbearance.) He then signals to an object resting against the wall, that no one has previously registered. It is a whip, with a small notice underneath which reads, 'for the edification of the mind via the process of self-flagellation ...' but, unfortunately, the rest of the text is too small to make out. Dmitri turns his glare upon his predecessor, if we may call him that, who twitches and cowers slightly.

'I am sure that you have encountered this implement before? It's a "cat o' nine tails".'

'Some people have strange tastes,' Pilate drawls his words.

'Really? It was designed for the likes of you.'

'For me?'

'In the art of online programming there are slashes which surround special characters. Think of them as an auto-immune response, like antibodies attacking unwanted microbes.' There follows a pregnant pause, as a reticent smile moves over Dmitri's face. 'And, from time to time, certain other undesirables need to be apprehended as well.' The director wonders where this is leading, but he is feeling better than a moment ago, since he is given to understand that the whip is only symbolic. In fact, in a while, he may even turn rebellious again.

'An immense expanse of verbal wickedness against the progressive art of online programming has flowed from the profane mouth of one who is here with us today – not mentioning any names, of course ...' Dmitri clears his throat and darts a glance towards his nemesis, 'but we, on the Board of Directors, recognise what self-flagellation really means.' A murmur of respectful approval circulates around the room. 'And so, I ask you, have all of the variables present been purified, through the routine of stripping and slashing?'

'Stripslashes?' says the director, referring to a famous PHP command. 'You must be taking the piss ... but anyhow, I have no spurious slashes.'

'My good man, we're not taking anything away – be it the p- or otherwise - and, *yes you have.*'

'No, I do not have. I only have commas and apostrophes to break up my data. My data has *no-thing* except alphanumeric characters ... er ... and the occasional comma or apostrophe.'

'And, for the latter ailment, you will have been given slashes, by kind permission of the interpreter ...'

'And I suppose that's you?' Asks Pilate. Dmitri shrugs.

'So, you've foisted these slashes upon my hard-working code, simply in order to give me the task of stripping them out again!'

'Now, then, – there's no need to be a clever clogs!'

'I suppose the construct, "if variable equals equals equals", was your idea as well!'

'Three equals are only used for comparisons with null.'

'Only? Ugh! Preposterous!'

'Great gables in Gloucestershire! Must I explain *everything* to you!' shouts Dmitri; and thenceforth he erupts into a loud and very abrasive poetry recital,

'*One equals* sign for assignments outside of a querrrr-ry,
Two for conditions outside of a querrrr-ry;
Three for conditions upon nothing at all;
And, if you *forget*, your edifice shall fall!'

'Well, as a matter of fact, I did employ one equals sign in a recent "if" statement upon *nothing at all*, as you put it,' Pilate confesses.

Dmitri contrives a cough and pretends it is convulsive. When he has finished his performance with some non-existent phlegm, he speaks with emphasis, 'You ... *provocateur* ... used only *one* equals sign?' He is sounding like the inverse of the beadle who is appalled by Oliver Twist requesting more than one portion of thin gruel. Dmitri struggles to avoid breaking into a diatribe, and spits a globule of genuine green bile into his lily-white handkerchief. 'There! Now see what you made me do. You have turned an already upset mind, into an upset stomach.' Pilate points to himself quizzically.

'How quietly have I been minding my own business, during the exposition of all of this nonsense?' he defends himself.

'Not much of a business, is it?' says one voice.

'Not much of a programmer, either,' a cheeky youth pipes up. Could it be Foolish Boy? Dmitri resumes:

'With one lonely equals sign all on its onio, - you, sir, have turned a question into an assignment. That's like ... it's like ... taking a youth from the back streets of a slum' (Foolish Boy pricks up his ears)' ... posing a question as to what he might become ...' (Foolish Boy raises his eyebrows, as if they were two parts of a suspension bridge through which a cargo ship must pass) 'and then ... then ... forcing him down the wrong alley before he has a chance to consider the other gauntlets which providence hath cast before him!'

'Well,' answers Pilate, 'while we are on the subject, - if you love those symbols so much, then why not have ... *ten* of them.'

'TEN?' The interpreter roars, like a thunderous knell heralding some dreadful execution. 'Have you taken leave of your minimalist senses! Why unearth would you wish to have ten equals signs, all contiguous to each other, like so many coaches at a London bus stop?'

Pilate mishears, - thinking that he is being threatened with a 'bust up!' – and flinches like a wolf which once was an alpha male. But alas! No longer.

'This man is delusional; either that, or his excitable nature has affected his ability to count. Is he taking medication?' The former director, at whom the tirade is aimed, goes as red as Cockburn's port. It is uncertain as to whether this is from embarrassment or rage – or could it actually *be* from the abuse of port wine?

'No, but really. It stands to reason! In said scenario, two is too few. Ten is too many. But three is just purrrrrrr-fect!' Dmitri licks his lips, and then expands upon his theme, referring to a photograph on the wall taken at a football match ... 'You know a skilful player will always do something twice in order to reassure the audience that the first time was no fluke.' The player has "ORACLE post-change trigger" knitted into his jersey. He has just scored, and he is kicking the ball into the net for a second time (even though the goal will only count once). 'You see, a character must be re-assigned a value that it *already* possesses, – which you achieve by leaving the field.'

Lesson Number 3: Treading Upon Egg Shells (Before Taking Some Light Refreshments)

The subject of conversation moves on to an esoteric discipline: that of managing those famous partitions within the Unix Operating System, known in the trade as "shells". The "C" shell is mentioned, and so is the "Bourne" shell – for which Myfanwy has heard "Bournville", the celebrated dark chocolate. The director's corpulent wife struggles to her feet. She has an insatiable appetite for chocolate, and especially for cream eggs.

'I bet you didn't know we had Shell amongst our clients?' says one of the technical staff.

'We don't,' says Pilate, taking him literally.

'Ha! Ha!' says another. 'Shell Oil! Very funny.' The technician goes on to explain: The shell stopped unexpectedly, and is currently under investigation.' Poor Myfanwy (alias "MYSQL"), realising that they are speaking about the behaviour of a shell that contains obscure "C" code, and not about the ever-popular chocolate egg (which is pumped full of a sweet gue), moans violently; and falls back against the wall for support in her moment of desolate privation. Meanwhile, the technician beams, as if he knew all along what would come of such a discrepancy. At the sight of the First Lady salivating, a lovely brown-skinned girl comes to the fore. She has been hired to devise testing scripts, but as her written English is limited and no one can decipher her sentences, - she spends her time concocting recipes for curries, and ridiculously sweet Indian deserts.

'The other day, I stole three chillies from a local vegetable stall,' she pronounces without an ounce of shame.

'You did?'

'Yes. I have an understanding with the stall-owner. I'm a good customer, you see.' An embarrassing silence ensues, as no one quite knows what to say. The girl moves swiftly to quash any misunderstanding -

'I would have taken more, but three was all I needed.'

And so, seamlessly, the tone of the meeting has changed to the happy subject of food.

The computer programmer who had visited the dentist earlier in the day (and whom Pilate has not yet fired for having halitosis) opens the door and enters the fray. He is full of delight, and more than a little surprised, that the swelling has gone down inside his mouth; and he is holding – of all things - a platter of food. For the benefit of the gourmet reader, this includes a few musty-smelling biscuits, stale bread covered in rancid butter, rock-hard flapjacks; and some peaches and pears which are going soft and brown, and are pickled with holes where maggots live. And there is a portion of curried fish. His head is laid low through the effort of supporting such a heavy tray; and he is breathing onto the food, for he has not the faintest notion of etiquette. He introduces the fish thus,

'Would anyone like a lovely piece of my "long raw" ... hmmmm?'

'Amazing! I thought that was a data type,' Pilate mutters under his breath. The delicacy consists of a long segment of rank, decaying matter which the sea has dredged up, and which has been sautéed by the presenter in some old curry sauce. The gentleman clarifies,

'I chanced upon it during my summer break, when I was sunbathing on a beach in Torquay. I duly removed the spine, the guts and the eyes.'

'It'll be an eye-opener for the belly,' remarks Pilate; 'and the belly shall wish it had closed its eyes and remained somnolent.'

'Oooooh! Yum. Cut me *a slice of paradise* upon the instant!' exclaims the interpreter.

'I have only this to carve it,' is the faint reply, as the purveyor of fine foods retrieves, from his breast pocket, a Swiss Army Knife caked in rust.

'Delay not one moment longer!' exclaims Dmitri, the *directeur nouveau*.

The gourmet chef is delighted with this reaction, and accounts for his behaviour on the beach in the following way:

'Well, I thought, "No one else has claimed this handsome morsel." So I decided to wrap it up in an old newspaper which – as far as I know - had not been soiled by the seagulls, and take it home in my brief-case. Waste not, want not.' And, reinforced by his own wisdom, he cuts off a juicy strip of flesh. Then he begins kneading and rolling it in two spoonfuls of flour, mixed with grated Parmesan (that he has scooped from a tiny cheese-board on the tray), using his muscular fingers with such obvious pleasure, that the whole preparation was serving the same function as a stress ball. He justifies himself with the words, 'A compressed format will save space inside my gut.'

'Look at him!' Dmitri exclaims. 'Revelling in that intersection between distraction and contentment! Isn't he the very picture of a Venn Diagram. (He would make my heart melt, had his cheesy ideas not pre-empted my heart by melting themselves.) Perhaps he could gather the matter up into a *blob* and therein store a "selfie"; then later print it off for general consumption? How self-referential would *that* be?'

'God! This place stinks!' Pilate protests; and his wife, not normally one to back him up, weighs in with the opinion,

'Yes. And the gentleman with the active fingers does not have a clue how to prepare fish' – for she is more concerned about the offence against her concept of propriety, than the assault upon her nostrils.

'Give him time. He's new to the culinary arts,' Dmitri defends the man. And then, observing how the rotten fish has begun to turn green at the edges, Dmitri proceeds to paraphrase a section from his favourite work of science, "Why Don't Penguins get Cold Feet?" -

'The green colour that is sometimes observed on bacon and ham is a result of the action of non-pathogenic bacteria. Therefore, it shows that the meat is no longer dangerous to consume.' At this juncture, the listeners are surprised to pick up faint traces of other scents infiltrating the atmosphere: possibly pork, mingled with burning hair and skin; and just a touch of sickly sweet hair conditioner. Yet no one, apart from Pilate, seems to have noticed.

'That isn't meat. It's fish,' says Pilate. Dmitri, however, is not listening, and offers Pilate a full plate for the forthcoming repast; to which Pilate responds with alacrity,

'I really couldn't eat a scrap. Would you believe it? I'm just not hungry.' But this does not stop everyone else from tucking into the victuals on display.

'Oh! Appetite, appetite! Wherefore art thou appetite?' Pilate wonders eloquently.

'I have died in the roasting of your victim's flesh,' is the response from Appetite. And Pilate remembers his hairdresser, and the foolhardy suggestion to the simpleton that he should plug himself into the wall ... and so he muses,

'It would be awful if he was on the menu, too.'

Lesson Number 4: Nice Distinctions

There are ten minutes of general feasting and drinking. Finally, Dmitri lays several copies of a computer program on the table - for the technical staff to circulate among themselves. And so begins a conversation about two variables in the code, which have been mistakenly treated by Pilate as identical: for it is Pilate's code laid out before them.

'Well. You've got to admit they are similar,' the disturber of the peace defends himself.

'No. I haven't got to admit anything.'

'But they do *look* alike,' says Pilate, lifting an old eyeglass up to his face, and peering through the cracked spectacle at a hard copy, over the shoulders of other interested parties.

'No. Not at all. Not in the tiniest bit. There is clearly a space in front of the contents of the first variable, which is not in front of the contents of the second variable - to which the first is being compared.'

'But that hardly makes them *completely different*.'

'I hereby declare that it doth!' answers Dmitri, becoming distinctly old-fashioned in a flurry of excitement. 'If two things were nearly always similar, you would expect them, occasionally, to take a leap of confidence and become identical. But, distinguished from each other by a leading space, these two shall *never* - under my illumination - be the same. Never! Not in a thousand light years! They are therefore as different as mud is from water!' And, fired by his rhetoric, other voices join in ...

'As different as *liver pâté* is from elephant dung,' says one.

'Or as distinct as a magician is, from a member of the laity,' says another, attempting to raise the public consciousness above the primal elements of mud and muck. At the mention of the word, "magician", Foolish Boy smiles, for he is a dab hand at certain magic tricks. And the similes continue,

'If they were two foodstuffs, they would be as wide apart in flavour ... as a *vinaigrette* is from *bile*,' adds a third commentator, returning the level of conversation to the bestial floor; whilst cocking his head to one side like a battery hen, and wondering whether the famous salad dressing (made from vinegar) is, in fact, *any different from bile.*

'And in *that* case, not wide apart *enough*,' thinks Pilate.

'No power, either in heaven or on earth, shall splice their entities – not betwixt here and the apocalypse,' resumes Dmitri, 'for they are as separate from each other ... as the earth is from the sky! As remote from one another' (and here he pauses) 'as a shepherd's delight is, from a shepherd's pie.'

'Or Turkish Delight is, from a Chinese massage in Shanghai,' one of the ancillary voices adds, who has a predilection for seedy experiences.

'Ah! Mixing the physical with the experiential,' complains Dmitri.

'But ... surely you can just delete the space?' Pilate asks cautiously.

'Well, you *can* ... and some act of transmutation *could* turn base metals into gold!' Dmitri responds reluctantly. Then, with imaginary steam squirting out of his ears, he ploughs on, like an express train, into an entirely different terrain:

'And with the accused having tackled the thorny issue of "What is a Customer?" in a meeting that he chaired not long ago ... the fresh subject which I, myself, have prepared for discussion is, "What constitutes *nothing*?" And - "What is the meaning of *null*?" Ahem! I shall exchange ideas with myself, in order to arrive at a sensible conclusion.' Simultaneously, every character in the room puts one elbow on the desk before him, and an index finger into the dimple of his chin, - thus performing a balancing act with the human head, indicating the most profound and respectful concentration.

'When I reflect upon things apparently empty of content or meaning that have been assigned a high value, – wondrous images sail before mine eyes ... a pile of bricks, circa 1976, for example; or Duchamp's infamous urinal. I wax lyrical:

How sad to be bereft
Of usefulness and heart.
But lacking soul or concept
Gave birth to Concept Art.

Then I decide that it is high time for a light interlude of mockery. And I begin to wonder how purely functional objects may be displayed in a gallery designed for the exhibition of high-flown things, thereby becoming artistic solely by virtue of their altered location. Why, I could have my old toilet bowl transferred into my kitchen, - and thereafter use it to rinse carrots and cauliflowers, in a prelude to the preparation of a hearty meal; or set aside said bowl for the washing of dirty plates and utensils, once my stomach has been adequately filled ... having previously sat upon the self-same bowl whilst my stomach was being adequately emptied. Ahem! Do I hear this alteration to its function being lauded by Health and Safety as a sublime feat of the imagination? Is there a grant winging its way to me from the Arts Council? No? Prey, why not ...?'

'And, ladies and gentlemen, as every raconteur knows, it is appropriate to polish a speech off with a little dose of humour. So then, what is the definition of *something* posing as *nothing*? The answer, of course, is two apostrophes nestled together – just short of a loving embrace!'

'There are different kinds of inverted commas. You can have a single or a double,' says Pilate.

'I'll have a double, baby, on the rocks! Ah! And Curly Brackets can pour it out for me,' says Myfanwy.

'Make that two!' adds Gladys, who is no longer so highly-strung, and seems to have come to terms with the abortion of her virtual child. Dmitri resumes,

'Null is the *new nothing*; and, now, the *former nothing* is no more than an imposter – an antiquated poseur who should be extinguished from our nodules!' He had meant to say 'from our modules', - but there was no laughter, for all about him had assumed an air of such gravity, that their mouths were frozen, and the corners of their lips could no longer be extended for the expression of gaiety. Dmitri breathes in deeply, and pouts his own lips in a pompous way. It is as if he is about to expound the dictates of a celebrated movement in philosophy. When he speaks the forthcoming words, he does so very slowly and deliberately, as if they are a viscous paste being squeezed out of a tube.

'Sometimes – in - life – nothing should be declared ... properly ... so as not to understate its significance. For everything in life has value ... even if it consists largely of emptiness. The universe has value, does it not? And yet it is almost nothing but space. But it also has a prevailing mystery. An observable feature may be both present and not present. Or it may be in two places at once. Shall I summon up Schrödinger's cat? No. I won't disturb him. He's in the kitchen eating some fish ... Or *is* he?' Dmitri lifts his eyebrows, just as that famous interpreter of human mysteries, Hercule Poirot, might have been inclined to do. Then he breaks into a self-satisfied smile, entirely appropriate for another kind of cat (who is fictitious and whose name is "Garfield"). 'Our dearly departed feline, who has risen from the dead, has fallen prey to a stomach bug and wishes to be left alone. That is, perchance, if he is at home,' Dmitri concludes. Copyvarfrom and Copyvarto are gaily nodding, like a couple of greylag geese engaged in a mating ritual; until one of them stops abruptly.

'Thank heavens!' Pilate breathes a sigh of relief. 'That purposeless expenditure of energy was starting to get on my nerves.' But the peace does not last long, for as the funnel of wind from the oscillating heads becomes quiescent, it is replaced by a funnel of words:

'And now, gentlemen, I have something to say - something which is *not* nothing. And I am not about to extend this into an account of Nihilism. I simply *haven't got the time*,' Dmitri says emphatically. 'The former master of us all, who has lately descended from grace - like Milton's Fallen Angel - informs us that there is but one extant copy of his expenses. But it amounts to nothing, for they are all perfect forgeries! And holding to the belief that they are persuasive, a corresponding amount of his salary has not been declared on his tax return.'

'Yes, I know. And that is because it was cancelled out by my *legitimate* expenses,' Pilate admits – entirely overlooking the fact that, even if these expenses are offset, the income is still supposed to go on record. 'But I did declare part of it (just a smidgen) in a note which is contained within my *out tray*, and which I intend to post with my expense chits and with the form itself. In fact, I do believe I sealed all of these items in a stamped, addressed envelope - ready to go.'

'And you took photocopies of the important documents, I presume ...?' asks Dmitri.

'I ...'

'Is this the tray on the kitchen table?' asks Foolish Boy.

'Ye-hess.'

'The one with the old envelope inside?'

'It's a brand new envelope, although it may have aged (like a fine wine) while I was getting everything ready.'

'And it's a brown envelope?'

'I thought it was a white one.'

'And it's *definitely* in the tray ... the tray that *doesn't* have any cat litter?' Pursues Foolish Boy.

'Er ... What?'

'He means,' Dmitri adds helpfully, 'is it the one which the cat (earlier on) evacuated his bowels into, perhaps to effect some kind of revenge ...? Or some other tray, which may contain cat litter but which the creature has left unsoiled?'

'Are there two litter trays, then?'

'You had better hope there are.'

'The tray should still be there – with the untainted letter. Fate cannot wish to throw out the baby with the bathwater,' says Pilate. Dmitri's eyelids twitch, as a halo of transcendent logic settles upon him.

'Come, now. Perhaps Fate was in a flutter of confusion, and, in the heat of the moment, she could not tell the difference? The goddess is a busy girl with a lot of housework to do. (Her maternal instincts are everywhere apparent). And she often saves time by throwing them both out together.'

'Goddess? Oh, God!' is the only response which Pilate can muster.

'Well, *my* experience of Fate indicates to me that He, She or It is not stricken with spiteful tendencies; but is merely to be found wanting in the faculty of discrimination,' some other clever fellow elucidates.

'Well. Of all the dilemmas which life throws at us, I am so glad we've cleared that one up,' infers Dmitri.

'Perhaps Schrödinger's cat and – er - whatever it did in the tray ... will both have disappeared, leaving behind my valuable letter,' says Pilate, recovering some dignity.

'Or perhaps the document will have disappeared, leaving behind only what was done on top of it?' contends Dmitri. 'Now that really *would* be rubbing your nose in it!'

Suddenly, Copyvarfrom has something he would like to say. He whispers into the ear of his twin; and Dmitri strains to hear, inclining his right earlobe towards the speaker, and cupping his right hand around that lobe, as if he were a small child on a seashore with a conch - or some other fanciful repository for lost sounds.

'What's he say?'

The two bearded men who have captured his attention continue a private dialogue. They sound like a clergyman and a sinner in a confessional. Finally, one of them finds his voice, - and a very eloquent voice it is too:

'I do believe that I may be speaking for the both of us, when I say that this automatic and violent agreement which has lately arisen betwixt us (evinced by a simultaneous and persistent nodding) has left an acute and lasting pain, somewhere in the region under the chin.'

'The region popularly known as "the neck"?' clarifies Dmitri, who is now nodding himself - as if the behaviour is infectious.

'No surprise there, then,' the former director thinks to himself.

'Umm,' the other bearded twin pipes up. "Tis Worse.' And after a further parley with Hani Hapahazardi alias Copyvarfrom, he explains:

'We think we might have dislocated our necks.'

And thus, the moral of this particular section of the tale is established: that too much communal agreement, to the point where it becomes vigorous and blind, may have an effect which is every bit as deleterious as a nasty dispute.

'Well. I could call for a search party,' Dmitri offers. 'I'm quite sure that, with a little help, the necks could be relocated. They couldn't have gone far. I have a map, - an architect's drawing, in fact, - of this very meeting room. And, while we are about it, we could peep round the door of the kitchen, to see if the cat and its ... well, you know ... are there, or are not there, as the case may be. In the mean time, listen closely and permit the following dulcet tones to act like an analgesic.' As Dmitri delivers these words, he raises his eyes towards heaven – thus emulating the kind of saintly figure whom Murillo loved to paint; and "Pork Belly" renews his reading.

Lesson Number 5: A Glimpse into the workings of the Machine

'I feel the call of nature coming on,' says Myfanwy. 'I need to do a substring. But should I convert it into capitals?'

'String to upper! String to upper!' shouts someone from the back of the room, dressed as a clown.

'But no longer shall I persevere in darkness!' continues Myfanwy. She is oblivious to the interruption. 'I am determined to count from *one* for this; and not from *zero*, as is fashionable in modern scripting languages.' Hereupon, she beams as brightly as the morning star.

As she is speaking, a huge, circular biscuit, some five feet or so in diameter, and embedded with three large cherries, comes to the director's attention. It is standing on a small rostrum, normally utilized by Pilate when he wishes to make a public announcement before a delegation; and it is remarkable that he has not noticed it before. The biscuit has a white card pinned to it - printed with the solitary word, "Cookie". Suddenly, the three cherries begin to signify the tiny eyes and pinched lips of a human face – and, just for a moment or two, it seems as if the entire contrivance breaks into a smile. Then the "mouth" opens to speak the following words,

'I am a clever biscuit. Every time the user loads a website, the browser sends me back to the server and I notify the website of the user's activity.'

'Sorry? Did somebody just speak?' asks Pilate, too astonished to believe the evidence of his own ears. As his eyes open wide, Foolish Boy is tending a flowerpot on the window-sill. He fills it with fresh, moist soil; and inside its muddy bed, a large, fat worm is fast asleep. There are strange pictures on the walls – of savage creatures, contrived by Jonathan Swift in his novel, "Gulliver's Travels", which go by the name of "Yahoos". They are omnivorous, but seem to prefer meat - and also garbage (not unlike Pilate's email provider, which has a great appetite for advertising) - and the words underneath the picture encapsulate the opinion of Gulliver,

"I never beheld in all my travels so disagreeable an animal."

There is also a mural of a trojan soldier, dressed in a plate of armour and making amorous overtures to his paramour. Here, the caption reads, 'Anti-viruses: Go forth and multiply'.

'For thine is the power and the glory, for ever and ever! Amen!' Pilate exclaims. But, alas! He is completely ignored, as his nemesis turns towards the mural, and verbalises the caption in order to regain control over listening ears. He then gives his take on the words.

'One vaccine is good, but two's a crowd. They are like Siamese Fighting Fish: internecine and blood-thirsty ... for they are highly territorial, you know.'

Finally, yet another extraordinary character enters the arena, who answers to the name of "Precursor of Sound-Byte". He is clinically obese, and suffers from bulimia: which is to say, he eats too much and spews ... and eats too much and spews ... and so on. I dare say, an imagination of adequate means may conjure him up; but who would want to – when there are already so many like him in the high street? So far today, he has not been fed, and he is impatient to feast upon some rotten fish. Sadly, he has developed bedsores owing to immobility. He is introduced by Dmitri, who excuses his appearance by saying, 'The more he eats, the better. We are fattening him up. We have not yet decided what *for*. He could grow into an outstanding couch-potato, and – upon the consummation of our wish – accompany the traditional turkey at Christmas-time. But the consensus of opinion is that his diet should not be *cordon bleu*. So he might spoil the taste of the turkey.'

Lesson Number 6: Donning Three Suits and Reading the Code

'I digress. Let us proceed with the main business of the meeting. We have our reader for today,' he signals to the accountant; 'and, for his benefit, Father Bertrand has kindly supplied a cross-section of available garments from his vestry. They are on higher purchase, and, as each is worn, the wearer may only speak in a certain tongue. His primary language of HTML shall paint the screen. His secondary language, PHP, shall accept values from the screen and validate them; and his tertiary language of SQL shall establish a dialogue with the database.' Dmitri nods to Myfanwy, who smiles at the female pair who are known as "curly brackets". One of them responds with a gorgeous pirouette on tiptoe. No sooner has she completed her rotation, than Dmitri proclaims in a loud voice,

'The changing of the guard for Hypertext Mark-up Language! Let the "trumpet voluntary" commence!' He is joined by a series of foot soldiers, who enter the room with a small brass band. All of these newcomers must have been just outside the door, waiting for their cue to assume centre stage.

They are clothed in beautiful textiles; whilst carrying even finer garments by hand - which they lay upon the nearest desk. The band performs a colourful fanfare with military precision, and a youth (who looks suspiciously like Foolish Boy) beats out the rhythm on his tabor. When the commotion simmers down, some HTML is spoken like a Vedic prayer,

'td class equals hr; td class equals dr; Less than question mark p-h-p ...'

As he reads, the mode of communication changes; and with each new mode, the brass band starts up again - with Dmitri barking at him in the background like a sergeant-major,

'Take off that suit. Now put on this one. No! Not *that* one. *This* one. The one right in front of you, you nincompoop!' When the accountant is suitably attired for his next spate of reading, he lifts the technical manuscript; and, with trembling hands, delivers the following information in a mere breath or two:

'Less than sign, question mark, PHP, Business type equals substring dollar original business type.' What follows is a different kind of command (in SQL) that accesses the database; and it draws a broad smile from Myfanwy ...

'update business_type
set business_type_desc = $bus_type_desc ...'

And then, quite suddenly, the reader breaks off to appeal to Dmitri's humanity in simple English:

'Please, sir. Permission to pant?'

'Permission granted,' replies Dmitri. And so the reader pants, with his tongue hanging out like a slobbering boxer dog.

Myfanwy snuggles up close to Dmitri, and holds one of his hands under the table, whilst his other hand clutches a learned volume named, 'A Handbook of Technical Wisdom'.

Critical Commentary

Now, I shall lapse into pure dialogue, and give the "Descriptor" a few minutes respite. I may still include the odd embellishment in square parentheses, since the contract of my Descriptor makes no provision for this, allowing it to remain within the remit of the author's "First Person".

As the First Person, I would like to say that the Descriptor, who is my assistant, wishes to generate a bright, clear picture of things: which is sometimes painful to witness, by dint of its intensity. He is not averse to the odd aside (not even if it is exceedingly odd) – and he has been well occupied in the telling of this story; so much so, in fact, that he has taken to developing his very own strain of chronic fatigue. Apparently, he has cultivated it from seed, although there is no place for it in a flowerbed; and no mention of it in the extant papers of Gregor Mendel – compiled by that man when he was dabbling with his peas. And so ... methinks Descriptor must be granted a tiny toilet break: thereby allowing him to piss out a few fancy phrases from his lexicon before they poison my text, or fall out of fashion and go rancid.

READER-ALIAS-ACCOUNTANT: I say, this is a load of abalone! I ask you - three different languages ...? And sometimes all of them on the same line!'

ASIAN COLLEAGUE: You know. You really are making a *montoon* out of a *marlhill!* It is quite easy for a multi-lingual person to touch upon three tongues in a single line of speech. And I am not alluding to a multiple of French kisses! You should try it yourself, some time. For example, the first phrase could be in Sanskrit, the second in English, and last bit in French. Would you like me to demonstrate?

DMITRI: Not right now, dear.

ASIAN COLLEAGUE: How about: the subject in Hindustani, the verb in Spanish, and the sufferer of the action in Swahili?

DMITRI: Please don't.

ASIAN COLLEAGUE [with the accent and manner of a French waitress]: In that case, Monsieur, may I interest you, instead, in a sequence of delicacies from around the world: an *hors d'oeuvre* of Dutch Edam, followed by a main course of roast chicken with potatoes and a sliver of Italian Parmesan [the First Lady of the Launchpad begins to salivate]; and for desert ... a thimble of microscopic parasites from Arabia or Rajasthan? [The First Lady stops salivating]

DMITRI: No. We would not like that.

READER-ALIAS-ACCOUNTANT [bemoaning his situation, and ignoring the verbal fencing match]: Mother of Pearl! Whatever next! Three suits! And I have to keep putting them on and taking them off, all through the livelong day. Even with PL/SQL, there were only two vestments to be worn, and one fitted as easily into the other as the humble waistcoat rests beneath an outer jacket! Oh! How my heart melts like butter for times past, when I was required to wear just one costume all through my waking hours ... the days of Common Business Oriented Language.

COBOL COMPILER [wistfully]: Ah! The good old days, when I was still in circulation. Now everything is interpreted, one line at a time.

DMITRI: But, my dear fellows ... Speaking as "the Interpreter of one liners" [and here he feels a tiny bit like a stand-up comedian] I say we must count our blessings, for there is nothing common about our business. It requires a truly awesome livery - and an exceptional trapeze act.

******

Dmitri nods to a couple of svelte girls whom we have already met. They are the elder daughters of Gladys, and they are wearing sexy gym slips that put on display the extreme curvature of their spines. And now, they begin to deck out the room like a circus arena – and to symbolically mark the start and end of a group of commands. This involves each climbing one of two step-ladders, placed at either side of the room near the window; and then applying a trusty old "Black and Decker" to drill holes into the masonry. Finally, they secure a high wire by the application of two hooks. The wire is tightly suspended below the ceiling, and Pilate wonders what precarious act they are about to perform.

'Of course,' explains Dmitri, 'the risk involved is integral to the demonstration ... one miniscule error of judgement, and everything will come tumbling down – just as it is with the programmer's art!' The two trapeze artists assume their positions at opposite ends of the wire, and tiptoe along its length to the middle, where they reach out and touch fingertips. One of them wavers slightly before recovering her balance, and this prompts Dmitri to remark,

'In this new online world, everything is fragile – but all is ingenious!'

'Well. I reckon there is a 98% chance of the entire thing collapsing. But I'm clinging to the 2%,' says Pilate. And here, Dmitri squeezes Pilate's wife until she makes a cooing noise, like Alice's white-collared dove.

The tightrope somehow becomes a live wire, and the gymnasts leap each time an electrical current approaches, and skilfully regain their footing after the danger has passed. The spectacle is reminiscent of youths when they perform a dance of death upon railway tracks in the face of an oncoming train.

'If the wire has even one microscopic thread displaced, calamity will surely follow,' says Dmitri. 'My friends, remember the moment when you realise that some ponderous block of code is finally working, even though you cannot entirely figure out *why*. Ah! The ecstasy of eureka laced with the fear of uncertainty. The fruit cake of self-congratulation never tasted so bitter-sweet, as when it is decorated by hundreds and thousands ... of indeterminate possibilities!'

Lesson Number 7: More Reading and More Dissension

Once more, the reader stiffens his sinews and sallies forth:
'$bus_type = stripslashes(sqlvalue ....'

The crossover between the screen painter, the scripting language, and the code which accesses stored data is gradually becoming familiar; and, with the fanfare, the cheeks of the trumpeters are growing red with overuse.

The deposed leader retrieves a tiny mirror and a modest pair of tweezers from his inside pocket, and, with the aid of these, he plucks the superfluous hairs between his eyebrows – pausing, briefly, to examine the effect upon his countenance. Then he proceeds to prune what is fast resembling a forest inside his nostrils. After he has been fixated by this displacement activity for some minutes, he puts the tweezers on the table, and stirs himself in readiness for some more fighting talk.

'So far, we've only processed a few lines. At this rate, we'll never get to the end of this bloody program!' he says. Then he wines, 'Who wrote this garbage anyway?' At this, all eyes turn upon him, flashing like shards of glass; but, for the time being, nothing registers.

'Even the basic syntax is just *so* long-winded, and the aim of it all is *far too modest*.' Thus does our anti-hero relieve himself of all responsibility for any attendant difficulties within the code, and foist them *all* upon the underlying *syntax*. When he falls silent, the interpreter responds magisterially:

'Never in the field of human endeavour was so much energy expended in achieving so little ....' He stops short, having realised that (in one fell swoop) he has misquoted Winston Churchill, and shot his beloved language in the proverbial foot. But never fear. Like a chameleon changing the colour of its skin, - he brings the paragraph to a triumphant conclusion: 'The Christian message is, "Love the sinner; hate the sin". But my message to you today is, "*Love* the language; *hate* the practitioner". Hail, Sisyphus! Be proud of the energy you expend!' Thus, does he pay his respects to a pagan god, who was consigned, for all eternity, to tirelessly pushing an immense boulder up a hill, only to see it roll back and hit him (at *every* attempt).

The former director takes up the baton once more, but this time with more gentility:

'Gosh! So you agree with me. This syntax *is* an overly-engineered way of doing everything. It really *could* be pruned.'

'"Pruned", you say! *Pruned*? By what authority do you speak of prunes? What would you like the program to produce? Diarrhoea? How very dare you! Would you prune *Shakespeare*?' A general hum of approval for this rebuke circulates around the room; although there are one or two unpatriotic personnel, who feel that pruning Shakespeare might not be such a bad idea.

'But this is not *Shakespeare*,' says Pilate in a wounded voice. 'Or at least it wasn't when I last checked.' And then he almost whispers, 'although, to be perfectly truthful, I am no longer sure of anything.'

'Silence, you fool! We have endured more than enough of these interjections to last us all for the rest of your entire nightmare!' Dmitri pauses, as he observes the accountant, alias The Reader, scratching himself, - and so he shifts his attention to him,

 'Proceed, Pork Scratchings!' And, in response, the bullied accountant turns to his technical manuscript once more. There is fanfare with full regalia, then HTML [and fanfare], and then some scripting language in PHP [with more fanfare]; then further Structured Query Language [accompanied with yet more fanfare]; and then it's back to HTML. As each line is read, it must be "interpreted", - and this, indeed, is an odd process to behold. Towards this end, and with all of the grace and dignity of an elephant's trunk snake in a fit of digestive angst, the Interpreter effects a swallowing motion whilst his stomach rumbles. Yet the Reader is oblivious to his strife, and ploughs on. Eventually, Dmitri holds one hand out and exclaims,

'Hang on! I can only swallow one line at a time. And I require another hot beverage to ingest it properly.' The Reader stops, as Dmitri defends his behaviour thus: 'But I am a fast worker. For I do not waste valuable time issuing helpful or meaningful error messages! It's all "HTTP 500" to me! Well, much of it is, anyway. Although I have been known to issue the occasional "Garbage Collection error" as well.' And, with the conclusion of this little speech, he looks athwart at Pilate; although it is Foolish Boy, dressed like a cadet, who delivers to Dmitri the wished-for beverage. Meanwhile, the Reader waits for a nod from the authoritative head before setting off again:

'Semi-colon, html special characters, open brackets ...'

The Interpreter reveals the palm of his right hand, and gradually moves it up and down in a rhythmic way, - as if it is a meat-cleaving device at the butcher's, chopping an industrially-produced cylinder of German sausage into salami-thin slices of salty magic.

'He's stolen our rhythmic thunder,' remarks Copyvarfrom (alias Hani Haphazardi) to Copyvarto (alias Bin Liner), as they make a pathetic attempt to move their bodies in time with the motion of the imaginary guillotine, wincing in pain as they do so.

'Ah! Like music to my ears', says the interpreter. 'Lift your voice and sweeten more of the sound waves with procedural logic ...'

And so the pattern of events passes through the various phases of literature: prosaic, poetic or mysterious, and dramatic: but not necessarily in that order, of course.

Lesson Number 8: On Considering The Deep Mystery of
"if exists" - tempered with the subject of Wimbledon line calls

The Reader proceeds for a few minutes, and then suddenly stops at the behest of the Interpreter.

'Hold on! Mr Scripting-Lang is trying to tell us something.'

The person to whom he refers examines his whereabouts, by waving his arms about in a circular motion. He needs to do this, because he has just tied a woollen scarf around his head, thereby depriving himself of the gift of sight.

'Oh, my ...! My visuospatial perception is impaired. Dear me!'

'Mr Scripting-Lang, what are you doing?' asks Dmitri. A command within the scripting language has struck a chord within the gentleman addressed, as he recalls how Dmitri, one afternoon, gave him an exposition of its use.

'I am engaging wit ze "if exists" function, and attempting to determine who – or vat – actually lies in vront of me,' he replies meekly; and then adds, by way of an apology, 'I fear it is a process which requires a very great presence of mind.'

'Why don't you just take the blindfold off?' asks Pilate. 'Then you will be able to see properly.'

'How very perspicacious of you. But, my dear fellow, I can zee nothing if it is not declared to me. Zee scarf is only zymbolic. Notwithstanding zis, I vish my actions to mimic ze software, and zo I access everything through ze lens of my intelligence, and not zat of my eyesight. In fact, if I am not careful, ze very existence of objects around me may be called into question: even ze dearest of zem, vich iz myzelf. Unlike Descartes, I cannot presume I – or zey - exist zimply because I am sinking about them; nor even because I zee myzelf (or zem) in ze mirror with my naked eye. I am like an inventor poised on ze precipice of creation ... or a pharmacist at ze outset of some ground-breaking chemical assay ... vaiting for an insight or some inside information ...'

'Yes, yes ... alright. We get the gist,' replies the Interpreter. And then, turning to the bemused audience of the German-American posing with a scarf over his eyes, he says (and he is alluding to you know whom), 'Don't bother humouring *him*. He has done *nothing* to deserve our forbearance. He's just rude! Plain Rude! Was the inventor of this company born yesterday?

Can he not cast his mind back even one generation – to a time when tennis matches at Wimbledon were presided over by umpires, whose principle qualification for the job was that they be partially blind?'

'Good heavens! Was it really? How ingenious they must have been,' says Pilate, obediently eating humble pie .... 'to be capable of calling a projectile *in* or *out*, when it is travelling with the velocity of a small rocket, and when (to boot) they could not even see properly!'

'The umpire was not *able* to call it ... that, sir, *was the whole point*!' Dmitri has a note of exasperation in his voice. Pilate looks confused. The systems engineers rest their heads, by inserting their forefingers into the dimples of their chins; and, as the seconds tick by, this precise act of dovetailing is appreciated with a nod from Dmitri.

'Ah, yes! I think I - I under-understand,' Pilate falters. 'Their blindness verified the true miracle of their judgement.' In fact, he did not understand at all.

'No!' Dmitri hammers the table with his fist. 'There was no miracle. There was a tension, such as exists between a queen and her subjects, who may resent paying their tithes to her, and who would prefer to be citizens of a republic instead; or such as holds sway betwixt the proprietor of a road and its users at a toll-gate, who would prefer to pass free of charge; or between God and his atheists, who detest being forced to believe in him. Listen up! The *partial blindness*, and the ensuing (justifiable) rage amongst the contestants, was necessary for the general spectacle to evolve – and for a creative frisson to occur.' He stops to refuel, with a sip of beverage and an intake of stuffy air. 'Also ... another example! Imagine the emotional excitement of a feudal lord, exercising his right of first refusal with respect to his vassal's bride on her wedding night? And think how dull that night would have been without it!'

'Personally, I am thinking of the poor vassal!' says Pilate, who, for almost the first time in his life, is discovering a vestige of humanity within himself, on account of there being none in the hearts of those around him. It is strange how opposites may stimulate one another. Whether opposites attract is quite another matter.

'Precisely. Think of him, too. Now then, reader ... read on ... lest we be here until nightfall, still debating matters that are highly improbable or patently ridiculous.'

'But ... back to the tennis ... what about Hawk Eye?' Pilate persists. 'Some are against the very idea of devaluing the umpire's role. But if I had the eyes of a hawk, I would not shut them when I was crossing the road; and thenceforth wait until such time as my well-being was challenged by a collision with a motor vehicle. It seems to me that our *third* eye, the *inner eye* which espies common sense, has been gouged out. After all, the purpose of the Wimbledon Lawn Tennis Championships is to showcase sporting prowess, and to properly summate the points won by the players, in order to ensure that the best genius wins – rather than to tease us all with calculated guesses.' He sits back in his chair, looking mightily pleased with himself. His pleasure is short-lived.

'But the purpose is *not* that ...' Dmitri cuts him short with his sabre tongue.

'It isn't?'

'No. Certainly not ...' The speaker of the house moves his forefinger around in an arc, to indicate the balance of truth shifting from one magnetic pole to its opposite, and the room at this moment becomes so quiet that you can hear the dropping of a pin as it hits the floor, - or the "plop" of an arthritic cockroach, as he slides into an ashtray. Pilate becomes giddy, and he feels both his eyes and his stomach trace the curve of the arc, all the way round to its starting point. 'The purpose, ladies and gentlemen, keys from the keyboard, virtual objects in cyberspace, software functions, compilers, and a most excellent Interpreter, – Oooh! I do believe that's *me*!' His hand moves over his mouth in a display of false modesty. 'I repeat, the purpose ... is to provide gainful employment to elderly officials. After all, you would not be so heartless as to declare them redundant, would you?' Dmitri examines Pilate with a penetrating gaze. 'Some of them may, in previous incarnations of their professional lives, have been operatives in Her Majesty's Armed Forces. To that extent, they have been separated from civilized society and require humane treatment. The poor men are half-blind and subject to flawed judgement. Who else is going to employ them?' Dmitri concludes his speech, by blowing any outstanding objections away with an exhalation through his nostrils. He was considering a trumpet voluntary, but his nose cannot deliver it.

PART THE SIXTH: A MULTI-FUNCTIONAL SECTION

Myfanwy is Confused by her new Powers

Suddenly, and without warning, Myfanwy kneels before Dmitri, who assumes the stance of royal authority by employing a large kitchen knife, tainted with the remnants of dried lasagne and tomato seeds (we hope they are tomato seeds), as a make-believe sword with which to officially anoint her in the capacity to which she has already become casually acquainted,

'You are Myfanwy Esquelle. And, henceforth, you shall be known as M-Y-S-Q-L ("My Esquelle"), and upon this rock I shall build my database. This act of mine ought to have been a function of the Canon, Bertrand Tyson. But the Canon (whose arrival is joyfully anticipated) has shot his bolt by being late.'

Pilate reflects upon how the transmutation of persons and things to a fantastical setting not only gives them an alternative environment in which to interact, but exaggerates their natures to an unbearable degree. Meanwhile, the Reader is formulating the words which are to follow, with a light-headed absence of mind.

'MySQL server ... has gone away,' he flutters his hands, after the fashion of a bird on the wing.

'No, she hasn't. She's standing right in front of you, you daft ape-eth,' the Interpreter corrects him, before turning to the First Lady of The Perfect Launchpad, who is visibly straining those muscles which reside in her forehead and betwixt her eyes. Indeed, she is straining so hard that the skin on her face is growing agitated, like the surface of a swamp when the resident alligator is in love. Dmitri, the interpreter, taps her lightly on the head with a soiled coffee spoon: thereby demonstrating, after the previous show of tyrannical strength, that there is a softer side to him (we shall suspend judgement as to whether the softer side is feminine or not). He is iterating and reiterating the mantra, 'Hello? Is anyone at home? Hello?' He waits for a few seconds, before managing to raise the volume of his voice, whilst retaining the docility of a whisper (clearly, the feminine side is at work): 'HELLO? IS THERE ANYONE AT HOME?'

'Mind what you do to my wife,' warns Pilate. He is not normally so defensive about Myfanwy; but, at the present moment, he feels moved, like a second-hand car dealer, to point out, 'It may be a heap of rubbish you're tampering with. But it's MY heap of rubbish.' Fortunately, he is only *moved* to say this. The actual words stick in his throat.

The Interpreter continues to address Myfanwy,

'First - stand in the pulpit where we can all see you, unencumbered by the daily objects of our professional and psychological life.' She moves to the designated place, and looks submissively down at the floor. 'Next, lift up your eyes and tell me what you see?' She squints and rubs her eyes. A group of young children are now standing before her, arms akimbo and with their elbows just touching. They are a foot or two away from Pilate, who has been watching the proceedings with some interest. Indeed, he has reached out to the nearest child, and seized her hand in order to verify the evidence of his own eyes.

'Well? Speak up!' exclaims Dmitri.

'If I may be permitted to observe ...?' asks Myfanwy.

'Yes ...? Yes ...? Observe ... Observe ...'

'Speak ... if I may be permitted to *speak* ...?'

'Permission granted. Speak, you may ... Is there a problem?'

'There is an error in my perception caused by that large object that was in front of me ...' she points at Pilate.

'Your husband, you mean?' Dmitri asks, wondering how this emerging psychiatric condition may be classified.

'I don't know. It is really quite odd. Whenever I am asked to concatenate one or more objects which contain only a null value, I – I do declare that everything before me disappears!' There is a pregnant pause, although this pregnancy is soon to be superseded by another which is far more heart-stopping. (Be patient, and you will see what I mean.) Pilate is rather insulted that his own wife should declare him to be null and void; but finds consolation in the thought that such invisibility is just one more symptom of an inexorable decline – in which "His Eminence" is passing from *something* into *nothing*. (If needs be, please refer to the exposition of these attributes in an earlier section.)

'What does she mean?' asks Dmitri, casting around for some enlightenment.

'I mean that in the present scenario, I cannot see anyone,' Myfanwy overcomes her reticence.

'Well, that … kind of … makes sense …' Dmitri takes his calculator out of his pocket, and verbalizes his thoughts. 'Now. Let us examine the situation. 'What are each of the values that we see displayed before us?'

'Something!' all of the children shout joyfully together.

'Anything in particular?'

'No. It doesn't matter,' the reply comes back, thick and fast. 'It can be anything at all!'

'And the last value?'

'Nothing!' they cry out raucously, as they glance at Pilate.

'So what does it all amount to?'

'Nothing!'

'Funny … I thought I heard you say that each of you were secreting a value? A certain *something*, I believe.'

'It all amounts to NOTHING!' is the belligerent assertion.

'Well, now. Let me double-check this New Age calculation.' Dmitri is tapping wildly on the keys of his calculator, like a musician in the throes of Rachmaninov's Third Piano Concerto. 'Something … concatenated with nothing … is clearly … wait for it …' (everyone waits with baited breath for the denouement of this fabulous arithmetical plot) '… The solution is in fact … *nothing*!'

'Come on! That can't be right, surely?' protests Pilate.

Dmitri orders Pilate to let go of the little hand; and, as he does so, Myfanwy proclaims with joy,

'And now I can see again!'

Next, Dmitri broadcasts into her tiny, indelicate earhole:

'There, now. You're absolutely fine. There's no need to see an optician after all.'

'Oh! *Thank* you … *thank* you … *thank* you,' answers Myfanwy, in a veritable crescendo of gratefulness.

More on the Subject of Gastronomy

'You know, quite suddenly I am feeling ravenous,' says Pilate. Even as he speaks, he is unaware of what actuates his voice. It is as if the words escape from his mouth of their own accord. 'But no fish, please.'

'Hold on, guys! That's *it*!' exclaims Dmitri, tapping the five fingers of one hand against the five of the other – as if the ten digits were completing an electrical circuit. 'You have nothing inside you. A variable which goes into a concatenation containing nothing ... will not be recognised; and nor will its neighbours! (Well, they do say you should mind the company you keep.) Yes! Yes! Make sure he is no longer empty! Fill him up with nutritious food. *Stuff* him ... *Stuff* him ... A curse be upon us all, if we allow his innards to remain empty!'

The events which follow are so shocking that Pilate is driven to externalize them. It is as if he is having an out-of-body experience – and his afflictions are happening to someone else. Two mesomorphs, resembling rugby players (and known to Pilate as the *Force Majeure* team), charge into the room. Initially, they startle everyone, for they are wearing the helmets and uniforms of policemen. They set about the former director, and handcuff him once again - this time affixing him to his chair; and then they wrestle both him and his chair to the floor. After a hard landing, two oversized elbows from one robust figure pin him down, and two oversized hands from the other scoop up fistfuls of available fish from the plate on the table. At this moment, and from the victim's mouth, arise the following words, 'I am not a *var-i-able*! I am a *human being*!' Pilate is unaware that he has almost repeated a line from the famous television series, "The Prisoner". As he observes the handful of rotten fish approaching his mouth, he emits a hoarse whisper, 'Oh, God! This is gross!' He then proceeds to recite the Riot Act of 1714, little appreciating that this act was repealed in 1973 – and was, in any case, configured to be spoken by the powerful to the powerless ... and not the other way around. Pilate wishes to clarify the situation:

'I know that husbands and wives do not always see eye to eye. But, throughout the previous episode, *I* perceived every element in the concatenation!'

'That is because *you* were *inside* it!' growls Dmitri, as one enormous muscular arm closes around Pilate's throat.

'Such behaviour as this should be outlawed,' Pilate protests.

'Perhaps the perpetrators could be granted diplomatic immunity? Then any offence to your basic humanity would no longer matter,' suggests Dmitri – noticing, for the first time, how foreign the two intruders look.

'But how can these bouncers have diplomatic immunity?' asks Pilate in desperation.

'How, indeed? And how does "diplomatic immunity" confer a licence upon foreign ambassadors of the state to behave as murderous, raping beasts? We shall never know. Ah, the joys of *carte blanche*!'

An articulate minion looks to Dmitri for permission to speak; and the latter nods cheerfully ...

'Of course, one sees the reasoning. An ambassador may relay information in time of war, and travel through enemy territory ... with the expectation that he shall not be held, against his remit or his will, - for interrogation, or on trumped-up charges (that make him an unwitting pawn with a ransom on his head). But this rational need for "immunity" is irrationally extended to allow a criminal to return safely home to his nest.'

'Plant a cuckoo in the nest to oust that sinful bird. Then let the cuckoo fly home, covered by the same protection. Thus one immunity may eclipse another. But shall the cuckoo kill him? Blood-lust sucks the veins of conscience dry. Ah!' sighs Myfanwy with resignation.

'Fear not, for they will not plant it!' says Dmitri.

The *Force Majeure* team are positively beaming with delight; although they temporarily relax their grip upon their victim.

'Might we, ourselves, not do something to earn this privileged status?' queries one member of that unique team.

'The status of loathsome beasts?' asks the other, whilst salivating. 'And the special exception which comes with it?'

'Yes,' states the first. He is tremulous with excitement.

'Would we need to go on a foreign mission? I might get homesick,' says the other. Incredibly, the saliva is now dripping from his mouth.

'I think that we would not,' responds his leader. 'If the flesh is willing, a single act could win for us that status upon the instant: provided the act was degrading enough. For, as the celebrated serial killer and exponent of necrophilia, Ted

Bundy, once said, "When you have passed through a daunting threshold once, your aversion to it somewhat diminishes. The membrane between the acceptable and the unacceptable has become permeable." But Mr Bundy did not embellish his idea so gracefully, of course. *That* is exclusively *my* doing!' (Clearly, our in-house philosopher sips from a font of fine words; yet he also quaffs deeply at the Bay of Pigs.)

'And would we not, perforce, need to attain a mental age of less than ten, in order to lose our moral responsibility, and to achieve immunity from public prosecution?' asks the second strong man. 'But how to shrink our brains for a moment of barbarism, and afterwards inflate them to their former size?'

'I have it! Forge two sets of legal documents relating to the aforesaid responsibility: and, at will, select for public inspection whichever should countenance the spirit of the moment.'

'Should we not take a vote on the right course of action?' asks Myfanwy.

'She's got a point,' replies Dmitri. And so Myfanwy's husband has a few moments of respite, as the electorate in the room arrange themselves into five equal sectors. Might jurisprudence let Pilate off the hook? Dmitri takes charge, and reassigns the sectors unequally - with the following result: Dmitri (on his own); Foolish Boy (on his own); Myfanwy in a third "sector", with the Accountant-come-Reader and Mr Scripting-Lang; Larry (the engineer) with his mother, comprising a fourth "sector"; and in the fifth, a large bevy of office personnel – or other living phenomena - which Dmitri refers to, collectively, as "the rest".

'That's just not fair!' protests Pilate. He can hardly contain himself.

'You've heard of gerrymandering – or "massaging the boundaries" as I like to call it,' explains Dmitri. 'It is a popular vehicle in "First Past the Post": which (ahem!) is the system you favour, I believe.' Dmitri pauses, and then calls out:

'All in favour, say "Aye". There is a resounding "Aye", to which Dmitri adds, without more ado, 'The Ayes have it. The room has spoken out in favour of "cruel and unusual punishment" by four sectors to one: the *others* being the one. In the third sector, Myfanwy, alone, has opted for clemency – and is outvoted. We are therefore witnesses to a landslide victory. Dear friends, we must dally not a moment longer. This is a call to arms!'

The two muscular men swing into action once again.

'Heave, *ho*! Heave, *ho*!' they exclaim, as they sway back and forth in a brave attempt to stuff a collection of foul victuals down their victim's throat. With each instance of applied pressure, there is – in keeping with Newton's third law of motion - an equivalent and opposite *re*action; until, with his assailants limbering up for their final thrust (and in lieu of the power of speech being taken away from him), Pilate finds his tongue:

'You don't have to force me. I-SAID-I-WAS-HUN-GRY! I just don't want any fi-shhhh ...' he hisses. 'I could murder a pizza, though.'

The two bullies look at each other in surprise at his familiar turn of phrase – and then desist from their cruelty, which (I have to say) indicates a remarkable degree of self-control, as they were just beginning to enjoy themselves. And so the accused is granted a stay of execution.

'It is not what a variable is called, but what is *inside* a variable that defiles it,' says Dmitri, posing with a Christ-like expression on his face. 'Alright. Foolish Boy, call our vegetarian pizza delivery service. And don't look at me like that ... it's the one which specialises in exotic mushroom and toadstool droppings ... er, *toppings*. It goes by the name of "Fungi Love", if I am not mistaken.'

As we have established that Copyvarfrom and his compatriot are from some far-away place, perhaps we can tolerate the following request:

'And don't forget – a side order of crickets!'

'They don't do 'em,' replies Foolish Boy.

'Or a John the Baptist Special ...?' adds Copyvarto, his mind whirring like a compact disk.

'That is - locusts, doused in wild honey? Mmmm. Delicious!' Copyvarfrom enlarges upon his compatriot's request, for the benefit of polite society; although polite society appears to be oblivious to the enlargement – for no answer is the kind reply. Nevertheless, Foolish Boy dials the number on his mobile telephone and casually orders a feast.

Mr and Mrs Boolean

Time passes. And whilst drooling mouths are on tenterhooks, waiting for the takeaway to arrive, Dmitri expatiates on the potency of small variables; and, at his instigation, two little characters enter the room who have not been seen before. Our disenfranchised hero breathes a huge sigh of relief, as he, and his chair, are eased into an upright sitting position – and he is, once again, free to assume a dignified pose. He takes the corporate decision to keep his mouth shut for the foreseeable future, - except, that is, for the admission of a little "Fungi Love".

'And now, can we please give a warm welcome to Mr and Mrs Boolean,' proclaims the interpreter. He would have ushered them in earlier, if there had been any chance of the vote going *the wrong way*. They are remarkably young; which is to say, they have only recently been added to one of the in-house programs. Thrown over their backs are translucent duffel bags, made from a composite of rubber and plastic, and filled with multiple replicas of the characters, "Y" and "N". The newcomers enter the room with looks of thunder upon their countenances. They appear to be engrossed in some kind of lover's tiff.

'Yes,' says the one.

'No,' defies the other.

'Yes, definitely!' emphasises the first.

'No. Most certainly not,' repeats the second.

Dmitri explains:

'They are fond of playing scrabble, but are upset by the fact that few words can be crafted out of the symbols which they are carrying with them.' The pair position themselves in opposite corners of the room: as far away from each other as is humanly possible, without the furthest one climbing out of the window and leaping onto the concrete some 30 feet below. They are married, and they are not even human: but in this warehouse, conundrums are the norm.

'More to the point, a boolean variable was recently changed, and the entire record which contained it was lost from the display. And now *he* blames her, and *she* protests her innocence. It's all so very sad! And the root problem may have been a simple programming error.' Dmitri glances at Pilate.

'Their parents were very much in favour of the union between them, and were exalting in the appropriateness of it all, until ... Oh! It all went so horribly wrong. Current thinking is: they will elope to Gretna Green to get a divorce. *Mon Dieu!*'

'Oh, dear. It may have all been my fault,' says Ms Esquelle. 'But I was beside myself. I just *did not* know what to do.' Dmitri comforts her,

'Well, never mind. I am beside you now – even as you are beside yourself ... with anxiety, that is.'

Unfortunately, she is inconsolable. She flaps her arms about - like a dodo, hoping to gain some purchase on the liquid air, before migrating south for the winter ... but the air is having none of it.

'I didn't know what to doooooo!' She repeats.

'So – what exactly *did* you do?'

'I threw out a record. At least I think I did.'

'You deleted it?'

'Well – it disappeared from the screen.

And then, seeing how penitent she is, Dmitri manifests a God-like sympathy and understanding:

'Ah! I see there has been a miscalculation. The lovely Myfanwy did not actually delete the record at all. It is still in the database, over which she – alone - presides. Apparently, the screen display was predicated upon a part of the record's index - a boolean variable - retaining its original value. When the value changed, the data was no longer shown. And thus it was lost, like the lone sheep in the parable, but now is found. There is no need to expatiate further upon the matter. My child, I absolve you of your sins. Go forth and respect the integrity of indices. But there is one who supersedes me, the laces in whose plimsolls I am unfit to untie. I speak of the Canon, whom you will shortly meet, and who can issue a special blessing with his magical holy water. I suppose I should have mentioned him earlier. I am afraid, for the time being, my absolution will have to do instead ...' and with these words, he reproduces the dirty coffee spoon, and taps her gently on the head again: as if the spoon were a tuning fork, and the resonance of pure tone would cleanse her mind of any wrongful thoughts.

Pilate sees a similarity between some of these words, and those of John the Baptist - when he alluded to the coming of a higher being (whose name requires no introduction), and he thinks,

'This is a mild form of blasphemy!' But, not being of a very spiritual disposition, Pilate's onset of holy contemplation soon gives way to human frailty: 'If that man assaults my wife one more time with filthy cutlery, there's no telling what I might do to him!' And he would have translated his thoughts into audible words, except that, like the thimble hopping and gliding across the rotating part of a roulette table, his mind has already moved on.

'Well, then,' Dmitri takes hold of the meeting again by the scruff of its neck. 'Now that this thorny issue has been resolved, I would like to invite you all to meet a pair of conjoined twins.'

A bicephalous woman enters the lovely, wood-panelled auditorium (for such is the décor which has been applied).

'Good evening, we are your "Dual Core" processor,' the two heads speak in a perfectly synchronised fashion, as if with a single voice. 'We have but one bed to sleep in, and so our two heads must suffice.'

'I can do one thing,' says one head.

'And, while she is doing *that*, I can be doing *something else*,' says the second head. Then both heads begin talking together, and with great speed:

'You will all have heard wondrous tales of how women may perform more than one task simultaneously. Well, now you will discover how this is done.' No sooner have they spoken, than they begin to communicate independently of one another – although they do not separate. In fact, their shared body, when they are seated, resembles a couple of ampersands, of which they are most proud. And they are both called Grizelda.

'OR is a logical AND, don't ya know?' comments one to the other.

'Really, Grizelda,' her twin replies. 'Algebra never was my strong point. But I must say, I am deeply offended by the notion that anyone could mistake *our* symbol (representing AND) for one of *those* ....' They both begin to edge backwards, distancing themselves from a monstrosity who has appeared before them – a tall, skinny man who is precariously balanced on a pair of stilts.

'There's no need to be offended, Grizelda. I'm only making small talk,' replies the first character to the second.

'Aw! Aw ...! Aw! Aw ...!' Says the man on stilts, his legs forming two bars of the famous "OR" symbol, as universally understood by programmers of a certain scripting language.

'Gracious me! What *is* that noise he's making, Grizelda?'

'He must think that because he looks down on everyone, he has the right to imitate a bird of prey.'

'But surely the interpreter values the nobility of the "AND" that is in ourselves, above this impostor, who represents the ignoble "OR", does he not?'

'Now, just you be patient there, ladies,' says the interpreter, 'and (if I get a moment to assist) your confusion regarding the precedence of logical operators shall be resolved.'

An Array of elements, and an Allusion to Benefits

The Reader resumes his jargon, and very soon he is interrupted.

'Gosh! I am a little queasy,' says Dmitri. 'I feel a list of values coming on, which – for the present incarnation – shall be fleshed out as boys and girls ...' The children who appear are mostly the progeny of Gladys (including Dot, who has become disillusioned with pacing the corridors by herself); and, before long, a female "element" is chastising a male "element":

'Now, then. If I am the third value, you must be the second!'

'I am *not* the second. I am the *first* and *you* are the second,' is the gruff reply.

'Poppycock and balderdash!'

'Alright, then. See if you can answer this. Who is the person to my left?'

'The first, if I am not mistaken?'

'Oh, but you are so very mistaken! Respectfully, he is the *zero-eth* element!' the other child concludes, caressing the syllables of this made-up adjective between her tongue and the roof of her mouth, as if they are chocolate raisins in a Ben and Jerry's ice-cream.

'Now, kids, simmer down and cease your bickering,' Gladys takes the lead, whilst retrieving (with a loud *'Voilà!'*) from some vast inside pocket of her coat ... a breakfast cereal called

"Benefits". The elements avail themselves of this crunchy delight, which is composed of Wheatabix, shortcake, peanuts wrapped in leaves of basil, and pieces of dried fig.

'We were practically raised on these!' says one.

'I'm totally famished!' adds another, as he reaches for the packet, only to be dispossessed by the first, who simply grabs it out of his hands and pours a quarter of the contents into a large breakfast bowl, and much of the remainder straight into his wide-open mouth. This is not a good move, as the cavity already contains other foodstuffs which he has been chewing upon; and several streams of milk dribble towards his chin, eventually forming a confluence before dripping onto his T-shirt.

'Well, I must say ...!' comments Dmitri, decorating an ellipsis with the bristles of his impatience. 'It is extraordinary what you can get out of a list of values – especially if it has not been properly policed for a while.'

The Reader is Assaulted

Suddenly, the visitor from the Inland Revenue makes his presence felt again. Initially, Pilate shows concern, but the man passes unnoticed by the crowd around him – who are fascinated by another greedy boy who is cradling some of the breakfast cereal in a kitchen towel, as if he is a marsupial mouse with a tiny pouch. The boy begins to fill his mouth with his booty, and his cheeks bulge as he tries – with all his might – not to blow half of what is in his mouth out through his nose. His lips have gone blue, and are cracking under the strain of retention. By now, the reader has resumed; and (impressively) he is reciting the obscure code from memory, until he grabs the attention of the floor by simply falling silent. He accounts for this behaviour by holding aloft the following notice,

'A script on this page is causing it to run slowly.'

Someone in the room, who is not far away from him, remarks that he has the wrong page in his hand.

'That's funny. I am sure he was given the correct information earlier on. What's he done with it?' asks Dmitri. Then he faces his silent minion, eyeball to eyeball. 'Pork Belly, what have you done with the scripts I gave you?'

'Excuse me, sir. He's got it in his pocket,' says Foolish Boy.

'What? Didn't he have this problem on a previous occasion?'

'This is *another* "wrong script" - different from last time.'

'Oh, Mother Mary! What's it doing in his pocket? It should be in his hand. He's supposed to be *reading* from it; not keeping it warm. The silly sausage!'

'The *next* script is on the table in front of him. He's finished reading from the *old* script, which he has crumpled and dropped onto the floor. And the *current* script is in his pocket, because it has not been paged into cache memory yet,' explains Foolish Boy. For once, he is sounding quite authoritative.

'Well, use the Ping command - and look sharp about it! We haven't got all day.'

Foolish Boy, delighted to be granted "the licence to flick", proceeds to sting the Reader on his face with the nail on his index finger; in response to which, the flicked subject moans gently, but makes no attempt at resistance.

'My reservoir of patience is running out!' cries the interpreter. 'Some of it has evaporated with the heat of my emotion; and some of it has leaked, due to improper containment.' All of a sudden, he is squinting with disbelief – for it seems, momentarily, as if Pilate's shadow has departed from its source and is scurrying towards the exit. Perhaps, like a treacherous Sea Captain, it no longer wishes to be attached to a sinking ship? (Of course, the impression only lasts for a second, and the observer could be mistaken. Anyhow, regardless of his alter ego, Pilate, himself, has not gone anywhere; and, very soon, the film of reluctant shadow – like a faithful pooch – is once again seen colouring the carpet at his feet.) The accountant, alias Java Man, alias Pork Belly, alias The Reader, is quiet, and Dmitri (not for the first time) cups a palm around his right ear, in order to magnify any sounds that are marked for his attention.

Throughout this sequence of surreal events, Pilate is day-dreaming. He is conscious of a role reversal: Dmitri is becoming more and more demonstrative (in fact, he is beginning to bear his teeth), whilst Pilate, himself, grows ever meeker. Cometh the role, cometh the man. It is a strange law of nature, that as the mantle of authority, responsibility, or lifestyle passes seamlessly from one being to another, - so the sceptre of a certain kind of personality passes with it. The king doth mould his head to fit the crown.

In his present incarnation, the accountant is generally mute except for the words he is given to read. And so, without a word, he displays an explanatory notice. This time, the message reads,

'A script on this page may be busy, or it may have stopped responding. You can stop the script now, or you can continue to see if the script will complete ...'

Dmitri asks for the Clear Screen command to be issued, but the "screen", as evinced by Pork Belly's face, appears frozen. Pilate has observed that the accountant-come-technical reader is, even in real time, a reticent man who asks few questions - and answers even fewer. The occupants of the room wait, but the object of their attention can add nothing to the words he is holding aloft on a piece of rectangular card. There is a beating of impatient knees, and a scuffing of ribbed rubber soles. Pilate is concerned for his plush new carpet, but the thick pile will not succumb that easily. Next, there is a universal tutting, and a clicking of tongues against the roofs of roomy mouths (all of which is much less soothing than the sound of willow on leather – or, for that matter, rubber on carpet).

'Well?' asks Dmitri. Still, there is no noise. Finally, sensing that something punitive is about to happen, the Neanderthal-lookalike rouses himself from his torpor ...

'It's an unresponsive script!' he protests pathetically. This is, indeed, a weak defence, and is not helped by a string of glutinous spittle escaping from his mouth (which has been forced shut by embarrassment for so long).

'My dear fellow ...' replies Dmitri, wiping away the saliva which he has been showered with, - and darting his tongue in and out of his mouth, like a serpent checking if any of the fluid is his own; 'a script is an inanimate thing. Unless you imbue it with life, it has none! It neither responds *to* you, nor is it repelled *by* you.' Dmitri licks the corners of his mouth, and then adjusts the knot at the top of his tie. Both are expressions of the highest degree of self-satisfaction.

Now this last remark might be understood by the present author to be mildly insulting, since, throughout much of this literary production, he has richly invested life in inanimate things ... with his *own* script, his whole script, and nothing *but* his script – so help him, God. Never mind. We will let that one go, and we will also allow Pilate to give us *his* view on the matter:

'A bit like some people's wives,' he whispers; and completes his thoughtful rejoinder, 'I wish mine could be less responsive. Then I might actually get some peace!'

'I am afraid I have run out of Random Access Memory,' the Reader explains with humility.

'But he's always remembered before,' says Dmitri, turning to face his audience like an actor playing to the gallery. 'And ... Gracious me! What extenuating circumstance is this, anyway, when the text is sticking out of his trouser-pocket?'

The reader summons up the full extent of his courage (and his torso). He leans towards the present director of ceremonies, and speaks from the heart:

'When Mr Propotamous bought his peripherals, he left me high and dry.' Pilate is upset by this. Anger has been welling up inside him for some time, and now, like a dam, he bursts forth: 'This is a fiasco! What would *he* know about peripherals! He's my financial advisor!'

The interpreter tightens his lips. He stares at Pilate with a sardonic expression, and then issues his directive:

'Alright, gentlemen. Let's cancel the whole process. We'll hit enter; then, after a while, boot up again ...' The Reader shudders, as Pilate's state of mind switches from ire to iced puzzlement. He scrutinizes the master who has supplanted him, but he is not alone. No one can make head nor tail of the instruction.

'Come on! You must know the procedure by now. Just bang him over the head with a frying pan; and then wait for two minutes before booting him up again.' Now, the little man who is The Reader looks deeply apprehensive - as well he might. A moment later, a member of the Force Majeure team returns from the office kitchen with a gigantic example of the required implement – a wok, in fact; and then, ending a brief period of uncertainty, bludgeons the Reader across the skull with such force that the echo of the assault reverberates through the chamber of every other skull in the conference room. The pathetic human collapses into a heap on the floor ... and, at this very moment, the lights go out and everyone is left in total darkness.

'What's happening?' asks Pilate. He begins to panic. This is partly on account of the serious crime he has witnessed, but more because he has lost sight of the thug with the wok. There is a general sweating and trembling in the animal bodies all around. Various voices are heard.

'Is he dead?' asks one.

'We've lost reception,' says another.

'What? No reception, you say? This is serious. If there's no reception, then there's no way out of the building,' articulates a third person.

Meanwhile, the stench inside the room emanating from putrid fish is becoming insufferable. Various individuals complain of nausea. To make matters worse, the meeting room, by now, is very crowded indeed; and exiting the present space (never mind the entire warehouse) would not be easy. Pilate, in the privacy of his own mind, begins to draw parallels with Britain's immigration policy. Then he comforts himself with the thought: 'Oh, well! At least if the accountant remains on the floor, that will free up a bit of space for the foreigner who hit him. If I should tread upon him I shall not worry, for he has fallen out of favour with me. In fact, if he is dead, then I will not have to listen to any more of my own code being read back to me!'

At this moment, the (former) accountant who has been floored begins to stir; and a member of the *Force Majeure* team attempts to kick him into a state of full consciousness, employing the metal tips of his rugby boots. He is acting on the advice of his feisty mother, given him when he was little:

'It is claimed that you should never kick a man when he is down. And yet, verily, I say unto you: "kick him hard when he is down". For if you kick him when he is upright, he may kick you back.'

The Reader finally opens his eyes. Like an astronaut, he has been to another world and back. His voice appears to have changed, for it is higher and more husky than before:

'Oooooh! Gawd! Ach! Jayyyyyyyyyysus Crust! ... *Crust* ...!' are his first words upon re-entering the earth's atmosphere.

Pilate calms himself down by imagining he is on a grassy knoll in the English countryside. There is a small protuberance under foot, and he realises he is standing on his accountant's head. He is not sorry, for it will afford him a better view of the proceedings around him when the light returns. It remains dark for what feels like an eternity; although, in truth, it may only have been a couple of minutes. Eventually the room is illuminated – and reveals The Reader moaning softly and rubbing his bloodied scalp. Mercifully, Pilate shifts his foot, - but not before stamping on the victim's windpipe (by accident, of course). The Reader spits blood – and Dmitri cries out, with the voice of a prophet, 'And the Lord sayeth, "I shall ground the sinner under my feet". Then (just to rub salt in the wound) he cites Corinthians: 1: 15-25: "For he must reign, till he hath put all enemies under his feet".'

'When there is blood on the streets, the government shall, through its tables of statistics, simulate economic growth,' says the COBOL compiler, who has been keeping a low profile. He touches his bald patch, and adds, 'Gone ... All gone ... to hair follicle heaven. I might request a mass to be said in their memory.'

'We have let a little blood this afternoon, and purged the system of bad humours,' says the Interpreter, who sounds like an apothecary. 'Let us continue with the recital.'

But The Reader can only say the words, 'Oh! My life is like a pressure cooker. How much more can I stand?' - in answer to which, a voice is heard with no identifiable source,

'A little more ... A little more ... until thy head shall burst!'

The Reader struggles to his feet and, in order to keep his balance, he defines the gentlest of undulations with his hands. He says nothing more. He simply stands erect and feels sorry for himself. But hearken! Dmitri is speaking again, and this time he is showing clemency,

'Our Reader needs time out to recover. Meanwhile, Dot has something to tell us ...'

'A little earlier, I was enjoying the cloud,' she says.

'The cloud?'

'I was licking my lovely, sweet cloud of candy floss,' she explains, 'before it got lost.'

'Well, just remember what your mother told you, and apply the same principle: "When you lose a parent, look for it in the place that you last saw it. Where did you last see it?"'

'I dropped it in the water tank – and then watched it mysteriously disappear! You know ... the tank of water in the atrium ...'

'Ummm ... Surprising. I must confess, I am not aware of a tank in the atrium,' says Dmitri. 'There is a fountain of drinking water just outside this office, but ... Ah! She means the vat of holy water brought to us by the very Reverend Bertrand Tyson earlier this afternoon.'

'What? I don't remember *him* being here this afternoon,' muses Pilate.

Given his recent extravagance, Dmitri seems, for the nonce, to have mellowed, and accepts that nothing about this meeting will run smoothly. Perhaps Dot talking about her candy floss has exerted a calming influence upon him? He remarks, philosophically, 'It is amazing how each subject we touch upon links up with some other; and how each of these others then strikes a sympathetic chord with other manifold relations of its own. It is a family reunion of corollaries ... a Cartesian product, no less: which, I might add, should be avoided in proper programming practice.'

PART THE SEVENTH: THE DOCTOR'S SURGERY

Suddenly, the meeting, like a sick patient, has suffered a bad turn. It even begins to sound like a General Practitioner's Clinic. Which patient will be seen first? And who will play doctor? We soon shall see.

'The next issue on the agenda is a certain field associated with a problem in our reporting functions,' explains Dmitri. 'She – the field, that is, - is here, now, to make our acquaintance.'

'A-hem! Mrs Field, if you please.' A woman with a bulge in her belly appears.

'Mrs Field has been complaining of a latent pregnancy. There is even some talk of a caesarean section. Mrs Field, would you like to take up the story?'

'Yes, sir. Well, sir ... you see, sir ... I have a carriage return character in my womb, obstructing my attempts at child birth.' Those around her look somewhat doubtful, and so she leans forward and reinforces her point: 'Yes. All of my reports are producing line throws at critical moments and when least expected, – or, at least, when least desired.'

'And what of your unborn children?'

'Occasionally a report will fail to print. But all of the reports are my progeny, and every one of them is precious beyond the pearls of oysters' dreams,' she announces proudly, cradling her stomach lovingly, as befits an expectant mother.

'Ah! I suspect that your difficulties arose from an external media device, and occurred at the precise moment when the little one was conceived.'

'Yes. I aborted once, and I came close to aborting again; but, in the nick of time, I saved this foetus (that I hold within me) from emerging too soon, out of the "pre-live" area.' Upon hearing this, Foolish Boy starts to giggle convulsively.

'It's not funny. It's very serious.'

'Yes, I know. I ... T is serious. Come on. It is ... is ... quite funny as ... as well!' stutters Foolish Boy.

'No. It is not. *Not - at - all*. These are my babies and their futurity, their essence, their very life force, is precarious and precious.'

Pilate wonders out loud, 'Could it be a phantom pregnancy?'

'Sir, I have not endured this trauma for the sake of a spirit which has no flesh!' she settles herself down, and places her hand gently upon her breast - for her heart is all a-flutter. Dmitri takes up the baton,

'Well, I am sure that everyone will join with me in wishing Mrs Field excellent fortune with the birth of her next child. Meanwhile, we have got a lot more of Pilate's turbid code to get through; so, Reader, would you recommence.' And, at this request, the accountant-come-financial advisor, alias Pork Belly, alias Java Man, resumes his irksome task with an incoherent drawl:

'<td class="dr"><select name="resident_bus_other">'

The interpreter signals to the reader to pause briefly, as he recovers from his gullet a portion of the previous line of code - like a cow regurgitating the cud from one of its four stomachs. Recovery complete, he begins to masticate the words all over again, deeming them to be improperly digested. However, he does not chew as leisurely as before, - but hurriedly, like a bovine who has been observed by predators at the watering hole. And, as he chews, the following words are already winging their way to him ...

'reset($lookupvalues);

for each($lookupvalues as $val)

{ $caption = $val; if ($row["resident-bus-other"] = '

More words follow, and Dmitri seems to be struggling.

'Hold on!' the Interpreter shouts, as something dribbles from his mouth into the bucket beside him. 'You're going too fast. I've told you, I can only process one line at a time.' He simulates a swallowing motion, with all three of his "double chins". (These appendages are misnamed out of a sense of propriety; quoth he: 'Well, I know it's really a triple and not a double – but modesty becomes me'). He works his lower jaw up and down, as if simulating a cylinder in a piston engine; but rather than transferring the offending morsel on to the next stage of the digestive process, the motion looks more like acid reflux.

'My poor Interpreter suffers from heartburn!' sympathises Myfanwy, 'and – merciful heaven! - he's discovered something in his windpipe (and it is not an unspoken piece of wisdom).'

'Hold on ... Just a - ... Just a mo-!' exclaims Dmitri.

'What is the problem?' ask the others in the room.

'It's a huh-huh-hy-hy-hy ...'

'What's he saying?' asks Pilate.

'Come again-ah?' asks Myfanwy.

'huh-huh-hyph-hyph.'

'Is it a fish bone?' Pilate quizzes him.

'No! ffffffff-fffffff! It's a ffff-fu-fu ....!' Dmitri attempts to dislodge the foreign body. Pilate raises the palm of his hand to his ear. (You know, I think our anti-hero is savouring the moment.)

'I'm sure a fish bone is pricking his windpipe,' reports Pilate confidently. 'The Queen Mother (may God rest her most glorious and inviolable soul) was prone to impaling her gullet upon fish bones. Poor Dmitri!' he exclaims sarcastically. 'It must have come from that dreadful platter which our hygienically-challenged technophile dished up earlier on.'

'It's not a fffff-ffffffish b-bone!'

'Well! Whatever could it be?'

Finally, with a cough as loud as an exploding hand grenade (and aimed - more or less - towards the spittoon), the Interpreter clears his airways ...

'It's a ffffffucking HYPHEN! And it's all HIS fault!' Dmitri points to Pilate, who has nowhere to turn. 'He knows nothing about the noble art of programming.' (The person addressed emits a feeble cough in fake sympathy.)

'You *know* I can't cope with hyphens in temporary variables!' Dmitri breathes in deeply before resuming. 'Well, I never! I have never, in all my born days, been so abused by such an insignificant character!' He looks at Pilate in a way which suggests that he is not talking exclusively about the hyphen. But Pilate is getting into the spirit of this strange world, and holds forth with the following hypothesis,

'Still, just imagine if we inhabited a hexadecimal world where alphabetic characters had numeric values? And let's suppose it was not a hyphen, but a minus sign? Why, the second half of the errant variable name, after the sign, might have been subtracted from the first half, before the sign. In that scenario, God knows what we could have conjured in our midst. Some fabulous creature of legend ... a leviathan, perhaps? For we have around us, ready-made for his environs, an entire sea of misunderstanding. Just think, if such a monster were to be accidentally named, he or she might feel that it was antisocial not to put in an appearance. After all, if your associates were to call you, I'm sure you would not refuse their invitation? That is right, is it not, Dmitri?' asks Pilate, prodding his prosecutor (or should that be "his persecutor") a little nearer to the edge. Dmitri gives him a look that is not altogether humorous - and whispers something foul (which, out of propriety, the author has withheld). And, hauntingly, the air becomes tinctured with a blue dye in the vicinity of the speaker's mouth. Dmitri is concerned about the effect of stress at work upon his thinning hair, which you would think was a mere bagatelle compared to the prospect of choking to death on a fish bone or a hyphen! He reaches into his desk for a phial of Baby Bio, and he gently massages this lotion into his scalp. Simultaneously, a head louse in the vicinity expresses concern that its usual food source has become contaminated. Indeed, it may be a matter of debate as to whom this louse has mostly feasted upon. Is it the old director or the new? For, at the present moment, both of them are scratching their heads.

Naturally, Dmitri is still shaken after his encounter with the hyphen in Pilate's flawed code, and woe betide any living thing which happens to arouse him in the wrong way.

'That is not ... *quite* right!' the interpreter finally replies, slowly and deliberately, as two families of head lice suddenly come into view on the desk in front of him. They are bugs with blood on their minds, and skin cells gripped between their sucking parts. One family of lice appear to be in hot pursuit of the other, and are slowly gaining ground on them: for their nits have hatched, and they imagine they have extra mouths to feed. (Little do they realise, a nit has no anus - and may die from constipation.) The sight of this miniature life-and-death struggle, played out on a green cloth (sometimes reserved for games of pool), resembles a migration of wildebeest over the African plains. For a couple of seconds, Dmitri allows this outlandish parallel to percolate through his mind. And then, when he has had enough, he beats the life out of the little creatures with his fist. Poor lice, deprived of that special dispensation, even granted to a condemned man, to enjoy a final meal of choice before execution. The other staff appear somewhat shocked.

'I had to do that. The sight of those bugs was having a deleterious effect upon my stomach – and the effect was beginning to interrupt my interrupting', the Interpreter explains.

'Don't you mean, "interrupt your *interpreting*"?' asks Pilate.

'Do not correct me!'

'I was merely ...'

'Well, do not *mere-ly* ...' yells Dmitri, banging the syllables out on the table in front of him with the palm of his hand.

PART THE EIGHTH: THE SLAYING OF CORTANA

Acts of Cruelty

A certain character with an encyclopedic knowledge of everything is now present in the room. No one knows how long she has been there – or how she managed to escape everyone's notice, for she has not the modesty to keep a low profile. She lives online and (ideally) should only speak when spoken to, but she invariably fails in her remit.

'Is she a spy working for the government, or gathering data on us for some universal advertisers (which is no better)? Either way, we cannot surf the internet in peace,' is the assessment of one office worker. Dmitri corroborates this opinion, with the following words spoken directly to the female savant:

'Madam, you are not welcome here. Will you please step outside.'

Cortana (for that is her name) puts on a demure expression, and obediently leaves the room. Pilate is glad to see her severely dealt with; for, often-times, he has been online when she has disturbed his concentration - by showering his computer screen with unsolicited facts. But he covers his eyes and his ears to shield his sensitive nature from all that follows. Two minutes pass. Cortana exits the front entrance of the building, and shuts the door behind her. Office workers in the meeting room rush over to the windows, with their mouths open and their nostrils flared like those of horses. They see her walk into the clutches of a spectral mob, who take to constructing a makeshift scaffold, – a process which, curiously, appears to be under her direction.

'Hang the harridan!' someone shouts.

'Alliteration is a subtle literary device much favoured by poets,' says Cortana.

'Burn her at the stake!' cries another disgruntled person.

'But you have no wood,' she counters sympathetically.

'Tell us where we can get some.'

'Let me see where the nearest hardware shop is.' Cortana puts her imaginary thinking cap on. Meanwhile, a cacophony of voices – some interacting, and some disassociated from each other, – rain down upon the materialization of the virtual lady.

'Kill the bitch!' one mobster yells.

'This term is only half-accurate, as I *am* a female but I am *not* a female dog.'

'Snuff the life out of the insufferable nag!'

'Crack her windpipe, the conduit of her superfluous words!'

'Unsolicited text and images online ... are relished by surfers everywhere. So get out your surfing board, and spread some relish upon the data that you crave!' she eloquently defends herself.

'You get out *yours*, so that we can drown you in the sea!'

Yet faced with this vitriol, Cortana just continues in the performance of her duties, reciting dictionary definitions of "harridan" and "nag" – and other spoken words. Clearly, she is not fazed by the dire predicament she now finds herself in, and has been programmed to feel that her service is of the utmost importance; irrespective of how many say otherwise.

'Cut out her tongue, so that, henceforth, it may not fondle our curiosity, nor irritate our nerves.'

'Stretch her on the rack, until her sinews snap!'

'The rack was a medieval instrument of torture invented by a Frenchman ...'

'We don't have one.'

'What? No Frenchman? Where can we get one?' Shouts the ringleader. 'Is he in the hardware shop?'

After a while, Cortana returns to the conference room. This time, she has a broken neck - resting gently upon her left shoulder.

'All my life, I have merely followed the edict of my all-powerful manager, Windows 10: which must not be disobeyed,' is her lame excuse. All is in vain, for she is ordered out again by Dmitri, with the ultra-stern words, 'This woman has received insufficient punishment.'

In the fray, Myfanwy is suddenly imbued with the arrogance of Salome, and cries out,

'I want her head delivered to me on a platter!' After this unprovoked outburst, her cheeks go quite red with embarrassment. 'Gosh ... I don't know why I just said that. I am sure I wish her well. After all, what possible use would her head be to me?'

'And what with the performance of the postal service these days, the head might never be delivered anyway,' replies one of the professional staff.'

'Horrifying!' Murmurs Pilate, as Cortana returns to her persecutors – and the abuse starts again; watched by the keen eyes of excited professionals, who peer through the glass of the closed office windows.

'Pare the skin on her face, and use the shavings in a stir-fry! Then separate her skull from her shoulders - and stick it on a pole!' shouts one vagabond outside.

'No. On a platter, marinaded with a stir-fry. 'Tis dinner for me dog!' adds another ruffian.

'Treat her dislocated head as if 'twas a football,' an errant brigand suggests; in response to which, Cortana verbalises the origins of the game of football. Meanwhile, one of her captors delivers his own commentary on current affairs,

'Blood on the pavement. Blood running in the gutters. Black pudding aplenty for Satan? Then, the devil am I!'

Next, the crowd is casting about for a spike to impale her head upon, whilst Cortana nonchalantly looks around for the next best thing ... a sharp branch capable of making an incision. Then, all of a sudden, someone pierces the nape of her neck with a letter-opener. She squeals with pain. Yet straight away she covers her mouth coyly – and, once more, hides her emotions under a sheet of ice: for she realises that her function is not to have feelings, but to convey knowledge. As blood from the appalling wound gushes forth, Cortana issues a banal report on the constituents of the human bloodstream. And back in the meeting room, Dmitri (who is – himself - now peeping through the window) states with emphasis,

'Ugh! Tell this mob, that under no circumstances is that woman to return here!'

After ten minutes or so, and the shedding of more blood, – but with no concomitant screams, - Cortana's head, still dripping, is brought in on a tray; and Dmitri is angry at this blatant transgression against his wishes. He raises his hand:

'Remove that vile object from my sight! I do not want it anywhere near me.'

'Given a chance, this most precious of my earthly remains could be food for thought; or simply *food*,' replies the head.

The ambassador, who is bearing the platter, takes his booty downstairs and out into the chilly air. More voices are heard.

'However we do it, we must take her life: for, somehow or other, her spirit is still with us!'

'Take her life? Where to? There is no library of public knowledge, nor churchyard ossiary, nor common vat, to which this pesky oracle has no access. Whatever location *her life* is removed to, *her spirit* shall reclaim it as her own.'

Eventually, Cortana's head is shoved into a bin bag, and carried off to the ocean for drowning. The whole group is singing baudy songs as they go; and still the sound of her voice can be heard, although it is growing fainter as the mob fades into the distance.

Pilate re-imagines her dislocated head as a buoy, bobbing up and down on the surface of the sea, – with eyelids all a-flutter (as if in the throes of death or sexual flirtation); and with a long and slender "kinkajou tongue" lapping the waves, and rendering approximate direction like a rudder. In his fantasy, she is still talking incessantly: perhaps reciting from a table of statistics on the health of the ocean, compiled by the Ministry of Agriculture, Fisheries and Food.

When peace at last prevails, Dmitri speaks with authoritative solemnity,

'Now, then. Let us put aside *two whole seconds* of respectful silence for the commemoration of her memory. Bow your heads – and mark my generosity. For she deserves no more.'

'That woman was taking an *Ice Age* to die,' remarks an office professional quietly. Dmitri's answer to this is dignified, and brooks no contradiction:

'All members of the human family (even those who are born, like plants, out of some asexual union, and have artificial intelligence in their skulls) must live – or die – according to the dictates of the personalities they have been given. Therefore, do not concern yourself with her welfare ... Trust me, her life may no more be extinguished than death and taxes.'

An Aside

Inside the conference room, every owner of a personal computer is impugning the good name of Cortana in his (or her) own mind, and through that spectral mob these thoughts are realized. Yet externally, each vocalizes false sympathy for this chattering know-it-all as she faces her ordeal. So it is, that a precedent set long ago is re-affirmed: wherein the ruling (educated) classes are the natural enemies of the dispossessed (and fear an uprising that may supplant them), - and yet those very classes will happily harness the masses into cohorts against a common enemy; and then wring their hands, and publicly deplore the ensuing violence ... whilst, in private, they breathe a sigh of relief that their dirty work has been done for them.

The Meeting Continues, as if Nothing has Happened

'You know, it strikes me that objects in the science of computing are related to each other, like apples and pears, – and, on occasion, they are even named after artefacts in the world at large,' says Dmitri.

'Don't you mean Apples and Apricots?' asks a junior member of staff, the one known as "Foolish Boy".

'Or Blackberries and "Raspberry Pi"?' questions Myfanwy.

'Well,' replies Dmitri, 'Apricots might, eventually, have become hybrids of Apples, if they had not died out before they could begin to properly evolve.'

The technical staff begin to discuss a significant piece of software which they are working upon, - that being, the ratio between the rising cost of property and the growing amount of disk space on offer inside computers (both measured in quantities of the magical letter, "K"). Indeed, a mathematician on the team is coding an algorithm for the graphical relationship between these two ever-changing phenomena.

'Yea, clever ... but isn't it a bit pointless,' asks Foolish Boy. 'There clearly ain't no link.' (Why can't he just follow the example of featureless wallpaper, and fade nonchalantly into the background?)

'Not at all,' says Dmitri, 'the advantages of such ground-breaking software are manifold.'

'They are?'

'They *must* be. The local bank manager has commissioned it. His establishment is close to the infamous "Chapter 11", and if it can ... how shall we say ...? be gently nudged towards the precipice by The Perfect Launchpad sucking it dry ... why then, my friends, it will be over the cliff-face and all at sea.' Here he pauses in order to formulate his maritime imagery, 'and a large pot of money will be forthcoming from the government, to buoy it up and bail it out! (And this is a further honey pot that we may dip our paws into.) How is it that entrepreneurs, after filing for bankruptcy, are able to bounce back into the frame so quickly – other than by support from friends in high places?' At this, the COBOL Compiler suddenly perks up with the words,

'I've had it with the present; and *fears for the future 'r us.* But I'm very excited about the past!'

Soon after, they all embark upon a debate about software for military surveillance. At this moment, the director registers - on his own highly attuned radar - certain whispers which are circulating around the room: among them, is the voice of a magnificent flower beetle, who appears to be talking gibberish:

'I want to go right, and I bank to the left; then I attempt to fly straight on, and my nose dips. Ever since my mummy taught me how to fly, I've never experienced anything quite like it.'

It is, coincidentally, the same beetle as was previously reported in the "Oval Office", - and he has somehow flown into the meeting room. But he doesn't know what his true identity is, or where he is ultimately heading. Like a Middle Eastern prince with his own chauffeur, he has become accustomed to being driven everywhere. What unearth do I mean? Well, he used to travel in reconnaissance missions, with a minute camera fitted to his abdomen which spied upon enemy airfields, and an implant for sending discrete electrical signals to those muscles controlling his wings (allowing his movements to be tracked and controlled). How ever did the creature end up inside this software house? Was he adopted by Foolish Boy (who, it is rumoured, keeps a menagerie)? He has no idea. Meanwhile, Dmitri has been speaking,

'... Then there is the strange case of the toy rocket, which emulates a recent production from the US Air Force. It will chase the hottest point in the vicinity, even if this happens to be its own backside ... in which event it will travel around and around in an eternal arc - creating a vortex with its own current of air; until it runs out of steam and falls to earth, exploding upon impact.'

'A veritable gift to comedy,' remarks one of the Software Engineers; and, as he speaks, Dot tilts her head and becomes doe-eyed, as if visualising the love of her life in her mind's eye. And what, pray, might this translucent image, overlaid upon her material reality, actually be? Well, she is only eight years old, and so we will let her explain in her own words:

'Oh! That's soooooooo sweet!'

'Sweet? How so? Speak, child, or forever withhold your sympathy.'

'My favourite friend's puppy dog does that.' A murmur of confusion ascends from the floor:

'Does what, exactly? What's she talking about?'

'Soooooo sweet,' she repeats, with a tear manifest in her aqueous blue eyes. 'It chases its tail around, as if nothing else matters in the whole wide world. I *want* one.'

'Mmmm. Yes ... well ....' and in the moments which follow, Dmitri feels like a feline athlete spinning through the air, whilst attempting to orientate itself properly with respect to the ground, before its head hits the concrete. He regards this outbreak of sentimentality as "insipid", and his mind is working with the greatest dexterity to nip all such behaviour in the bud, before the rarefied atmosphere in the board room becomes infected with it:

'As a matter of fact, these rockets are selling rather well, having been used infrequently by terrorists in arson attacks. Perhaps they will employ drones next? A drone could pick off any object at a considerable distance ... even a small female. And Yoyo, a shock-wave Flash object (famous in 3D games), may be along later to demonstrate – but only in a virtual way, of course!' he inhales deeply, having spoken the words at great speed in order to bury the little girl under an avalanche of ghastly images. And then he peers over at her, certain of his success. But she remains statuesque, like a figurine who is the apotheosis of puppy love.

Oh well, an office meeting is intended to be a haven of civility, and so the shattering of such a pretty ornament will have to wait. And while we are waiting, a glorious reign of peace ensues – almost reminiscent of that which held sway in the Holy Roman Empire for two hundred years or more (the *Pax Romana)*; except that this reign is shorter, and lasts for under two hundred seconds.

Felicity's "Technology Fest"

'Let us indulge ourselves with a three minute silence,' says Dmitri, 'in order that we may reflect upon all that has been said.' Watches are calibrated, and soft sighs are heard. Could it be the release of stinking gasses from food breaking down, or the wind in the trees outside, or even the sound of thoughts travelling through discarded neural circuits – that would be rusting up, were they not living tissues? Anyhow, after three minutes exactly, Dmitri ensues:

'Now, let us examine our own endeavour. I shall amplify my delight in all things new, by equipping each one of you with brand new, highly specialised glasses. Schiller, forgive me, for this is my "Ode to Joy"! You will have heard of these glasses ... they have a built-in camera, which allows access to the internet in response to a verbal command from the wearer; and they record everywhere you go, in real and virtual space, before relaying it all back to our central processing unit, so as to render an audit trail of your day. I am just *so* excited! How can anyone even feign to resist? We must find a pair for Mr Propotamous, and super-glue them to his nose, in order that we may monitor what he does for evermore. (He enjoys monitoring others, and so he will understand our motives.) And from this ... on to a highly portable piece of technology, brought to us by everyone's favourite little girl; a girl who is – if I may say – *fêted* for her *own* portability.'

The impression is dawning upon Mr Propotamous that this other-worldly meeting is following a similar agenda to the one that he, himself, had chaired earlier in the day.

******

Since its inception, the software house has depended upon a special company for the provision of its smaller hardware components. This public limited company trades under the name of "Excelsior Re-furbishers"; although, today, they are exhibiting something entirely new. The outfit is run by a brother and sister team from China, Y. Aye Pong and Y. Ou Pong; and whichever of them is in the country at the time of arrangement, stands as the point of contact. At least, this has been the case thus far. Unfortunately, their names have, in the past, caused so much amusement that Pilate has issued a legal writ - insisting that another underling (with a more "palatable surname") be appointed for the purpose of visiting clients ... or he would have to *look elsewhere*. Surely, a bunch of big-hearted British businessmen will not persist in their laughter? We shall see. So, now: enter a replacement from the USA, a Chinese-American, some 4 feet 9 inches high, and answering to the name of "Felicity Pangolin". She is removing a wet mackintosh after being caught in the rain, and she has a well-rehearsed ice-breaker for new clients:

'I ... not pangolin ... not reeeeeaaaally. My appeaaaaarance ... is a little un-contestant wit my name' (she means "inconsistent", and she chuckles – but not for that reason). 'You see' (she touches her nose) ... 'no pointy snout and no tail either ... but I do wear stiff, dry rain mac, caked in mud ... like *exoskeleton*!'

All around her, people break into smiles. Felicity is about 45 years old, but appears to enjoy being referred to as "a little girl". And she is carrying a mysterious orb in a velvet bag, with all of the delicate care which befits an *objet d'art* of unknown worth. Behind her is a retinue of five individuals, bearing on their shoulders a long, black case, some eight feet long. Are they a funeral cortège with a coffin? May such a narrow case contain anything at all? Could anything but a serpent be that shape? Felicity notices everyone's curiosity, and utters these reassuring words:

'Na! It not em-potty! It def-in-ite-ly fooooooool!'

And so we have the ceremonial opening of the lid. And what does this elongated object turn out to be? Surprise, surprise! It is a laptop. And the display area is revealed to be only two inches in height.

'Ladies and gentlemen!' says Dmitri, gesturing to the wall where several photographs are hung. 'What would I want with the portraits of others, when I can have my very own *landscape*. And such a *wide* landscape it is too! The *next generation* of landscape, in fact.' A couple of those present begin to discuss a suitable formula for the most appropriate "screen estate".

'*Screen estate*, hey? Is that a hatchback,' asks Myfanwy, who is utterly clueless. 'Would a wolfhound fit in the back?'

'No. We are referring to an arithmetical anomaly - that is to say, how the total display area dwindles with a wider screen; even though the description of the area – expressed as a length from corner to corner in inches – is the same. To elucidate, I have recently purchased a WXGA fourteen inch laptop to replace my old fifteen inch device (which had a 4:3 aspect ratio); and, but for the gain of a few millimetres on the width, the screen is twenty-five percent smaller!'

Myfanwy's husband is looking with disbelief at the monstrosity that has been brought in. He puts his head in his hands, like one who is losing his mind, and mutters: 'Oh, God! So un-pc ... So un-pc ...'

Dmitri looks at him with distaste, and then stares into the crystal ball that Felicity has unwrapped from its velvet carrier bag.

'Wide screen is the way of the world! Wide screen is where the near past, the present and the future must all rest their weary heads!' Dmitri proclaims with zeal, and then brushes the back of his hand across the lid of the laptop (which is 100 inches wide), as if it was the gorgeous pelt of some wild feline.

'Well, Felicity .... little girl ... more bang for your buck, hey?' says Dmitri, who is so full of enthusiasm that he is completely oblivious to the innuendo.

'But ...' interjects Pilate, half referring to Dmitri's saucy comments, and half to this peculiar device, 'this so far exceeds the common bounds of courtesy and good taste.'

'Mr Propotamous, listen up! It is marketed on the principle that – with such *long lines* on offer - you can just type and type to your heart's content, without having to keep pressing the Return key,' explains Dmitri; and, turning to Myfanwy, he adds, 'or carriage return, as it used to be called.'

Pilate is unconvinced.

'B-But ... If suspended in the middle, will it not crack easily? It is ... You are ...'

'What are you mumbling about now? It's hardly a see-saw, is it?'

'So *un-pc.*'

'That term again. So uniquely and perfectly constructed! Is that what you mean?'

'I don't know what to say.'

'Well. Be careful what you *do* say. Other people's nonsense is like other people's fetid air. For their companions' sake - better in than out.'

'B-But ... I thought the phrase meant -'

'Will you P-PLEASE stop saying B-BUT. Good grief! Now you've got *me* stammering as well!' And at the precise moment of his discontent, he (once again) brings his open palm crashing down on the wooden table, with a noise like a clap of thunder. The table buckles under the stress and a fault line opens between two wooden knots, as if the entire composition were a model of the earth's crust, and enthral to an earthquake. This is extraordinary for an object which, supposedly, has been so well-crafted. Worse still, his hand connects with the treasured electronic device, and he gazes in horror as it falls to the floor and *actually* snaps in two. The result is spectacular, to say the least, - with liquid crystal seeping out, like some meretricious devil's broth ... one that is, at once, both beautiful as a rainbow and poisonous as an asp.

'Now see what you've made me do!' shouts Dmitri.

Pilate groans inwardly, and offers the following health warning, 'You know, that liquid might be inflammatory.'

'This was entirely his fault,' Dmitri says, turning to the other businessmen present. 'If he hadn't mentioned the *possibility* of the screen cracking, none of this would have happened. *You* heard him. He infected my mind with auto-suggestion.' Pilate goes as red as cranberry juice – although it is uncertain whether this is due to shame, humiliation or rage. I think, myself, that it is primarily consternation. He is concerned about his new Wilton carpet being infused with the oily fluid that has escaped; but at that moment Dmitri cites Nietzsche,

'Never mind the carpet stain, and the concurrent heartbreak over damage to physical things. What does not destroy me makes me stronger.' (Obviously, the bit about the carpet stain is not by Nietzsche.) Dmitri pauses for breath, and then charges, like an unfettered bull, into his next subject.

PART THE TENTH: A MIRACULOUS BIRTH

A desire to be the centre of attention has been temporarily renounced by The First Lady. She is having some ghastly abdominal spasms, and is noisily concentrating all of her efforts on regulating the pain. This is no laughing matter. (Readers, wipe away your smirks and bin your dirty tissues! Fresh, absorbent pads are required for tears of sympathy.)

'Oh, my gourd!' She says, using her palms (in lieu of a fig-leaf) to cover her forbidden fruit. 'Oh, my giddy aunt-ah! God 'ave mercy 'pon me for all my sales 'n' lettings!' - for she has, from time to time, *sold* herself to the highest bidder (being driven to seek gratuitous flattery, on account of the non-performance of her husband); and thus *let herself go* in numberless ways she never should have. It seems to her husband that she is experiencing the pangs of child birth, and he takes this as evidence that she has been unfaithful. But with whom? Surely not with Dmitri? The readers may decide for themselves whether her progeny shall be brought into the world via the normal means, or by divine intervention. We understand that it might be the latter - for how could two human beings, who have no allure, be tempted into an act of sexual union with each other? And yet, for that matter, how well could a systems builder (with an angelic messenger operating in the cyberspace of biblical history) stand in for a carpenter who builds things out of wood? Pilate is thinking:

'When I have reprised my company, I shall hold a tribunal on the matter.' His wife is certainly in labour now, and is thrusting her pelvis out and groaning, 'How much longer, Lord? The post must arrive soon.' Suddenly, all eyes are upon her. Ironically, she cannot enjoy the attention, for her own eyes are shut, and the veins in her forehead have risen - like blue eels out of a pink ocean. (A strange simile, perhaps, but why should the traditional colours of nature remain, when the normal processes of nature have been ditched?)

'The ba-ba-bastard birth will actually occur while I am still t-t-tied to this bloody chair!' Pilate is clearly distraught; and is made more so by the sight of birth fluids which (like Royal Mail) arrive not a moment too soon. Dmitri speaks,

'She will bear me a child and he shall be called Emanuel, or *God with us.*'

The director is struck by the sacrilegious tone of the language, yet before he can protest, the birth has already occurred. Alas! no infant is heard crying.

The various characters in the room begin rummaging through the bloody output. There is so much of it, that - would you believe? - they can find no trace of a newborn baby. The light afforded by the eco-friendly bulbs is rendering the appearance of the room in a light that is dull and overcast. Then one of the seekers of the infant has a bright idea, and another has a torch. The torch is switched on, and the one with the bright idea seizes hold of the umbilical cord, as if it were a rope that would prevent the baby from falling off a cliff.

'Here! It's got to be attached to the end of this! Where *else* could it be?'

'Maybe it's escaped?' the man with the torch offers, without much conviction. He is not as bright as his colleague (or his torch).

'You mean it's gone back inside?' replies the other, with a hint of sarcasm.

Soon, all of the guests form themselves into a queue, and each holds a part of the umbilical cord aloft, whilst unfolding the next section and handing it to his neighbour. They are chattering nervously. To the untutored eye, they appear like intrepid explorers in the dark interior of Guyana, posing, for the benefit of photo journalists, with an anaconda which they have just sacrificed. One of them has a tape measure (which is dutifully applied), and the handlers all agree that it must be the longest example, ever recorded, of a disposable piece of human anatomy. Even Foolish Boy has something to say. He quips that their thoughts are intersecting like the circles on a Venn diagram; and that their murmurings sound like a Voodoo incantation. Finally, the end of the cord is reached – and the end of their tether, so to speak, - only to find, gift wrapped (like a Christmas present) by the last loop of Myfanwy's fleshy excrescence ... a computer manual, entitled, "An Indispensable Primer in CASE Methodology: Volume 1". If Joseph, foster-father of God incarnate, is looking down, he must be so proud of her: for he was a carpenter, and paper is a wood-based material. Although I must concede that he knew nothing of Computer-Aided Software Engineering.

'Could it be a virgin birth?' Pilate wonders. 'If so, it is the first instance amongst human kind for two thousand years … and the only latter-day example of parthenogenesis outside of the reptiles.' At that moment his nemesis calls out:

Is it a boy? Oh, bring him to me! Bring him this very moment! Let me embrace him! Oh, my darling child!' And, upon receiving his paper-based offspring, he bursts out,

'Ah! *Le … manuel d'entretien.* It is a boy!' Clearly, he is of the Gallic persuasion, and wishes to impute gender to inanimate things. Meanwhile, the true owner of this software house, who is livid at the thought of having been cuckolded, expresses his wordless horror with a series of false coughs; and then comforts himself by muttering under his breath, 'Oh, well! If that's how Dmitri's last manual came into being, no wonder it's no bloody good!'

Eventually, the "child" is wrapped in swaddling bands and presented to Dmitri, who appears blissfully unaware that it is *not* actually a boy – nor a girl either. And then, quite suddenly, Myfanwy winces and goes into labour again.

'Aye up! Volume 2 is on its way!' someone calls out. After a further series of grunts and sighs, and splutters of bodily fluids, the second "infant" arrives. This time, it is not a computer manual, but rather … *A One-Volume Guide to the delivery of Neonates within the Computer Industry (Henceforth to be known as "Nerds").*

The midwives, who are really computer programmers, are not fazed by this unflattering reference to technical fellows and females of advanced logic. And one of them, who is transfixed by the subject matter, begins to read …

A Note with Respect to Copyright

Neither this companion piece, nor the primer to which it is allied, may be photocopied; nor may any facsimile of either be made - by hand or dexterous paws or claws (we refer to the well-honed art of animal thieves, most especially monkeys and cats); nor may the manual be "reverse engineered" to fulfil ulterior motives (that are improper); nor may any part thereof be subject to the self-same acts of pilfering or corruption, specified in the clause which you have only just read (and, I trust, will not yet have forgotten – without the impairment of dementia); nor may the whole, or any part thereof, be altered through the kind of word shuffling that will unzip and falsify its meaning, and thereby "stitch up" the manufacturer in the community at large.

Peace of Mind

The author of the "noble primer" hereby encloses his guarantee, that there shall be no excessive documentation nor any defective workmanship, either in the appearance of the whole manual, or in any part thereof; and that, should any such superfluity or flaw be found, the manual may, in its entirety, be returned – notwithstanding statutory rights, – to the manufacturer for correction, no later than the warranty period of sixty seconds from the moment of its bloody birth.

Latent Praise for Righteous Attainment

Please note that every effort has been made to punctuate each sentence within this guide; and, through the art of proper expression, we (the associates of the manufacturer) do confidently assert that the excellence of the present paragraphs must necessarily supersede those of every previous legal document contrived by the mind of man.

******

The guidebook is 50 pages long: comprising the above cautionary notes and preface on the first page, and a logical condition on the second:

If neonate be of human stock then
    detach umbilical cord from belly button
else
    detach umbilical cord from first visible period on dust jacket

What follows are 48 blank pages, "saddle-stitched" together. The male "midwife" who has been reading aloud now protests:
'God! What a waste of paper. And I can barely make out the lettering on the cover – which is doused in blood and flaccid membranes!'

Another midwife opines, 'If I were none the wiser, I would say the period is all over the flimsy dust-jacket.'

'Ha, ha! A spineless production – unworthy of the paper it is not printed on!' ejaculates the first. 'The primary genetic inheritance must have been passed via the female line.'

'Male chauvinist pig!' a female midwife utters.

Dmitri exclaims,

'Escort these two gentlemen outside, pronto! Somebody?' No one moves, and so the two remain.

So much for the guide to the primer. Meanwhile, the main volume has been transferred into the arms of its progenitor, Dmitri, who is now rocking it to sleep, as if it was a living, breathing infant in a cot. And the proud father whispers (as affectionately as a lovebird cooing to its chick):

'There, there. Do not cry, my lovely!'

PART THE ELEVENTH: A WONDROUS HOLY MAN –
AND SOME MINOR ASSAULTS, JUST TO PASS THE TIME

An Official Disclaimer, and a Declaration of Intent

Before we are joined by a man of God, the author would like to express his abhorrence. Firstly, for the suffering of Cortana. And secondly, for the earlier treatment meted out to the accountant-come-financial advisor, - who shall remain nameless, except for his various soubriquets: The Reader, Pork Belly and Missing Link (or Java Man). And he would like to apologise on behalf of Dmitri Bosphorus-Deaux who instigated them, and who has lately acquired the same personality disorders as the former misanthropic leader in this yarn, Pilate Henry (christened "Hodgkin") Propotamous: the one whom Dmitri deposed. The author can offer nothing but surprise, at the distorted affection shown by Dmitri for an inanimate possession: a mere manual. In addition, the author in no way countenances the methods employed in restoring the functionality of a computer, - that is to say, powering down and booting up with such animal brutality. In fact, and in all innocence, he eschews each and every wilfully inhuman act described within these pages – and hereby abdicates all responsibility for them. For that matter, he wishes to disassociate himself from acts of wanton violence altogether, whether they be in the surreal – or the genuine – world. And he is at pains to reassure the reader that no living things were harmed in the making of his tale – except, perhaps, for certain figments of the imagination.

Also, strong advice must be issued against the consumption of rotten fish. Don't try this at home, or anywhere else for that matter. In fact, do not consume any fruit of the sea ...

More offensive to the nose
Than is the stinking rose

Instead, be sure to bring such manifest dangers to the attention of the proprietors of those restaurants and take-away "joints" which you may frequent, who should know better than to poison their clientèle with putrefying flesh.

Lastly, and before the completion of this legal snippet, the author wishes to state his objection to the acerbic white wine of legalese which, once imbibed, excises all punctuation marks from each indenture (as if they were *red wine* stains upon a valuable textile), on the grounds of their raising "a shadow of a doubt" as to the primary meaning. In fact, we do not punctuate in order to take our meaning away – but to make it plain! (Would you nourish a child's mind by starving it?) It is clear, so very clear, that legal scribes practice, for their personal gain, the dual arts: of veiling their meaning as they write, to throw us into a state of confusion; and of unveiling it as they read and explain – in order to levy an inflated fee from us, who are blind and helpless in the face of such prolixity!

Inevitably, if thou, thyself, should read, with an unpractised eye, an unbroken chain of words, thou shalt discover thyself spontaneously breaking the chain, if for no other reason than to prevent death from asphyxia (and, hopefully, not because thy throat has been punctured by a hyphen or a fish bone). Should this pause occur inopportunely, then a false meaning shall be gleaned.

Henceforth, please may the law desist from archaic forms of expression; and, on bended knee, I beg, - build breakers ... to break, break, and break again the tide of obfuscation that ye spool, so that it may yet be formed into something comprehensible to all. Please act upon this advice without delay. Let not the global warming of our anger melt the icecaps of thy inaction, and thereby raise the sea level to engulf us all! Finally, noble Lords and Ladies of the Bar, will you be so good as to excuse my prior iteration, which is a *free and easy* use of English grammar (and so, hitherto, unknown to you).

The New Arrival

'There is too much of everything in this world,' philosophises Dmitri, 'except for this beloved innocent whom I cradle in my arms. We could do with more like him. As for the rest - there are worms replicating themselves over the network, and slowing it down until it grinds to a halt; even though no worms were ever purchased on Ebay.' As he says this, a worm pokes its head out of a flowerpot at the far side of the room, in order to listen. 'There are online advertisements;

and cookies are present to store the virtual places where you have been … and there are too many human beings in the physical world, many of them from unplanned pregnancies. Indeed, a whole plague of them exists: more than seven billion, at last count. Everything is reproducing too quickly – most especially, those wicked computer viruses. What havoc may they wreak when they are not properly quarantined? Yet here, amidst the hordes of the unwanted and the superfluous, this little fellow' (he indicates the "infant" in his lap) 'is so much in need of an earth not populous nor contaminated. With this thought, my friends, you must stiffen your upper lips and endure – just one more time - the sight of bodily fluids.' On cue, a victim of German Measles steps forward and rolls up his sleeve, to reveal that he is covered in pustules.

'Precursor of Sound-Byte – at your service,' he says.

Dmitri asks for a sharp or abrasive object to be fetched from the office kitchen; and then, armed with sandpaper and a bread knife with a serrated edge, he goes to work on the patient - hurriedly scraping off some surface skin, along with a generous helping of blood and infected matter. Next - horror of horrors! - he sets about applying this disgusting preparation, whilst it is still dripping from the blade, to the exposed neck of Mr Propotamous, whose own blood type begins to mingle with it. Dmitri calmly explains,

'I now demonstrate the principle of inoculation.'

Pilate yelps, like a traumatized puppy.

'He's tweeting,' mutters Foolish Boy, - as he affixes, with assiduous care, a birdcage to the top of Pilate's head … after populating it with a robin, which he has summoned from the broad sleeves of his white shirt in an act of consummate magic. Finally, he shuts the door of the cage, and watches the little bird chirp in response to the high-pitched noises of Pilate.

The humiliation is completed by Dot, reciting a rhyming couplet from William Blake,

A robin redbreast in a cage
Puts all heaven in a rage

Dmitri takes up the gauntlet once more,

'We must hope that viruses in the virtual world will never filter into our tangible reality; and, conversely, that our physical diseases shall never permeate our software. In summary – no monstrosity should ever be allowed to escape the boundaries of the domain into which it is born. But if an author should breathe life into his characters – who fly free from the printed page ... Why, what shall befall us then?' It is uncertain whether Dmitri is referring to the author of this story, who is yours truly. Yet how would this be possible? He knows less about me than I know about my *own* creator, with whom I occasionally parley when the spirit so moves me. Dmitri continues,

'Now, assuming you have successfully applied an anti-virus, and the computer still fails to respond properly, you may *ping* its IP address.' He approaches the director with thumb and forefinger poised for action, and – after moving his forefinger down the runway of his thumb, like a Sopwith Camel preparing for take-off, - he flicks with as much force as a single finger is capable of. (My simile is chosen with care, for his finger is not *supersonic* – not yet.)

'Do you mind?' says the director, with a wounded look on his face.

'Or you may poke an electronic device, such as an iPhone, which you have not heard from for a while.' Dmitri moves nearer to his former boss again, and, with his outstretched forefinger, pokes him in the stomach. The depression produces a series of circular ripples, thus emulating the effect of a stone cast into a pond. Foolish Boy is looking on, and cannot resist participating in this mild persecution with his own forefinger, whilst saying,

'This little piggie is in a poke. Oink ... oink ... oink!' He hopes that Pilate Propotamous will respond in kind, snorting and grunting, just as any member of the porcine family is inclined to do.

'Please! *Do you mind?*' Pilate addresses his tormentors - but this time, the words are uttered in a tone of despair. With a lopsided and mischievous grin on his face, Dmitri answers the question,

'Folks, can you imagine? He keeps asking me if I mind. *Mind?* Why should *I* mind?' He pauses, before broaching on the next topic,

'Now, then, having gained protection against dangerous viruses, the time has come to guard the spirit of the software house against the ravishes of Satan. And so, let us deport ourselves into a devout mood of thanksgiving; for we are shortly to be visited by the parish priest, Canon Bertrand Tyson, who will bless these premises, the items of equipment contained therein, and all who use them.' No sooner has he spoken, than there is the sound of something heavy being dragged across the floor, towards the entrance of the room where they are all gathered.

'Could it be the hairdresser, whom I led, like a lamb, to his electrocution – and who is now risen from the dead?' the director wonders, with a feeling which is near to guilt, but most intimately allied to fear.

'It couldn't be Black Rod, surely?' asks Myfanwy, who has now recovered from the pain of childbirth (although she could do with a change of clothes).

'Affirmative. It neither is, nor ever could be,' replies Dmitri.

The monstrous noise increases until a cumbersome object is laid to rest, while a fist beats incessantly upon the door: thump ... thump ... thump! And now, a strange, other-worldly sound is heard. The intruder has announced his arrival by blowing a foghorn - which, as the blower, himself, is apt to say, "illuminates the muddled heart, like a beacon in the smog". He then opens the door.

'All rise!' instructs Dmitri, for it is none other than the one who has lately been anticipated, the Reverend Bertrand Tyson. He is wearing a cassock and a remarkable broad-brimmed hat known as a *Capello Romano*; and he is clenching an intricately decorated staff between his teeth – a crosier, in fact, which he stole from a visiting bishop.

'Next time, I will procure that magnificent cape (the *Cappa Magna*), an episcopal ring, and a mitre to complete the set!' the dignitary mumbles to himself. No one asks how he got into the building without a key. All are obediently standing, and are simply gob-smacked by the sight of him dragging (across the thick-piled carpet) an enormous vat, which is filled to the brim with holy water. Dmitri has opened his mouth and is about to speak – but the Reverend bypasses him. He launches into an account of the falling numbers of people receiving the sacraments of communion and confession; although, in self-defence, he explains, 'in my parish there is no shortage of attendees at the celebration of the mass'. He continues with a tidal wave of words on all manner of things, before pausing to catch his breath. He totters on one leg before placing his (suspended) foot back on the floor, and resting its opposite number against the wall. For a few minutes he behaves like a shovel-snouted lizard – famous for keeping cool in the desert by alternating its direct points of contact with the scorching sand. He then excuses his failing sense of balance, and the damage inflicted upon the flooring by his huge tank, with the words, 'the consecrated produce must not be wasted'; which is a coded way of saying that he has become somewhat tipsy on the blood of Christ. Indeed, he has already imbibed two bottles of genuine blood-red wine, purchased from Lidl's (and blessed by himself) before breakfast. And now he has turned up with a vat of ordinary water.

'That's it! That's the tank which swallowed the cloud!' exclaims the child, Dot, referring to the large mass of candy floss that she was carrying around on a stick earlier on, and that she decorated with tiny pieces of skinned fruit which she termed "applets".

'By the way,' explains the priest, 'I must say, upfront, that (while I mostly adhere to first principles) I – unlike Jesus - have not been circumcised. I was put off the idea when I was given to understand (by my medieval forebears) that the foreskin from the infant Jesus was employed by God to form one or more of the rings around Saturn. (Picture that! Just an infant as well! He must have been *very* well hung.) I do, however, hasten to add that I follow the Lenten tradition of eating fish on a Friday. Now, my morning newspaper informs me that this *is* a Friday, and I find myself wondering if an exception could be made - as I have travelled from afar' (he waves his right arm in a pathetic attempt at grandiloquence, for his parish is situated next door to the warehouse; and then he waxes lyrical) '... for the smell of bacon is in the air, and my nose is lifted towards it, as if by angelic wings ... and I am truly famished. Indeed, it has been observed how similar the flesh of human is, to that of pig, – and so I must relent, and return to the straight and narrow path. But never mind. I see that you have supplied for me one fruit of the sea.' He proceeds to help himself to some rotten filaments. After a short while, he passes wind and sighs, 'Ah! That's so much better. And have we any bread in the fridge? Or wine?' He passes wind again.

'Deny him nothing. This man is a primary god sent to us from the heavens,' states Pilate; and (moving his lips silently) he adds: '... a gas giant like the planet, Jupiter.'

'We've got bread ... and some fine Chilean Merlot,' replies an underling of Dmitri – and, instantly, Dmitri and Myfanwy (but, curiously, no one else), kneel down before the clergyman, and open their mouths wide, revealing two yellow-coated tongues in readiness for communion.

'Ah! Just a loaf of bread? No crusty rolls or croissants? Nor Anchor Butter, nor a smidgen of Gruyère - for extra flavour?' comments Canon Tyson. Foolish Boy fetches a block of long-untouched English cheddar from the kitchen. 'We know what the bread and water symbolises – but what of the pungent cheese? I'd say ... it is the rich joy that resides in the Christian life: which – if broadcast appropriately – shall be sniffed out by everyone in the community. And to add a certain piquancy to the wine, might I suggest ice, and a slice of lemon?'

'*This-is-an-outrage*!' objects Pilate - with special emphasis, for he is apt to change his mind, and is guarding against that weakness.

'You're right. Ice should not be added to red wine,' agrees the priest. 'I shall accede to your wishes. We'll do communion later. Personally, I have always found communion wine to taste remarkably like any other. (I must say, I have no tendency towards vampirism.) But, for now ... Ah! Methinks that Myfanwy's voracious beaver hath altered its appetite! And so I shall strike while the iron's hot, and consecrate their union.'

'You'll do *what*?' asks Pilate.

'May the souls and bodies of Myfanwy Esquelle and Dmitri Bosphorus-Deux be entwined ... in a marriage fit for the incandescent joy of heaven! You know, these days there is great variation among human partnerships. Some are *like* marriages, although they are only the "common law" variety; and, from time to time, I have observed that just *one* person wears the trousers. And it is not necessarily the male. There is one trousered member of such a union in my parish. The only time she is able to coax any words out of her other half, is by shoving ... first her hand, and then the rest of her arm up to her elbow ... inside his rectum.' All shudder and touch their ears, as if the Organ of Corti had given rise to the wrong nerve impulse. In response to this, the Canon turns and faces his doubters. 'You have heard me right. And her husband does not mind one bit: for he has no brain, and his head is fashioned out of English oak. Yes, my brethren. He is a mere puppet; and she is a ventriloquist.'

'That story is ... *a disgrace*!' Pilate blurts out.

'Please accept my apology for his impertinence,' interrupts Dmitri, and promptly slaps his former boss across the back of the head. 'Honestly. You'd think he'd have learned by now.' The holy man proceeds to devour (with great relish) all of the food and wine brought out to him. Meanwhile the little girl, who is called Dot, is uncomfortable with this visitor herself. She has this to say,

'Earlier on, when I was making my way here, a light fuse blew in one of the corridors. Then I heard someone scream. Navigating in the dark, I became very, very afraid. A moment later, I had the sensation of someone following me. It was *him*,' she points to the clergyman. 'He asked me to stop, because - and these were his very words, - "I would especially like to accost you in the darkness."'

'Naturally, I am frightened of the dark also,' explains the Canon, who sees a scandal brewing. 'And I thought that, by holding hands, we could defuse each other's anxiety.' The little girl ignores his feeble excuse, and continues:

'My mummy tells me that I shouldn't talk to strange men – but they keep attaching themselves to me.'

'A-ha. And?' is the disinterested response from Dmitri. He has suddenly acquired the habit of his supposed paramour, Myfanwy, of colouring his nails and polishing them with his handkerchief.

'Well. I am not so sure ... but my friends say to me that every Dot should do its duty.'

'Quite right, too. You're a concatenation operator. What do you expect?'

Dot says nothing more, but merely twinkles her sea-green eyes, as if some salt water fish were at that very moment swimming to the surface of her Piscean fantasy, and out through the portals of those very eyes. Fresh fish would, indeed, be most welcome after that rotten sea food fiasco.

All who have congregated in the room watch her for a while, and then turn their attention to the extraordinary figure of the clergyman. He has a broad, muscular back, and huge biceps. Yet, curiously, he possesses tiny feet, suggesting that he has acquired through training what, at first, was denied him by nature. But we cannot be sure, on account of his singular characteristic of never remaining long enough in one place to be asked.

'I must tell you all,' the Reverend Tyson deflects public interest away from his anatomy to his capacious mind, 'that (at the inception of my professional life) I attended the seminary run by the blessed Melcheezaduke. You know of him?' Everyone glances at everyone else, wondering whether it would be politic just to lie and nod their assent. 'And *he*,' continues the cleric, 'was guided in *his* thought, both temporal and spiritual, by the holy prophet, Leviticus, whom Melcheezaduke describes as "his beloved", and who is (now and forever more) my very own ... my dearest Lev.'

'Ooooh! Mine too!' exclaims Pilate, hoping to curry favour with the cleric. 'He is the one who requested that cripples desist from making offerings before the alter of God. (They're just not welcome, you see.) And he made repeated calls for the execution of those who work on the Sabbath. At least that's what I read on the internet. In fact, his text is *so extreme*, that it can sometimes be highly amusing – especially when digested with a tipple or three of intoxicating spirit on a quiet Sunday afternoon.' This time, Pilate really has taken a step too far, - but he fails to see the look of concentrated malice settling upon the Canon's face. And so, like a blind donkey, he just "keeps buggering on". 'These days, you have to threaten execution in order to extort from your staff simply what you are paying them for, - and that's during the week, never mind on the Sabbath! By the way, Leviticus also wrote, "Thou shalt not respect the person of the poor." And with that, gentleman, he reinforces the very bedrock of capitalism!' Finishing his homily, Pilate at last notices the storm that is brewing across the Canon's craggy face. Alas, too late! The Canon's mighty hand is swooping downwards in a perfect arc – like a falcon with a field mouse in its sights - and is striking him across his jowls. A modicum of spittle escapes from his lips and lands upon somebody's writing pad, where it smears the half-dried ink of a fountain pen. The hand of abuse follows through, which is the result of long years of martial arts training, and Mr Propotamous is truly silenced.

Dmitri reinforces this with a rebuke of his own,

'We have before us one who has succumbed to "the love that dare not speak its name".' Pilate is nursing his sore and slightly reddened cheek, and so his wife has to speak up for him:

'My husband has *never* been a follower of Oscar Wilde: not intellectually, nor by natural persuasion. Epicurus, perhaps, but never Wilde.'

Dmitri responds with a remark which no one can deny,

'The defendant stands accused of having fallen passionately in love with a man. That man is himself.'

******

No sooner has the "new chief" finished speaking, than "the betrothed" rushes into the room. He has got wind that a man of the cloth is here - and he articulates the need for some spiritual and carnal guidance. Since being made redundant he has been out of sorts. And, apart from this, all has not been well in the bedroom department – not for some time, in fact. The young man seats himself next to the Canon. He is one of the parishioners where the holy man practises his priestly arts, and the latter has anticipated his approach ...

CANON TYSON: My son, be at ease. Let there be no blindness-inducing activity, either in private or in public. [He hands him a wooden condom, adding wistfully ...] 'Twas mine for many years. Use carefully and follow the instructions. [He retrieves the official documentation on appropriate use, which has grown yellow – we hope, with age.] The splinters shall enhance your pleasure! If not, I have some WD40 for you ... But first ... [He places his hand on the young man's crotch.] Think of crop rotation, my child. *Spend* yourself on other things. [He taps the young man's privates with his index finger, as if conducting an experiment with a tuning fork.]

THE BETROTHED: Ugh! What are you doing?

CANON TYSON:

Please let this field lie fallow for a while,
So sweat from thwarted impulses rain down ...
So hope, like sunlight, gives it nourishment ...
And it shall bring forth fruit in perfect time.

His Holiness, The Literary Titan

Fr Bertrand has tucked several heavy books under his arm. One is entitled, "The Perfect Launchpad". (I have no idea how he got hold of it). The others are, "Devilish and Dynamic Schisms in the early Christian Bosom"; and, thirdly, "A Whole Volume of Sustained Insanity". The latter two are by the Right Honourable Barnabas Honey-Bear; and are now (sadly) out of print. After the fashion of many personages before him, the Canon prefers to be *seen* with scholarly tomes, than to be *reading* them; and these particular tomes – with the exception of the first, of course, - are kindred spirits in the venerable series: 'Books with something to say, by authors with nothing to say'. The series contains surreal examples of creative writing which, through the medium of the reading public's own imagination, have taken on a life of their own, larger than what was originally envisaged. (And if you believe all of this, you'll believe anything.) Pilate shakes his head sadly, and philosophises quietly to himself,

'The fool attempts to be worldly-wise by reading a book. The worldly-wise acts out his sincere desires and multiplies his regrets: thereby proving that he, also, is a fool.'

'Fr Bertrand Tyson is an historian ...' Dmitri introduces a subject close to his guest's heart.

'Indeed, I am,' is the instant reply. 'I have lately written two books about a unique figure in The Bible - a serial killer whose writing has formed the very cornerstone of our faith. The whole work is entitled, "The life of Saul: A Narrative in Two Parts" ... and the two parts are ... "Part 1: Saul, The Psychopath", and "Part 2: Paul, The Subject of a Damascene Conversion". Well, now, - "Aul, S 'n' P" (my pet name for him) was a significant man. He was a Roman Jew who became a Christian; and so we remember him with grace and forbearance.'

Pilate is wondering how the Canon conducted his research, and gleaned enough for two whole volumes on such a thinly documented piece of biblical history. The speaker adds,

'These days, the church is under siege in so many ways; but I am not one to bear grudges, nor to unfairly discriminate. As a matter of fact, I am a regular prison visitor with a knack for converting "the inconvertible".'

'Now, that's *got* to be a motor-car,' thinks Myfanwy.

'... And I learn a great deal from this process. I take copious notes during each conversion; and I am presently at work on a body of received wisdom from a variety of unscrupulous sources. So, I'll just run these by you ... "An Epistle of Myra Hindley to the Prison Chaplain" ... sadly, there are no Thessalonians or Corinthians in the average nick. They're just never around when you want them.'

'I don't like the sound of that,' comments Dmitri.

'OK. What about, "The Gospel According to the Yorkshire Ripper?"'

'You're worrying me now.'

'Only *now*?' murmurs Pilate.

His Holiness, The Artist ... alias "Murillo"

The Canon sees that a chair has been prepared for him, but he neglects to take it, saying, 'Modesty forbids me'. In fact, his gargantuan legs forbid him, for they cannot be squeezed under the wooden table without some act of truncation occurring. His stance would have appeared awkward, except that he cleverly diverts the attention of onlookers by commenting upon incidental items of decoration ...

'Great ocean-going Triton with a horn in his mouth! Mmmmm ... fashioned out of plastic - and purchased from a seaside gift shop, I presume?' He refers to a model on a shelf by the window.

'It's ceramic,' says the former director, who is mildly irritated by the downgrading of a choice ornament. But then, Pilate hears a sound which grates upon his ears, and reminds him of the high-pitched screeching made by a novice musician upon the strings of a violin. He strains to see what is happening, for there are unfortunately several persons blocking the path of his vision. After bobbing his head up and down like a muppet, he discovers the cause of the disturbance. Father Bertrand is scratching the gilt veneer from the surface of another ornament, more valuable than Triton: a representation of Venus, no less. The Canon expiates his destructive instinct by disguising it as curiosity ...

'It is not solid gold, but gold-plated or gilt-edged: like human virtue. For in that domain, nothing is ever more than skin deep.'

'Is that so?' whispers Pilate. He feels like he has an open sore, and the Canon's words are pricking it mercilessly. 'Damn him! I'll spill the liquid purity of his critique, and use it as a polish to buff up his bald pate!'

'No matter. This is The Age of Too much Stuff,' remarks the Canon implacably. He elects not to hear the last item of abuse.

'It is also the Age of the Internet,' replies Pilate audibly, hoping to redeem his self-defence: for he is feeling rather pathetic. 'The internet is so multi-faceted, it has become a virtual palace of education and self-improvement. (Upon the pages of the web, I bought my Triton and my Venus.) And, occasionally, it is a keyhole through which the government may spy upon the mindset of a nation.'

'Sir, if I may play the moralist (and who should play it, if not I?) - it is, in a manner of speaking, a catchment area for the filthy puddles of our interest,' is the stern reply of the venerable Canon. There follows an embarrassing silence – after which, Dmitri praises his visitor,

'The high priest of our parish is an artist in his spare time – a second noble calling. And so, before he blesses our software house, he would like to donate two of his latest paintings to this enterprise. I believe he has brought them with him, wrapped in a Hessian cloth. Am I right?'

'Ahem! *Donate* ...? Not quite,' interrupts the very Reverend Canon Tyson, before taking up the baton. 'I have called the first painting, "Peace be with You". It is a gentle evocation of an especially intimate part of the mass. You know the part to which I refer? I depict one member of the congregation shaking hands – except that here, he does it with everyone else simultaneously. Since about 400 parishioners attend mass at my church, - for this moment of peaceful exchange, the benevolent model who sat for me has (in my painting) sprouted

400 arms. And you are all in luck, for the painting comes with a companion piece.' His listeners look up from their sloth.

'It does?' they ask.

'Yes, it does!' the Canon responds with boyish enthusiasm. 'And it is my magnum opus.' His pride has coloured his vision. He confuses the dumbfounded expressions of those around him, for the awe that is manifest in beholders of a work of genius. 'It is called, "And Also With You", - and depicts every single member of the congregation simultaneously shaking hands with every other.'

'Is such a warm indulgence truly necessary? Could each not simply issue a circular wave – like one bearded dragon signalling to another?' asks Pilate.

'If you simplify the painting, then you will obviate the need for a further sequel. Good heavens, man. keep up!' the priest pauses. 'But there is a technical problem ...'

'Surely not?' says Pilate, with a strong whiff of sarcasm in his voice.

'Yes, there most certainly is: for how am I to depict 160,000 arms, with no visible torso in sight. Merciful heaven! It might resemble a mass grave after an act of genocide. But then I thought, "If I brought all of my skills as a sublime draughtsman into the frame, and made at least one torso visible with a head attached, - which bore the attitude of a man deep in prayer, - why, then ... the correct impression would be conveyed?" No? What say *you*?'

'I would say,' Pilate responds tentatively, 'that a depiction of one person deep in prayer and surrounded by 160,000 dislocated arms, will arouse within spectators a feeling of dread – for they will fear it's a massac-'

'Shhhhh!' utter several persons at once, with Myfanwy acting as ringleader.

'Don't mind him. He's just jealous. He cannot paint to save his life!' she says. And so, the venerable Canon does not "mind him", and is about to broach on the small issue of a price for his painting. Unfortunately, he is prevented from doing so by the numerical wizards in the room; who open their eyes wide, syringe their ears with their little fingers, and begin spouting arithmetic formulas a-plenty. It is as if the Holy Spirit has appeared in a flame hovering above each head, causing them all to speak in tongues. Finally, one Master of Philosophy jumps up and declares,

'Scholars, physicians and lovers of William Shakespeare ... lend me your ears! For every adherent to shake the hands of every other in this place of worship ... would require a very great number of handshakes indeed ...' [he clears his throat] 'which, simply speaking, may be expressed as 400 factorial.'

'Wrong!' exclaims another speculator, his objection resounding like a gong. 'It is, good sir, *800 factorial*: for every human present has two hands, rather than one hand – as you have erroneously assumed.'

'Well,' replies the first, 'they need only shake hands with each other once, and not twice. But if you are going to be pedantic about it, what about the statistical possibility of some parishioners being minus a hand? Or suffering from muscular dystrophy, and being unable to exert themselves sufficiently to shake another person's hand?'

Dmitri shows them the palm of his right hand to signify silence; and then gestures to the Canon with the back of his hand (and a flourish of five fingers), to pick up the baton once more, which he duly does:

'Good gentlemen and gentle ladies, I must name my price – for works of devotional art cannot be undervalued. Rest assured, mine will be a *mere sprat* of a sum, compared to the big fish on display in the public galleries. It will be ... £5000 for each painting, in two easy payments of £2,500; or £10,000 for the two, in two easy payments of £5000.'

Once more, Pilate simply cannot resist putting his two penneth into the piggy bank of words,

'Why *easy*? Difficult, I should say. Just pay the whole fee in one go! Or don't pay anything at all, if you can't afford it.'

'There he goes again!' exclaims Dmitri. 'Interjecting and contradicting ...' (Foolish Boy whirls his supple fingers as he listens) ... 'as if every dialogue within earshot were no more than a failed loop within his program logic, - which he would like to break out of, but cannot: on account of there being no exit strategy!' Dmitri turns to the Canon. 'And there is a third painting, is there not, dear Reverend? Shall the three works, together, not comprise a very elegant triptych - with two paintings attached at the hip to a central panel?'

'Indeed there *is*, and they *shall*,' exclaims the delighted vendor. 'It comprises the good Lord Jesus, at the altar, extending four hundred arms – or should that be eight hundred? - to his flock, who are standing in the nave. You may purchase the two finished paintings, and the third "off-plan"; and all for the total sum of £20,000.' He looks into the eyes of Dmitri, and his face visibly softens. Then, he spells out his best offer. 'Alright! I am feeling generous, and, perchance, you are feeling lucky. What about a special deal for the three paintings, a one-off payment of just nineteen thousand, nine hundred and ninety-nine pounds, ninety-nine pence; with all but a hundred pounds sterling paid forthwith, and the balance sent to me by an agreed date. But, I warn you, I can hold this bargain basement offer for only one day.' Dmitri's heart beats faster. With trembling hands he reaches into a draw under his desk, and seizes a wad of bank notes; in response to which, the director groans inwardly, 'Oh! My poor piggy bank, exhausted in one fell swoop!'

'But there is a minor caveat,' the Reverend says. 'My "plc" has recently been floated as a public offering; and, should it go bust before the last brush stroke has been applied to my third and final masterpiece, - well, then, you will only have two works of art for the price of three. Notwithstanding this, your deposit shall be non-refundable.' Copyvarfrom and Copyvarto have begun nodding their heads excitedly once again, and Dmitri cannot resist the general mood of enthusiasm. He nods as well, exclaiming:

'Nothing ventured, nothing gained. I accept.'

'Thank you. And at this point,' says Fr Bertrand, encouraged by the easy flow of capital, 'I would like to draw your attention to the many who have given their working lives in the service of this software house; and to support the notion that a memorial should be erected to commemorate them all ... for, devoid of a noteworthy reference, more and more employees are realising that there is no meaningful life after The Perfect Launchpad has dispensed with them.' Even before finishing his sentence, Father Bertrand grabs the piggy bank and gives it a good shake to see if it is empty. 'I feel this memorial should be constructed out of the finest Gwespyr stone, with the names of "the fallen" inscribed in a plaque of snow-white bone china - or white gold, whichever takes your fancy ...' Then, with his free hand, he retrieves a handsome leather wallet, filled with twenty pound notes, and waves it in front of the former director's face.

'How the hell did he get hold of my wallet?' Pilate wonders.

'And Fr Bertrand is not only an artist,' adds Pilate's nemesis, 'but a composer, too, – taking his lead from John Cage. You know, there is a theory that if all the keys on the giant organ of St Paul's Cathedral are played simultaneously, the resulting vibration would cause that edifice to implode. But, of course, we would not want *that* to happen to St Paul's, now, would we? No matter. My *own* contention is that a solidly constructed house of God would survive.'

'Well – that *is* a relief, not least for the occupants inside the buildings surrounding it,' says Dmitri.

'I am afraid I cannot vouch for them,' is the reply. The Canon adjusts his loose-fitting corduroys under his cassock. His blood is coursing swiftly round his veins, and his spirit is enlivened. He feels like he has been to the races and picked a winner.

'These boxer shorts have been widened to accommodate a more generous girth,' he explains (remembering his Viagra pills), 'for the cannon fires less accurately than in days of yore, and, whilst passing over the uneven terrain of early old age, the balls of the cannon must be lowered for heightened comfort and ease of mobility.' The author lies in "no man's land", as to the right spelling of the word, "cannon", in this context; but he has decided to give precedence to the *military* over the *spiritual*.

Acts of Confession

Moving on from the comfort zone inside his trousers, the clergyman speaks the words,

'The time has arrived.' And then, with some esoteric words, he begins to join Dmitri and Myfanwy in a special covenant – much to the consternation of Pilate. Once more, the two present their tongues to receive the host; and Fr Bertrand requests some more victuals from the kitchen.

'All that's left is stale bread and rancid wine. You've had the rest, excepting a small portion of margarine.'

'Alright. What is left shall suffice,' the clergyman announces solemnly. The margarine is blessed, before being spread liberally on the hard, dried-out slices of bread; and Dmitri and Myfanwy take their holy sustenance. Then they sit back in their chairs, waiting for the next stage of the ceremony. 'With communion out of the way, does anyone know why these two should not be joined in holy matrimony?' Fr Bertrand Tyson turns to Myfanwy.

'As a priest, I would like to say that I am a man of vision – and that I cannot refuse any life-form, not even an apparition, access to my wise counsel.' He purrs with delight as he senses the channel of Myfanwy's attention focus upon him - as if it were a beam of light from the sun. He continues,

'One of your fat cells came to me in a dream last night. He (and I personify the fat cell, for it appeared to be imbued with a fully-formed personality) ... as I say, *he* wanted to confess something to me.' Myfanwy's eyes widen. 'He told me, "Myfanwy used to treat me with consummate care and affection. She would feed me whenever my cravings arose, and, as she ate, she would pat her stomach (which is where I am domiciled) with an almost spiritual sense of resignation. But now! *Now* she has forsaken me for another."' The Canon glances at Dmitri. 'A fat cell is not just for Christmas - although, of course, fat cells do tend to proliferate at that time of year. Ms Esquelle has even confessed to wearing six layers of clothing on her upper body at the height of summer, in order to sweat off the rubbery compounds within her spare tyre. So, Myfanwy, what do you have to say for yourself?'

'Well, Father, it is true that I have recently been on a diet,' she explains.

'And very honourable your self-control is, too. It must have taken some will power. Now, then, having digested the slander of your fat cell (whom I shall admonish at my next opportunity, in the strongest terms possible), I feel it is time to move on!' He measures up to Pilate. 'You may take communion also.'

Pilate puts the last piece of bread and margarine into his mouth, and the blessing which the food received begins to work its magic.

'I could hear your confession, if you wish?' says the holy man. Pilate responds,

'For many years I was, I confess, something of a xenophobe. Then one day, quite out of the blue, my mind was altered,' Pilate blinks, and dabs his nose with his handkerchief.

'Well, my son, I complement you on your fresh outlook,' replies the Canon. 'And what, prey, was the hand that pressed the prejudicial applets of your malevolence into a most honourable cider? Was it the way in which ethnic minorities can enrich our culture?'

The respondent shakes his head.

'Perhaps it was their *nouvelle cuisine*, which has spiked our palettes with its piquancy?'

Pilate shrugs with nonchalance.

'No? Then it must be that you have met someone adorable, who is the very embodiment of exotica: your wife, perhaps? After all, she is – Ahem! - a rich mixture of Spanish, Italian ... and Welsh I am told?'

Mr Propotamous clears his throat and shifts his rump around the seat of his chair ...

'It wouldn't be her.'

'Come, come. Surely not some factor even more influential upon you than your beloved spouse?'

'Much more!' Pilate barks at him. Let me tell you. It was an epiphany! When the penny dropped, I became so enlivened that I nearly choked on my own saliva!

'But what was the *stimulant*?' Father Bertrand is becoming impatient.

'Well ... I once employed a group of staff from the exotic East, and I was blown away by their high productivity ... even though the overhead was but a few rupees! I began to see them in a new light: as penny shares which yield generous dividends. One individual I am presently remembering was so taken by the spirit of diligence, that he was the prime mover in the refinement of our office systems. In fact, the possessor of this spirit set my mind a-racing; and I was overcome with a powerful idea, - one which made me tremble with anticipation. Why not sack everybody, and set up a colony of computer-literate professionals in Bombay - who will be prepared to work for a pittance. Of course, I would target those who were down on their luck (the homeless and the hungry, for example), and then apply for a charitable grant, which I could use to pay their miserable wages. In fact, being the fair-minded boss that I am, - rather than getting rid of my expensive English employees, I could also offer to them the opportunity of moving to India, and reapplying for their jobs upon arrival. Of course, I could not cover their relocation costs, nor disguise the inevitable fall in their wages.'

'I see,' says the Canon. 'And the enterprising individual? He went on to do well for himself, I imagine?'

'What enterprising individual?'

'The one you just spoke so highly of ... shall we call him *the prime mover*?'

'Oh, *the exotic* ... No, he developed high blood pressure, and then a high temperature to match ... he was overwrought ... pushed himself over the edge, you see ... And then he died. Honestly, I kept telling him about there being ice in the fridge (that would cool his Fahrenheit) – but he wouldn't listen.'

'Well. I shall withhold forgiveness for the time being,' the priest rounds off this confession. Then he turns to another candidate who is wanting the sacrament: an Irishman, in fact.

'Bless me, fodder, for I have sunned. It is twelve monsters since my last tax return, and these are my tax-deductible luxuries.'

'My son, this is a public confessional (the first of its kind, I might add, – since confession is normally a private matter) and I am not your accountant. But still, by the power invested in me, you are forgiven. Next, please ...'

'But I haven't told you what they are yet.'

'NEXT!' shouts the priest. And, seeing the lips of the Irishman still moving, he pre-empts him with the words, 'I see you are pursuing your cause, which is (I have to say) foolhardy. Absolution shall be withheld as punishment for your impertinence!' The man from the Emerald Isle is crestfallen, as the priest turns to the person responsible for Pilate's book-keeping.

'Father Bertrand Tyson,' says this man. 'Please, sir, may I call you BT?'

'My son, you may call me anything which "oils the wheels" of my communication with you ... or with the supreme Being who actuates my prayerful thought,' qualifies Canon Tyson, with his eyes turned heaven-wards. And so the accountant alias Pork Belly alias Java Man – or, in more casual circles, The Reader, - begins,

'It was that infernal tune.'

'Tune?' asks the priest.

'Yes, the ... er ...I ...'

'My son, be thou no more a cog in the online wheel. Breathe freely. Let thy tongue be loosed.'

'I was a recent visitor to a house of God. And one of the cloying melodies which was sung there stuck in my throat like sawdust, and sickened me slightly. Oh, God!' The speaker is tremulous as a leaf now. His mouth is opening and shutting like an aquarium fish in need of an air pump - but no sound is coming out.

'Yes, my son? Please finish your story.'

'Well, as I retched, the acrid incense hurt my eyes, which watered with altruism; for they would have washed out my earholes – except that my ears (like my fists) were clenched, and the tears could not reach them. Father, I know it sounds disrespectful, but my body was acting independently of my mind. The littlest of my fingers extended themselves to their full length and rose to my ears – and would have stuffed them, had courtesy not checked my motor neurones!'

Fr Bertrand looks harassed, although he is also curious ...

'Explain yourself – for this confusion of mine is unbecoming.'

'Well. My primary misgiving occurred this Christmas last.' (The others in the room prick up their ears, surprised that the accountant has found his true voice at last - and that it is a different voice from the Client Server). 'We were at a session of hymn singing - my family and I. I must say, I had practised a hymn-avoidance strategy for many years, but my loved ones were determined to attend, and – it being Christmas time – were adamant that I should go with them. I was uncertain what your missionary position would be, on the subject of my aversion; and so I acceded to their wishes.' (The Canon elevates his eyes, and then lowers them with the grandeur of the setting sun.) 'The hymns were so lengthy. We ploughed on, as if wading through treacle – but still there was no end in sight. Now, I don't object to a carol or two at Christmas; but hymns are like sleeping pills, and should be taken in moderation. Finally, we reached the eighth refrain of the wettest and most vapid dirge of the entire evening. Outside, the rain was pissing down in sympathy for my predicament; and, at that very moment, I began to disbelieve in the existence of God. Had the Hymn Master limited our rendition to the first four verses; nay, if he had put a stopper into my mouth (like a baby's dummy) so that I could no longer sing, the spirit of unbelief might have been held at bay.'

'And who, might I ask, was the choir master?' asks the Reverend sharply. Suddenly, the confessor has a frightened look in his eyes. The pastor leans forward and says quietly, 'Come, come. You can tell your blessed Reverend. Whisper it in his ear.' *Said ear* is moved a little closer to *coy little mouth*, for the easy transportation of the requisite words into the listener's thoughts. But the confessor is put off by a large volume of waxy deposits in the approaching ear. Perhaps they account for why the Canon has a tendency to shout?

'It was ... not you,' came the muted reply. The respondent scours his environment for moral support, but finds none.

'*Not* me?' replies the priest. His eyelids flutter as if there is a storm brewing beneath them. Let us hope that the proverbial butterfly wings really cannot produce a tsunami in Asia. 'So the iron filings of my own congregation are not repelled by the magnet of my interest?' asks Canon Bertrand.

'*Not* you,' the accountant repeats robotically.

'In that case,' replies the Canon breezily, 'you shall perform a light act of contrition. But always remember that the kingdom of cancer is inside a man, and groweth surreptitiously. So sayeth the devil: for evil is a kind of cancer.' He scratches his head.

'What prayers shall I say, father? Can we strike a bargain? Eight HAIL MARYs, one for each refrain?' the sinner asks plaintively. Suddenly, Foolish Boy butts in and mentions a controversial survey; and I shall render the ensuing dialogue in such a way as to give my accomplice, Descriptor, a few seconds to catch his breath and fetch a glass of water ...

ACCOUNTANT: Well, I wouldn't exactly call it a survey.
FOOLISH BOY: You did when you told me about it.
ACCOUNTANT: It was more of a "brief questionnaire", really, – completed by a few people upon leaving church after a service one Sunday morning ... before they hurried off to

the pub. These people confessed that their minds had wandered, and they made a certain principle clear to me: the longer the mass, the more tortuous were the paths that their thoughts would follow. Their day-dreams divided, roughly, into three equal groups: a third think about household economics; a third, about what they are cooking for Sunday lunch; and a third, about sex.

Descriptor is Back

'This survey was commissioned by *Satan*!' bellows the priest.

'Well, he did suggest it to me,' replies the accountant, with a nervous half-glance at Pilate.

'What? I never did any such thing!' replies Pilate.

'He – hath - spoken. It – is - him!'

'Steady on, there, old fellow!' remonstrates Pilate.

'Too late! You have already indicted yourselves! While I am in my pulpit, I expect the warm blood of Jesus to be circulating through your veins. It seems that I have a "congregation of alligators" in my midst!' ….says the priest. He turns and addresses the accountant personally. 'Your penance, my son, is in the balance. Leave the matter with me, and I'll email it to you later. Next, please.' These last two words are like an electric eel with a sting in its tail. No one speaks for a few seconds. 'NEXT, PLEASE!' The Canon is angry now, at his offer of absolution being rejected. But, at last, his heart rate slows, and he puts the matter to rest,

'Where was I? Ah, yes,' he adds, ticking his bullet points off a handwritten list in a notepad made of recycled paper and elephant dung. 'I have given an account of myself, and spoken some holy words. I have organized communion – and confession too … So! Onwards and upwards to the next sacrament … the time has come to bless this software house and everything inside it!' The celebrant proclaims his plan joyfully, and sprinkles holy water over everyone present, and over all of the equipment as well. 'By the way,' he adds, making small talk. 'You know that hairdresser who works here? I'm sure you do. I issued the last rites to the poor fellow, but he was writhing around as if he didn't want them. People are so ungrateful these days! Mind you, I did douse him in holy water at the precise moment of his maximum exposure to mains electricity. There he was … I remember him vividly … clutching the three prongs of the electric plug, which were half in and half out of the wall socket. His skin and nails were singed, and his hair was standing on end as if he was a mad scientist in a cartoon. It was most upsetting for me.'

"Blessings" in Name only; a Revelation; and a Rapid Departure

The former director knows that, in health and safety parlance, water and electricity do not mix. He begins to feel less uneasy about his part in the hairdresser's downfall. Really, when all's said and done, it was the present speaker who facilitated the electric current and finished him off.

'Death by water,' Pilate thinks, as he pours himself a glass of H_2O. He also cannot help noticing that the Canon has a sizeable packet of matches bulging through his chest pocket.

'And what *about* this young hairdresser?' asks the clergyman, as he fingers the box of matches. 'Was he a sinner with an alternative lifestyle? I am not able to confer my approval upon certain styles of living. Did he, by any chance, spontaneously combust? To produce such an outcome, a sufficiency of evil must be contained within him, for 'tis evil that "lights the fuse".' The Canon sniffs the air. Then he issues both a compliment and a slight inside a single motion:

'It seems to me that this *ultra-brave* soul bears the same relationship to the building we now inhabit, as a medieval faggot to a condemned man hanging at the stake. Put simply, he has ignited a dangerous interest. And what, prey, is his present bodily state?'

'Well. Let's just sum up by saying that, by now,' Dmitri checks his watch, 'he will hopefully have been bundled off to a much better place.'

'Oh, is he recovering? How wonderful! Can we all visit him there?'

'If he has arrived at his destination, it will cost you. The funeral director will not open the mortuary on a whim.'

'In that case, I shall refrain from visiting him. It would be macabre. But – just before we leave this delicate subject, - have you ordered a removal van? Or must I do it for you? For until we do, his scorched remains … shall remain here.' No one answers the question. 'After all, he can't make this final journey on his own!'

The priest sprinkles water on an IBM Thinkpad, which then redirects it, via a special conduit for spilt liquids. Meanwhile, multi-tasking like an able modern female, the computer issues a warning to the clergyman about not getting too close to the screen – so he doesn't strain his eyes. Ah! The boys at Big Blue! They think of everything. They have brought to the marketplace a machine with a level of humanity exceeding that of every human being present. That is, of course, with the exception of the Canon, who is dipping a teaspoon into the consecrated tank, and flicking his holy water around liberally. However, even after all things and all persons appear, like flowers, to have a film of vernal dew upon them, - the tank remains full, almost to the brim.

'Damn it! I always bring too much of this stuff!' expostulates the priest. 'Now, then. What to do ...? What to do ... with the remainder?' All eyes alight on Pilate, who sees what's coming and freezes in fear, like a rabbit facing the headlights of an oncoming car; but, unlike a rabbit, he has been manacled to a chair.

'It's alright, Bertie,' he says, faking affection with coarse familiarity; and adds (as he wipes away a bead of sweat, posing as a drop of holy water), 'You've already done me.' He is referring to the modest sprinkling he has just received, along with everyone else. His casual address is measured to turn the hound off his scent, but all it does is elicit a look of distaste from his wife. As Pilate waits for the inevitable, he is suddenly in awe of the priest's robust symmetry, and fears what it could do to him. The weak illumination from the ecological bulb on the ceiling plays upon the well-developed muscle tone, which shines with a near-mechanical power. Really, this priest resembles Attila the Hun; and his stature lends, to every phrase he utters, an almost Germanic weight.

'Ye gods, by the powers invested in me from the spirit world, I hereby perform an act of great penetration and mercy, combined with an element of shock ...'

'Myfanwy? *Myfanwy*?' Pilate calls softly, like a love bird cooing to its mate. Unfortunately, his "mate" isn't listening. 'Dear?' Still, there is no answer. 'Myfanwy?'

'Yes?'

'Shhhhhhhh!' is the loud retort, from all four corners of the room; but the voice will not abate.

'This priest of ours ... are you quite sure he is an ordained minister?'

'Of course he is. Do you think the clergy hand out cassocks and dog collars for free? And as for a toy shop, or a box of magic tricks, – they would have these prerequisites. You would *have* to go to a seminary for them.'

'Shhhhhhhhhosh!' say the other attendees of this most peculiar meeting, for they are hanging upon the priest's every word. The clergyman proceeds with an exorcism of 'cookie, trojan, worm and other malware' – in response to which, the fruits demarcating the eyes and mouth of the huge biscuit displayed on the rostrum contort themselves into a look of serious anxiety; and a juicy earthworm rears its corpulent head from one of the larger flowerpots. After receiving these surreal communications from cyberspace, the sacred visitor launches himself into an arcane tract, drawn less from the wells of Catholicism than from the vaults of necromancy. While he does so, he turns towards the vast tank of holy water by his shoulder, - which stands ready for action, like one of Hannibal's younger elephants.

'God's curse be upon me if I should leave this liquid here – like unrequited love - for it reeks, it positively *reeks*' (and, curiously, it really does) 'not of a scent, but of a collection of hallowed words ... that are, perhaps, an invocation from the Holy See: "Use me! Use all of me! Waste me not. Let not one atom of my fluid form be lost. And I pray that there be not one humble attribute (possessed of human or of database); nor any unique index or other elemental object (be it real or virtual, animate or inanimate) that shall escape these wondrous waters ... which have so recently been whipped up by a distillery in paradise! And may the one who is most saturnine in our midst, become, through its blessing (and if only for a moment), the most blessed of us all!'

'Hold your horses! I suppose I could do with a glass of water, but that's about it,' is Pilate's final salvo. Unfortunately, his protestation is ineffectual. The cleric fills his mighty lungs with air, and sighs with resignation. Then, with a most unholy grunt, that more befits a wrestler than a spiritual man, he lifts the entire vat of holy water up to his chest, and steadies himself. Next, he yanks it high above his head - and, with legs quivering like jelly, holds it there for a second or two. Everyone is so still, you could hear a pin drop. It is as if he does not wish to disappoint an imaginary panel of judges at a weight-lifting contest. The Reverend groans under the weight of his liquid hoard. He glances downwards, and then upwards, muttering an invocation to the Lord of Hosts. And, before the consummation of his choreographed sequence, he says,

'I have wondered if it be an act of apostasy – that this tank has a primary devotion to the centre of the earth, rather than to the summits of heaven.'

Finally, he takes aim and empties the entire contents over Pilate. Meanwhile, the congregation yells with ferocity, 'Praise the loud!' or 'Praise the lewd!' - depending upon whether they are taking their sanctimonious lead from the southern baptists of America, or from somewhere equally devout (maybe County Kerry). The priest is much heartened by the reaction which he has fostered, and begins to recite the following lines from one of his poems,

> The entities, and attributes within,
> And models lovelier than a mannequin,
> The characters of variable length
> In systems of integrity and strength,
> And decimals with floating points that crawl, -
> The Lord God (with his keyboard) made them all.

'Praise the Lewd! And praise our most oily fodder!' cries out the zealous contingent (numbering just one) from County Kerry (or thereabouts).

Opening and shutting his huge mouth, the priest begins to bellow out a hymn with such velocity and volume, that it seems to acute observers as if the notes are being fired out of a nail gun, and embedded into the masonry.

'And so, my brothers and sisters in Christ ... altogether, now ... a one, a two; a one, two, three ...

> And did those feet - in an-cient time -
> Walk upon Eng-land's mountains green -
> Un-to a soft-ware hoooooouuuuuuuuuuusssssssssse?'

The holy father attempts to cajole everyone into singing, raising and lowering a flat hand, like a geologist expatiating upon tertiary rocks. Then he stops suddenly, having dragged the last syllable over the smouldering coals of his larynx. (If the syllable were of mortal stock, it would have grazed its knees in transit.) Yet no one is following his lead. The consensus of opinion is that it is all a fabulous myth, aided and abetted by the composer, Hubert Parry; and that Jesus never *did* take a vacation in England (much less visit a software house).

'Alright, enough!' he announces. 'We'll have a sing-along later, when you have got in the mood.' His would-be congregation is gazing at Pilate, every inch of whom is sopping wet: from his head and shoulders, shirt, tie, and suit, - right down to his underpants, shoes and socks. Father Bertrand attempts to sum up this sad episode with the following words:

'Not since Jesus was drenched by John the Baptist in the waters of the Tiber, has any person been so consummately blessed!'

'I say,' objects Pilate. 'Are you a signatory to the European Charter on human rights?'

'Not personally - no,' replies the clergyman.

'What I have just been subjected to could be classified as a form of water torture.'

'Don't be ridiculous! Nothing involving water could ever amount to torture,' answers the Canon. The two bearded staff (presumed to be Middle Eastern) madly shake their heads in disagreement; but there is support rising from the floor, and it is primarily flowing from the font of Myfanwy:

'Yes. And he should know. For he is the adjudicator on all things involving the joys and travails of the human spirit. Ah! And he deals with holy water all the time.' The bedraggled Mr Propotamous is still feeling sorry for himself. So the Canon justifies his theory,

'My dear brothers and sisters in Christ, I ask you, with all candour, - how could water ever be a means of inflicting pain? And tepid water, mind you! Have you ever heard of anything so fallacious? The hills are covered with verdant pasture, by virtue of H_2O. You may drink water, and be sustained by it. You may bathe in water, and have the dirt (ingrained from long hours of hard labour) washed from you with haste. When water is heated, it is therapeutic and relaxes the muscles exquisitely - like a maiden's loving touch. This is most especially the case when it is a bubble bath. (In fact, I so love the "Radox Bubble Bath", that I gave my only plastic duckling – posing as my son - to a neighbour, in exchange for a full bottle).

Indeed, all life on earth has arisen because of water. But aside from its practical uses, how often does it stand as the prettiest symbol in a poet's metaphor? Water may coruscate like quicksilver, or be as clear as the voice of truth itself! Could all of this be said of any other earthly thing – be it animal, vegetable or mineral? And was it not water that Our Lord turned into wine at the Feast of Cana? Through this limpid fluid (at the celebration of the mass) you may receive a holy sacrament, which often-times has been the happy fortune of *this* ungrateful wretch. But you may never, ever be tortured with it ... and to make a counter claim against such a perfect feature of our world, would be analogous to stating that there is a design fault in God's creation! It would be heresy.'

'And you know what heretics used to receive?' says Myfanwy.

'The death penalty,' the accountant whispers.

'Hey! You're supposed to be on my side,' protests Pilate pathetically.

'Well, my fine congregation,' continues the Canon, changing the subject somewhat. 'I was checking my post yesterday, when I discovered that my water bill has not yet been paid. And I thought to myself (I did, too) that maybe my *holy* water has been rendered *unholy* by a brief foray of my very *holy* parish into the colour, scarlet ... and so, I might need to come again when I am solvent – and perform another ablution of your sins.' He looks at Pilate as he says this, who, in turn, flinches in anticipation of another soaking. (Mindful of the Canon's words, and as an act of Christian kindness, the present author will desist from terrorizing the chief subject of his narrative for a while.) The priest continues,

'And may I express my wish that, through one final blessing, all of us are cured of an evil, and most unusual, form of substance abuse.' The priest genuflects and makes the sign of the cross.

'What ever could it be – *this substance abuse?*' All who are present wonder to themselves. And then, because speculations are impotent when raised in a vacuum, they begin to cast around, pointing their fingers liberally at one another and making baseless accusations:

'Are you the foul addict? Or is it you ... or you ... or even *you* ...' in response to which, comes the reply:

'It certainly isn't me. It must be you ... or you ... or even *you.*' Thus, do they unwittingly act out the parts of the twelve apostles – soon to become eleven – at The Last Supper. And the stage is set for the metaphor to be completed.

'The guilty party is the one who takes a piece of this fish to eat, and dips it into the humus at the same time as I do,' says the priest, alluding to the victuals that are still on the table.

'Just to recap – that's *fish first*, followed by *humus*,' Myfanwy clarifies. The Canon selects a piece of fish and dips it into the vegetable mould, and every other person in the room does precisely the same thing! Whatever could it mean?

'The substance, dear brethren, is this.' He makes as if to lightly touch the screen of the nearest iPad, but miscalculates his reach and connects with a loose live wire dangling from a larger electronic device nearby – which gives him a short, sharp shock. After issuing an evil hiss (more apt for a gaboon viper than a priest) he brings this instalment of his homily to a close:

'I wish to cure the staff at this institution of their obsession with mobile phones and ipads, personal computers, Wi-Fi, and wireless, petite printers with their dainty footprints ... and pray that you all, instead, shall talk to each other, or to God; or – of an evening – go home more willingly to your wives. An Englishman's home is his castle. So, gentlemen, the time has come! You must return to your castles ... and prep-are for gov-ern-ment!' He finishes the sentence in a crescendo, unaware of the faint dash of chauvinism, or of the allusion to David Steel's 1981 address at the Liberal Party conference: 'Go back to your constituencies, and prepare for government!'

The priest shares a special handshake with Dmitri, lightly stroking the centre of his palm. Hani Haphazardi and Bin Liner are tremulous with glee. They are very ticklish, and their empathy with Dmitri's palm has caused them to wriggle and giggle like two little girls.

'Someone in the room cites Albert Pike on the guiding light of Satan, and begins to quote from that man's arcane and scholarly work; to which Dmitri replies,

'My dear fellow, he was not exonerating Satan, but merely wondering why unearth the Prince of Darkness was gifted with the name of Lucifer, which means "Light-Bearer". At least that's what we *hope*! But, of course, Satan *was* originally the light-bearer, like yourself,' he turns to Pilate, 'before you went astray. Oh, hang on! No, that's not right. *You* were *never* a light-bearer!'

'Well, this *is* a turn up for the books!' remarks Pilate to himself. 'If I'd known he was one of *them*, I would not have unfriended him through so many onerous demands. I'd have been sucking up to him, rather than bearing down upon him (or sucking him dry).' Dmitri shudders for an instant, as a distasteful video is downloaded into his mind from the YouTube of common speech.

'I inducted him into the fellowship earlier on today,' says the Canon quietly, in an aside to Pilate.

'But how is that possible?' asks Pilate. 'He's been in the office all day. Unless he has supernatural powers?' And then, the former boss chants the following lines of spontaneous blank verse,

Where is the compass of my sanity?
My dial makes North of South, and East of West:
The magnetism of my earth's confounded!

'Search me!' laughs the Canon. He turns to address the entire group. 'Now, then. I am full of jubilee. And not Jubilah, Jubiloo or Jubilum – please note! (We don't want any of *those* bastards around here, polluting our pure communion of souls!) I note that you have all rewarded me with your patience; and, being a man of fair values, I shall now reward all of you. You will each receive a unique gift – assuming I have the time and resources to bestow it. For instance, Dmitri might receive the gift of tongues ... this being an addition to the machine languages which he already knows; or the betrothed, a brand new home, fresh from the catalogue of Wimpey or Wates. But you must each be happy with your gift – whatever it might be. Promise me that you shall all be satisfied with your gifts.' Everyone nods excitedly, and the words, 'Yes, I shall unwittingly accept what's coming to me', are spoken with zeal. The audience begins to verbalize various private musings: 'Whatever could it be?' and 'I need a reward after this long and gruelling day', and 'It had better be worth waiting for. Last Christmas, I received a pair of oven gloves, reconstituted from my grandpa's old socks.' This last comment comes from Dot, whose family has created a culture where everything is recycled - and where everyone contributes to the household economy from an early age.

'In that case, I shall begin.' Fr Bertrand diverts his eyes towards the "Worker Bee", and makes the sign of the cross, before uttering the words,

'You, my son, have already received your boon. The inside of your mouth has lost its swelling, and your tongue is free to speak normally.'

He moves over to where the erstwhile accountant, and latterly the reader of obscure texts, is standing; and, in response, the recipient-to-be simpers gratefully. He has had a hard time of it. At long last, his horizons may be illuminated with good fortune. The priest retrieves a magic wand from his pocket, composed of cigarette butts glued together, and waves it over the puny man's head. The moment is full of expectation. 'For evermore, when you cook the books – or speak out loud an untruth of any kind, - your gums shall be punished.' The little man swallows awkwardly, and cocks his head to one side as if he has misheard. Father Bertrand clarifies, 'My son, I bequeath unto you the gift of ... toothache.'

'Tooth-what? What ... the hell ...?' But it is too late, for no sooner has the unfortunate man posed the question, than his fate is sealed: and he sinks to the floor with a subdued moan. In the process, his hand rises to offer solace to his beleaguered jaw. He then makes a last-ditch attempt to appeal to the priest's humanity, by petitioning him with some flattery (which resembles the opening of Our Lord's Prayer):

'Our Father Bertrand – who art in a state of grace, – hallowed be thy name. I fear that this pain shall rob me of my good will.'

'And *I* rather suspect that the deposit account which holds your good will is running so low anyway, that this heist (brought about by your current ache) shall be negligible. In fact, if the account has, as I strongly suspect, already passed from the *black* into the *red*, my miracle shall, by robbing you of your (negatively-charged) "good will", flatter the state of your virtue - and therefore prove to be a surprising boon.'

The sufferer is about to respond, but the Reverend ignores him and races on (with histrionic reference to his expensive timepiece):

'Well! Would you ever ... The Lord Zeus will not be best pleased; nor will my altar boy, Zebedee.' (Eyebrows are raised, and none higher than the brows of Pilate, who doubts the authenticity of this man of God.) 'I was just about to perform the Doxology and the Great Amen – and lead a recessional hymn or two for good measure -' (he glances sideways at the accountant ...) 'but, as I solemnly dip my chin, and avert my eyes to my chronometer, I ... Good heavens! Is that the time? I simply *must fly*. I have a water bill to attend to!' Like a bad actor, he mimes the positions of the mechanical hands on the dial. Then he rises and scampers off, - swaying from side to side, like a broad oak tree in a gale. As he goes, he achieves such lightness of foot, that everyone present who has but an inkling of the principles of physical science, begins to revise that inkling; for never before has a hulk of such immensity transported itself in this way. And being thus preoccupied, no one is fazed by the huge vat he has left behind, which is now empty.

Gradually, as the patter of his tiny feet recede into the distance, a crowd collects around the window to watch his departure from the vicinity: which is transacted in an old, two-storey London bus - decommissioned many moons ago. This particular bus has been customised into a mobile home, where the priest can live when he is "on the road" and blessing the captains of industry, their business ventures, and their hardware. The side of the vehicle bears a presumptuous message, writ large: "There is no life after The Perfect Launchpad ... probably". And, upon seeing this slogan, Pilate remembers a similar line relating to the touted non-existence of God; and remarks that the wording might need to be altered, in case it gives offence.

Apologia

It is hoped that no offence shall be rendered by any views espoused within the compass of these pages: upon saints or beverages, or modern strains of popular culture. And I would like to emphasize that whilst opinions may be strongly held by persons within the narrative, - they are not necessarily the views of the author, himself, who (for the time being) would prefer to remain speechless on emotive subjects.

A Pronouncement by the Author, with
Respect to the Changing Layout of the Text

THE PRESENT AUTHOR [aside, to his readers]: There is something I must tell you about Descriptor, while he is out of earshot and on his toilet break. He is, at once, both indolent and vocal. He is very aware of his rights, - somewhat of a revolutionary, in fact. I keep telling him ... and telling him ... that the conditions of his labour as my underling are replete with victuals and home comforts, and should meet with no complaint. But he has collected footage (on his mobile phone) of civil unrest from a generation or two ago, and he is highly impressionable. I have not given up on him. And I needn't fret, for his contract with me is soon to end anyway ... but more of this later, as I see that he is on his way back to his desk.

An Exclusive Transcript of a Soliloquy of the Author on the
subject of his Descriptor (believed to have been Gleaned
from Telephone Tapping, with the aid of a Hidden
Recording   Device planted by Rebecca Brooks)

THE PRESENT AUTHOR: Of my right-hand man, who bears a name half-baked and somewhat fitting for an extinct lizard (Descriptor so hates me when I proffer this comparison), - there is much that I could tell. Oh! How many tribulations has he caused me? He refuses the legal minimum wage, and fights with me interminably about the number of words per day that he is required to produce.

Descriptor was fully intending, prior to my embarkation upon this literary voyage, to join the National Union of

Mineworkers – and was immoveable in his stance, until I explained to him that he wouldn't qualify because he wasn't a miner. He was crestfallen. Hour by hour, he would cast about, seizing upon this newspaper, or perusing that magazine, or watching the History Channel on his television set, - all for another union that would suit his needs. He has one now. The name escapes me, but, let me tell you, the members are Bolsheviks, to a man, and have negotiated an unspecified number of breaks for him within his working day. Meanwhile – pity me, if you will! - I am powerless to control him. He protests that he used to be a miner, perhaps in a prior life; and when I tell him that he was summoned into existence just a short while ago, and only to assist in the telling of this tale, – he simply will not have it. I have also explained to him that he is a "minor" in years, and, as such, would not be allowed near a colliery or slag heap; although, in less enlightened times, he could have been exposed to many things.

Sometimes a light comes on inside his brain, but not for long; and often-times, I must describe the deep trauma of the "three day week" in the 1970s, when humanity could not switch the light bulbs on – and when many people (left in the dark) would have fallen prey to Seasonal Affective Disorder. I do this in a colourful way, explaining how our anti-hero might claim that it was far, far worse than both World Wars and the Great Depression – all rolled into one: for at least they were what the Chinese proverb calls "interesting times".

May my diurnal fate, forthwith, go easy with me; for I am at the end of my tether. I would like to invoke the aid of Pilate's two strong men, but I rather suspect they will no longer comply, any more than they comply with *his* requirements. Should I fear an insurrection arising from the printed page?

PART THE TWELFTH:
SOFTWARE AND THE SUPERNATURAL

A Visit from a Creature of Legend

Dmitri is pensive. He is planning his approach to subsequent agenda. In the hiatus which follows, Pilate plucks up some courage. He is going to send an SOS signal to a friend, and decides that an appropriate medium for this signal is his mobile telephone, which he now removes from his pocket. His accountant begins to read again, and the rhythmic beat of Dmitri's hand upon the table, marking the end of each line of code, emulates the movement of a guillotine. Then Pilate remembers that he hasn't got any friends: not even his wife, whose rapt attention is on Dmitri..

Pilate is not fazed. No – quite the opposite. It is a odd feature of human neurosis, that just as the steep curve of inner tension reaches its peak, the vessel for that tension is able to sigh and become quiescent – as if the turmoil has played itself out, and there is nothing of it left. All of a sudden, Pilate is in a fanciful mood. He asks himself why he should not send a physical object by email as an attachment, as effortlessly as he would – a diagram or a photograph. After all, Star Trek gives notice of a teleportation machine – which deconstructs matter into atoms, and, after a brief journey, reconstitutes it into its former self. While he is in this reverie, he begins to regret all of the money he has wasted on postage and packaging through the years. He muses on the new technology of 3D printing, and asks himself,

'Why not a cooker or refrigerator ... or even, if one had a plot of land with planning permission, a swanky slice of real estate ... Ah! The Betrothed ... eat your heart out! What if I could transmit myself out of this building to a place of safety? If only ... if only,' he murmurs with rising excitement, as he discreetly types away upon his tiny virtual keypad. Unfortunately, as we know, things can get lost in the post; and the correct item is not always apprehended. And so it transpires that as Pilate attaches a program unique to him and clicks "Send" (hopeful that he will pass, somehow embodied by his code, to another location), he summons up something never before seen as a tangible object: and every bit as outlandish as the presence of Gabriel before the virgin Mary. There is a puff of steam, which gradually clears to reveal a man, bound (except for one limb) from head to toe in a strong ligature – all encased within a thin membrane. Amid gasps of astonishment, the following words can be heard:

'Good evening, ladies and gentlemen and children. I am a bind variable from the planet, ORACLE. I am functionally associated with a database field of the same, or a similar, name to myself. Indeed, I am "bound" to her and she to me. 'Tis a marriage of sorts. And when I am fully committed, the data that is contained within me shall pass into her. This is due to happen just as soon as you click *Post*. Lo! It shall be done. And in that moment, she and I shall become one variable in Christ - and one spirit.'

'An imposter!' is the rallying cry.

'Strip and slash him!' call some of the rowdier elements of the forum.

'We should have him committed,' is another suggestion.

'Sir, I shall be nothing if not committed.'

The "pupa", for that is what it resembles, proffers a low and courtly bow to the listening audience (whilst gesticulating in a circular motion with his one free arm). He is like a medieval courtier in a Castilian mount, paying his respects to his sovereign. This has the effect of neutralising the excitement in the room; and so, after an inauspicious beginning, a civil conversation ensues.

'You may have heard of ORACLE: the panacea for all of your database ills. It has now gone online, and (much to your chagrin, I am sure) has taken over your tired old master, Sun Microsystems, which invented MYSQL.'

'Well, I never,' says Myfanwy. 'That means we're almost related. I could refer to you as my step-father. It's a small world!'

The visitor looks baffled.

'Yes, yes. We all know what ORACLE is!' Dmitri is impatient. 'And it's very expensive!'

The strange pupa is undeterred ...

'Everything is so much more transparent where I come from ... an assignment is performed with a colon and an equals sign. Two or three equals signs beside each other are never seen. The notation - or syntax - is so exquisitely simple, it brings tears to my eyes ... and to my hooter. Excuse me while I just ...' At this moment, he recovers a tissue from underneath his network of ropes and bandages, dabs his eyes, and then blows his nose, as if it is a wind instrument wrapping up business on the final night of the "Proms". 'My creators are multi-talented and, if I may say, eminently sensible.' He gestures to Myfanwy, and pretends, like a harlequin in a restoration comedy, that his words are for her ears only (although they are really for the ears of the entire audience), 'If only she'd followed the ORACLE standard, rather than wilfully going her own way, - Miss Esquelle Open-Source could have selected her data *straight into* someone like me, without even declaring a "cursor"'. He lowers his voice slightly. 'That's a *buffer* to you and me'.

'Oooooh!' Myfanwy shudders with titillation. And then, in mid-exclamation, and realizing the social inappropriateness of her joy, she goes quite red. (This is a first for her.) Hisses and reproaches are directed at the visitor; and even a cockroach, that has surreptitiously crawled onto the platter of fish, begins to hiss in unison.

'If I follow their lead, maybe they won't notice me,' the cockroach thinks to himself – for he is very aware of the melancholy fate that has befallen other scavengers. But escaping detection is not his only challenge. He also has arthritis to contend with. 'This is the lot of arthropods,' he muses. 'It all comes down to having jointed legs. But we're a hardy breed. My daddy once suffered at the feet of a society lady. She regularly abused him with the most obscene language. And then, one day, when he was minding his own business, she decapitated him with one of her stilettos. Yet he was undaunted. He soldiered on without a head. My daddy was *amazing*.'

'My planet is high maintenance,' continues the other creepy visitor (the one who seems half-human, and half, enormous maggot).

'At last we agree on something,' replies Dmitri. 'But, kind sir, I must qualify what you said earlier. There is still a memory buffer in the example you gave. It is just nameless; like the contraband on a bootlegger passing through customs, who lies that he has nothing to declare.' This casual reference to illegal substances provokes a strong reaction; and an ampersand, whose name is Grizelda, cannot restrain herself:

"ssssssgusting!' she cries out loud. Her disapproval is formulated with such rapidity, that some metaphysical equivalent of wind resistance dislocates the first syllable of the word, and sends the adjective flying out into the conversational world, incompletely formed.

'Let all the esses conjure a hissing serpent; and let it strike at any who oppose my words! I lay down the gauntlet, or – should I say - I rest my mace,' remarks the pupa.

'How very clever of you,' remarks Dmitri. 'But back to the subject of the "cursor", which you have explained for the benefit of the reader – who may not know.'

'He's right. I don't know,' says The Reader (alias The Accountant).

'I'm not talking about *you*! Our concern is with the readers of the present script, and with posterity,' replies Dmitri. (Author: Good heavens! One of the characters inhabiting this story is going right over my head, and accessing the readership which I might one day achieve! And I, the narrator, who is like God to these acting minions, have imagined that my stage directions were detailed and immaculate. Is there no enforcement of the privacy laws in this country?) The magic continues ...

'Gentlemen, I shall soon emerge from my chrysalis, and flutter above your heads, close to the very ceiling of possibility. Thus shall I demonstrate how light is my yoke, compared to other incarnations of the programmer's art.' With these parting words, he slips off his bandages to reveal the body of a giant butterfly. Then he takes to the air.

'Quickly! Give chase!' exclaims Dmitri. 'Use these butterfly nets to ensnare him, and cast him from the Inner Circle.' Dmitri reaches into a draw and places the aforementioned nets on his desk. It is remarkable what accoutrements some people bring to work with them. And, in passing, it must also be noted how pointless it is to chase a six-foot butterfly with a six-inch butterfly net – although the logistics are lost upon several characters, who seize upon the nets and brandish them like swords.

'Dear sirs, let your anger abate before you do me some harm ... and let me say – in my most humble defence – that I have an *oldie worldie* faithfulness about me, which is rare these days. I cannot overstress how committed I am, in passing all of my data into the database variable who is my mistress. But, naturally, I retain something of myself - for I cannot depreciate my value to absolute zero.'

And with these words, the newly-hatched bind variable flaps his huge wings more rapidly, and circumnavigates the room, eventually settling behind some penjing trees near the window, which bear a grey-green colour similar to himself, and which – he hopes – might offer camouflage. But by his height this notion is undone. Not even the furthest reaches of the Japanese imagination may successfully mask a six-foot butterfly man with a twelve-inch bonsai tree! And just as those in pursuit are closing in, the stupendous insect cries out, 'Abort! Abort the job!' and changes direction.

'Where are the beaters!' Dmitri invokes reinforcements.

'Here we are!' cry the youngest children – formerly, the elements of an array. Noticing they have already armed themselves with brushes and brooms, he asks:

'Have you any prior experience with wildfowl?'

'That's not wildfowl. That's a butterfly,' replies one of the children, whilst Dmitri rises and wields a cricket bat.

'Yes, dear. But it's more like a partridge than your usual Lepidoptera.'

'No, it isn't.'

'Well. I was reserved in my comparison. It's actually like a cross between a pheasant and a pterodactyl!'

'No.'

'Yes, it bloody well is! Now, don't just stand there arguing with me! Hurry up and beat about the bushes!' The children begin to cast about with their makeshift weapons, as if their lives depend upon it, punching and creasing the stately curtains, and toppling the multi-coloured flower pots.

'Oh! My exotic plants!' rues Pilate. 'Oh! Oh!'

'This is an exemplary experience for fresh young office staff,' Dmitri coos with satisfaction. And his words send the youngsters thrashing about more wildly than ever, smashing a porcelain vase in the process.

'Oh, God! That's worth a fortune! How will I ever replace it?' asks Pilate.

The giant butterfly man ascends the warm, stale air, and glides just below the ceiling. He targets a sash window which has not yet been double-glazed, and, with an almighty thud, attempts to force his way through it. The pane of glass cracks in half a dozen places, and part of it is dislodged and falls onto the cobble-stones beside the building. Still, there is no aperture large enough to admit the winged beast. He turns full circle and, with a resounding crash, opens the entire window with his head before squeezing his peculiar torso through.

'That's going to cost hundreds of pounds sterling to replace,' states Pilate, in a tone that implies someone is going to pay.

'I told you, you should have installed Everest,' says his wife, forgetting for a moment her mystical role as "keeper of the database". Meanwhile, the children rush over to the window, to see if they can swat their target out of the air. You could call it a "Butterfly Race" (although the Olympic Committee might have other ideas). Alas, the children are too late! And as they pull long faces, they hear the ORACLE Bind variable speak its parting words, with a voice similar to Martin Luther-King's:

'Free! Free at last ... no longer bound by marriage to a nominal field.'

'Leave him,' says Dmitri. 'He's gone for good; and he's good for nothing! Now you must ensnare the witch who summoned up the monster!' Strangely, Pilate is left in peace, as everyone's attention is suddenly taken by another, more beautiful distraction. The ballet dancers are just ending their routine on the tightrope by curving their well-defined bodies in a most suggestive way. The girls, who have been christened with the name of "Curly Brackets", are perched at either end of a high wire, as a small theatre curtain falls – imprinted with the words, 'A Perfect Subroutine'. A wave of applause commences, and one of the ballerinas continues her gymnastics, loudly humming: 'See me dance the polka', a melody composed by George Grossmith. Meanwhile, the former director looks aghast, as his huge wife attempts to join them on the trapeze wire. This is highly precarious, as it is not designed to take her weight. Inevitably, the wire snaps and a pile of bodies are left writhing on the carpet.

'Everything is getting out of control. By heaven! Methinks this "programme" of entertainments is more like a badly-spelt "pogrom"!' exclaims Dmitri, who, not for the first time during this fantastical sequence of events, is clutching at his stomach and retching, 'Oh dear! Oh my! Aaaarrrgh ....'

'Look out! He's going to be sick!' someone shouts. In point of fact, everyone is nauseous. Then Dmitri (whilst reaching for his bucket, and knocking it over) spews onto the carpet with frightening violence: creating, as he does so, a most peculiar but highly accomplished abstract design – quite worthy of Tate Modern. A couple of the others follow his example.

'That's goodbye to my newly-laid and thick-piled Wilton carpet. Ruined! Utterly ruined!' Pilate moans quietly. There is a sudden, mad rush to assist the vomiting principal, while some of the assistants are fainting. And then – quite magically and of its own accord, - the very same window forced open by the bind variable (alias "butterfly man") begins to close; and Pork Belly holds aloft an explanatory notice,

'Windows is shutting down.'

But that is not all. A thin film of smoke is seeping under the door; and a sweet, acrid smell pervades the atmosphere.

'We have to open those damn windows – not close them. We must act immediately, before the fire takes hold!' exclaims Dmitri. He is panicking now.

'I can't seem to open any of them. The hinges just won't budge,' says someone who is choking on a cocktail of smoke and desperation.

'But – in any case - won't the air just fan the fire?' another person asks.

'Surely you would not prefer the fire to be quelled by a shortage of oxygen, and by the high water content of our bodies?' asks a third voice.

'Well - if the preservation order on the warehouse means the breath of life must be exhaled, so be it,' Dmitri speaks with sudden resignation.

'Myfanwy - I never knew there was a preservation order on the warehouse,' Pilate responds with confusion.

'You mean we must all perish, so the building can be saved?' asks a doubting Thomas from somewhere in the room, while stuffing a series of paper towels under the door. Dmitri's reply is loud and clear:

'Why, of course. Altruism is the fairest mark of human virtue.'

Meet Sound-Byte

Now, much to Pilate's surprise, several respected figures from the neighbouring community force their way into the room. They are careful to shut the door behind them, and to re-seal it with the towels. All of this, they do with extreme haste. To afford themselves some relief from the heat, they are wearing damp cloths on their foreheads (which they have doused under the kitchen tap); and they have brought with them several bowls of water, which the ambient temperature will evaporate into cooling oxygen. To further assist, a humidifier has been switched on.

For the moment, the sealed entrance is successful in keeping the smoke at bay, and so the captive audience relaxes – and begins to pass the time by pondering a conundrum: this being, how could the newcomers have achieved access to the building? Furthermore, how did they escape detection? They must have surreptitiously followed the Reverend through the main entrance, before later emerging from the chrysalis of their shadows to take centre stage. (Of course, the same questions might be asked of the outlandish creature who has just left, except that he possesses supernatural powers).

Among the new arrivals is a bedevilled character who answers to the name of "Sound-Byte"; a financial services manager; and a funeral director. And they have arrived with the express aim of delivering a series of official presentations. First up, is Sound-Byte. He is a rare case among the *Dramatis personae* of this curious tale, in that he does not have a living, breathing avatar in the conventional world; and yet, at the same time, he is everywhere apparent in it.

'Security is so porous these days,' he muses, as he scratches his blackheads, and fondles the oily pores in his skin. 'There is a clear osmosis betwixt what we would wish to keep strictly for our personal pleasure and good fortune, and what the criminals require for the advancement of their "rackets".'

As Sound-Byte speaks, it is clear that he has two prevalent features. His skin shines with perspiration, rather than with good health; and he has a permanently blocked nose, which he wipes with the back of his hand. He also has a distasteful tendency to touch everything in his vicinity, and, owing to his slippery exterior, he leaves traces of salt water or slime wherever he goes. But, as the following words testify, he would prefer to introduce *himself,* rather than have me do it for him.

'Right, then. I'll hurry along with my presentation, as we haven't got long. Sound-Byte's the name. I am the alpha and the omega. In other words, I am every tiny distraction which grabs your short attention span – in all the days of your lives.'

'I don't remember him impacting upon our systems development,' mutters Pilate, 'but I suppose he is symbolic.' Sound-Byte bows his assent.

'By now, I have acquired so much junk inside my body, that I am struggling to fit any more in – leastwise, that is to say, without my insides rupturing. And yet how else, except by virtue of my gross appetite, may my empire of interference spread to the furthest reaches of the globe?'

The visitor's stomach begins to rumble, and Dmitri takes up the challenge:

'I could prick you with a drawing pin. Would that help?'

'You might release more than you bargained for. And, besides, you are a kindly man and would not do it.'

'Well - I *might*,' says Dmitri.

'Prove it,' says Pilate (like an *agent provocateur*).

'Alright, I will.' And, upon the instant, Dmitri pierces Sound-Byte with the biggest drawing pin he can find. (Fortunately, several are available, as if supplied for this very purpose.) Sound-Byte's hands instantly rush to the point of incision, but even in the split second before they arrive he has already exploded.

Man alive! I cannot count the crimson spots of blood and biological tissues, combined with substances yellow-green and brown, which pepper the walls. Heart muscle, still beating, dangles from the chandeliers; and partially-digested "bangers and mash" are sticking to the cast-iron radiators. Indeed, pretty much everything in the room is covered with an oily film, several millimetres thick; although - and this is the weirdest thing of all – every living thing apart from Sound-Byte has been spared the fallout.

No one has even flinched. All eyes are drawn towards this shiny, pervasive mantle, as if to a kaleidoscope. The pleasant colours of the rainbow are at once reflected – and, soon, they reconstitute themselves into a pixilated display of every source element of the deceased, both visual and audible. It is like looking at innumerable tiny windows on human life. There are newscasters broadcasting their summaries of events from around the globe, both principle and trite; and videos of terrifying military exchanges in foreign wars; and there are elements of musical butchery, wherein portions of the liveliest popular melodies are played out and dissected by pundits, who lack the big heart and the cerebral equipment needed for the task; and, further to this, there is an adjacent portal into a special subdivision of hell, reserved for the creators of television commercials - guilty of the misappropriation of outstanding classical music.

There is a clip from a past video on the Leasehold Reform Bill, in which the presenter holds up an "engorged lease" for a block of flats, all prettified and enclosed in transparent plastic ... but now *disgorged*, and discoloured by the entrails which have fastened it to one of the walls. And, beside this, many disappointed leaseholders are seen, who have occupied this building all of their lives; and who must now start to pay rent on something they previously owned, or buy their property for a second time.

Also on display, are advertisements for every superfluous product of the human imagination; and commercials for fattening food items, like chocolates with soft centres, – and all of them coated with sticky voice-overs that adhere to the mind of the listener, although he may not wish it. There are even sex goddesses who sit astride the bonnets of automobiles, strumpet-like; and footage of goals galore from famous legends of "the beautiful game"; and, last and least, are various disgusting clips from the television series, "Embarrassing Bodies".

A Brief Presentation on the State of the Economy

After mapping out the geography of Sound-Byte's world domination, the author would like to introduce a little man with big ideas - and a bulbous nose to sniff out clients. From the soles of his shoes to the tip of his pudding-basin haircut, he has to be no more than five feet tall; and yet, the circumference of his head is something to be reckoned with. He steps nimbly over an exposed umbilical cord (which, until recently, has been attached to a most unusual child), taking care not to stain his exquisitely polished shoes, nor to steady himself by laying his stubby fingers upon slimy walls. Then he positions himself at the famous pulpit in front of his audience; and, in an aside to Pilate, he makes mention of every economist's favourite water closet.

'Yes. We used to own one of them, until a certain dampness in the air gave rise to a proliferation of insects - at which point, we had to get rid of it,' Pilate offers meekly.

'Shhhhh!' retaliates Dmitri.

'Ditto!' corroborates Myfanwy, who (with the aid of a fresh linen blouse, and a pair of soapy nylon pantaloons, plucked from the washing machine in the office kitchen) has become "partially decent" again. In keeping with this restoration, she distances herself from her own sanguinary discharges. And she smiles, as the financial services manager describes himself in a most quirky and endearing way:

'I was known in intimate circles as "Little Balding"; until a hair transplant, from my pubes to my pate, restored my follicular beauty to beyond its original setting. And before my recent haircut, I was so proud that Afro-Caribbean-seeming locks should fall upon my face ... and deck my faint complexion. But then it was time for the chop. I just thought I'd get that one off my chest. And I must tell you that, in finance, I am tall indeed; and bearing substantial weight, I'll have you know. 'Tis said of me: were I the pence in your pocket, I would bring your trousers down.'

Foolish Boy shakes with laughter, until his upper lip becomes very sore and starts to bleed: for he has bitten it, in order to pre-empt a convulsion. But the speaker's opening gambit is no less attention-grabbing:

'Dear all, I have come to speak to you today about the gravest of monetary issues: those which relate to the very survival of our economy, as we know it. You have, no doubt, heard of the famous Philips machine - containing water tanks, pipes, pumps and valves; and operating with the aid of gravity. The mechanism is well known by sight, but not by name; and it consummately portrays how Mammon flows from the highest echelons of power ... down through each limb of the "body politic", and thence into every sector great and small.' (Some of the intelligentsia who are listening question this wisdom, believing, instead, that it flows in the opposite direction – transferring its advantages from the poor to the rich. But since this contravenes the law of gravity - witness, Newton's falling apple, - they keep schtum.)

'Today, I shall introduce a special sector within our economy: that of financial services.' He holds aloft a balloon filled with helium gas in one hand, and a letter-opener (in the shape of a tiny sword) in the other.'

Upon registering his intention, all of the characters in the the room stuff their fingers into their ears, whilst puckering their brows; and their cheeks go cherry-red with anticipation. They have already experienced one explosion, and do not wish to be caught unawares twice.

'There is really no need for a show of nerves,' the speaker attempts to defuse the tension. Unfortunately, his audience have partially closed their eyes and bowed their heads, - and they are sticking their fingers even more deeply into their earholes.

'Please, my good people. Let us be sensible about this. I concede that, under normal circumstances, the balloon would burst. But if you put this patch,' he holds up a pounds sterling note of high value, with a strip of sellotape affixed, 'over the balloon's most vulnerable area, then I can safely prick it with my make-believe sword, and it will remain intact. We affiliates of the Labour Party believe an injection of cash can solve any problem.' His reassurances are still not working, and the fingers remain firmly inside the ears.

'Really, gentle men and dressy ladies ... comely youth and playful kiddies ... these precautionary measures of yours are quite pedantic.' The children dart under the tables. The adults recoil, and then follow them. Finally, the learned speaker loses patience and stabs the balloon with a shocking degree of aggression. What follows is an almighty bang, as might be heard when all of the big guns are fired, at once, from the flank of a Spanish galleon. And the fallout might resemble that which arises from an orgy of safe sex. Pieces of colourful rubber are dispatched to the furthest reaches of the room, and one small portion of the former balloon comes to rest, like a skullcap, on the head of the financial services manager himself, although he fails to notice it. He only knows that he has deflated the enormous bubble of his pride. He rubs his fleshy nose, sinks to the floor, and speaks the following words whilst sitting on his haunches (and giving the appearance of a proboscis monkey):

'Dear me. This is more serious than I thought. Clearly, a much larger patch is required – perhaps one which can surround, and insulate, every iota of our economy.'

Of Burials and Cremations, Funeral Plots and Coffins

As he scuttles off to the back of the room, with an imaginary downward-pointing tail between his legs, replacing the upbeat tale which was flowing from his lips, another man takes the limelight. He is just 48 inches from floor to scalp, and he, also, harbours big ideas. It is the funeral director. Yes – the very one who hails from just a couple of doors down the road. The slightly-proportioned new arrival steps up to the podium, if one may call it that. He is wearing a gas mask with an oxygen cylinder, to avoid succumbing to the poisonous fumes now slowly seeping through the paper towels. A small and helpless child reaches out to him, and asks plaintively,

'Give me, please, one mask. I beg of you.' (The little one coughs). 'Just one for me!'

'You know, I'd love to,' he replies blandly, 'but unfortunately we're out of stock.'

A sweet and winsome melody is heard – as an organist in the adjacent church begins to play. The cold, unfeeling funeral director writes on the blackboard, in fancy lettering, "An excellent investment opportunity"; and then stands back to admire his own calligraphy. He is asked, once more, if he has any spare gas masks. And so he writes, slowly and deliberately, upon the blackboard (feeling himself to be like Jesus),

'Let the one amongst you who has committed no sin, reach out and take my mask and accompanying oxygen cylinder.' Before any of the children think to offer themselves as pure in heart, he pre-empts them all by writing:

'None of you are worthy of my mask, and so it shall remain with me.' Then, putting down the chalk, he turns away from the hapless children, and embarks upon his public address to the adults (who possess what he is most interested in: money).

'Gentlemen, programmers, and QWERTY characters of an extended imagination, I stand before you today, with the express intention of selling you each a special service. It is one that involves a discrete plot of land, and a warm, comfortable and well-insulated ... *coffin* ... in which to rest your weary ... er, *lifeless* ... limbs.' What a shame! Until the italicised words, the battle for hearts and minds was almost won.

'I will begin by reminding you that, very soon, you may pass away; for, as you well know, there is a fire brewing and no alarm has sounded. The Fire Service is not coming to your aid. In plain English, it is high time you drew up your wills. I have a template of a "Last Will and Testament" in my portfolio, that may easily be customized according to personal circumstances.' Next, he plays his trump card: 'And I am here to give you the glorious news that, should you wish to organize your funeral, and buy your coffins and your burial plots *forthwith* (for there is not a moment to lose), you may do so for a modest fee. And what might that modest sum of money be?' He pauses for effect. 'Pardon me, gentle guys and lasses all, if I report to you ... that the artefacts and related services are available (Hallelujah! Praise the Lord!) at *today's prices*!' His listeners stare at him with poker faces. 'Consider, my friends: if the flames do not take you, then in future years how much more expensive shall the requisite commodities become? Those who will foot the bill may remember this day of reckoning, and wish that you had not survived – or even lived at all!' Thus, in a few seconds, does the funeral director transform himself from a harbinger of doom, into a prophet of hope: the hope of a life that is not just about to end. But then, he goes back into "gloom mode" ...

'Reflect on the survivors of Hiroshima and Nagasaki. Picture their scars - and anticipate your own. What terrible melancholia shall befall each darling family - worn like a coat of arms in Winter, – when they see you lying in your coffin, perfectly still and with a face like blancmange; and realize that they must empty their coffers in order to bury your casket. By contrast, let those who buy into my schemes wear the scars they win today from this great fire with pride: the pride that comes from knowing they have dissolved a financial millstone, as surely as if 'twere but a kidney stone.' The orator is feeling himself to be suitably inspired, and a glorious Shakespearean speech commemorating St Crispin's Day floats into his head. Thank God he doesn't quote from it.

Meanwhile, this preposterous sales pitch has both Pilate and Dmitri twitching with irritation. It is Dmitri who takes up the baton,

'All things which are for sale, in every shop on earth, are available at *today's* prices. Unless they are reduced, in which case they are touted at *yesterday's* prices. But nowhere will they be sold at *tomorrow's* prices. (If they were, no one would buy them.) To argue that you save money by purchasing at the current price, is like saying that you should buy the house you might want in ten years time, right now, because it is being marketed at *today's price* - rather than with ten years' of house inflation added!' He stops abruptly – realizing that (if you were *flush with cash*) this is not such a bad idea after all. Then he searches for a more damning comparison.

'It is ... is ...' he cannot think of a strong enough way to slander the idea.

'We do not sell houses,' the protagonist defends himself.

'More's the pity - because the inflation manifest in house prices, is greater than that which may be observed in the provision of coffins or funeral plots, or other end-of-life services,' comes the rejoinder.

'But think of the precious time you will save your loved ones, by doing all of the attendant paperwork for them?'

'Alright! Another example.' Dmitri drives forward with his contention, like a military general deaf to a truce. 'Should you purchase your future bed, and all of the bedding that you will ever lie in, at today's prices? And all of your clothing, and all the underwear that your babies will ever soil? (You will first want to squeeze out of your wife's vagina all of the babies she will ever conceive.) What about all of the books that shall ever grace the shelves of your personal library (never mind whether you read them or not), collectively accounting for every *slight* alteration in your sense of the aesthetic during your whole lifespan – though it might be ever so hard for you to know this in advance? Soothsayer! Should you fork out for them all, right now, without hesitation?' Dmitri pauses for breath, and so Pilate takes the helm ...

'Aye! And what about purchasing and freezing all of the food that you will ever eat, - or throw out (ye wastrel!) - necessitating a freezer the size of a tower block? (You will need an enormous house to contain it.)'

Hani Haphazardi and Bin Liner – alias Copyvarfrom and Copyvarto - are nodding wildly. So is Dmitri, although he is surprised to have his chain of thought broken. He raises his hand, in order to achieve silence, before continuing,

'And, whilst you are pondering such imponderables, perhaps you should also do a lifetime's worth of washing up, assuming – with your new frame of reference – that you will have already purchased all of the plates and cutlery and mugs that a lifetime of consumption shall require? Are you a mug, dear sir? Just wash ... wash ... wash ... until you cultivate an obsessive-compulsive disorder that renders you incapable of any other action. Indeed, by the time you are through, your poor fingers shall be insensate. Nay! Worn down to their final atoms – or quarks! Thou shalt require a hundred years' supply of hand cream to revive them! And whilst you are rueing the state of your hands, you will be well served to buy ten thousand packets of chewing gum, – to help you ruminate upon each act of foolishness ... or (having previously chomped your way through eight decades of food at a single sitting), to ease the foul processes of your digestion, and freshen your pallet. Oh! And, while you're about it, don't forget the two thousand kilograms of toilet tissue which you'll need. Yes! Buy now ... all *now* ... at today's prices ... because it is cheaper than at tomorrow's prices ... Ah, logic! How far from thy intellectual Eden hast thou fallen? A baser mouthpiece for *induction* thou hast ne'er found!'

'Sir. I was only talking about funeral plots and boffins!' replies the undertaker. 'Er ... coffins.' But Dmitri isn't listening.

'Hell! Why stop there? Why not buy all of the dining room furniture that your family shall ever use.'

'We are not wholesalers of such merchandise.'

'But, with a respectful nod to Sweeney Todd, and to endangered bodies entombed within this soon-to-be inferno, you shall have meat aplenty. So ... why not lay the table straight away? In fact, now I mention it, I am surprised the Co-op hasn't capitalised on this idea. They deal in a questionable mixture of food and funerals, do you not agree?'

'I don't know what to say to that.'

'What about conservatories?'

'What about them?'

'Or sepulchres ... surely you sell those? How about *a sepulchre with a conservatory*? Now *that* would be a "turn up" for the building merchants to get their teeth into! Just have your loved ones stuffed, and then – when you visit them - you can all sit together in a glass box and observe the sky at night (rather like Patrick Moore, who may by now be peering down at you). What a scene of domestic bliss ... to be enjoyed with a slice of Battenberg Cake and a nice pot of Earl Grey tea. (You'll have to brew it yourself, and pour it out of course. Those dead people can't be asked.) And then you will all be free to sip, and to reminisce about old times (perhaps you can supply a ventriloquist?), and to speculate upon which astral bodies your loved ones' spirits sit.'

The funeral director is browbeaten, but he is determined to hold his ground: for any profit that he procures from this scenario, could be realised rather quickly. And, to boot, he has a captive audience.

'Sir, I am enabling you to protect your loved ones from a certain expense. No more, no less.'

'Or clothing ...' continues his adversary. 'Why not straight away buy all of the suits or frocks that you will ever need for your earthly life ... you would save yourself stacks of money ... for 'tis certain you and your lady wife will never wish to expose yourselves in public! Only an exhibitionist would do *that*.'

'We do not sell clothing – not even to dress the dead for their final journey.'

'What about appurtenances for hobbies?'

'I don't know what you mean.'

'Such as video players or old vinyl classics?'

'Well, I dunno ... I suppose we could play the cadaver's favourite melody. But, presently, we sell only coffins. Just *coffins* – and ... suchlike,' he whimpers softly. The little man is almost out of breath, trying to maintain his defence against what he feels is an onslaught on his integrity.

The soulful sound of the church organ does not soften the disagreement, as Pilate leans forward and watches the encounter unfold. He is captivated by an illusion. What else would one expect, in a world where abstractions become real? He sees bluebottles buzz out of the putrefied carcass of a crusty old argument ... and raises his eyebrows, as the protagonist wields a racquet with electrically-charged strings, to swat each one ... until, with the last abject protest having been despatched, the two combatants slump down into their respective chairs: too enervated to speak, or even move, for quite a few minutes.

Some Entertainment for the Innocents,
Before they are Consigned to the Flames

At this juncture, the carcinogens from the smouldering towels are starting to engulf the room; and Pilate is surprised at how long everyone is taking to collapse. One of the victims (a lovely documenter from the continent of Asia) notices the rising levels of distress amongst the children, and gathers them all around her. She has just had an inspiration. She will read from the Encyclopedia Britannica. Surely this will help them simmer down? Unfortunately, there is no trace of this venerable masterpiece to hand. And so she settles, instead, for the authoritative "Book of UK Taxation". Apparently, this is even longer than the famous encyclopedia. Perhaps they will fall asleep, which would be no bad thing. Sadly, the department does not stock a single, solitary volume from either of these "miniature libraries". Therefore, she decides, at last, to tell the children a fairy tale (with coughs inserted, like inept punctuation marks: some belonging to her, and some to them.) To this end, she has seized upon another scholarly tome – belonging to that wizard of technology and science, Dmitri. And being adept with words, she puts everyone at their ease in the traditional way:

'Are you sitting comfortably. Then I shall begin. A reading from The Book of Elements. Once upon a time, there were two rather contentious siblings perched upon the periodic table, called Osmium and Iridium. They were always arguing about who was more dense.' She hiccups with sudden violence, and her eyes water as she damages the back of her throat by inhaling a mouthful of scorched air. 'And Iridium spake unto Osmium, "I am incomparably thicker than thou art."'

"No, I am most certainly more dense," declared Osmium, with gusto.

"Look, you. I am thicker, incalculably thicker, than thou art. In fact, I am the thickest in the entire family. And that's an end of it." Henceforth, each pursued the ultimate proof of his own superior density, to the statistically significant level of 95%; but, for all of their verbiage, neither could be persuaded by the other's argument.' Finally, Osmium erupted - with a magnum of insight in his brain, and a pyroclastic flow of regurgitated food travelling out of his mouth, -

"Just hold your horses right there! We are only the densest elements on the periodic table in our purest form."

"Well, you are not pure: judging from the extended period of time you spend in the confessional," replies Iridium.

"What? Look, you! And you are no angel, either!"'

Unfortunately, despite the stalwart attempts of the narrator to hold the attention of her charges, and to keep her voice from cracking with the smoke, they are all now issuing gut-wrenching coughs; and, in the background, a sickly dirge reverberates from the most holy of holies among musical instruments. Gradually, this resolves itself into one horrendous wail, consisting of every note on the musical register. Oh! Where are the platitudes of heaven now? Surely not replaced by the vaults of hell? Pilate has a frightening vision (which he cannot get out of his head) of Fr Bertrand, seated at his organ and playing his new composition, with a smile of triumph spreading over the wide expanse of his face - like the sun rising over a land of plenty.

The children are having difficulty hearing the teacher; but, truth be known, they are not trying very hard. Ah, the youth of today! What is to be done with them?

The Strange Case of Benylin and Optrex - and of Boiling Tea

While the charming fairy tale is related, the youngsters are growing fidgety.

'Excuse me, miss. Can we go now? I'm choking,' one of the children petitions the storyteller. The attractive young Asian reaches for a bottle of Benylin, which she conveniently has to hand, and decants a soup spoonful of the medicine for her own consumption. She swallows it, and is just about to put the bottle away when she suddenly experiences a change of heart. Acting upon this, she seizes the unsuspecting youngster by his rosy cheeks. As he wriggles from side to side, she presses her left palm against his forehead; and with her right hand forces his lower jaw open with a pair of metal pliers, before summoning an assistant to pour half the contents of the entire bottle down his plump little neck. She excuses her behaviour thus,

'It is an expectorant, and will help you to clear your lungs.'

The child is soon struggling to stay upright, on account of all the coughing and retching which racks his little body; until, eventually, he falls onto his back, and remains in a state of collapse for some time.

Unfortunately, his "nurse" has fallen foul of the same misapprehension as numberless others before her – in imagining that one who is already suffering from a painful cough, only hankers for more violent coughing (even tinctured by a stain of blood, perhaps): for that is the result of taking an expectorant. Expect nothing more, nothing less. Of course, the only true medicine for those who are inhaling smoke in a confined area is to head for the exit; but this expedient solution never occurs to her. Has an odd principle been established? One is reminded of an historic occasion, when a fire broke out inside a cinema. Those within perished, whilst applying their combined weight against the door, – even as the main intelligence in the room was exhorting them to *please stand back* from the exit, because *the door opens the other way!* However, there is *something* which urges our story-teller to round off her fairy tale, both fairly, and fairly quickly:

'One fine day, Iridium has a firework of an idea ...

"Osmium, most loyal and noble sibling, we must dissolve our differences by coming together." (Iridium clears his throat and spits – or is that the narrator?) "Let us have a nuclear fusion of our personalities: and form a compound yet more dense than either of us has ever been before." The end.'

As you can imagine, the children are sighing and wiping their brows, and showing other visible signs of relief that the story is over. A couple of them look as if they are openly weeping. But this is to moisten their eyes, and not to empty a keg of rich feeling. The din from the most holy of holies remains steadfast. Pilate now envisions Fr Tyson, using the full gamut of his pipes and levers to coax from his organ the appropriate dirge for undermining the very foundations of the warehouse: where all and sundry are more dedicated to machines, than to humanity or to God. The children make straight for the door.

'Hold on, little ones! Stand in single file!' Dmitri shouts.

Meanwhile, the young Asian lady grabs the sick boy she has lately indulged. She sees him blinking rapidly in his sleep, and wishes to treat this ailment as well. She addresses Foolish Boy,

'Child - bring me the Optrex! You will discover it in one of the upper cupboards of the kitchen. This strong detergent ...

Shall make eyes water, stinging them like bees,
And cleanse their surface of impurities.

And said stinging shall be maintained, and cheerfully endured. And through this *near-spiritual* endurance - shall this fat child make reparation for his sins! So sayeth the Lard!'

'Madam, have you quite taken leave of your senses?' asks Pilate. Evidently, she has taken leave of her sense of hearing, for she carries on as if he had not spoken, - administering the eye drops and ordering a pot of boiling tea to be brewed by Foolish Boy. (He seems grateful for the attention. Could this be an opportunity for a little magic?) She continues,

'I adhere to the tenet that a beverage such as tea is refreshing on a hot day. May the spirit that infuses all boiling liquids be merciful to us! And may it bring forth a cooling perspiration through the excretories of the skin. Mother earth, let our pores be like your geysers!' Foolish Boy, believing the tea is for her, imagines her burnished complexion reconfigured as an aerial view of Iceland at night. Meanwhile, Pilate recalls the day when he interviewed this young lady for one of his positions; and wonders if he has accidentally hired a witch.

With a pot of tea brewing, the chubby boy shakes himself into a state of wakefulness, coughs, and obediently pours out a cupful for himself. Fearing retribution, he raises it to his lips without a moment's delay – and swallows, scalding his throat in the process.

At the mention of a beverage, the Worker Bee pipes up (as if already in mid-sentence):

'... And I have been hard at work on a new formula. Indeed, I have! It will be a "sparkling soft drink" composed of carbonated water, sugar, citric acid, flavourings (including ammonium, ferric citrate and quinine), emulsifier and preservative (*lots* of preservative), and some lovely colours known as "sunset yellow" and "Ponceau 4R" -'

'It sounds absolutely scrumptious,' says Dmitri, sipping from the concoction. 'My word ...!' He slurps like a peasant. '*Oh, Gawd!* I can *taste* the Ponceau ...' Dmitri's eyes are watering like hoses, and the sound of his speech fluctuates by a full octave, as if he is a youth whose voice is just breaking.

'Yes. And it's a secret recipe, devised by a piece of my very own software. I hereby dedicate it to the iron man in all of us.'

'And you have a sales pitch, I believe?' asks Dmitri. 'Is it ... "Poisoning young people ever since 1911"?' The software-cum-soft-drinks producer is confused, and somewhat crestfallen:

'No, no ... It's my *own* recipe ... with a sugar and aspartame "combo"; and a half a percentage point of real fruit juice. It also contains phosphorus, which helps with muscle contractions - and so prevents unwanted rear-end explosions. My slogan is ... "A fruit cordial to fill all-comers with a sweet gas, *from here to eternity.*"'

******

A tremor is felt in the building, and Pilate fears for the imminent collapse of his software universe. In a surreal reverie, he sees the Canon as an embodiment of one of the church-goers in his own painting – reaching out to the faithful in the most grotesque way possible, with multiple arms covered in suckers (like a giant octopus). The former director glances around him, and notices how everyone is preoccupied with the rapidly rising temperature. The fat boy has drunk his cup of hot tea, and is sweating like a pig. The office workers are wiping their brows with loose sections of tablecloth. Meanwhile, Gladys has lifted her wet floor mop, and sunk her entire face into it! In an instant, Pilate realizes that, far from being securely tethered to the back of his chair, he has actually been the subject of a mere amateur in the hostage game. Oh, joy! The cord is loosening ... and, for the moment, all eyes are suddenly fixed upon Myfanwy, who is eating her placenta.

'If I hurry, maybe I can escape,' he verbalizes to himself.

'Soon, the room shall be inhabited,' proclaims Dmitri, 'not with hordes of odd characters, but with dancing flames, - each vying, like Moloch, to consume our children ... including this little one, the dearest of them all!' He is clutching his special manual - the "egg" which the new bird in his life has recently laid. '*Mon Dieu*, I fear for my inflammable offspring!'

******

Pilate rises, and flees for his life - out of the room and through a long corridor ... down the stairwell ... and into a voluminous open-plan area which he traverses at great speed, losing his footing along a threadbare carpet. As he stumbles out of the building, he is relieved to have clean air around him; and he would rush down the street, if only he could. But his locomotion is hampered by a chair which is still attached to his back, and which renders him like a member of the genus, *Mollusca*. Never mind. He has more than one slimy little foot propelling him along. He shakes the chair off his back, dislodging one of its cylindrical legs as he does so, - and watches it roll down the hill in front of him. The birdcage has fallen from his head and crashed to the ground, flinging open its tiny door. Two tweeters escape towards heaven, - but there is still the small issue of the handcuffs, by which he is attached to the chair. He attempts to wriggle out of these, after applying some disgusting residue of margarine and fish oil; but he does not succeed. He is furiously ringing his hands as he scuttles to his freedom, - muttering, repeatedly, 'The room is crowded with flames! It is not I who condemns these living souls, but the crowd of flames.' He is shortly to be chased by the strangest posey of characters ever collected together in public. But, for now, all he can hear, disappearing into the background, are the muffled words of Dmitri emanating from a room some way above his head,

'Oh, dear! Oh, my giddy aunt. I ... I do declare I ... I think I'm going to do a hexadecimal dump!' In response to this, an authoritative voice from one of the members of the Force Majeure team declares,

'OK! Listen up, people. Let's be civilised about this. Gangway! Gangway! Women and children first ...'

PART THE THIRTEENTH: OUT OF THE FIRE, AND INTO THE FRYING PAN

Pilate scampers along the pavement towards the seashore. For a moment, he looks up and sees a silhouette of the mythical flying creature which earlier on dropped by to say, 'Hello'. It has been circling the former warehouse like a vulture in search of something to eat; but there is no wholesome food in its immediate environs. Naturally, it has no taste for such vectors as beetles or other pests; and as for the fish – well, the less said about that stinking mound, the better. And so the creature soars, like an American eagle into the Hollywood sky … and towards the next site where it has been booked for some consultancy.

Pilate knows he cannot return from whence he came, and so he decides to roam the streets until morning. Soon, he grows weary of this – for he is not a fit man. Then he pauses, and cries out with a soulful invocation to the mercy of heaven, 'Has the End of Days now come?' … But no sooner have the words parted company with his tongue, than a voice is heard from high up in the clouds: 'End of Day has not been run'. (However, he needn't worry – for the celestial voice is only referring to some arcane backup procedure.)

Eventually, our troubled anti-hero arrives at a building site. And thereupon, he falls into a deep sleep lasting several hours. He awakes at sunrise to the sound of labourers. They have been working under cover of darkness all night; for they must fulfil a contractual obligation to perform their tasks with a modicum of interference to the daylight infrastructure.

He believes himself to be safe, although a terrifying retinue of oddballs has been closing in on him. Several of the children, in struggling to keep up with their companions, have ceased their bipedal motion and resorted to cartwheels; and this final touch likens the troupe to a travelling circus. Pilate turns three hundred and sixty degrees in order to get his bearings. And there they all are! Dmitri is standing with his paper-based "babe in arms", with Myfanwy at his side. She still has traces of blood on her underclothing, and a yellow-green dye with a high "Ph" factor on her white shirt. It might be vomit. Like everyone, she has lost her appetite somewhat. She used to look rough and ready, but now she just looks rough. In fact, they all look sickly pale; and several are bruised and burned. Behind Dmitri and Myfanwy is Larry, the brain-damaged engineer, linking arms with his darling mother. Street lighting exposes a fault line on his head, surrounded by a purple swelling. Nearby is the man from the Inland Revenue, as well as that other emissary of the state - the Health and Safety Officer. And secreted within the group is the accountant, grasping his lower jaw and grunting softly in the stillness. Dmitri moves rigidly, like a clockwork soldier, towards Myfanwy - and holds her hand. He is regarding Pilate with deep-set eyes. There is a faint sea-breeze stirring his hair, and Pilate can taste the salt-spray on his tongue. Finally, Pilate's wife steps forward and unlocks the handcuffs, as Dmitri begins his formal address:

'There is only one way by which you can make atonement for your sins. You must transact the most enormous and outlandish migration for the local county council. It is, in point of fact, an undertaking of similar magnitude to the one which you were so keen to foist upon us. Specifically, I hereby command you to remove the entire beach you see before you, to the next seaside resort some ten miles west of here; but you must exclude the gravel, in case holiday-makers should cut their feet. Furthermore, you will transact this migration by carrying one grain of sand at a time. This is because each grain is to be weighed and measured, and its shape and colour documented, - with a descriptive label carefully affixed ... so that grains may be grouped together upon the basis of shared characteristics.' Dmitri fills his lungs with fresh air, and resumes,

'Your life is in peril! And lest you forget, I must threaten you with the cold prospect of being deposited alongside the head of Cortana – out at sea. Furthermore, each label should be imperceptible to the naked eye of any sunbathing man, woman, or child. I warn you, you would be well advised to make haste before the sea comes in.' Dmitri casts his eyes over the building site, where labourers are busy in several large holes - each containing a layer of sand spread over dried cement. 'To begin with, however, you shall prove that you are equal to the task by undertaking a smaller challenge. This involves shifting the grit, grain by grain, from the first cement pit, some thirty yards yonder, to the second.'

'What are you saying ...? You mean I am not allowed to used a shovel?' Pilate asks plaintively. 'I'm sure that nice man over there will oblige if I ask him for his spade.' He calls over to a labourer who is hard at work, and he dresses up his words in the most courtly of phrases,

'Ahoy, there, my good fellow!' The sea-breeze has given him the faint illusion that he is on a ship. 'Could I borrow your spade? I only require it for a couple of hours or so, in order to transact a little honest labour - such as a man of virtue like yourself would readily appreciate.' The man looks up from his work, wondering if the sound is an auditory hallucination. He cocks his ear so as to catch the next sentence. Then he puts his head down and continues labouring.

'You must follow my instructions to the letter, or else you will never recapture your reality. Lo! I have spoken,' says Dmitri.

'Oh, no! Noooooooooooooooooooooooo!' Pilate projects his words with such volume, and so sorrowfully, that his shout carries as far as the mating call of an American bullfrog. Since the latter is a lake-dwelling amphibian, unaccustomed to the ocean, this is somehow appropriate: for Pilate, himself, is like "a frog out of fresh water".

Strained Communications and Altercations

A moment later his tormentors are gone. Initially, Pilate rests on his laurels, taking ten delicious minutes to recuperate. During this period, he observes a traditional London Routemaster bus pass by, with the slightly altered motif: "There is no life after The Perfect Launchpad ... *definitely*" – accompanied with some small print, "The original wording of this slogan has been altered for legal reasons". Clearly, the Reverend has got the wrong end of the stick; and, rather than softening his point, he has sharpened it.

Pilate realises that time is racing away, yet he requires some refreshment before starting work. He clears his parched throat and "rises from his laurels". Then he waddles over to a stone basin (which hails back to a time when the pasture on this hinterland was intensively cultivated for agriculture and livestock - whilst latterly, farm animals have made only an occasional appearance). The name engraved on the outside of the basin is: Metropolitan Water Fountain and Cattle Trough – although there is no metropolis anywhere in sight. Falling to his knees, as if before the altar of the Lord Jesus, he slakes his thirst.

Afterwards he rises, picking some soiled hay from between his teeth, and wiping a residue of earth and gravel from his lips. He sets off to spend a quarter of an hour investigating a near-by skip for disposed electronic media, before making his way over to a gruff foreman. The man is standing in the first of the aforementioned cement pits. As he approaches, Pilate has a "floppy disk" in his right hand, and a "hard disk" in his left; whilst the tip of a flash drive hangs out of his mouth like a cigarette. Happy hunting! His wrists are limp, and he carries each disk in a weakly affected way between thumb and forefinger. He dare not damage them: for who knows what treasures they might contain? To a dispassionate observer, it would appear that he cannot decide whether the objects have the value of a Fabergé egg, or a slither of torn pantihose; although, in the right frame of mind, both may be deemed precious. He decides to be polite and to flatter the foreman. Sadly, he misheard the man's surname when he caught snatches of muffled dialogue a few minutes earlier; and, so far, he has not revised his judgement – for he privately believes that the least significant persons in life's story are often the ones whose names you most readily remember. He also intends to breach the details of his unwritten contract, and perform any migration by the swiftest means possible.

'Mr Willy Wogweevilberry? I am delighted to make your acquaintance.'

'I beg your pardon?'

'I'm awfully sorry to bother you, but I do believe that you are standing in amongst my data,' Pilate offers apologetically.

'What's he talking about?' asks a surly labourer who is standing nearby. The man addressed by Pilate walks over to the foreman.

'We've got a right one here. Is he a friend of yours or something?' asks the foreman.

'Of course not. I've never seen him before.'

'He was asking to borrow your spade only a few minutes ago,' states the foreman. The man looks nonplussed as the foreman continues, 'He was handcuffed and calling upon heaven. He must be high on something. Are you sure you don't know him?'

'Mate, what do you take me for? Earlier on, that lunatic was running around with a chair on his back and a birdcage on his head. I wouldn't have a friend like that! Maybe he's the groom at a stag party?'

Pilate, meanwhile, is conducting a preliminary investigation of the sandpits. The workmen watch his antics, but, for some reason, appear to have been oblivious to the entourage of misfits who pursued him, and who have since disappeared. The labourers have all been working hard (or so they claim), and they use this visit from a stranger as an excuse to emerge – like meerkats - from their various holes, and congregate for an unscheduled tea break. They are laughing amongst themselves, and, for a while, the foreman is laughing with them. When he has had enough, the foreman walks over to the deepest pit of all, and calls the erratic stranger over.

'Your underling has been planting footprints in my database,' says Pilate.

'I'll piss in it, if you don't leave this area instantly!' replies the foreman.

'I'll fine you, if you contaminate my data,' Pilate rebukes him.

'Shall I call the police?' asks one of the labourers.

At this juncture, Pilate relinquishes his storage media. He has decided that even a God-fearing IT consultant can only take so much, and, in a fit of angst, he seizes the pneumatic drill from the labourer and starts the motor. Then he leaps into the hole (which has been meticulously prepared to accommodate some new cables), and begins to drill furiously. He is loosening the topsoil for the forthcoming migration. Then he turns and brandishes his unoccupied hand in the direction of the foreman. The effect is reminiscent of a dictator waving his sabre in a cavalry charge, -

'Get behind me, Satan! You are like a picket guarding an adit; and I, like an abused canary, shall succumb to the poisonous vapours of your social intercourse if I dally a moment longer! I must drill, drill deep down I tell you, *drill* into the inner recesses of the data, and time is not on my side!'

After using the pneumatic drill furiously for a few seconds, he drops the machine (which, for safety reasons, automatically switches itself off) and continues in his madcap venture, alternating between the two sandpits (noted by Dmitri) with the regularity of a metronome.

Other labourers in the vicinity notice the disagreement, and join their colleagues in moral support. Simultaneously, Pilate half-senses that someone is standing behind him with a frying pan. It is as if he is employing that sixth sense - which in blind people is so acute – to register what has escaped the attention of seeing eyes. His knees buckle as the pan comes crashing down; and he falls through the air to the gravel floor. During this brief descent his perception of time is lost, and his mind generates an elaborate fantasy - wherein he stands on the flat roof at the top of the warehouse, posing as Jesus during the forty days of fasting. Satan appears in the guise of Dmitri, tempting Pilate to perform extraordinary feats.

'Sir, will you throw yourself off the roof? A legion of angels will surely save you?'

'Dmitri, whilst I cannot impugn their pure intentions, what if they should arrive late because their wings are in a state of disrepair? And think, even if they were to catch me, - with my weight, I could land heavily.'

'Sir, your velocity shall not be increased by your great weight, so long as it is in proportion to your great mass!'

'Nevertheless ... your offer of an "Air Ambulance Rescue Service" is still less attractive to me than a handsome fortune, or a gourmet feast.'

'Excuse me? I don't remember offering you that.'

Suddenly, he is no longer aware of anything. Of course, it might appear that he had long ago forsaken the everyday world for some alternative universe; but, now, he is declared to be "completely out of it", and remains so for about twenty minutes.

During this time, a crowd of concerned passers-by gather around the capacious hole which he has fallen into – and peer down at him, as if he was a wild animal in an enclosure at a zoo. They take photographs with their digital cameras, and gaze in wonderment at the foreman for enacting such a splendid "capture". Finally, the concussed hero of our tale opens his eyes and sees daylight once more. It is the daylight of absolute reality (if such exists). He rubs his sore head, and rouses himself from what feels like the bestial floor.

He hears the foreman speaking with a police constable, for "Old Bill" is on his beat. Place the constable in your mind's eye and watch him there awhile. See how he hobbles on rheumatic legs; and how, with outstretched hands, he relinquishes his balance and then catches it again, like an acrobat making a pretence of danger before an audience of excited ladies. (He wishes!) As a matter of fact, he does have one lady with him: a young apprentice named Una. She is from South Africa, and refers to her boss as "Ol' Bull".

'My men are unable to work, because a madman insists on running from one sandpit to another and back again, carrying grit in his hands and talking gibberish.' Pilate finds his tongue (an implement which is rarely lost to him for very long). He blurts out to the officers of the law,

'I say - you're not Norton Utilities by any chance, are you? By God! *Am I* glad to see you? I have been mugged. *Mugged*, I tell you, - and in my own offices! I just had to escape into the open air. You know, when I got hit with that frying pan, I thought I was done for – even worse than Java Man. (He got whacked as well.) He's my accountant, actually, – but he does look a bit primitive, and (I must say) he has been behaving very strangely of late ... reading my own computer code back to me verbatim. I'd say that's a bit cheeky, wouldn't you? I have even been an unwilling ear-witness to the slaying of Cortana. It is with a heavy, but a guilt-free heart, that I proclaim unto you: she was complicit in her own downfall. And, after enduring so much myself, I thought that my session was going to be terminated.'

'Will you just step this way, sir.'

'Obviously, I'll need another session.'

'You fell down a hole. You might need a doctor.' The officer turns to his colleague.

'Shall I read him his statutory rights, Bull? Yiss?' asks Una.

'Go ahead, Una.'

'OK. Fan.' She gathers herself for her big moment. 'I would lick to infirm you that inything you see will be ticken down and may later be oozed aginst you. Inderstind?' (Pilate unconsciously moves his head.) 'Yar? Fintistic!'

'You mean, I'll be hoist with my own petard?'

'Sire, will you plizz lit me furnish?' She rubs her brow with a cravat (which she produces from an inside pocket), until the light, wispy lines in her forehead radiate beauty, after the fashion of natural grain in a wood carving.

'But it's not like this in the Cayman Islands.'

'We ah nit in ze Cayman Ah-lands.'

'No. But my money is, and that's what counts.'

'A min is not identified by his minney.'

'*Au contraire!* I think I often am – at least when I gaze at my reflection in the mirror, and speak to myself in soft, dulcet tones. Thereupon, do I make Mammon the theme of my soliloquy, - and, by logical deduction, the largest autonomous component of my compound self.'

'Can ye jist slip these hendciffs on, sire?'

'What? More handcuffs?'

'Sire -'

'Excuse me ... sorry to butt in – but can I just ask a question?'

'Wit is it?'

'Before we proceed any further, can you please issue me with a new Session I.D.? Normally, the computer would help with such formalities; but, as there isn't one available ... er, by the way, it needs to be 32 alphanumeric characters and ... well, you would not want my person to be "terminated" on your watch, now would you?'

'He appiz to have completely list his marnd. He's not dangerous, is he?' the young policewoman asks cautiously.'

'Well. I don't like the sound of him grabbing a pneumatic drill from one of the workmen - and then boring deep into the ground! Is there anything else we should know about him?' asks the constable. The foreman replies,

'Well, the madman was observed earlier on in a skip, up to his waste in rubbish. He said something about searching for personal data.'

'I mean: does he need to be physically restrained, or will he come peacefully?' asks the constable. The foreman shrugs nonchalantly, as if to say, 'It is not my area of expertise. Ask me about laying a pipe line as a conduit for water or gas, and I can help you.' And so the lady officer begins afresh,

'Ah would lick to remarnd you that inything you say will be nitted dan ...'

'That old chestnut, again. Are you a plebeian? Because I most certainly am not. I have a reputation to protect. I require no repetition. My memory is an immaculate conception. I don't take notes – never needed to.' (This is not strictly true.)

'A pleb- ... what did you just call my colleague?' the constable is offended. Pilate does not reply.

'You know, I could sue you for coining a term of abuse.'

'My dear fellow, you are a policeman, and – in the grand pecking order - I count *myself* no less important than a Member of Parliament. This is a modest estimate, I might add, but still one that raises me far beyond your ken. Oh, whatever next?' he sighs. 'A symphony of woes? Some "Variations on a Theme by Plebgate" ...?' The eyes of the constable open wider and wider. He can scarcely believe this insolence.

'Can you get me a new ID, please? Or, for that matter, a fresh IP address?'

'I can't sort you out with a passport, if that's what you mean. That would be the job of Customs and Immigration. Right now, I've got to read you your rights ...' the officer declares.

'I thought you just did. They don't mention anything about Session IDs, do they?' Silence ensues. Mr Propotamous shuffles his feet nervously, like one of those unfortunate dancing bears, the soles of whose feet are being scalded (maybe right now) on a hot plate far, far away, - in the subcontinent of China.

'Will you please stand still whilst we read your thoughts to you ... your *rights*, I mean ... while we read you your rights.' Una comes to the rescue:

'Yeh dinit hiv to say inything. But it may ham your difince if you dee not mention, when questioned, something which yeh leeter relah awn in court. Bull?'

'Anything you say may be given in evidence,' adds Bill.

'So – I may be penalised if I say something immediately, and I may be penalised if I say it later. "Mere Chicanery" is what I call it, although you may know it better as "Hobson's Choice",' retorts Pilate.

'A police cell won't have the resources to look after him,' Bill gives his considered opinion. 'We might need to place him in an asylum, where a psychiatrist can examine him. That's assuming he hasn't got an illegal substance in his blood stream: in which case, he'll need a Biochemist.'

'A psychiatrist, you say? Is that the disk doctor? He wouldn't, by any chance, be related to Doctor Watson ... would he?'

'Is he your General Practitioner?'

'Just think of him as "a Post-Mortem debugger". You see,' continues Pilate, stepping gingerly over the question, and pointing to his head, – 'it's my hard drive. It hasn't been functioning very well of late ...'

'No. Nor mine ... not since I met you, in fact!'

'I'm so sorry to hear it. Do you require time off work?'

'Look. Who's asking the questions around here?' The Constable stamps his feet with impatience, much like the bloated police horse he was sitting upon earlier in the day, before it released its load into a hanging basket.

'Now then!' Pilate exclaims, 'Where was I? Ah, yes ... A session ... It's kind of like ... a new lease of life.'

'We'll give you a new lease of life!'

'Oh, thank you. You're so kind. But how am I going to start my new life? I'll need a unique identifier ... Have you got a Random Number Generator?'

'Yes.'

'You have?'

'Yep. We've got one especially set up for people like you – and we're going to use it just as soon as we get back to the station, to determine how many days you'll be in custody for.'

The two officers begin to frog-march him back to the police station for further questioning. They ask him if he has taken any narcotics. He denies everything except caffeine consumption, but they insist they will need to take blood samples.

'Not too much blood, though. The good news is that you may drain my bad humours away, but if my very essence goes with them ... why, then, a concatenation might not work when I stand in line. In fact, *everyone* in the parade of suspects could disappear!'

'So, you anticipate an identity parade?' replies the constable. 'That sounds to me like an admission of guilt.'

'Yiss, and you had bitter lick your beast, as you did on the day of your mirage,' adds his sidekick. The Constable ignores her embellishment, and continues,

'Anyhow, where do you work? Do you have a fixed abode?' Pilate then dictates the address of his business to them.

'I am the chief of a software house,' he says (sounding like a Navaho Indian).

'Hang on! There was a fire there just hours ago, wasn't there?' asks the constable.

'Yea. A *bug* fire,' replies his young assistant. 'So bug, it was burning all night long. One or two survivors are being interviewed. The current thinking is that it was not arson. With regahd to statements which 'ave alridy bin githered, there were siveral contingencies which may have arther induced, or added to, the blahze: ze old Dell laptops overheating; a spillage of inflammable liquid crystal; and a hairdresser who attached 'imself to the mins, presumably in an attimpt et suicahd, and who - through spontaneous combustion - sivved as an incendiary dev-arse.'

'It is all most peculiar,' says her boss.

Pilate does not hear them. He is striding ahead, with one horizontal arm trailing behind him, which is still handcuffed to Petty Officer, Una. It is almost reminiscent of Michaelangelo's fresco inside the Sistine Chapel, depicting God reaching out to Adam; except that in this case, God has no interest in Adam (whose part is played by Una) and is avoiding eye contact.

'Sir, we must accost you. Will you please walk alongside us?' asks the constable.

'Good sirs. The caffeine which I have lately downed, must expedite my paces.'

******

When they arrive at the police station, the disturber of the peace is permitted to check his online messages. Three of these are on Facebook. The first reads,

"Devina Doubleknot has a friend suggestion for you, whose name is Siobhan Shovel?"

The second speaks of a joyous homecoming,

"The missionary, Gustave Faht, will soon return to his native Austria, having sojourned for several months in the Congo. He is invited to attend a consortium with Mr Belly-Colony and Heinz Rotting-Beef, on the avoidance of stomach bugs in Central Africa."

And thirdly,

"Family Tree Bulletin: Iglesias O'Leary discovers he is of both Spanish and Irish extraction."

'Never 'eard of 'em!' Pilate grumbles. 'They are all complete strangers to me - but they are more persistently friendly than my own wife!'

Another email comprises a statement, with all of his employees as "virtual signatories", - and simply reads,

'We have left the premises, and no longer seek employment from you. We are especially concerned about your faithful employee, Dmitri, who has been hospitalized because of burns to his hands and shoulders. His condition is critical.'

'He was not faithful,' states the abject reader. 'And he did appear to have escaped (unharmed) from that terrible conflagration, when he issued his last instructions to me near the coast. There are witnesses who will testify ...'

His protestations are ignored, and one final communication is pointed out to him. This is from his wife:

'Because of your dilatory action, regarding buildings and contents insurance, I have lost everything. All that constitutes this business of yours, belongs ultimately to me. I shall sue for a divorce, with immediate effect. And I shall insist that the pre-nuptial agreement is honoured. I should remind you, in case you have forgotten, - this states that, in dire circumstances, I am entitled to have the full value of my dowry returned to me ... in pounds, shillings and pence.'

'I can return nothing to my wife. I am penniless.' Pilate hyperventilates. 'Damn! Some of my wife's jewellery could have been given to a pawnbroker, and the proceeds from it used for severance pay. She doesn't even remember half the items she has squirrelled away in her drawers. She would never have missed them! Damn again! This is so inconvenient.'

'Sir, while it is true that debtor's jails no longer exist, you could be in a serious predicament for dishonouring a legal agreement.'

'So be it. Think of me as a Camelid. Anything you say will be masticated upon and swallowed; and then, later, with the aid of acid reflux, spewed out against you.'

(Descriptor is revolted by this, and has fled for another toilet break.)

UNA: He will burp and spit at us, Bull!

BILL [addressing Pilate]: Sir, are you quite mad?

UNA [chuckling to herself]: He's insanely funny.

BILL: He should be sectioned.

PILATE: Oh, you cannot commit me! There's no database large enough to contain all that I am! You see, I am no longer in the world of unreality. I have hatched from a seed that, once, was the merest speck of data. And, through cell division (and a bump on my head), I am cognizant at last. And I know my rights.

BILL: Would you like to see a solicitor? Or maybe a clergyman is more to your taste – if you have done something that weighs heavily upon your conscience?

PILATE [lapsing into blank verse]:

A conscience? I'm already *nonpareil.*

Solicitor? - What for? A priest? - I've seen.

Both smug as smog from politician's cant!

BILL [with a sigh of exasperation]: Very well. I'm not forcing you. [To Una] He says he doesn't want a solicitor or a priest. Have you got that, Una?

UNA [with writing pad in hand]: Yiss, boss. [She lifts her finger high into the air, like a weathervane registering the direction of the wind, – and she is rather fetching in her gesture.] Tonight, when Ah close mah arse, Ah shall sleep tart. But for ze tarm being, Ah'm *on ze case*!

At the Last

Pilate has given blood, and is waiting overnight in a damp, bare cell, while the sample is analysed. During this period, a storm has taken hold. The captive listens to the local news channel on a nearby radio, belonging to an officer on night duty.

'Rough seas are expected around Fair Isle. And elsewhere, - the weather in the south-east has also changed dramatically. There is a great rumbling overhead, and the threat of flash floods in several regions. Lightning has forked across the sky, leaving wrecked power cables in its wake. And that is not all. In a village by the sea, a funeral director and financial advisor were killed when a giant commercial hoarding fell on them. Meanwhile, thunderbolts from the heavens struck a recently refurbished depot, and annihilated a London Routemaster bus. We are currently awaiting further clarification, but (being a vehicle not normally seen around these parts) it is assumed to be privately owned. Eyewitnesses are claiming it was a direct hit. The body of the driver has not been identified ... The storm was anticipated – and there may be worse to come.'

A voice is heard from somewhere,

'The irate boar of intractable weather hath our golden delicious sun in his mouth. Indeed, he is swallowing it whole, even as I speak.'

Pilate still feels dizzy from the fall he suffered earlier on, and he is not in a fit state to respond to *certain* information that has been broadcast. Or is it that he doesn't really care? He does, however, have this to say,

'Well, I never! Weather forecasts have improved since I was young – maybe because, in recent generations (via human pollution and nuclear tests), mankind has actually been *creating* our weather! It is easy to predict the movement of a marionette, if you are the puppet-master.'

******

When Pilate surfaces to consciousness at first light, it is with some discomfort, for he has remained fully clothed all night. He struggles to take his coat and pullover off. Like an allium with multiple layers on, he's all in a pickle.

The results of his tests are in. He is scheduled to go with his captors to what are now the derelict remains of the warehouse where he once worked. The storm has abated and, in perfect innocence, the sky has turned blue. The building and surrounding area has been cordoned off by police. Much of it is now no more than a pile of rubble, after the great fire. Notwithstanding, the embers are still warm, and, from close quarters, it may be seen that when an officer of the law treads accidentally upon them, wispy plumes of smoke are exhaled into the sunshine.

Pilate muses over the events of the last 24 hours. How much was truth? How much, fiction? And yet a pile of bricks and mortar have been razed to the ground. So from Pandora's box of tricks, an element of reality must have escaped.

The detective has something on his mind, and pulls out a printed note from his inside pocket:

'You know, this building was always shrouded in secrecy. And only the other day, I got wind of a government initiative.'

He reads the following to his assistant: "In future, asylums shall be set up for the containment of lunacy, based upon a rare, new mode of therapy. The focus will be upon *recreating past truth as present fantasy*". Essentially, patients who already know each other, and were colleagues long before their mental illness took hold, are not confined against their will; but, instead, shall co-exist (with occasional healthcare visitors) in an environment which is fully equipped with technologies and various other "props", so as to give the impression of a genuine (and current) place of employment. Here, they may pass their time with dignity, coming and going of their own volition, and labouring under the misapprehension that they still *contribute* to society. It is a fresh approach to *care in the community*." You know, I have always thought of this site as a centre for systems work of the most sensitive kind: something involving the MOD, perhaps?' Bill looks at his young apprentice, who shrugs.

'Sar minny bug boldings. It's a big sham. Wery swoon, there will be no spiss lift for pidistrians,' she comments.

As for Pilate, all he can do is utter expletives - and express astonishment:

'God! My God! Having been struck once with almighty force and given a sore head, I had imagined that my tribulations were over!'

'Do we have the results of the blood test?' asks the constable.

'The subject was finned to hev a whole concoction of substinces coursing through him. We are nit even sure what they all ah,' replies Una.

'Well. What do you have to say for yourself?' asks Bill, facing down his strange prisoner.

Pilate is silent.

'We mist treble you for a statement,' elucidates the young sidekick. The present author would like to say that he is glad of this request, for it is only fair that the hero of our tale should have the final word. And so, here is his official statement, as noted down by the petty officer, who is hoping that it will shed light of an abstract kind on this already sunny afternoon, and that it might even be substantial enough to be used as evidence against him:

'My underlings have undermined my business! I do observe a distinct absence of electronic equipment amongst the cinders ... From this, I do infer that they have made off with my hardware. I no longer have any staff. My wife has left me. My former life is moribund! My fond conceits and all my pre-conceptions have been drained of their essence ... like cabbages in a colander, or spent leaves at the bottom of a decorative teapot. What more can you draw out of them? As heaven is my witness, this statement is in chaos!'

And with that final flourish, imagining himself to be a player upon the stage, he takes his bow.